ZECHARIAH

ZECHARIAH

PROPHET OF MESSIAH'S GLORY

by

MERRILL F. UNGER, TH.D., PH.D.

Academie
Books Grand Rapids, Michigan
Zondervan Publishing House

Zechariah: Prophet of Messiah's Glory

Academie Books are published by Zondervan
Publishing House, 1415 Lake Drive, S.E.,
Grand Rapids, Michigan 49506

ISBN 0-310-33421-7

Printed in the United States of America

85   86   87   88   89   90   91   92 / 15   14   13

CONTENTS

CONTENTS

COMMENTARY ON ZECHARIAH

INTRODUCTION

INTRODUCTION

I. THE HISTORICAL PERSPECTIVE OF ZECHARIAH'S DAY — CHRONOLOGY OF THE EXILE AND THE RESTORATION

The years 633–612 B.C. witnessed the decline and fall of Assyria ("the giant among the Semites"), which as a far-flung empire had been a controlling political factor in ancient Bible lands from about 1000–633 B.C.

1. The New Babylonian Empire (612–539 B.C.) and the Captivity of Judah

625–605 B.C. Rise of Nabopolassar, king of Babylon
614 B.C. Fall of Asshur to the Medes
612 B.C. Fall of Nineveh to the Medes and Babylonians
612–609 B.C. Remnant of Assyrian power holds out in Haran
609 B.C. Defeat of Assyrians and Egyptians under Pharaoh-Necho at Haran
605 B.C. Defeat of Pharaoh-Necho at Carchemish
605–562 B.C. Nebuchadnezzar II's long and brilliant reign
605 B.C. Nebuchadnezzar II assumes control of Palestine-Syria; Judah becomes a client state; Daniel and other choice youths taken to Babylon
598 B.C. Jehoiachin taken captive together with Ezekiel, etc.
587 B.C. Fall of Jerusalem
562–560 B.C. Amel-Marduk (Evil-Merodach, II Kings 25:27) ascends the throne; liberates Jehoiachin (II Kings 25:27–30); is slain by Neriglisar, his brother-in-law
560–556 B.C. Neriglisar seizes the throne
556 B.C. Labashi-Marduk, son of Neriglisar, rules briefly, is slain by conspirators
556 B.C. Nabunaid, one of the conspirators, ascends to power
556–539 B.C. Nabunaid (Nabonidus) co-rules with his eldest son, Belshazzar
549–530 B.C. Rise to world-rule of Cyrus the Persian
549 B.C. Cyrus unites Persia and Media
546 B.C. Cyrus conquers Lydia
539 B.C. Cyrus conquers Babylon (end of the Chaldean Empire)

2. The Persian Empire (539–331 B.C.) and the Restoration of Judah

538 B.C. Edict of Cyrus permitting Jewish repatriation of Judah (Ezra 1)
537–536 B.C. Return of 49,897 Jews to Jerusalem (Ezra 2; Neh. 7)
536 B.C. Altar rebuilt and sacrifices offered (seventh month)
535 B.C. Work on the temple started, but then stopped (Ezra 3:1–4)
535–520 B.C. Hardships, economic depression in Jerusalem; people forget the temple and selfishly concentrate on their own needs (Hag. 1, 2)
530 B.C. Death of Cyrus
530–522 B.C. Reign of Cyrus' son, Cambyses II, who conquered Egypt
522–486 B.C. Darius I, the Great, saved the empire from civil war, erected the Behistun Inscription, and was friendly to the Jews
520 B.C. Darius confirms the decree of Cyrus and aids in the construction of the Jewish temple in Jerusalem (Ezra 6:1–14)
520 B.C. Sixth month (Sept.–Oct.), first day of the month, Haggai's first sermon (Hag. 1:3–11)

Sixth month, twenty-fourth day, Haggai's second sermon (Hag. 1:12–15)

Seventh month (Oct.–Nov.), first day, Haggai's third sermon (Hag. 2:1–9)

Eighth month (Nov.–Dec.), day, Zechariah's opening sermon Zech. 1:1–6)

Eighth month, twenty-fourth day, Haggai's last sermons (Hag. 2:10–23)

520 B.C. Eleventh month (Feb.–March), twenty-fourth day, Zechariah's eight night visions (Zech. 1:7–6:8)

Eleventh month, twenty-fourth or twenty-fifth day, the symbolic crowning of Joshua prefiguring Messiah King-Priest

518 B.C. Ninth month (Dec.–Jan.), fourth day, delegation from Bethel; Zechariah's message of repentance and promised blessing (Zech. chaps. 7 and 8)

516 B.C. Twelfth month (March-Apr.), third day, completion and dedication of the temple (Ezra 6:15)

490 B.C. Darius I's campaign against Greece. Defeat at Marathon

486–465 B.C. Xerxes I (Ahasuerus), husband of Esther (Esther 2:16), reigns

480 B.C. Persians defeated at Thermopylae and Salamis by the Greeks

478 B.C. Esther becomes queen

465–424 B.C. Reign of Artaxerxes I

458 B.C. Ezra returns to Palestine (some scholars date this event later)

445 B.C. Artaxerxes I authorizes Nehemiah to restore Jerusalem's walls

445–432 B.C. (or somewhat later) Malachi's ministry

424–423 B.C. Xerxes II

423–404 B.C. Darius II

404–358 B.C. Artaxerxes II

358–338 B.C. Artaxerxes III

338–336 B.C. Arses

336–331 B.C. Darius III. Defeated by Alexander of Macedon

II. THE PROPHETIC PERSPECTIVE OF ZECHARIAH 9–14 (FROM ALEXANDER THE GREAT TO MESSIAH)

It is possible that Zechariah lived as late as 460 B.C. and on into the reign of Artaxerxes I. As the author of chapters 9–14, he certainly outlived Darius I and envisioned the rise of Greece after the Persian setbacks at Marathon (490 B.C.) and Thermopylae and Salamis (480 B.C.). At any rate, his prophetic vista in chapters 9–14, like Daniel's, scans the centuries from the rise of Alexander to the first advent of Messiah, which Zechariah sees, as do the Old Testament seers so frequently, in blended view with the second advent and the establishment of the kingdom over Israel.

1. *The Macedonian Empire* (336–323 B.C.)

359–336 B.C. Philip of Macedon extends his power over the Greek states

338 B.C. Battle of Chaeronea. End of individual power of Greek states

336–323 B.C. Death of Philip and the rise to power of his son Alexander

334 B.C. Alexander's victory at Granicus

333 B.C. Alexander's victory at Issus, opening up Palestine-Syria to his conquests

332 B.C. Tyre, Gaza, and Egypt fall to Greek arms

331 B.C. Victory at Gaugamela and the destruction of Persian power
327 B.C. Alexander reaches India
323 B.C. Alexander dies in Babylon

2. *The Ptolemaic Dynasty in Egypt* (323–30 B.C.)

323–285 B.C. Ptolemy I. Many Jews emigrate to Egypt
285–246 B.C. Ptolemy II. Alexandria is center of Jewish culture
246–221 B.C. Ptolemy II. Egyptian Jewry prospers
221–203 B.C. Ptolemy IV. Translation of Old Testament into Greek proceeds
203–181 B.C. Ptolemy V
181– 30 B.C. Ptolemaic line continues under Roman control
     30 B.C. Egypt becomes a Roman province

3. *The Seleucid Dynasty in Syria* (312–64 B.C.)

312–280 B.C. Seleucus I
280–261 B.C. Antiochus I
261–247 B.C. Antiochus II
247–226 B.C. Seleucus II
226–223 B.C. Seleucus III
223–187 B.C. Antiochus III, the Great. Jews come under Seleucid influence
187–175 B.C. Seleucus IV
175–163 B.C. Antiochus IV, Epiphanes. Intense persecution of the Jews
163–162 B.C. Antiochus V
162–150 B.C. Demetrius I
150–129 B.C. Alexander Balas, Demetrius II, Antiochus VI, and Antiochus VII
129– 64 B.C. Weak dynasty under Roman domination
     64 B.C. Syria becomes a Roman province

4. *Palestine from Alexander to Messiah* (323–4 B.C.)

323–198 B.C. Palestine under Egyptian control
     198 B.C. Seleucids gain control
175–163 B.C. Ruthless paganizing attempts of Antiochus Epiphanes
     167 B.C. The Maccabean revolt
165–160 B.C. Judas Maccabaeus heroically resists Greek paganism
160–142 B.C. Jonathan
142–134 B.C. Simon
134–104 B.C. John Hyrcanus
104–103 B.C. Aristobulus I
103– 76 B.C. Alexander Jannaeus
 76– 67 B.C. Alexandra, second queen of Jewish history
 66– 63 B.C. Aristobulus II
     63 B.C. Pompey brings Palestine under Roman control
 55– 43 B.C. Antipater, the Idumaean, controls Palestine under Roman grant
     41 B.C. Herod and Phasael, Antipater's sons, are tetrarchs
 40– 37 B.C. Aristobulus' son, Antigonus, is high priest and king by aid of Parthians
 40– 4 B.C. Herod the Great, king of Judaea
      5 B.C. Birth of Messiah

5. *Palestine from Messiah's Birth till Jerusalem's Fall* (5 B.C.–A.D. 70)

  4 B.C.   Herod's kingdom divided

4 B.C.–A.D.	6.	Archelaus, tetrarch of Judea, Samaria, and Idumaea
4 B.C.–A.D.	39.	Herod Antipas, tetrarch of Galilee and Peraea
4 B.C.–A.D.	34.	Philip, tetrarch of Gaulonitis, Trachonitis, Batanaea, Auranitis, and Panias
A.D.	6–41.	Rule of Roman procurators
A.D.	26–36.	Pontius Pilate procurator
A.D.	27–30.	Public ministry, death, and resurrection of the Messiah
A.D.	37–44.	Herod Agrippa I
A.D.	44–66.	Roman procurators
A.D.	66–70.	Jewish revolt against Rome
A.D.	70.	Destruction of Jerusalem. End of Jewish nation

III. THE PROBLEM OF THE AUTHORSHIP AND DATE OF ZECHARIAH 9–14

1. *The Traditional and Conservative View.* This position maintains that Zechariah is the author of the entire prophecy, the last six chapters as well as the first eight. The Zecharian authorship of the so-called "Deutero," or in the case of some critics, "Trito" Zechariah, is maintained despite the fact that the second part of the prophecy (chapters 9–14) is not dated and contains no references to actual authorship by Zechariah, the son of Berechiah, the grandson of Iddo, as does the first part of the book (cf. 1:1, 7; 6:9; 7:1; 8:1). Chapters 1–8 have never seriously been placed in question as to their genuineness and authenticity as the product of Zechariah, and as having been written between 520 and 518 B.C., or somewhat later.

After a lapse, apparently of many years, when perhaps the active ministry of a long life was completed, Zechariah was once more called to pen canonical prophecy. The product of that ministry is the section of this book which has evoked so much critical discussion and disagreement.

2. *The Higher Critical View of the Authorship of Zechariah 9–14.* The first eight chapters are the genuine work of Zechariah, but the last six, it is maintained, are the work of at least one other writer, or two, or even three or more. These writings when collected were brought together under the name of Zechariah. Some critics consider one or more of these writers pre-exilic, others one or more of them post-exilic. Great disparity of opinion prevails regarding the number of authors, their dates, and the events to which they refer. The vast disharmony among the critics who abandon the Zecharian authorship constitutes a potent warning against hasty acceptance of any view except the traditional position, which is capable of logical and scholarly defense.

3. *The Rise of the Critical View.* The traditional authorship of chapters 9–14 does not seem to have been questioned either by Jew or Christian until Hugo Grotius (1644) declared chapters 9–14 were post-Zecharian. He was shortly followed by an English critic, Joseph Mede, around 1650. The latter was led to posit a pre-Babylonian-exile date for this section and to maintain that Jeremiah was the author, by comparing Matthew 27:9 with Zechariah 11:12, 13 (*Works*, pp. 786, 833).

Several English scholars followed Mede, such as Hammond (1653), Kidder (1700), Whiston (1722), and others. These opinions, however, were strongly opposed by English scholars in general, especially by Blayney (1797), and the hypothesis fell into disrepute in England.

The doubts expressed by English scholars spread to Germany, and Flügge (1784) opposed the unity of the prophecy and was echoed by Seiler, G. L. Bauer, and J. Doederlein. After 1814 and the publication of Berthold's *Einleitung*, the conjecture there put forward that Zechariah, the son of Jeberechiah, was the author of the second portion, became current. This view received the approval of Wilhelm Gesenius in his *Commentary on Isaiah*, Rosenmüller in his *Scholia* (1828) and Hitzig in his *Studien und Kritiken* (1830) and held that the author or authors of the second part of the prophecy lived at some time previous to the Babylonian Captivity. Bernhard Stade held to a 300–280 B.C. date for chapters 9–14, and was followed substantially by Cornill, Hoelscher, Budde, and to some extent, by Wellhausen. In Nowack's opinion two to four authors are responsible for the second portion of the prophecy. Rubikam lists eight authors and assigns a Maccabean date (166–160 B.C.), as do Marti and Duhm. Baudissin, Kuenen, and Steuernagel were of the opinion that chapters 9–11 were pre-exilic in date but suffered a post-exilic revamping in the Greek era. They posit chapters 12–14 as post-exilic. Sellin took a complete critical somersault, originally assigning chapters 9–13 to a pre-exilic date, but later concluding that he was wrong and that the entire section 9–14 was penned by an apocalyptic author of the third century B.C. (*Einleitung* p. 123; *Zwölfprophetenbuch*, p. 543). More recently Robert Pfeiffer has relegated the whole second part of the book to the third century B.C. (*Introduction to the Old Testament*, p. 611).

The unity and Zecharian authorship of the prophecy have been ably defended by Köster, De Wette, Hengstenberg, Kliefoth, Keil, Delitzsch, Lange, Pusey, Moeller, C. H. H. Wright (*Zechariah and His Prophecies*, pp. xxxv-xlii). Also defending the unity of the book are T. T. Perowne ("Haggai and Zechariah" in *The Cambridge Bible for Schools and Colleges*, pp. 49–57). David Baron (*The Visions and Prophecies of Zechariah*, 4th printing, 1951, pp. 261–282). Recent writers who maintain the conservative position are C. H. Leupold (*Exposition of Zechariah*, 1956, pp. 6–13) and Theodore Laetsch (*The Minor Prophets*, 1956, pp. 404–406).

IV. ARGUMENTS AGAINST THE UNITY OF AUTHORSHIP ANSWERED

1. *Alleged Differences of Style and Content.* Chapters 1–8 are claimed to be prosaic and unimpassioned in style and diction, while chapters 9–14 are said to be full of fire and fervor. But if the prophet in the bulk of chapters 1–6 records a series of visions seen by him, as is repeatedly stated, why should we expect an elevated and imaginative style, if he simply recounted what he saw, as he was supposed to do? In the latter portion, although the writer was predicting events yet to occur, he was at least free on the human plane to use imagination, etc., as consonant with divine inspiration. Certainly the contention that in chapters 1–8 many visions occur and in chapters 9–14 prophecies, but no visions, is only partly true, as Zech. 11:4–17 borders very closely on a vision. And why should it be thought impossible for a prophet on one occasion to be given visions, and on another to be graced only with far-reaching prophecies? Since when has the Spirit of God been placed in a narrow groove of operation?

2. *Alleged Chronological Problems.* It is said that the first part of the book encourages the building of the temple, but that chapters 9–14, if they had appeared at the same time, would have discouraged this venture, abounding as they do in predictions of the capture of the city and future disasters. But such a criticism loses sight of the fact that part 2 was probably penned many years after part 1, when Zechariah, then a young man had become an old man. Moreover, both parts of the prophecy are equally characterized by *a unifying message of ultimate hope.* Both, *correctly* interpreted, have the *terminus ad quem* of their encouraging message in the future establishment of Messiah's kingdom over Israel and symmetrically dovetail.

Criticism which maintains that such details as the reference to the Ionian

Greeks (Javan) in chapter 9:13 necessitate a date after 300 B.C. ignores the fact that the prophet evidently lived into the era when Greek power clashed with Persia in 490 B.C. at Marathon and at Thermopylae and Salamis in 480 B.C., well within the span of ministry of Zechariah. Long before Zechariah's day Ionian Greeks had bought and sold Jewish captives as slaves (Joel 3:6; Obadiah 1:20).

3. *Alleged Religious Difficulties.* "One who denies salvation to the Samaritans as harshly as Zechariah did in chapters 5, 7, 8, certainly cannot a few years later include these Samaritans in his promises of salvation, chapters 9, 10" (Sellin, *Zwölfprophetenbuch,* p. 540). But such criticism, besides ignoring the predicted grace of God manifested in Messiah, arbitrarily assumes that the Samaritans are harshly denied salvation by Zechariah in the passages cited.

V. ARGUMENTS FOR THE UNITY OF AUTHORSHIP OF ZECHARIAH

1. *Echoes and Allusions to the Former Prophets throughout the Prophecy Bind It Together as a Unit.* Both parts abound in such references, but C. H. H. Wright shows that the second part contains even more such echoes than the first portion (*op. cit.,* pp. xxxv-xxxviii). Compare Zech. 13:2 with Hos. 2:17 [19]; Zech. 13:8, 9 with Ezek. 5:2, 12; Zech. 13:9 with Hos. 2:23 [25]; Zech. 14:8 with Ezek. 47:1-12; Zech. 14:10 with Jer. 31:38, 40; Zech. 14:16-19 with Isa. 60:12, 66:23; Zech. 14:20 with Ezek. 43:12; Zech. 14:21 with Ezek. 44:9. For the numerous allusions to the former prophets in chapters 1-8 see the exposition.

2. *The Historical Perspective of Chapters 9-14 Is Post-exilic.* Significant is the complete absence of any reference to a reigning king of Judah or Israel. King-Messiah, the Branch of "the house of David," is the only king mentioned throughout the prophecy (6:12, 13; 9:9). Various attempts to demonstrate an alleged disparity in the picture of the Messianic reign in chapters 1-8 over against 9-14 have been dismal failures.

In both parts the house of Israel and Judah are viewed as essentially one (1:19 [2:2]; 8:13; 9:9, 10, 13; 10:3, 6, 7). Likewise the ties of "brotherhood" are represented as existing even after the Good Shepherd has been rejected by the people. Like Jeremiah (23:6) and Ezekiel (37:16-19), Zechariah presents the future covenant people united, and the prophet's ultimate hope for Israel *is absolutely identical* in both parts of the prophecy.

3. *Similar Rare Expressions Are Found in Both Parts of the Prophecy.* For example, the infrequent phrase "from one going out and from one coming in" (*me'over umishshav*) occurs both in 7:14 and in 9:8. The archaic formula, "is the oracle of the Lord" (*ne'um Yhwh*) which occurs fourteen times in chapters 1-8, also is found in 10:12; 12:1, 4; 13:2, 7, 8. The expression "remove" (*he'evir*) occurs in 3:4 and 13:2, being uncommon in the sense in which Zechariah employs it.

In both parts of the prophecy the people are similarly styled "the house of Israel and the house of Judah" (8:13) or "the house of Judah and the house of Joseph" (10:6), or "Judah and Israel" (11:14). Compare "Judah, Israel, and Jerusalem" (1:19) [2:2], and "Judah and Ephraim" (9:13).

In summary it may be said that to hold the unity of the prophecy of Zechariah is consonant with the highest scholarship and is in agreement with the internal evidence of the book itself, being witnessed to by both Jewish and Christian students from earliest times. The fact may be safely rested in that the book is not only an intrinsic part of God's inspired Word, but that it is throughout the work of the author whose name it bears.

ZECHARIAH

CHAPTER ONE
THE PREREQUISITE
FOR SPIRITUAL BLESSING

INTRODUCTION TO THE WHOLE BOOK

(ZECH. 1:1-6)

THE prophecy of Zechariah is pro-foundly precious to the Christian because of its unique Messianic em-phasis and its panoramic unfolding of the events connected with the first and especially the second advent of Christ and the consequent millennial restoration of the nation Israel. George L. Robinson gives an accurate ap-praisal of the book as a whole when he describes it as "the most Messianic, the most truly apocalyptic and escha-tological of all the writings of the Old Testament" ("The Book of Zechariah" in the *International Standard Bible Encyclopaedia*, p. 3136).

While some may disagree with this description of the general character of the book, it does enunciate its salient emphasis. The prophecy abounds in far-reaching predictive allusions to the person, work, and future glory of the Coming One. Messianic flashes occur everywhere. The whole gamut of events clustering around Messiah's rejection at His first coming and His acceptance at His second coming, as these affect Israel and the nations, is unfolded with singular fulness and clarity. Nowhere else in the Old Testament is there such a concentrated and rich revelation of Messianic prophecy. The book is the Apocalypse of the Old Testament. The scope and profundity of its visions are striking.

Important Messianic predictions of Zechariah include Jehovah's Servant, the Branch (3:8); the Man the Branch (6:12); King-Priest, Christ (6:13); the True Shepherd, Christ (11:4-11; 13:7) versus the False Shepherd, Anti-christ (11:15-17); Betrayal of the Good Shepherd (11:12, 13); His Crucifixion (12:10); His Sufferings (13:7); His Second Advent in Glory (14:4).

Not only does Zechariah's prophecy rank high in Messianic content and eschatological importance, but it is one of the most difficult books to interpret. Many Jewish expositors like Jarchi and Abarbanel and Christian exegetical writers like Jerome have lamented their inability to interpret the book satisfactorily; but the great teacher Jarchi and the honored ex-egete Abarbanel, not accepting the

1 In the eighth month, in the second year of Darius, came the word of the Lord unto Zechariah, the son of Berechiah, the son of Iddo the prophet, saying,

1   In the eighth month, in the second year of Darius, came the word of Jehovah unto Zechariah the son of Berechiah, the son of Iddo, the prophet, saying,

Messiah of whom Zechariah prophesied, could scarcely be expected to fathom this book which has more to say about Christ than all the other minor prophets combined. Rejecting the Messiah, these Jewish teachers have rejected the key which opens the treasuries of truth contained in these age-spanning predictions.

Little wonder Jarchi complained that Zechariah's prophecy "is abstruse, for it contains visions resembling dreams which lack interpreting"; and "we shall never," says he, "be able to discover the true interpretation until the Teacher of Righteousness arrives."

This Teacher, the Holy Spirit, has arrived (John 16:13; Acts 2:4). He is "the Spirit of truth" and guides us "into all truth." He does not speak "from Himself," but whatsoever He hears, He speaks, and pre-eminently shows us "things to come" (John 16:13). His sphere of tuition prominently involves the realm of prophecy and eschatology. By "the Spirit of prophecy" we shall understand the "testimony of Jesus" (Rev. 19:10), which two of the greatest of the Hebrew teachers declared inexplicable.

I. ZECHARIAH'S CALL TO REPENTANCE (Zech. 1:1-3)

1. *Preface to the Call to Repentance: The Time and the Prophet's Name and Ancestry* (Zech. 1:1). *The time.* By virtue of their emphatic grammatical position the time notations to these prophecies and visions are highlighted. **In the eighth month in the second year of Darius came the word of the Lord...** (1:1; cf. 1:7; 7:1). The reason for this emphasis on the time of the prophecies lies beyond the fact that a mere chronological signpost is given. The prophecies are dated in the second

year of Darius I, the Great (522-486 B.C.), in the eighth month (November, 520 B.C.). The grammar, as well as the method of reckoning by a heathen monarch, instead of by Israel's or Judah's own kings, as was the uniform custom before the exile, forcefully expresses the salient fact that the "times of the Gentiles" (Luke 21:24) were in full progress and that God's covenant people were without their own king and under the dominion of a foreign nation (Hos. 3:4, 5). The "times of the Gentiles," thus stressed in Zechariah's prophecies and which began with Judah's exile under Nebuchadnezzar (605 B.C.) and will last until Jerusalem has been fully liberated from Gentile overlordship at the second advent, form the important background for the visions and prophecies which look forward to the consummation of this period of Israel's misfortune and to the nation's establishment in millennial glory.

Darius I, the Great, was an Achemaenid prince, the son of Hystaspes, who saved the Persian empire in the revolt which followed the death of his predecessor, Cambyses II (530-522 B.C.), who in turn succeeded Cyrus the Great who founded the mighty Persian empire which ruled the world for over two centuries (539-331 B.C.). It was this Darius who is so prominent in the datings of the books of Haggai and Zechariah, who is no less famous archaeologically. It was he who recorded his triumph over his enemies trilingually on the rock of Behistun, the decipherment of which furnished the key to unlocking Babylonian-Assyrian cuneiform, the wedge-shaped writing of antiquity.

Darius founded a new capital at Persepolis and beautified and enlarged Susa (Biblical Shushan, Neh. 1:1;

Esther 2:8; 3:15) and Ecbatana (Achmetha, Ezra 6:2). He displayed unusual humanity and restraint, as did in general the Achemaenian kings, and like them exercised a more liberal rule than was generally true of oriental despots of the ancient world. The Persian rulers, moreover, showed wisdom in administration. As devotees of Ahura Mazda, they adhered to a relatively high moral code. For two hundred years peace was maintained throughout the East.

Different nations which fell under Persian sway were allowed to continue, and religious toleration was practiced. Peace and prosperity were the result (cf. Zech. 1:11). The Jews, moreover, had an appreciation of their Achemaenid conquerors, which strongly contrasted with their resentment against all their other overlords, Egyptian, Assyrian, Chaldean, Seleucid, and Roman.

When Zechariah began his ministry of encouragement and hope to the returned remnant, sixteen years had already elapsed since Cyrus had issued his decree in 536 B.C. (Ezra 1:1–4) and some 50,000 exiles had returned to Jerusalem from Babylon. With high hopes they planned to resettle in the land and rebuild the temple. By the second month of the following year (535 B.C.) they had laid the foundation of the structure (Ezra 3:11–13); but due to opposition from the Samaritans (Ezra 4:5), spiritual declension, and other causes, the work fell into abeyance for almost fourteen years while the people gave themselves to building their own homes and other selfish pursuits.

When Darius succeeded to the Persian throne, the prophets, Haggai and Zechariah, fearing that the decrees of former kings were void, began an arduous campaign under divine direction to resume the building of the temple. Inquiring and questioning of this by Persian officials led to the referral of the matter to Babylon. The original decree of Cyrus being brought to light, permission was

confirmed by the Persian government and the project went forward until its completion four years later in the sixth year of Cyrus (Ezra 5:1 – 6:18).

The prophet's name (vs. 1). The name *Zechariah* is a very common one, being borne by more than twenty people in the Old Testament. Jerome regarded the name as meaning *memoria domini*, "memory of the Lord," interpreting the first part of the name as a noun. It is more satisfactory, however, to construe *zakar*, "remember," as a verb and render "whom the Lord (*Yah*) remembers." This is better, and more conformable to Hebrew usage than to make *Yah* the object "who remembers *Yah*," particularly since the entire prophecy is an exposition of the fact that *the Lord remembers Israel.*

In Hebrew proper names compounded with *Yah*, as Wright points out (*Zechariah and His Prophecies*, p. xxi), the sacred name is the subject when it is compounded with the verb in the third person singular, "and there is no reason to treat this as an exception." The explanation of the name as derived from *zakar*, "male," (i.e., "a hero") must be rejected as without a parallel and as being meaningless in relation to the prophecy.

The prophet's ancestry (vs. 1). Zechariah was the son of Berechiah, the grandson of Iddo (1:1, 7). The name Iddo is apparently mentioned among the priests who returned from Babylon under Zerubbabel in 536 B.C. (Neh. 12:4; Ezra 5:1; 6:14). Zechariah was therefore a priest as well as a prophet. Presumably he was a very young man (cf. 2:4 [2:8]), while his contemporary Haggai was a very old man when Zechariah began his prophetic ministry, since Haggai apparently saw the first temple standing (Hag. 2:3).

Although in the book of Ezra (6:14) Zechariah is styled "the son of Iddo" and no mention is made of his father Berechiah, the usage refers to "the grandson of Iddo." Berechiah is doubtless passed over because he

2 The Lord hath been sore displeased with your fathers.
3 Therefore say thou unto them, Thus saith the Lord of hosts; Turn ye unto me, saith the Lord of hosts, and I will turn unto you, saith the Lord of hosts.

2   Jehovah was sore displeased with your fathers.
3   Therefore say thou unto them, Thus saith Jehovah of hosts: Return unto me, saith Jehovah of hosts, and I will return unto you, saith Jehovah of of hosts.

likely died young, never being distinguished as the head of a family. On the other hand, Zechariah is careful to mention his actual father along with his grandfather.

Zechariah was certainly born and educated in Babylon and, in common with Ezekiel and Daniel, makes extensive use of visions and symbols. He spent his prime under the Persian empire, and his visions reflect, to some extent, Persian imagery. He saw the enlarged earth comprising the mighty Persian realm, far-flung from the Indus River to the Hellespont and from Egypt to the Caucasus Mountains, forming the mightiest empire up to that time. He saw the celestial messenger riding on varicolored horses through the myrtle groves which then adorned the base of Olivet (1:8-11) or he glimpsed chariots hitched to steeds and speeding across the vast empire. This recalled to him the swift couriers in the vast machinery of the posts, bringing back tidings of war or peace (cf. Herodotus VIII:98; Esther 3:13, 15).

2. *Zechariah's Warning to Repentance* (Zech. 1:2, 3). The initial six verses of the first chapter of Zechariah constitute a synopsis of a sermon of the prophet. Its theme strikes the keynote of the entire book and forms an indispensable introduction to it. The truth it enunciates is one which runs throughout the revealed ways of God with man; namely, *the appropriation and enjoyment of God's promises of blessing must be prefaced by genuine repentance.* Zechariah's prophecies are filled with such assurances of blessing for God's people Israel, promises that center in the Messiah and which are immutable and sure, based upon the

efficacy and the certainty of the Word of God, and not at all dependent upon Israel's unfaithfulness and sin.

But, although the immutability of God's Word and the certainty of His plans for Israel assure the fulfillment of these purposes, nevertheless the people are not to divorce divine grace from human responsibility. God's covenant people must put themselves in line for the manifestation of these far-reaching favors by genuinely turning away from sin. **Return unto Me, and I will return unto you** (Zech. 1:3) sounds the clarion call that furnishes the background for the message of hope that is the pre-eminent emphasis throughout the entire book.

The prophet emphasizes the divine wrath (vs. 2). The Hebrew is expressive: **Angry** [displeased] **was the Lord with anger** [displeasure]. Three grammatical devices stress the acuteness of the divine displeasure. First, the initial position of the verb **Angry was the Lord** in the sentence. Second, the use of the cognate accusative — to be "angry *with anger*," a Hebraism meaning to be "severely angry." The Septuagint inserts the adjective "great" (*orgēn megalēn*), which, although absent from the Hebrew idiom here, is often present elsewhere (cf. Zech. 1:15). Third, the choice of the word "to be angry" (*qatsaph*) further emphasizes God's keen displeasure. The term actually means "to be wroth" or "wrathful" and is used both of God as here (Deut. 1:34; Isa. 57:16, 17; 64:5 [4], 9 [8]) and of man (II Kings 5:11; Esther 1:12; 2:21).

Whether dealing with His ancient covenant nation Israel or with us, as members of the church and as sons, or with the unsaved, God in His infinite holiness must always deal with sin. Those who have experienced His electing grace, He chastens, scourges, and disciplines, as a father with a son. Those who have no experience of His electing grace in Christ are under His unmitigated wrath and in danger of eternal hell. "For the wrath of God is revealed from heaven against all ungodliness and wickedness of men who by their wickedness suppress the truth" (Rom. 1:18). Those who abuse the truth that "God is love" (I John 4:16) and make Him a doting indulgent Father to those who sustain no genuine relationship to Him as sons, forget that "our God is a consuming fire" (Heb. 12:29).

Zechariah fervently declares, **God was acutely displeased with your fathers.** One would have expected *"our* fathers," with the prophet identifying himself with the sinning people, even though not guilty of their sin. Codex A of the Septuagint thus renders the expression, "our fathers." But even though Zechariah undoubtedly used **your fathers** instead of "our fathers," it must not be supposed therefore that he was disassociating himself from the past generation, or playing the role of an innovator. He was a reformer, but not an innovator, as John Adams points out (*The Man among the Myrtles,* p. 5f.). The seer was crying out to his countrymen to return to the ideals and spiritual values of the past which they had forgotten.

The prophet sets forth the divine grace (vs. 3). The warning of divine wrath is a prerequisite to the acceptance of the divine grace. **Return unto me and I will return unto you.** Does the **and** (*waw*) in this instance express a subordinate idea of purpose, *"in order that* I may return unto you," or does the conjunction connect two coordinate ideas? The thought must be taken as coordinate, as in Genesis 17:1, 2: "Walk before me, *and* be thou perfect. And I will make my covenant between me and thee ..." The **and** here is not subordinate in the sense

that the framing of the covenant was made dependent on the perfect allegiance of the patriarch. Neither in Zechariah's sermon is God's preventing grace made contingent upon their initial response.

God had already taken the initiative. The fact that Haggai and Zechariah had been raised up for this revival is proof that God had turned to His people. They were, therefore, on their part freely to return to Him. *God's love for Israel is in order to incite* God's love in Israel and *Israel's love for God.* Any idea of legal righteousness in the reception of the hope and promises contained in the book must hence be excluded. But, on the other hand, divine grace must not be divorced from human responsibility.

It is remarkable how this call to repentance (for such it is, the Hebrew *shubh,* "turn, return," being equivalent to Greek *metanoeō,* "repent") is buttressed by the authority of the command of **the Lord of armies.** Three times this expression is used. Twice to introduce the command itself, once to conclude it, and twice more in the warning and illustration (vs. 4) which enforces it (five times in all), demonstrating *the complete necessity of obeying the injunction to turn away from sin* so that the blessings of God's grace about to be announced may be enjoyed. This fact alone should impress upon every preacher the necessity of proclaiming the Word of God with the authority of "Thus says the Lord." Nothing is more urgently needed in the present-day pulpit when men's philosophies and men's opinions are studied and expounded instead of God's counsels and the enunciation of God's truth backed up by God's authority.

II. ZECHARIAH'S WARNING FROM HISTORY (Zech. 1:4-6)

1. *The Command to the People Not to Be Disobedient like Their Fathers* (Zech. 1:4). Four times in the course of his introductory sermon Zechariah uses the expression **your fathers**

4 Be ye not as your fathers, unto whom the former prophets have cried, saying, Thus saith the Lord of hosts; Turn ye now from your evil ways, and from your evil doings: but they did not hear, nor hearken unto me, saith the Lord.

4 Be ye not as your fathers, unto whom the former prophets cried, saying, Thus saith Jehovah of hosts, Return ye now from your evil ways, and from your evil doings: but they did not hear, nor hearken unto me, saith Jehovah.

(vss. 2, 4, 5, 6). Their example of disobedience and apostasy is employed as a severe warning. **Do not be like your fathers.** The prophet employs the negative imperative (prohibition). People look with pride, if possible, to their ancestors and frequently try to follow their example. But this is prohibited by Zechariah in the case of his auditors. The reason is plain. Their **fathers** (forbears) were not only neglectful but inattentive to the word of the Lord which was ministered unto them by **the former prophets** (Isaiah, Jeremiah, Hosea, Joel, Amos, Micah, Habakkuk, Zephaniah, etc.).

These **former prophets** are called **my servants** (vs. 6), because they faithfully ministered the Word of God to their generation in the will of God. They fearlessly proclaimed *repentance* to their sinning and backsliding auditors in the name of **Thus says the Lord of armies.** The word which they preached, accordingly, came with the power and authority of God. As the Lord commands them as His servants (vs. 6), so they command the people as their servants (vs. 4). They enjoined repentance (*shubhu* is imperative, second personal plural, **repent!**).

However, that the prophets despite their faithful zeal used tact and grace is also indicated by the employment of the polite particle *na'* ("if you please," "please") with the imperative. **Return** [repent], **please.** There was authority of divine command, but there was also the urging constraining love of the Spirit in their stern utterances to the people to forsake sin manifested in their **evil ways and evil deeds.**

Their **evil ways** constituted the common everyday "course" of their lives, their general "manner of living."

The Hebrew word *derek* means a "road," a "way," a "path." (Cf. Gen. 35:3; 48:7; I Sam. 15:2.) Here it is used figuratively of the "road of life" or "path walked in everyday activity" (Deut. 28:29; Josh. 1:8; I Sam. 18:14). Their **evil deeds** describe the "practices" or "doings" of their daily "activities" (Heb. *ma'alalim;* cf. the Arabic *'alla*, "do a thing twice"). This word is used particularly of the bad *practices* of men, growing out of their wrong orientation in the "road" or "path" of life (I Sam. 25:3; Hos. 9:15; Isa. 1:16; Jer. 4:4). Hence repentance is enjoined both from the *cause* of their sin, their **evil ways**, and the *result* of their sin, their **evil deeds.**

This incisive call to repentance runs throughout the former prophets. Isaiah cries:

"Seek the Lord while he may be found,
    call upon him while he is near;
let the wicked forsake his way [*derek*],
    and the unrighteous man his thoughts;
let him return to the Lord, that He
    may have mercy on him
and to our God, for he will abundantly
        pardon" (Isaiah 55:6, 7).

Joel says:

"Yet even now, says the Lord,
    return to me with all your heart,
with fasting, with weeping, and
    with mourning;
and rend your hearts and not your garments.
Return, to the Lord, your God,
    for he is gracious and merciful,
slow to anger, and abounding in kindness
    and repents of evil" (Joel 2:12, 13).

Amos declares:

"For thus says the Lord to the house of
        Israel:
    Seek me and live . . .
Seek the Lord and live,
    lest he break out like fire in the house of
        Joseph,
and it devour with none to quench it for
        Beth-el" (Amos 5:4, 6).

5 Your fathers, where are they? and the prophets, do they live for ever?

5ʹ Your fathers, where are they? and the prophets, do they live for ever?

Jeremiah calls:

"Return, faithless Israel, says the Lord.
I will not look on you in anger,
for I am merciful, says the Lord;
I will not be angry forever" (Jer. 3:12).

Hosea warns:

"The pride of Israel witnesses against him;
yet *they do not return* to the Lord their
God,
nor seek him, for all this" (Hos. 7:10).

Malachi berates the people as follows: "From the days of your fathers you have turned aside from my statutes and not kept them. *Return to me and I will return to you*, says the Lord of hosts. But you say, How shall we *return?*" (Mal. 3:7).

The message of repentance was emphasized by John the Baptist (Matt. 3:2, 8, 11), Jesus (Matt. 4:17; Luke 24:46–49), Peter (Acts 2:38; 3:19; 5:31), Paul (Acts 20:21; 26:20; II Cor. 7:10), and James (Jas. 4:8). Saving faith is always inextricably bound up with conviction for sin and repentance. Moreover, fellowship with God in any age is dependent upon confession and consequent cleansing (I John 1:6–9). Zechariah was announcing an ageless truth. The prelude to the experience of God's blessing must involve dealing with sin which is offensive to a holy God.

2. *The Warning against the Peril of the Passing of Religious Opportunity* (Zech. 1:5). Despite the authoritative and gracious presentation of the message of repentance through the former prophets, their hearers **neither heard nor heeded me, says the Lord** (vs. 4). Whereupon the prophet asks dramatically concerning these stiff-necked and disobedient sinners. **Your fathers! Where are they? And the prophets! do they live forever?** (vs. 5). Baron, Keil, and some other Christian commentators, apply this first question to Zechariah: **Your fathers! Where are they?** and the second to the people as they im-

pudently retort, **And the prophets! Do they live forever?** "Have they too not shared in the common calamities of the disobedient nation?"

Although this is confessedly a possible interpretation, it can scarcely be true. Both questions are the prophet's because they form a part of his sermon. Both the disobedient people and God's faithful servants the prophets, it is true, are pictured as temporary. Both have passed off the scene, suffering in the common calamities that overtook the nation for its sins. But the second question calls attention not to the common fate that overtook the prophets, but to the brevity of opportunity to repent and obey God offered by their ministry. It stresses the fact that spiritual opportunity neglected is spiritual opportunity lost. There is a calamity worse than all other calamities. It is the passing of religious opportunity. Zechariah would call attention to the ominous peril.

3. *The Warning Concerning the Effectiveness and Certain Fulfilment of the Word of God* (Zech. 1:6). In the light of the temporariness both of the sinner and his religious opportunity to repent, the prophet sets forth the permanency and the unchangeable certainty of the word of the Lord. **But did not my words and my statutes which I commanded my servants overtake your fathers?** (vs. 6). Emphatic by position is the compound subject **my words and my statutes**. These words and statutes constituted the word of the Lord to the people, and are hence set forth prominently by their syntactical position in the sentence.

The adverbial restrictive particle **but** (vs. 6) (Hebrew *akh*, "only," "but") presents the contrast of the temporariness of the sinning people and their short-lived religious opportunity (vs. 5) with the permanency and

6 But my words and my statutes, which I commanded my servants the prophets, did they not take hold of your fathers? and they returned and said, Like as the Lord of hosts thought to do unto us, according to our ways, and according to our doings, so hath he dealt with us.

6   But my words and my statutes, which I commanded my servants the prophets, did they not overtake your fathers? and they turned and said, Like as Jehovah of hosts thought to do unto us, according to our ways, and according to our doings, so hath he dealt with us.

immutable operation of the word of the Lord. **Did not** [*halo'* negative interrogative adverb, expecting the answer "yes"] **the words and ordinances of the Lord through the former prophets overtake the people?** The verb **overtake** (Hebrew *nasag* in the causative stem means "to reach," "catch up with"). Its clear meaning appears from Deuteronomy 19:6: "Lest the avenger of blood pursue the slayer and *overtake* him, because the way is long, and slay him. . . ." The word is used of both blessings and cursings "overtaking one." "And all these blessings shall come on thee and *overtake* thee, if thou shalt hearken unto the voice of the Lord thy God" (Deut. 28:2). "But if you do not obey the voice of the Lord your God or be careful to do all his commandments and his statutes, which I command you this day, then all these curses shall come upon you and *overtake* you" (Deut. 28:15; cf. vs. 45). Zechariah undoubtedly had these great Deuteronomic passages in mind in his sermon. (Compare Psalm 69:24 [25]; 40:12 [13]; Isaiah 59:9; Job 27:20.)

When the word of God overtook the people, *caught up* with their sin and unrepentance, then they said, **Exactly as the Lord of armies purposed to deal with us according to our ways and our deeds, so has he dealt with us** (vs. 6). The word translated **purposed** (*zamam* means "to devise" or "plan") is especially used of the Lord's purpose in punishment and discipline (Jer. 4:28; 51:12; Lam. 2:17; but cf. Zech. 8:15, where it alone is used of blessing, in contrast to its normal use in the preceding verse 14).

It is interesting to note that it was **according to** [their] **ways** [and] **deeds** (vs. 6) of which they did not repent (vs. 4) that the Lord punished them. God's disciplinary punishment of His people is always on the basis of their **ways** (their general course or manner of living) and the result in their **deeds** or manifestation of those ways in everyday conduct.

Having thus laid the spiritual foundation for the visions and prophecies of blessing and the message of hope which constitute the book, the prophet proceeds with this aspect of the divine revelation.

CHAPTER ONE

(Continued)

HOPE FOR DISPERSED
AND DOWNTRODDEN ISRAEL

(THE FIRST VISION)

THE RED-HORSE RIDER AMONG THE MYRTLE TREES

(ZECH. 1:7-17)

I. THE VISION AND ITS IMAGERY
(Zech. 1:7, 8)
1. *The Time of the Vision*
(Zech. 1:7)
2. *The Persons of the Vision and
Their Identity* (Zech. 1:8a)
3. *The Places and Things of the
Vision and Their Identity*
(Zech. 1:8b)

II. THE VISION AND ITS MEANING
(Zech. 1:9-12)
1. *An Explanatory Word Concerning the Meaning*
(Zech. 1:9-11)
2. *A Symbolic Act Concerning the
Meaning* (Zech. 1:12)

III. THE VISION AND ITS MESSAGE
(Zech. 1:13-17)
1. *The Lord Declares His Great
Love for Israel* (Zech. 1:14)
2. *The Lord Declares His Great
Displeasure with the Nations*
(Zech. 1:15)
3. *The Lord Gives Good and Comforting Words* (Zech. 1:16, 17)
(1) The personal second advent of Messiah (vs. 16a)
(2) The building of the millennial temple (vs. 16b)
(3) Jerusalem's great growth
and expansion (vs. 16c)
(4) God's comfort for Israel
is assured (vs. 17a)
(5) Israel's divine election will
be vindicated (vs. 17b)

AFTER the introduction to the entire book, presented in Zechariah's opening sermon on repentance (1:1-6), a new section of the prophecy takes the form of a series of eight night visions (1:7 – 6:8). All of these visions have the same scope. They bridge the centuries and extend to the period of the restoration of the kingdom to Israel (Acts 1:6). They realize the ultimate in Jewish hopes and Jewish eschatology. Although all of them had an immediate and significant ministry of consolation and encouragement to the poor and feeble remnant of that day lately returned from the Babylonian exile, and desperately struggling to establish themselves in a ruined

city under the heel of a foreign power, yet in *no case, nor in any sense,* can any of these eight night visions be said to be *fulfilled* in the prophet's day. They had an application and a service to perform at that time, and sprang out of the historical exigencies of that period of trial and discouragement. But this is an entirely different matter from confusing such an application with fulfilment in any sense.

The fulfilment of these visions is yet future and awaits the events of the end of the times of the Gentiles and the second advent of the Messiah, who alone will destroy the Satanic world system and set up His kingdom of righteousness and peace.

25

7 Upon the four and twentieth day of the eleventh month, which is the month Sebat, in the second year of Darius, came the word of the Lord unto Zechariah, the son of Berechiah, the son of Iddo the prophet, saying,

8 I saw by night, and behold a man riding upon a red horse, and he stood among the myrtle trees, that were in the bottom; and behind him were there red horses, speckled, and white.

---

7 Upon the four and twentieth day of the eleventh month, which is the month Shebat, in the second year of Darius, came the word of Jehovah unto Zechariah the son of Berechiah, the son of Iddo, the prophet, saying,

8 I saw in the night, and, behold, a man riding upon a red horse, and he stood among the myrtle-trees, that were in the bottom; and behind him there were horses, red, sorrel, and white.

I. THE VISION AND ITS IMAGERY (Zech. 1:7, 8)

1. *The Time of the Vision* (Zech. 1:7). As in verse 1, the time notation is emphatic by its grammatical position (first in sentence). This is consonant with its importance since it gives the time when the entire series of eight visions, extending from chapter 1:7 through 6:8, was given. In contrast to the notation in 1:1, however, the day of the month is included. This is **the twenty-fourth day of the eleventh month Shebat** [February] **in Darius' second year** (520 B.C.). Thus the night visions were given approximately three months after Zechariah's opening sermon on repentance (1:1).

The **twenty-fourth day** of the month is obviously of special significance for on that day five months before, work on "the house of the Lord of hosts" had been resumed (Hag. 1:14, 15; 2:18). Also on that day two months previously Haggai had delivered a stern rebuke to the priests for their impurity and to the people for their delay in building the temple (Hag. 2:10–17). On that day, moreover, Haggai had received the far-reaching revelation (Hag. 2:20) of the destruction of Gentile world power previous to the establishment of millennial rule of the greater Zerubbabel-Messiah (Hag. 2:21–23). The day was, therefore, of unusual meaning and was peculiarly suitable for the vast prophetic disclosures contained in the eight visions of the prophet Zechariah.

2. *The Persons of the Vision and Their Identity* (Zech. 1:8a). The vehicle of revelation is not a dream (given when the recipient is asleep), but a vision (given when the subject is awake and fully conscious). He sees, hears, and understands the spiritual communications through the medium of his alerted physical senses. **I saw** [*ra'ithi*, not "I dreamed," *halamti*] **in the night** or "during the night" (an adverbial accusative). The most important person seen is **a red-horse rider.** This importance is stressed by the interjection **look! behold!** which precedes the noun **man** and fastens attention dramatically upon it. **Look a man!** The participle modifying the noun indicates the man is envisioned *in the act of riding*, that is, *astride* **a red horse** and he [i.e., the horse] **was standing** [another participle] **among the myrtle** [bushes] **in the glen.**

Behind the red-horse rider was *a company of horsemen.* The stress is altogether on the red-horse rider. This appears in the interesting detail that it is *not* said, "behind him [the red-horse rider] were *men riding* upon red, spotted, and white horses," but simply **behind him were red, spotted, and white horses** (vs. 8). To be sure the company of horses had riders. But the vision wishes to stress that the preeminently significant person was the red-horse rider, who is to be carefully distinguished from the other riders, yet in a sense one with them.

The *young prophet Zechariah* appears

in verse 9. **And I said, What are these, my lord?** Also appearing at this juncture and in verse 10 is **the interpreting angel.** The messenger [angel] **who was speaking** [participle] **with me** [*bî*] or perhaps, with Pusey, "*in* me," signifies an intimate heart-to-heart communication and impartation of the meaning of the vision.

The **red-horse rider** was an angel in human form, yet not merely an angel, since He is clearly differentiated from the other angelic riders. He is emphatically presented while they are presented only by implication. He can be none other than the Angel of Jehovah, since He is styled **Jehovah** (vs. 13). In addition, He possesses an authoritative dignity different from the others, who report their findings to Him in a way that suggests His preeminent position over them (cf. Judg. 6:12; 13:20; Num. 22:23). He thus appears to be none other than the Angel of the Presence (Exod. 23:23), Jehovah Himself, the Messiah in His preincarnate glory.

Does the color red speak of bloodshed and war and identify Him as the One who, as the result of the redemption He wrought at His first advent, will come to "judge and *to make war*" at His second advent (Rev. 19:11)? Is this not the portrayal of Him who will come "from Edom, in crimsoned garments from Bozrah, He that is glorious in His apparel, marching in the greatness of His strength"? He whose apparel is red and His garments like a treader of the wine press, who will trample His foes in His anger and whose lifeblood has stained all His raiment? (Cf. Isa. 63:1–6).

Although the **red-horse rider** is thus identified with Christ, the other riders in this first vision are mere angels. They appear in the role of scouts or military reconnoiterers under the direction of the red-horse rider and with responsibility to report their findings to Him. He, in turn, is seen as the overseer of Israel and the intercessor for the nation's welfare throughout the centuries of their humiliation and suffering, rather than as the Warrior and Avenger of His people against their enemies (Rev. 5–19), which role He will assume when He finally delivers them previous to the establishment of the kingdom.

The colors of the other horses (the riders are implied), namely, **red, dappled, and white** (vs. 8) are meaningful, contrary to Wright's contention (*Zechariah and His Prophecies*, p. 19). The red horses symbolize war, bloodshed, and judgment, but in this vision *not* as these are unleashed against the nations in the last night vision (Zech. 6:1–8), but *as the condition* of the earth is *ascertained* with regard to these calamities as they constitute a necessary prelude to Israel's restoration to millennial blessing (cf. Hag. 2:21, 22; Zech. 1:11, 12). The same is true of the colors of the other horses.

The **tawny** (*seruqqim* from root *saraq*, "to intertwine," "plait") probably means **sorrel** as translated by the A.V. and R.S.V. Baron interprets it in the sense "of mixed color," a combination of the red and the white (*The Visions and Prophecies of Zechariah*, p. 27), being sent on a variegated mission of judgment and mercy. The white portray victory and triumph (Rev. 6:2).

3. *The Places and Things of the Vision and Their Identity* (Zech. 1:8b). As important as the persons in the vision are the places and things. These constitute first, the myrtle trees and second, the deep valley where the red-horse rider was standing, with a company of horsed riders behind him (vs. 8).

The **myrtle trees** or shrubs beautifully symbolize Israel, the covenant people, in the role of an eternally elect nation, loved by the Lord, and the object of His unchanging purposes of grace (Rom. 11:29). The myrtle itself is a common indigenous shrub growing all over Palestine. Usually it is a low bush, adorning the barren hillsides. Under more favorable conditions of shade and moisture, as in the case of Zechariah's reference to it in the deep glen, it attains considerable height. It possesses dark-green, scented leaves, delicate starlike flowers, and dark-colored berries, which are edible.

Isaiah in millennial context refers to the myrtle as one of the choice plants of the land:

"I will put in the wilderness the cedar,
    the acacia, the myrtle, and the olive;
I will set in the desert the cypress,
    the plane and the pine together"
                                (Isa. 41:19).

"Instead of the thorn shall come up the
                                cypress,
    instead of the brier shall come up the
                                myrtle;
And it shall be to the Lord for a memorial
    for an everlasting sign which shall not
        be cut off" (Isa. 55:13).

Myrtle branches together with palm and willow twigs were used in the ritual of constructing booths in celebration of the Feast of Tabernacles (Neh. 8:15; Lev. 23:33–44). This feast was both retrospective, memorializing the redemption out of Egypt (Lev. 23:43), as well as prophetic of the kingdom rest of Israel after her final regathering from Egypt and the world. Peculiarly fitting is the use of the myrtle in this connection, since this lively shrub symbolizes Israel as the object of God's promises of restoration and blessing culminating in all the Feast of Tabernacles typifies.

Hadassah, the Jewish form of the name Esther (Esther 2:7) marks the occurrence of the word "Myrtle" as a proper name, which must have been popular in Israel.

The myrtle trees (symbolizing Israel) are said to be in the bottom (vs. 8). The Hebrew word is *metsulah*, "a deep place" or "glen" or "a low ravine," from the root *tsul* — the verb *tsollal* employed of "sinking in the water":

"Thou didst blow with thy wind.
    the sea covered them;
they *sank* as lead in the mighty waters"
                                (Exod. 15:10).

The noun *tsulah* (from the root *tsul*, "to be deep") means "the depth of the sea" or "abyss" (Isa. 44:27). The word

used by Zechariah occurs in the sense of "the depths" or "deep places" of the pit (*metsoloth*), as in Psalm 88:6 [1]. Similarly it occurs with the meaning of "the deep" or "ocean depth" in Psalm 107:23, 24:

"Some went down to the sea in ships
    doing business in the great waters;
they saw the deeds of the Lord,
    his wondrous works in the deep"
                                (*metsulah*).

Hence Zechariah sees the **myrtle trees in a deep glen** or ravine and not, as the R.V. margin, following the Septuagint, in "a shady place," *metsillah* (from root *tsalal*, "to be dark," "shady").

Aptly is "the bottom" or **deep glen** an expressive figure of the condition of Israel **(the myrtles)** as one of deep humiliation, degradation, and suffering during the *entire* period of "the times of the Gentiles" (Luke 21:24) from Nebuchadnezzar's day, 605 B.C., until the destruction of Gentile world power and the establishment of the kingdom at the second advent of Christ.

II. THE VISION AND ITS MEANING
    (Zech. 1:9–12)

1. *An Explanatory Word Concerning the Meaning of the Vision* (Zech. 1:9–11). Seeing the red-horse rider and the company of horsemen in the background, the prophet Zechariah, desiring to know their identity, asks, **What are these?** He is thereupon told by the interpreting angel that **These are they whom the Lord has sent** [dispatched] **to patrol the earth** (vs. 10). The words **to patrol** (the *hithpael* of *halak*, "to walk," "to go") have the idea of "walking up and down" (Gen. 3:8; Job 1:7), "to go about," "walk about" (Exod. 21:19; II Sam. 11:2). In the present context (Zech. 1:10, 11; 6:7), the idea of "walking up and down" occurs in a military sense with the significance of "patrolling," "making a careful military survey" or "reconnoitering," with the purpose of ascertaining the exact state of anything militarily.

The sphere of the reconnoitering

9 Then said I, O my lord, what are these? And the angel that talked with me said unto me, I will shew thee what these be.

10 And the man that stood among the myrtle trees answered and said, These are they whom the Lord hath sent to walk to and fro through the earth.

11 And they answered the angel of the Lord that stood among the myrtle trees, and said, We have walked to and fro through the earth, and, behold, all the earth sitteth still, and is at rest.

12 Then the angel of the Lord answered and said, O Lord of hosts, how long wilt thou not have mercy on Jerusalem and on the cities of Judah, against which thou hast had indignation these threescore and ten years?

---

9   Then said I, O my lord, what are these? And the angel that talked with me said unto me, I will show thee what these are.

10   And the man that stood among the myrtle trees answered and said, These are they whom Jehovah hath sent to walk to and fro through the earth.

11   And they answered the angel of Jehovah that stood among the myrtle-trees, and said, We have walked to and fro through the earth, and, behold, all the earth sitteth still, and is at rest.

12   Then the angel of Jehovah answered and said, O Jehovah of hosts, how long wilt thou not have mercy on Jerusalem and on the cities of Judah, against which thou hast had indignation these threescore and ten years?

---

expedition is said to be in the earth. This designates not only the far-flung Persian Empire from the Hellespont to the Indus and from the Caucasus to Egypt, but the *entire earth*, for the scope of the vision extends to the establishment of the world-wide kingdom of Messiah.

The report of the angelic scouts is a disconcerting one. The words, the whole earth, are highlighted. Look, the entire earth is quiet and at rest (vs. 11). The expression is quiet (*yosheveth*) is a participle denoting continuous action, and meaning "sitting," "sitting down relaxedly." When used of a place, city, or country, it has a passive force, "to be peacefully inhabited" (Isa. 13:20; Jer. 17:6, 25; Ezek. 26:20).

The verb "to be at rest" (*shaqat*, "to be quiet, to lie down, to be tranquil") is employed of one whom nobody harasses (Judg. 3:11; 5:31; 8:28; Jer. 30:10), particularly in the phrase, *shaqetah mimmilhamah*, "to have respite from war" (Josh. 11:23; 14:15). What the scouts reported to the red-horse rider was the fact that "lo, the entire earth is being peacefully inhabited and is in a state of respite from war."

2. *A Symbolic Act Concerning the Meaning* (Zech. 1:12). This was amazingly disappointing and disquieting news. It contained no suggestion of the fulfilment of God's promise that before the destruction of Gentile world power, preceding Israel's restoration to kingdom blessing, He would "shake the heavens and the earth . . . overthrow the throne of kingdoms and . . . destroy the strength of the kingdoms of the nations . . ." (Hag. 2:21, 22).

Because of this bad news that the nations were at peace and there was no sign that the time for the redemption of Judah and Jerusalem was at hand, the angel of the Lord becomes the intercessor. Then the angel of the Lord replied and said, O Lord of armies, how long wilt thou not have mercy upon Jerusalem and upon the cities of Judah with which thou hast been angry these seventy years? (vs. 12).

The how long query has stretched to almost two and a half millennia and still the cry is, "how long, O Lord?" Despite modern Zionism and the establishment of the Israeli state, Jerusalem is yet partially under the heel of Gentile power, and Jewry is still scattered throughout the world in unbelief and still persecuted with

13 And the Lord answered the angel that talked with me **with good words and comfortable words.**

14 So the angel that communed with me said unto me, Cry thou, saying, Thus saith the Lord of hosts; I am jealous for Jerusalem and for Zion with a great jealousy.

---

13   And Jehovah answered the angel that talked with me with good words, **even** comfortable words.

14   So the angel that talked with me said unto me, Cry thou, saying, Thus saith Jehovah of hosts: I am jealous for Jerusalem and for Zion with a great jealousy.

---

frightful cruelty in the modern world.

It is a great consolation to Zechariah, however, to know that the redhorse rider (the preincarnate Christ) is identified with His people in their sufferings, degradation, and woe. He is still standing **among the myrtle trees** [Israel] **in the glen.** He is still interceding for them. The Angel of the Presence, Jehovah-Christ, who had so wonderfully delivered their father Jacob is even now in the process of restoring His ancient people and preparing them for the revelation of His salvation at the end of the age.

He who is the great High Priest installed in the Heavenly Tabernacle, is according to the flesh the posterity of Abraham and carries on His intercessory ministry in His glorified humanity. We may be sure, moreover, that if the earthly high priest used to carry the names of the twelve tribes of Israel upon the breastplate nearest his heart (Exod. 28:29), the true High Priest, who is the King of Israel as well, has them just as near His loving heart. He loves Israel and yearns for the day when they will repent of their unbelief and sin and crown Him Lord of all.

III. THE VISION AND ITS MESSAGE (Zech. 1:13–17)

As a messenger proceeding from the vision and as an answer to the Angel of the Lord's fervent intercession, the Lord gives a consolatory message to Zechariah through the medium of the interpreting angel. This message is said to consist of **good words** – **comforting words** (vs. 13).

1. *The Lord Declares His Great Love for Israel* (Zech. 1:14). So the angel who was speaking with me said to me, Cry out, Thus says the Lord of armies: I am exceedingly jealous for Jerusalem and for Zion (vs. 14). Numerous syntactical devices here express the *greatness of God's love* for His covenant people Israel. (1) By the direction of the interpreting angel, **Cry out** (*qera'*, "to call with energy and spirit," to cry out as a herald or a prophet [Isa. 40:6; 58:1; Prov. 1:21, Greek *kerussein*]). (2) By the prefixed, **Thus says the Lord of armies,** intimating that all heavenly intelligences (angels) know God's love for Israel. (3) By the position of the verb first in the clause, **Jealous am I.** (4) By the meaning of the verb, from the root "to be jealous," because of the redness of the face when suffused by this burning passion; cf. Arabic *qana'a*, "to become very red" (Ps. 106:16; Gen. 30:1; Num. 5:14; 25:11, 13; I Kings 19:10). (5) By the position of the objects, **for Jerusalem and for Zion,** *before* the adverbial idea **with jealousy.** (6) By the use of the cognate accusative, **I am jealous ... with jealousy,** that is, "I am very jealous." Cf. Zech. 1:2, "angry ... *with anger*," i.e., *greatly* angry. (7) By the use of a qualifying adjective modifying the cognate accusative, **I am jealous ... with a great jealousy,** that is, "I am *exceedingly* jealous."

Jealousy is a burning, fiery passion. Men are jealous if that which is their own and dear to them falls into the hands of another, and is in danger of being taken away from them or

15 And I am very sore displeased with the heathen that are at ease; for I was but a little displeased, and they helped forward the affliction.

15   And I am very sore displeased with the nations that are at ease; for I was but a little displeased, and they helped forward the affliction.

abused. In this sense, and with infinitely holy connotations, God is likewise jealous of His own people Israel, abused and exappropriated by the nations. Jerusalem and Zion are distinctively His by sovereign, gracious choice (Zech. 3:2). The Gentiles have taken them and dispersed their inhabitants, mistreating God's inheritance. God has been conscious of the desolation of the land and city throughout the centuries. He is fully aware of the world-wide woe of oppressed Jewry. He is jealous for His people exceedingly. He is soon to arise to take vengeance on their foes.

"For the Lord has chosen Zion,
He has desired it for his habitation:
This is my resting place forever;
here I will dwell, for I have desired it.
. . . .
There will I make a horn to sprout for
David;
I have prepared a lamp for my anointed.
His enemies I will clothe with shame,
but upon himself his crown will flourish
(Ps. 132:13, 14, 17, 18).

He rejected the tabernacle of Joseph,
He did not choose the tribe of Ephraim;
but he chose the tribe of Judah,
Mount Zion, which he loves" (Ps. 78:67, 68).

2. *The Lord Declares His Great Displeasure with the Nations* (Zech. 1:15). And I am intensely angry with the nations that are at ease; with whom I was angry a little but they furthered the disaster (vs. 15). The *intensity of God's displeasure* against the nations is indicated: (1) By the cognate accusative appearing in the first position of emphasis in the Hebrew sentence. With . . . anger I am angry. (2) By the use of the adjective to modify the noun in the adverbial accusative, With great anger I am angry. (3) By the use of the participle with the separate pronoun I, showing the continuousness of the anger, I am

continually being angry (*qotseph*). (4) By the repetition of the verb "to be angry" in a finite form (historic perfect showing completed action in past time), with whom I was angry. (5) By the use of the separate pronoun in addition to the pronominal idea already in the finite verb. I [Myself] was angry for a little while (time expressed here, not degree as in 1:2). (6) By the adversative use of and (*waw*), plus the separate pronoun. But they [contrast to I] furthered (*'azeru,* "aided, helped, abetted"; cf. II Sam. 8:5; 21:17). (7) By the fact that the nations abetted the calamity or "disaster" which was the inevitable punishment meted out by the Lord's wrath for their mistreatment of His people.

The word for calamity (*ra'ah*) is a feminine adjective, (masculine *ra',* "evil," "bad") used substantivally of "evil" which anyone perpetrates (Job 20:12; Ps. 97:10). It is also employed of anything "evil" or "bad" which happens to one in the sense of "calamity," "harm," "disaster" (Gen. 19:19; 26:29; 44:4). Its use by Zechariah denotes the inevitable consequences which God's wrath visits upon men and nation's sins, in this case the sin of anti-Semitism, the crime of the nations.

That the Lord was for a little time (*me'at*) angry with the nations who were at ease was primarily true of the seventy-year exile in Babylonia. But God's anger has been stretched out over the millennia and increases as the centuries still roll on and the Jew suffers new butcheries and pogroms at the hands of a modern Antiochus Epiphanes, like Hitler or Mussolini, as cruel Gentile leaders go far beyond what God had in mind in using them to discipline and correct His erring people.

16 Therefore thus saith the Lord; I am returned to Jerusalem with mercies: my house shall be built in it, saith the Lord of hosts, and a line shall be stretched forth upon Jerusalem.

17 Cry yet, saying, Thus saith the Lord of hosts; My cities through prosperity shall yet be spread abroad; and the Lord shall yet comfort Zion, and shall yet choose Jerusalem.

16 Therefore thus saith Jehovah: I am returned to Jerusalem with mercies; my house shall be built in it, saith Jehovah of hosts, and a line shall be stretched forth over Jerusalem.

17 Cry yet again, saying, Thus saith Jehovah of hosts: My cities shall yet overflow with prosperity; and Jehovah shall yet comfort Zion, and shall yet choose Jerusalem.

The guilty nations under God's wrath are said to be at ease, *sha'anan* from the *pilel* of the verb "to be tranquil," "to live in carnal tranquillity" (Jer. 30:10; Job 3:18). Hence the adjective, denoting a settled state, is used both in a good sense, "tranquil, peaceful" (Isa. 33:20; Job 12:5) and with a bad connotation, "living at ease," "secularly and carnally secure," "tranquilly careless" (Amos 6:1; Isa. 32:9, 11, 18; Ps. 123:4). In Isaiah 37:29 and II Kings 19:28, the substantive is used in the sense of "pride," "arrogance," the natural result of living in carnal, God-denying security and tranquillity.

The divine anger will be one day revealed in full measure against the sinning nations. The pre-kingdom age will terminate in the judgment of the nations (Zech. 6:1–8). That judgment is a necessary prelude to all that the millennium will be (Israel as the head of the nations restored to full high priestly ministry as in Zechariah, chapter 3). The judgment of the nations will eventuate in a recompense for sins committed by *individuals* of these nations against Christ's people, the Jews (Joel 3:1–3, 17 [4:1–3, 17]). The nations are punished or rewarded according to their treatment of the Lord's "brothers" (Matt. 25:31–46).

3. *The Lord Gives Good and Comforting Words* (Zech. 1:16, 17). **Therefore, thus says the Lord of armies** (vs. 16). These words form the introduction to the "good *words* and comforting *words*" (repetition which

emphasizes the importance of these words). **Therefore** (*lakhen*, "on that account" [Judg. 10:13; Isa. 5:24; 8:7; 30:7; Job 32:10]) is a causal adverb and sums up logically the reasons for the good and comforting words; namely, the vision of the red-horse rider among the myrtles in the glen and the great truth springing out of it that God loves His people intensely and is grievously provoked at their enemies. **Therefore, thus says the Lord!** fortifies this concluding message of the first vision.

The first good and comforting word declares *the personal second advent of Messiah* (vs. 16a). **I have returned** (*shavti*) construed as a simple past historical perfect had a definite application of comfort to that poor, harassed community of the prophet's day which was struggling to reclaim the ruined city and country of their forefathers. But in its fulfilment the expression is to be taken as a *prophetic perfect*, declaring with the sureness of a past event an occurrence that has not yet taken place. **I will surely return to Jerusalem.** The Shekinah glory as it was manifest in the wilderness and as it appeared in the Solomonic temple will be restored. "I will go away and return to my place" (Hos. 5:15). "For, behold, your house is left unto you desolate. For I say unto you, Ye shall not see me henceforth till you shall say, Blessed is he that cometh in the name of the Lord" (Matt. 23:38, 39). The people being nationally set aside, the

Lord is absent in person. Israel is forsaken. The land has been desolate throughout the centuries. The coming of Messiah will be foundational and indispensable to Israel's true restoration. Little wonder this great prediction stands first among the good and comforting words vouchsafed to Zechariah.

The Lord's return, moreover, will be attended with mercies (*rahamîm*, "the bowels," Greek *ta splagchna*), designating the ancient idea that the *viscera* were the seat of the emotions (Prov. 20:10); hence, *very tender affection, love, natural affection* towards kindred (Gen. 43:30; Amos 1:11). Zechariah uses the term of God's love in action in *pity, grace,* and *favor* (Ps. 25:6; 40:11; Isa. 47:6).

The second good and comforting word embraces *the building of the (millennial) temple* (vs.16b). **My house** [emphatic by position] **shall be built in it** [Jerusalem], **is the saying of the Lord of hosts.** This promise, of course, had an incipient application (as do all eight night visions) to the prophet's time and supplied the need for encouragement in the construction of the second temple. That application, however, was only *partial.* The fulfilment of this glorious promise will not be realized until millennial times in the construction of that temple which Ezekiel saw in prophetic vision (Ezek. 40–42). This edifice will be a house of prayer for representatives of the saved millennial nations. Isaiah glimpsed this future temple clearly:

It shall come to pass in the latter days that the *mountain of the house of the Lord* shall be established in the top of the
                                    mountains
and shall be raised above the hills;
and all the nations shall flow to *it,*
and many peoples shall come, and say:
Come, let us go up to the mountain of the
                                    Lord,
to the house of the God of Jacob;
That he may teach us his ways
and that we may walk in his paths.
For out of Zion shall go forth the law,
and the word of the Lord from Jerusalem
                              (Isa. 2:2, 3).

So universally doubted, even among scholars who take these great prophecies literally at their face value, are these predictions that the Spirit of God buttresses this promise of an actual temple to be constructed in Palestine for the universal worship of God, with the assuring words, **is the saying of the Lord of armies.** His testimony is to be received in preference to the specious skepticism of men.

The third good and comforting word is that *Jerusalem shall enjoy great growth and expansion* (vs. 16c). **And a line shall be stretched over Jerusalem.** This is a tape measure, *qaw, qere* reading, "a rope," "a cord," Arabic *quwwatun,* from root *qawah,* "to twist," "to bind"; "a measuring line or cord," Ezek. 47:3; Job 38:5; Isa. 44:13. "To stretch a line over" is "to pull a tape taut to measure anything."

The imagery of the surveyor's measuring line suggests the growth and prosperity of the city in that day, but particularly in the millennial era when Jerusalem is to be the capital and center of the earth (Ezek. 38:12). **My cities through prosperity shall yet be spread abroad** (*tephutsenah, qal* imperfect 3rd feminine plural from *puts,* "to disperse," "to scatter," "to overflow"). Zechariah employs the word here in the sense of "overflow," "to be superabundant," as in Proverbs 5:16: "Should your springs *overflow abroad,* streams of water in the streets?" *My* cities shall yet overflow *by reason of* prosperity (*mittobh,* the *min* being causal).

The fourth good and comforting word is that *God's comfort for Israel is assured* (vs. 17a). **And the Lord shall yet** [despite all appearances to the contrary] **have mercy upon Zion.** The words, **have mercy upon** (*niham* [Septuagint *eleēsei*], "to be tender," *piel* "to treat with the tenderest affection," "to console" with the fulfilment of gracious promises; cf. Exod. 33:19; Deut. 13:17 [18]; 30:3; Ps. 103:13; 116:5; Isa. 49:15), express

God's love for Israel as it will be put into action in the day of their conversion and blessing. The Masoretic Text, however, has *niham* instead of *riham*, "to comfort, console," i.e., "to declare grief or pity" (Gen. 50:21; Job 2:11). It frequently includes the idea of help and deliverance especially in the case of God, as in this passage (Isa. 12:1; 49:13; 51:3; 52:9; Ps. 23:4; 71:21; 86:17). The Lord in that future day will comfort Zion with gracious help and wonderful deliverance from their enemies.

The fifth good and comforting word is that *Israel's divine election will be vindicated* (vs. 17b). **And the Lord will yet** [despite all appearances of her apparent rejection] **choose Jerusalem.** The word **choose** is from *bahar*, "prove, try, examine"; Syriac *behar* (Job 34:4); then "to approve, choose, select" (Gen. 13:11; Exod. 17:9; Josh. 24:15). Yet will Zechariah's words as well as the Apostle Paul's record in Romans 11:29 be proved true: "For the gifts and call of God [of Israel] are irrevocable." If God proved forgetful of His covenants and promises regarding Israel in the Old Testament, what basis would the Christian have that God would validate His promises made to him in the New Testament?

CHAPTER ONE

(Continued)

ISRAEL TRIUMPHANT OVER HER FOES

(THE SECOND VISION)

THE FOUR HORNS AND FOUR SMITHS

(ZECH. 1:18–24) [Hebrew 2:1–4]

I. THE FOUR HORNS AND THEIR IDENTITY (Zech. 1:18, 19) [2:1, 2]

   1. *The Prophet Envisions Four Horns* (Zech. 1:18) [2:1]

   2. *The Identity of the Four Horns* (Zech. 1:19) [2:2]

II. THE FOUR SMITHS AND THEIR TASK (Zech. 1:20, 21) [2:3, 4]

   1. *Four Smiths Appear* (Zech. 1:20) [2:3]

   2. *The Task of the Four Smiths* (Zech. 1:21) [2:4]

   3. *The Identity of the Four Smiths* (1:21) [2:4]

---

18 Then lifted I up mine eyes, and saw, and behold four horns.

---

18 And I lifted up mine eyes, and saw, and, behold, four horns.

IN the preceding vision of the red-horse rider among the myrtle trees, the Lord's great anger against the nations because of their treatment of Israel has been mentioned and the threat of their punishment has been hinted at (Zech. 1:15). Glimmerings of hope for eventual restoration from the nation's dispersed and downtrodden condition appear. Now the question arises: How would God deal with their enemies and their persecutors? Would the nation in its smallness and weakness ever hope to have deliverance from its powerful oppressors, who during the whole span of "the times of the Gentiles" (Luke 21:24) have mercilessly ground the Jew into the dust? The answer to this problem constitutes the theme of the second night vision revealed to the prophet. This is the vision of the four horns and the four smiths.

I. THE FOUR HORNS AND THEIR IDENTITY (Zech. 1:18, 19) [2:1, 2]

This vision resumes the gracious and consolatory note struck in the first vision. The nations who have scattered and crushed Israel shall themselves be scattered and crushed.

1. *The Prophet Envisions Four Horns* (Zech. 1:18) [2:1]. **Then I raised my eyes and looked, and lo! four horns.** This second vision opens in a temporal sequence, following immediately on the first vision. **Then I raised my eyes.** Likely with head bowed in meditation upon the meaning of the preceding vision, the prophet is doubtless directed to the second vision by the ministry of the interpreting angel although this is not specifically said. **And looked,** literally "and *saw*," not only with his physical eyes, but with the inner vision of his soul and spirit as these

35

19 And I said unto the angel that talked with me, What be these? And he answered me, These are the horns which have scattered Judah, Israel, and Jerusalem.

19   And I said unto the angel that talked with me, What are these? And he answered me, These are the horns which have scattered Judah, Israel, and Jerusalem.

are stimulated by the supernatural communication of the vision itself.

The arresting objects in the vision that strike Zechariah's spiritual consciousness are **four horns**. This is indicated by the adverbial interjection, **behold! lo!** (*hinneh*, which is a lively demonstrative particle widely used to fasten attention upon that which it points out to set it apart for careful scrutiny or as an object of special interest). Here the **four horns** are the focal point of concern.

These are animal horns, likely those f a ram, but the beast or beasts who ore the horns are hidden from the prophet's view. Nevertheless, the beasts are not to be supposed to be absent because the strength or destructive power of an animal's horn is in its connection with the beast which possesses it.

The Hebrew word (*qeren*) denotes "a horn" of a ram, goat, or ox, and is common in all the cognate languages (Assyrian *qarnu*, Arabic *qarnun*). The Latin has *cornu*, Gothic *haurns*, German *horn*, and English "horn." Whereas the word often means a horn for blowing (Josh. 6:5) or an animal's horn used as a receptacle (I Sam. 16:1, 13; I Kings 1:39), it very frequently is employed as a symbol of *strength* and *power*, particularly of nations or individuals, being a figure borrowed from the great strength or destructive power of bulls, wild oxen, etc., centering in their horns. "The horn of Moab is cut off, and his arm is broken" (Jer. 48:25). "He hath cut off in his fierce anger all the horn [might] of Israel..." (Lam. 2:3). "All the horns of the wicked also I will cut off" (Ps. 75:10 [11]). "To lift up the horn" is to increase one's power or prestige (Ps. 89:17[18]; 92:10 [11]).

David calls the Lord "the horn [*qeren*] of my deliverance" (Ps. 18:2 [3]), by which he means the Lord is his protection, procuring his liberation, just like a horned animal uses its horns as a defense.

Since a "horn" commonly symbolizes strength or power of nations or individuals, it often symbolizes a *Gentile king as representing his kingdom.* "And the ten *horns* out of this *kingdom* are ten *kings...*" (Dan. 7:24). "And the ten *horns* which thou sawest are ten *kings...*" (Rev. 17:12).

The "ram which had two horns" (Dan. 8:3) represents "the *kings* of Media and Persia" (Dan. 8:20). "The goat [Macedonia-Greece] had a conspicuous horn [Alexander the Great] between his eyes..." (Dan. 8:6). Thus in prophecy a "horn" represents a Gentile *king closely identified with his kingdom*, symbolizing the beastlike (from God's point of view and that of His people Israel) power and strength of such rule. Compare Daniel 7:7, 8 where kingdoms are represented as (horned) beasts. Accordingly, the **four horns** envisioned by Zechariah represent four kingdoms.

2. *The Identity of the Four Horns* (Zech. 1:19) [2:2]. **And I** [the prophet] **said to the angel who was talking with me** [*qal* active participle denoting continuous time, here in past], **What are these** [horns]? Glimpsing just the horns, apparently apart from the animals who possessed them, Zechariah is puzzled to know what they represented or symbolized, not certainly that he did not recognize them as "horns."

Then [temporal sequence] he [the interpreting angel] **replied and said: These are the horns which have scattered Judah, Israel, and Jeru-**

salem (1:19) [2:2]. The horns plainly signify ruthless kingdoms which through their kings have "thoroughly winnowed" God's covenant nation as grain is beaten out and the chaff separated from it in the summer threshing floor. The form used is the *piel* of the root "to scatter," "to disperse," as dust is driven by the wind (Exod. 32:20; Isa. 30:22). But the particular meaning in the *qal* is "to winnow" (Isa. 30:24; Jer. 4:11; Ruth 3:2) and with figurative force, "to rout enemies" (Jer. 15:7; Isa. 41:16; Ezek. 5:2). But in the *piel*, as in the case of Zechariah's use, the idea of *winnowing* is even more pronounced, and the word as used thus by the prophet is very strong and intensive. The nations have "unmercifully sifted" God's covenant people, suggesting the cruel and relentless rage of the nations and their drastic dispersing of them (Lev. 26:33; Ezek. 5:10; 6:5; 30:26; Prov. 20:8).

In dealing with the question of the identity of the four horns the important truth must be kept in mind that the scope of this vision is the *same* as that of the other seven night visions (Zech. 1:7 – 6:8). All of them (and this one is no exception) extend through the centuries and on to the establishment of the kingdom over Israel. All of them have their fulfilment in events preparatory to the setting up of that kingdom or to the established order which will prevail in the millennium itself.

The four horns then must symbolize the four great world powers which will be coterminous with "the times of the Gentiles" (Luke 21:24), which period began with Judah's captivity under Nebuchadnezzar (605 B.C.) and runs to the second advent of Christ. During this interval Jerusalem has been under Gentile dominion. Even today after the marvelous events in Palestine consequent upon the establishment of the Israeli state, Jerusalem is not yet fully liberated from Gentile control. But every indication points to the fact that "the times of the Gentiles" are running out like the sands of an hourglass.

The four great empires revealed in Scripture to be coeval with "the times of the Gentiles" are, according to Daniel's interpretation of the colossus (Dan. 2:37–45) and his vision of the four beasts (Dan. 7:2–8, 17–28): Babylon, Medo-Persia, Macedonia, Greece, and Rome. The latter was divided in the fifth century into the Eastern and Western Empires and subsequently fell into dissolution. However, the Roman power will be revived in a federation of ten kingdoms corresponding to the feet and toes of the colossus (Dan. 2:42–44; 7:7, 8, 20; Rev. 13:1).

Inasmuch as the word **scattered** (*zeru* is a perfect tense) *may* be interpreted as a past completed action, some scholars are inclined to reject Babylon, Medo-Persia, Macedonian Greece, and Rome and to specify Egypt, Assyria, Babylon, and Persia as Gentile powers which had already overrun Israel and Judah. But the Hebrew verbal system describes the *kind* of action, and *not* past, present, or future tense. The perfect presents *finished* or *completed* action either in past, present, or future depending upon the *context*. In line with the scope of *all* the other night visions, it is certainly preferable to interpret this one as a *present* perfect. **These are the [four] horns which scatter** (that is, characteristically do so). It is gratuitous for Wright to object that "the vision appears to refer to the past and not to the future" (*Zechariah and His Prophecies*, p. 27) when all the other night visions do so, and the verb in this instance by no means compels such a view.

Some critics doubt the textual genuineness of **Israel** in verse 4 [2:2], especially as this expression is not found in verse 21 [2:4]. If the name **Israel** is a textual intrusion, it is very early, at least pre-Septuagintal, for the Greek version has it both in verse 19 [2:2] and verse 21 [2:4].

20 And the Lord shewed me four carpenters.

20   And Jehovah showed me four smiths.

But it seems possible that it may be a gloss since Israel in conjunction with Judah regularly denotes the Northern Kingdom in distinction from its southern neighbor (Jer. 3:8, 11, 18; Ezek. 9:9; 27:17, etc.). In addition, this explanation appears likely since in the first night vision, which this second follows closely, as well as in the later visions, the prophet clearly has the Judaean dispersions in mind, and employs the "four horns" to picture the powers instrumental in those catastrophes (in 586 B.C. and A.D. 70) and lasting till the final regathering).

It is to be noted also that the **four horns** symbolizing Gentile persecutions of the Jew were successive and not contemporaneous. Only the Persian power existed in Zechariah's day, the Babylonian having passed off the scene some sixteen years previously. The empires of Nebuchadnezzar's colossus (Dan. 2:31–45) are seen all at one time, but followed each other in historical succession, as well as the wild beasts of chapter 7:2–13. Prophecy has this perspective aspect which appears here.

That Zechariah had the four world empires of the "times of the Gentiles" in mind, rather than a vague reference to the universality of the enmity against Israel by allusion to "the four winds of heaven" or "the four corners of the earth" is further corroborated by the fact that the prophet largely bases his visions and prophecies on revelations already granted to the prophets who preceded him. In this case he shows indebtedness to Daniel, in the sense that the same Spirit who inspired Daniel inspired him in similar vein.

II. THE FOUR SMITHS AND THEIR TASK
    (Zech. 1:20, 21) [2:3, 4]

These verses do not constitute a new vision, as some would suppose,

but form an intrinsic and inseparable part of the same prophetic disclosure — the second night vision.

1. *Four Smiths Appear* (Zech. 1:20) [2:3]. **And the Lord showed me four smiths.** It is interesting that the prophet automatically saw the "four horns" (Judah's enemies) when he looked up (1:18) [2:1], but that when it was a matter of divine help against these destructive Gentile horns, the Lord Himself **caused him to see** [*hifil*] **four smiths.** God's deliverances are often made more delightful and memorable by His revelations of Himself.

These **four smiths** stand over against the *four* horns to demonstrate to the Lord's people that every hostile world power that rises up against them to extirpate them, shall in turn be extirpated and destroyed, and that, as has often been proved, for *every* enemy of God's people God has provided a counteracting power adequate to destroy it.

It is possible Zechariah himself and the people to whom he preached the word given to him in prophetic vision did not see much more than these simple practical lessons of encouragement and uplift. But this consolation was of superlative value to inspire them and fortify them for the onerous tasks and the severe trials they were called upon to face. All prophecy has this wider role. It has a message and ministry to God's people in any age, and not only to those who may live in the era in which it is fulfilled and realized as a present reality. As the Apostle Peter says, "And we have the prophetic words made more sure. You will do well to pay attention to this as to a lamp shining in a dark place, until the day dawns and the morning star rises in your hearts" (II Pet. 1:19, R.S.V.).

However, whatever the degree of comprehension of the full meaning of

21 Then said I, What come these to do? And he spake, saying, These are the horns which have scattered Judah, so that no man did lift up his head: but these are come to fray them, to cast out the horns of the Gentiles, which lifted up their horn over the land of Judah to scatter it.

---

21 Then said I, What come these to do? And he spake, saying, These are the horns which scattered Judah, so that no man did lift up his head; but these are come to terrify them, to cast down the horns of the nations, which lifted up their horn against the land of Judah to scatter it.

---

the vision granted the people of that day, the scope of this and of all these night visions is panoramic. This fact appears all the more obvious to us from our superior vantage point much nearer their ultimate fulfilment.

The smiths are "technicians" (Septuagint, *tektones*), skilled workers in metal, stone, or wood. The Hebrew term *ḥarash* is a *piel* substantival form with the middle radical doubled, here with compensatory vowel lengthening since the *resh* cannot be doubled. This characteristic form denotes a trade or professional worker – "an artisan or artificer of iron, bronze, or wood" (Exod. 35:35; Deut. 27:15) from the root *ḥarash*, "to cut, engrave, or forge." Since the idea here is a worker in metal, a smith is a good rendering, rather than a "carpenter" or worker in wood (Isa. 44:12) or a "stone mason" or engraver (Exod. 28:11).

2. *The Task of the Four Smiths* (Zech. 1:21) [2:4]. Then [or "afterwards" – the *waw* consecutive denotes temporal sequence] I said, What are these [smiths] coming to do? Zechariah does not say, "*Who* are these?" but, What are these coming to do? The prophet instantly recognizes *who* they are, doubtless by the garb of their guild and by their tools. He is interested in their task. The demonstrative pronoun these points out these artificers, and the participle coming (*ba'im*) indicates that the prophet sees these artisans *in the act* of advancing to accomplish their purpose.

To the prophet's question the interpreting angel replies forthrightly. These are the horns which thoroughly winnow [*piel*] Judah so that a man

[i.e., "one"] did not lift up his head; and these have come to terrify them to cast down the horns of the nations who lifted up [their] horn against the land of Judah to scatter it.

The verb "winnow, thoroughly disperse" (*zeru*) is identical with the form in Zechariah 1:19 [2:4] and has the same lively force and meaning. The words, These are the horns which have scattered Judah, constitute a repetition (for *emphasis* on the ruthless cruelty of the persecuting nations). In the repetition, however, it is noteworthy that both "Israel" and "Jerusalem" are omitted (although the Septuagint has "Israel" in both passages).

So thoroughly did the nations *scatter* "Judah" that [*kephi*] a man [here purely a pronoun in Hebrew, "one"] did not lift up his head, because he could not, demonstrating the terrible severity of the nations' maltreatment of the Jew through the centuries. "To lift up the head" is a movement that shows a little strength, but Israel's sufferings at the hands of the Gentile nations have been so inhuman that not even this sparse display of strength was possible.

Following the emphatic repetition of the fact of the nations' barbarity against Israel, appended with an additional note stressing its diabolic cruelty (no one did lift up his head), the interpreting angel with this introduction presents the work the smiths are seen coming to do, So that these [smiths] have come to terrify them, to cast down the horns of the nations. . . . The *waw* consecutive (And these have come) here expresses logical result – so that these have come. Their *purpose* for coming is indicated by the infinitive prefixed by *lamedh*, in regular Hebrew idiom: to terrify or "to affray" (*lehaharid*) and to cast [or throw] down (*leyaddoth*). "To terrify" with the added purpose "of throwing down," their consternation being a necessary prelude to their destruction.

The verb terrify is the causative form of the *qal* stative *ḥarad* (Assyrian *ḥaradu*, "to tremble, be afraid"), "to be frightened or scared" (Exod. 19:16; I Sam. 28:5), so that the *hifil* form means "to terrify," "to make afraid" (Lev. 26:6; Zeph. 3:13); "to throw into a panic," "to drive away in terror" (Judg. 8:12; II Sam. 17:2). The four smiths will "throw the persecuting nations into a panic," making their destruction an easier job.

The verb, to cast down, is the *piel* from the *qal yadah*, "to throw or cast" with the meaning of "profess," "confess," i.e., by the gesture of the hand cast forth or extended (Ps. 32:5), then with the idea of "give thanks," "praise" (Gen. 29:35; 49:8). The *piel* form used here means "to *throw* or *cast down*" in the sense of destroying (Lam. 3:53). That which the artisans "throw down" is the horns of the nations who lift up [participle denoting not a sporadic but a continuous persecution] the horn against the land of Judah to scatter it.

To lift up [the] horn is the figure of a horned animal charging its victim to maim it or kill it outright (Ps. 75:5 [6]). In this figure the persecuting nations are tacitly likened to ferocious beasts who charge Israel in their anger to gore her to death and destroy her. In a similar idiom used in a good sense, compare Psalm 92:10 [11]: "But my horn [power, strength] shalt thou exalt like the horn of the wild ox" (I Sam. 2:10; Ps. 89:17 [18]; 148:14).

Having *twice* used the same word (*zeru*) "thoroughly to winnow" or "disperse," Zechariah employs it a *third* time, thus *thrice* emphasizing the malignant scattering of Judah effected by her enemies.

3. *The Identity of the Four Smiths*

(1:21) [2:4]. It is possible to interpret these four smiths, following Jerome, Cyril, Calvin and many others, as symbolic of the *supernatural means* through which the Lord accomplishes His purposes of punishment against the persecutors of His people, Israel, with the truth enunciated that the injury done Judah will be as far-reaching and as thorough as the evil inflicted.

But since the four horns are symbolic of four successive world empires spanning "the times of the Gentiles," extending "from Nebuchadnezzar to the second advent of Christ, it is consonant with the scope of the vision to treat the four smiths in a similar fashion. They also must represent four successive powers likewise running coterminously with the very same period and used by God to terrify and to cast down the enemies of God's people Israel.

In line with Daniel's great prophecies concerning "the times of the Gentiles" (Dan. 2:31–45; 7:2–13) three of the horns in turn and under the punitive hand of God *become* smiths, while the fourth and last horn is cast down by the world-wide kingdom set up by the returning Christ, coming to dash to pieces His enemies who are at the same time His peoples' enemies (Ps. 2:1–12). Thus the first horn (Babylon) is cast down by Medo-Persia, the second horn. The second horn (Medo-Persia), accordingly, in turn becomes the first smith. The second horn (Medo-Persia) is cast down by the third horn, and thus becomes the second smith. The third horn (Macedonian Greece) is in turn cast down by the fourth horn (Rome), which thus becomes the third smith. The fourth horn (Rome), the most dreadful of all, *does not* become a smith but in its revived ten-kingdom form of the last days is destroyed by the fourth smith, *the millennial kingdom* set up by the returning "King of kings and Lord of lords" (Rev. 19:16).

Zechariah sees all four smiths together; the fourth, however, being diverse from the three, is only included with them to fill out the scope of the vision and to complete the symbolism of the overthrow of Gentile world power preparatory to the establishment of the kingdom over Israel.

In the colossus vision of chapter 2 of Daniel the casting down of the fourth horn corresponds to the "stone . . . cut out without hands [Christ]" "smiting the image" [symbol of Gentile world power] "upon its feet" (the fourth horn, Rome, in its final form so that the iron, the clay, the brass, the silver, and the gold of which it was made are "broken to pieces" and become "like the chaff of the summer threshingfloors." And "the stone that smote the image" becomes "a great mountain" (the millennial kingdom, Zechariah's fourth smith) and fills "the whole earth" (Dan. 2:34, 35).

In the vision of the same overthrow of Gentile world power under the symbolism of wild beasts in Daniel 7, Zechariah's fourth horn (Rome) appears as "the fourth beast, dreadful and terrible, and strong exceedingly." It has "great iron teeth" and devours and breaks in pieces, and stamps "the residue with its feet," and it is "different from all the beasts that were before it"; and it has "ten horns" (Dan. 7:7). These "ten horns . . . are ten kings that shall arise" (Dan. 7:24).

It is "in the days of these kings" (final form of the revived Roman power) that "the God of heaven" shall set up "a kingdom, which shall never be destroyed: and the kingdom shall not be left to other people, but *it shall break to pieces and consume all these kingdoms* [this is the fourth smith of Zechariah's vision] and shall stand forever" (Dan. 2:44).

Daniel had a magnificent foreview of the investiture of Christ with the kingdom before His departure from heaven. "I saw in the night visions and, behold, one like the Son of man came with the clouds of heaven, and came to the Ancient of days and they

brought him near before him. And there was given him dominion, and glory, *and a kingdom that all people, nations, and languages shall serve him: his dominion is an everlasting dominion*, which shall not pass away, and *his kingdom that which shall not be destroyed* (Dan. 7:13, 14).

How wonderful does this vision portray the truth that "the most High rules the kingdom of men, and gives it to whomsoever he will" (Dan. 4:32). At first blush it would appear that the first three kingdoms came to an end purely by *human* instrumentality and that only the fourth is *supernaturally* destroyed by the kingdom set up by the returning Christ. Actually, however, *all* the kingdoms are cast down by "the most High" ruling in the kingdom of men.

Nebuchadnezzar was God's "servant" raised up to chastise God's sinning people (Jer. 25:9; 27:6; 43:10). Concerning Cyrus, the Persian who cast down Babylon, the Lord declares "He is *my* shepherd, and *he shall fulfill all my purpose*" (Isa. 44:28). "Thus says the Lord *to his anointed, to Cyrus, whose right hand I have grasped,* to subdue nations before him and ungird the loins of kings, to open doors before him, that gates may not be closed" (Isa. 45:1).

Alexander the Great, who destroyed the mighty Persian power, was similarly God's instrument to execute His purposes. One of Alexander's most notable exploits, the taking of rich and powerful city of Tyre, is attributed to the Lord and not to Alexander:

"Tyre has built herself a rampart,
    and heaped up silver like dust
    and gold like the dirt of the streets,
But lo, *the Lord will strip her of her
            possessions*
and hurl her wealth into the sea,
and she shall be devoured by fire" (Zech.
                                9:3, 4).

Similarly the dreadful Roman power was an instrument in the hands of the most High to destroy the Macedonian Greek kingdoms into which Alexander's world empire disintegrated after his death. But the last form of Gentile world power, reaching the peak of iniquity and blasphemy under the Antichrist, the man of sin himself, will be destroyed by the personal Christ appearing to set up His kingdom of righteousness and peace which "shall break to pieces and consume" all other kingdoms "and shall stand forever" (Dan. 2:44). Zechariah saw this great event and the panoramic sweep of events which are a prelude to it in the vision of the four horns and the four smiths. In synoptic symbolism he envisioned Israel triumphant over her enemies and the foes who have persecuted her throughout the long and wearisome centuries of the "times of the Gentiles". He envisioned "the indestructible Jew" preserved to inherit the kingdom and to realize the reliability of the divine promises and covenants made to the nation in the Old Testament.

CHAPTER TWO

JERUSALEM IN MILLENNIAL GLORY

(THE THIRD VISION)

THE MAN WITH THE MEASURING LINE

(ZECH. 2:1–13) [Hebrew 2:5–17]

THE purpose of this third night vision (in the series of eight) is to set forth prophetically the restoration of Jerusalem with reference to Zechariah's time, but also in larger scope, to describe the yet future *fulfilment* in the kingdom age, when the city will become the capital of the millennial earth. Particularly emphasized is the great increase in size, population, wealth, spirituality, and security of the city.

This third vision foreshadowing Jerusalem in millennial glory is inseparably connected with the first, predicating hope for downtrodden Israel, and the second, presenting the nation triumphant over her foes. The message of the first vision was crystallized in "the good *words* and comfortable *words*" (1:13), the essence of which declared God's passionate love for *Jerusalem* (1:14), His keen anger at her persecutors, the *nations* (1:15), His sure "return to *Jerusalem* with mercies" (1:16), the latter indicated by the rebuilding of the temple and the expansive growth of *the city*. As in the present vision, a measuring line is "stretched over *Jerusalem*" (1:16), with the whole land experiencing the beneficent effects of this grand visitation: "*My* cities through prosperity shall yet be spread abroad; and the Lord will yet have mercy *upon Zion* and will yet choose *Jerusalem*" (1:17).

The second vision also springs out

43

1 I lifted up mine eyes again, and looked, and behold a man with a measuring line in his hand.

1   And I lifted up mine eyes, and saw, and, behold, a man with a measuring line in his hand.

of the first. It amplifies that portion of "the good words and comfortable words" which assert God's anger at Zion's enemies (1:15). It demonstrates how the Gentile nations who "helped forward the disaster" of Israel's terrible dispersion and sufferings shall themselves be destroyed. This paves the way for the third vision developing the consoling thought of Jerusalem's growth and future greatness.

The inseparable unity of these visions not only appears in their content or subject matter, but from grammatical considerations. The Hebrew conjunction (*waw* consecutive), introducing each one, not only binds them together as a unit, but unites them in a connecting narrative form that tells the coherent story of Israel's restoration and blessing in the coming kingdom.

I. THE VISION PRESENTED (Zech. 2: 1-3) [2:5-7]

Important to this vision, which has less symbolic imagery than either the first or second vision, are the persons.

1. *The Surveyor and His Identity* (Zech. 2:1) [2:5]. Thereupon [temporal sequence] I lifted up my eyes and looked [*wa'ere'*, saw with the physical sense of sight] and look a man with a measuring rod in his hand! The important person pointed out by the demonstrative adverb with strong interjectional force, behold! (*hinneh*, "look!"), is a man (*'ish* "a male"), as opposed to woman (Gen. 4:1); a man (*homo*) in distinction from God (Job 9:32; Isa. 31:8); in distinction from a beast (Gen. 49:6; Exod. 11:7). The man to whom attention is directed is described by a circumstantial clause and in his [the man's] hand was a line of measurement, i.e., a measuring tape. This

clause is rendered in English idiom as a *phrase:* and look a man with a measuring tape in his hand!

Since the man's appearance as well as his task of measuring the city of Jerusalem (vs. 2) [6] indicates that he is a surveyor and no other data are specified giving a cue as to his identity, it is to be expected that contrariety of opinion prevails concerning him. Some expositors would make the man simply an unidentifiable part of the scenery, introduced merely to perform the symbolical act of the vision, and then to pass out of view. While this is undeniably a possible interpretation, it is scarcely correct in a series of visions where each character is significant. The red-horse rider in the first vision, the four horns and four smiths of the second vision possess identifiable importance, and so with characters and symbols in succeeding visions. Is this an exception?

Since the man with the measuring rod cannot be the "interpreting angel" as verse 3 [7] proves, nor "the other angel" who meets the interpreting angel, nor yet the prophet who is "that young man," verse 4 [8], he is to be identified with the Angel of the Lord, the same glorious preincarnate Christ as appeared in the first vision (1:8) as the red-horse rider among the myrtle trees (Israel) in the deep glen (Israel's deep degradation in her world-wide dispersion).

But how can the surveyor be said to be the Angel of the Lord when he is styled simply a man? The answer is that in an indisputably Messianic passage Messiah the Branch is so named. "Behold, *a man* [*'ish*] *whose name is the Branch*, and he shall grow up out of his place, and he shall build the temple of the Lord" (Zech. 6:12).

2 Then said I, Whither goest thou? And he said unto me, To measure Jerusalem, to see what is the breadth thereof, and what is the length thereof. 3 And, behold, the angel that talked with me went forth, and another angel went out to meet him,

2   Then said I, Whither goest thou? And he said unto me, To measure Jerusalem, to see what is the breadth thereof, and what is the length thereof. 3   And, behold, the angel that talked with me went forth, and another angel went out to meet him,

In similar vein the prophet Ezekiel was brought "in the visions of God . . . into the land of Israel" and set down upon a very high mountain to see a divine surveyor measuring for the construction of the millennial temple. "And behold, there was a man ['ish], whose appearance was like the appearance of brass, with a line of flax in his hand, and a measuring reed" (Ezek. 40:2, 3). This surveyor whom Ezekiel saw is clearly the Angel of Jehovah, the appearance of Christ in theophanic form. Therefore, the surveyor Zechariah saw appears to be best taken as the Angel of the Lord.

2. The Other Persons of the Vision and Their Identity (Zech. 2:2, 3) [2:6, 7]. The prophet Zechariah himself appears as the interrogator of the man with the measuring rod in verse 2 [6]. Then I said, Where are you going? He [the surveyor] replied, To measure Jerusalem, to ascertain what is its breadth and what is its width.

At this juncture appear two other persons beside the surveyor and the prophet. Then, behold, the angel who was talking with me was coming forth [participle, portraying the action as going on before the seer's eyes] and another angel was going out [participle] to meet him (vs. 3) [7].

It is gratuitous to identify the another angel with the Angel of Jehovah, as Chambers and others do. Both his indefinite designation and his implied attendance on the surveyor put him in a subordinate position. Moreover, he is dispatched to meet the interpreting angel with the message the latter in turn was to deliver to the prophet. He is, therefore,

merely an angel who assists the Angel of the Lord, like the interpreting angel.

Zechariah appears not only as the questioner in verse 2 [6] but also as the young man in verse 4 [8]: Then he [the another angel] said unto him [i.e., the interpreting angel], Run, speak unto that young man. . . . The term young man (na'ar) is employed both of a newborn male child (Exod. 2:6; Judg. 13:5, 7; I Sam. 4:21) as well as of a youth as old as about twenty (Gen. 34:19; 41:12; I Kings 3:7; Jer. 1:6, 7). Thus the word, as Baron correctly states, "denotes a male from infancy . . . to the prime of life" (The Visions and Prophecies of Zechariah, p. 60). Sporadically it is used for a "servant," like the French garçon (Exod. 33:11; II Kings 4:12; 5:20; 8:4). But the reference here points out Zechariah to be a young man or "youth," like David when Saul discouraged him from going forth to fight Goliath. "Thou art but a youth" (na'ar), thereby intimating that he was not fit to go forth to fight with Goliath who was a warrior "from his youth" (I Sam. 17:33).

Some expositors deny that the reference to that young man (Zech. 2:4 [8]) is to the prophet. In reply it is sufficient to remark that if the allusion is not to Zechariah, it can be to no other, for angels are ageless and it would be pointless to describe an angel as a "youth."

II. THE PROMISES PROCEEDING FROM THE VISION (Zech. 2:4-13) [2: 8-17]

Simple as the vision is, it contains thrilling good news for both Zechariah

4 And said unto him, Run, speak to this young man, saying, Jerusalem shall be inhabited as towns without walls for the multitude of men and cattle therein:
5 For I, saith the Lord, will be unto her a wall of fire round about, and will be the glory in the midst of her.

---

4   and said unto him, Run, speak to this young man, saying, Jerusalem shall be inhabited as villages without walls, by reason of the multitude of men and cattle therein.
5   For I, saith Jehovah, will be unto her a wall of fire round about, and I will be the glory in the midst of her.

---

and his contemporaries, struggling to rebuild a ruined city and its temple, as well as for every Israelite looking to a brighter future for the Jewish people.

1. *Jerusalem Will Enjoy Prosperous Expansion* (Zech. 2:4) [2:8]. The "other angel" instructs the interpreting angel to **Run, speak** (two imperatives giving direct commands) to Zechariah. The importance of the message proceeding out of the vision is far-reaching. Such good news as it contains demands dispatch and diligence in its publication.

Jerusalem shall inhabit open rural country (objective accusative) or "be inhabited *as open rural country*" (adverbial accusative). The term *perazoth* is from the root *paraz*, "to exceed limits, overflow bounds, spread, expand" and is a feminine plural substantive describing open, unprotected country outside a walled town. The northern invader of Palestine at the end time will say, "I will go up *against the land of unwalled villages* [*'al 'erets perazoth*]; I will fall upon the quiet people who dwell securely, all of them dwelling without walls, and having no bars or gates" (Ezek. 38:11). In the book of Esther the Jews of the villages who dwelt in the unwalled towns (*perazoth*), the suburbs unprotected by walled fortifications, are distinguished from those residing in the fortified capital, Susa (Esther 9:19). In I Samuel 6:18 the "fortified cities" of the Philistines are differentiated from their "unwalled villages" (*perazoth*). Deuteronomy 3:5, in noting the Trans-

jordanic cities taken by Israel, describes these as "cities fortified with high walls, gates and bars, besides very many unwalled villages" (*perazoth*).

Thus the vision of the surveyor portrays the phenomenal growth of Jerusalem so that the city overflows its walls and expands into the open country. The reason given is **because of** [causal *min*] **the multitude** [from *robh*, infinitive of verb *rabhah*, "to become much or many," "be increased," therefore, "increase, abundance" (Lev. 25:16; Isa. 1:11)] **of human beings** [*'adam*] **and animals in it.** The city shall bulge out beyond its borders because of increased population and material prosperity (cf. Isa. 49:19, 20). The fact of Jerusalem's prosperous growth is emphasized by the primary position in the sentence of *perazoth*. **Open rural country shall Jerusalem inhabit**, or "*As unwalled villages* shall Jerusalem be [peacefully] inhabited."

2. *Jerusalem Will Experience Special Divine Protection and Glory* (Zech. 2:5) [2:9]. **For I, saith the Lord, will be a wall of fire to her** [Jerusalem] **round about and will be glory in the midst of her.** This grand promise is buttressed by (1) the emphatic **I** or **I Myself** (the separate pronoun *'ani*, "I," being used in addition to the regularly inflected form which contains in itself the pronominal element); and by (2) the assured word of the Lord behind the promise, **is the saying** [oracle] **of the Lord.**

This emphasis is highly significant in the light of the fact that many otherwise able commentators, such as Pusey, Wright, etc., deny the real fulfilment of these verses in a still future period. They maintain these promises of the second chapter of Zechariah were fulfilled in the growth and prosperity of Jerusalem in the succeeding centuries previous to the Christian era. To support this erroneous position, Hecataeus' reference to the city at the time of Alexander the Great as being ". . . fifty stadia in circumference and inhabited by 120,000 men" is cited, as well as Josephus' description of the restored city as it is referred to in the letter of Aristeas to Philocrates (*Jewish Antiquities XII*), as well as the expansive growth of the place in the time of Herod Agrippa (*Jewish Wars V*, 4, 2).

But this exegesis violates several hermeneutical principles: (1) It fails to differentiate between a *prophetic application* to the immediate future with reference to the prophet's own and subsequent times and the *real* fulfilment of the prophecy in a culminative eschatological sense. (2) It violates the scope of the eight night visions *all of which* extend to the establishment of the millennial kingdom over Israel. (3) It adopts a "phantomizing" or "mysticalizing" (*not* spiritualizing) method of exegesis, which for the obvious and plain sense of the prophetic oracles, substitutes an unnatural and shadowy meaning, which beclouds prophecy with uncertainty and confusion. To call this method of exposition "spiritualizing" is a misnomer for it rather *hides* the meaning and real application of the Holy Spirit, who alone can make the Word of God "spiritual" and profitable to the reader. (4) It has an erroneous concept of "spirituality," arbitrarily making it incompatible with a literal earthly kingdom with material conditions of prosperity. Since when have matter, material wealth, and earthly government in, and of themselves, become "unspiritual"?

Jerusalem will be able to overflow and be peacefully inhabited in open rural country without city walls because the **Lord himself** shall be a protective **wall of fire round about her.** As a fire keeps away the marauding wolf from the sheep while the shepherd slumbers, and as the "pillar of cloud and fire" separated Israel from the Egyptians so that it was a protective wall between God's people and their pursuing enemies (Exod. 14:19-24), so the Lord Himself will be Israel's sure wall of defense against threatening forces without.

But the *Lord Himself* will be more than a wall of protection against external foes. He Himself will be the **glory in the midst of her** [His people]. Then the entire nation will realize the psalmist's testimony: "But thou, O Lord, art a shield about me, *my glory*, and the lifter up of my head" (Ps. 3:3 [4]). Then the glory of the Lord, the Shekinah Presence which Ezekiel saw depart from Jerusalem (Ezek. 11:22, 23) as the "times of the Gentiles" dawned upon Israel and the nation passed under the dominion of the outside nations, shall *return* in the glad millennial day.

"Afterward he brought me to the gate, even the gate that looketh toward the east. And, behold, *the glory of the God of Israel* came from the way of the east: and his voice was like a noise of many waters: and the *earth shined with his glory*. And it was according to the appearance of the vision which I saw, even according to the vision that I saw when I came to destroy the city: and the visions were like the vision I saw by the river Chebar: and I fell upon my face. And *the glory* of the Lord came into the house by the way of the gate whose prospect is toward the east. So the Spirit took me, and brought me into the inner court; and, *behold*, the *glory* of the Lord filled the house. And I heard him speaking unto me out of the house; and the man stood by me. And he said unto me, Son of man, this is the place of my throne, and the place of the soles of my feet,

6 Ho, ho, come forth, and flee from the land of the north, saith the Lord: for I have spread you abroad as the four winds of the heaven, saith the Lord. 7 Deliver thyself, O Zion, that dwellest with the daughter of Babylon.

---

6   Ho, ho, flee from the land of the north, saith Jehovah; for I have spread you abroad as the four winds of the heavens, saith Jehovah.
7   Ho Zion, escape, thou that dwellest with the daughter of Babylon.

---

where I will dwell in the midst of the children of Israel forever, and my holy name shall the house of Israel no more defile . . ." (Ezek. 43:1–7). Then *"the glory of the Lord* shall be revealed, and all flesh shall see it together"* (Isa. 40:5). Then the Angel of the Lord, with whom the cloud of glory was associated in the Old Testament (Exod. 13:21, 22; 14:19, 20), will be manifest visibly and personally to rule upon the Davidic throne.

After the revelation of the Lord the Branch with the consequent cleansing of Israel (Isa. 4:2, 3), "the Lord will create over the whole site of Mount Zion and over her assemblies *a cloud by day,* and smoke and the *shining of a flaming fire by night;* for over *all the glory* there will be a canopy and a pavilion. It will be for a *shade* by day from the heat, and for a refuge and a shelter from the storm and rain" (Isa. 4:5, 6).

3. *Israel Will Be Restored and Repatriated* (Zech. 2:6, 7) [2:10, 11]. **Ho! ho! Flee from the land of the north, says the Lord; for I have scattered you abroad as the four winds of the heavens, says the Lord. Ho! Escape to Zion, you who dwell with the daughter of Babylon.** Three times in these two verses the onomatopoetic interjection **Ho!** (*hoy*) is employed to arrest attention for the purpose of giving a warning and a solemn admonition for Israel to flee from Babylon. Called **the land of the north** although actually in a southeastern direction from Palestine, Babylon is so styled because invading armies and trading caravans from this land to Jerusalem came around the "fertile crescent" and entered

Palestine from the north (Jer. 1:13, 14).

These warnings to flee and escape presage impending peril upon Babylon, which did befall her two years after this prophecy, but the fulfilment of the prediction envisions the age-end destruction of both ecclesiastical Babylon (Rev. 17) and political and commercial Babylon (Rev. 18) of the Satanic world system at the second advent of Christ. John the Revelator makes a similar plea (Rev. 18:4–8) which had been issued again and again by the former prophets (Isa. 48:20; 52:11; Jer. 51:6, 45). This call was only meagerly heeded in the return from Babylon, but will be fulfilled in a future day (Isa. 11:10–16).

The word **spread** (*perasti,* Assyrian *parâshu,* "fly," i.e., "spread the wings," Arabic *farasha*) here does *not* mean a beneficent diffusion in the sense of multiply by dissemination as Chambers (Lange's *Commentary,* Vol. 14, p. 32) and others correctly point out, but "to scatter, disperse" as in Psalm 68:14 [15] and Ezekiel 17:21. This appears: (1) from the context which envisions fulfilment in the *final* regathering of Israel from her worldwide dispersion *in political Babylon,* i.e., among the nations organized in the Satanic world system with Israel, out of her rightful place, **scattered** among them; (2) from the fact that they have not been beneficently spread to the four winds but **scattered** world-wide **as the four winds of heaven,** that is, with a violence such as would result from the combined action of all the winds of heaven" (Feinberg, *God Remembers,* p. 48); (3) from the fact that the call to leave Babylon and to flee back to

8 For thus saith the Lord of hosts; After the glory hath he sent me unto the nations which spoiled you: for he that toucheth you toucheth the apple of his eye.

9 For, behold, I will shake mine hand upon them, and they shall be a spoil to their servants: and ye shall know that the Lord of hosts hath sent me.

---

8 For thus saith Jehovah of hosts: After glory hath he sent me unto the nations which plundered you; for he that toucheth you toucheth the apple of his eye.

9 For, behold, I will shake my hand over them, and they shall be a spoil to those that served them; and ye shall know that Jehovah of hosts hath sent me.

Zion (Jerusalem) is because (causal *ki* introducing a causal clause) they have been violently scattered over the entire earth for their sins.

4. *The Nations Despoiling Israel Will Be Judged and Punished* (Zech. 2:8, 9) [2:12, 13]. For thus [in this manner, as follows] the Lord of armies says, After glory has he sent me unto the nations who are despoiling you, because he who is touching you is touching his [God's] pupil [eye gate]. This important declaration is, as is so often the case in Zechariah and the prophets in general, prefaced by the authoritative Thus says the Lord of armies. In this case a solemn warning is issued to the nations molesting Israel. Their certain punishment is emphatically stressed.

The difficult adverbial phrase after glory is emphatic by being placed *before* the verb it modifies. A possible interpretation is: "*After glory* has He [God] sent me [Zechariah]." This would mean that Zechariah's divine commission had as its goal the demonstration and vindication of the glory of God. Against this view, however, is the fact that (1) the context concerns not Zechariah, despite the explicit reference to him in the *dramatis personae* of the vision in verse 4 [8], but the Lord Himself; (2) in only a very limited sense could the passage be applied to Zechariah's ministry, which is presumptive evidence that the pronoun "me," object of the verb "send," does not refer to the prophet.

Another possible view is that the phrase after glory has reference to the promise of the second advent of Messiah already alluded to in verse 5 [9]: "And the *glory* [emphatic] will I [Messiah] become in the midst of her [Jerusalem]." This is substantially the position of the Jewish exegete Kimchi as well as that of some Christian expositors, including Hengstenberg, Dennett, Kelly, and Chambers. But the indefinite "glory," not "the glory" would scarcely refer to the glorious second advent.

It is best to take the words with Von Orelli and Baron in the sense: After glory has He [the Lord] sent Me [the Servant of the Lord]. This statement anticipates the New Testament revelation of the Father sending the Son to glorify Him, both in His first advent (John 17:4, cf. Isa. 61:1, 2; Luke 4:17–19) and in His second advent (Isa. 61:2, 3). In the Isaiah passage the whole glorious ministry of Messiah, combined in both advents, is summed up in the words: "that they [the recipients of Messiah's salvation] might be called trees of righteousness, the planting of the Lord, *that he might be glorified*" (Isa. 61:3).

The phrase after glory accordingly describes the ministry of Messiah in which He *vindicates* and *demonstrates* the glory of God, particularly as He will punish Israel's enemies and deliver and establish His own people in kingdom blessing. After glory has he sent me unto the nations who are making a spoil of you [My people]. The participle "despoiling" has the article and is equivalent to a relative clause, and describes the *continual* plundering activity of the nations.

Why will Messiah's mission of punishing the nations at His second advent be attended with, and be directed toward, the realization of **glory** (*kabhod*, from *kabhed*, "to be heavy or weighty" in the sense of "honor or splendor" both of men [Gen. 45:13, Job 19:9] and of God [Exod. 33:18; Lev. 9:6; Num. 14:10; Ezek. 8:4])? The answer is God's word and promises toward Israel will be thereby vindicated, demonstrating God's truthfulness and faithfulness. God's love toward His people will be proved, His power displayed, His wisdom proclaimed, and His whole infinitely holy and gracious character revealed. His glory is inseparably linked with the fortunes of His people. He cannot be glorified as long as His people are disgraced and persecuted by their enemies who, in a vital sense, are His enemies.

This fact is beautifully set forth by the causal clause. **For** [because] **he who touches you** [graphic articular participle] **is touching** [participle] **the pupil of his** [God's] **eye.** These are the words of the Messenger of the Lord, the preincarnate Messiah, concerning the Lord of armies (and should *not* be read "*My* eye," *'eni*). What tender affection they express concerning His love for His people Israel! How acutely sensitive is the Lord of armies concerning their mistreatment! The metaphor used to express this thought is exquisite, despite its being boldly anthropomorphic. "To touch [*naga'*] the pupil of His [God's] eye" means to come in contact with it to *harm* it (followed by the prefixed preposition *beth*, as in Gen. 26:11; Josh. 9:19; II Sam. 14:10; Jer. 12:14).

The **pupil** (Latin "little boy," from the diminutive image reflected on the contractile aperture of the iris of the eye) is in the Hebrew "the gate" of the eye (*babhah*, "gate," Arabic *babun*, "gate"). This contractile opening by

which rays of light reflect images on the retina, is the tenderest and most sensitive part of the visual organ. It feels most acutely the slightest injury and is meticulously guarded as extremely precious, the loss of which is irreparable. This figure eloquently expresses God's keen feelings toward Israel mistreated by the nations.

The same tender concern of the Lord for His elect nation Israel is found in Deuteronomy 32:10: "He found him [Jacob] in a desert land, and in the waste howling wilderness. He led him about, he instructed him, he kept him as *the apple of his eye* [*'ishon 'eyno*, "the little man," i.e., *pupil* of his eye]." Similarly Psalm 17:8: "Keep me as the apple of the eye [*'ishon bath 'ayin*, "little man, daughter of the eye"], Hide me under the shadow of thy wings."

For lo, I will brandish my hand against them so that they shall be spoil to their servants in order that you may know that the Lord of armies has sent me (vs. 9) [13]. This verse presents a demonstration of the truth that whoever harms Israel touches the pupil of God's eye. The *future instans* (*hinneni meniph*, the interjection plus a personal pronoun plus a participle) presents in lively fashion that which is about to happen (imminent), or certain to happen. Here the latter idea occurs. **I will shake** [brandish] **my hand against them.** The verb **shake** (causative of *nuph*, "to move to and fro") signifies to "swing" or "to cause to move to and fro," "to shake or brandish against" (Isa. 10:15; 11:15; 19:16). The figure is of the Lord as a puissant Champion of His oppressed people. He needs only to *brandish* His hand, that is *wave it threateningly against* the enemies of His people and they become as women (Isa. 19:16). In this reference, Zechariah as frequently echoes the former prophets, in this instance Isaiah (cf. Isa. 10:15; 11:15).

Zechariah has Isaiah also in mind in the remainder of this verse. In this passage the prophet sees Israel re-

10 Sing and rejoice, O daughter of Zion: for, lo, I come, and I will dwell in the midst of thee, saith the Lord.

11 And many nations shall be joined to the Lord in that day, and shall be my people: and I will dwell in the midst of thee, and thou shalt know that the Lord of hosts hath sent me unto thee.

12 And the Lord shall inherit Judah his portion in the holy land, and shall choose Jerusalem again.

13 Be silent, O all flesh, before the Lord: for he is raised up out of his holy habitation.

---

10   Sing and rejoice, O daughter of Zion; for, lo, I come, and I will dwell in the midst of thee, saith Jehovah.

11   And many nations shall join themselves to Jehovah in that day, and shall be my people; and I will dwell in the midst of thee, and thou shalt know that Jehovah of hosts hath sent me unto thee.

12   And Jehovah shall inherit Judah as his portion in the holy land, and shall yet choose Jerusalem.

13   Be silent, all flesh, before Jehovah; for he is waked up out of his holy habitation.

---

stored and exalted when "the house of Israel will possess them [their foes] in the Lord's land as male and female slaves; they will take captive those who were their captors, and rule over those who oppressed them" (Isa. 14:1, 2).

The nations who were *plundering* them **shall become plunder to their servants** (literally '*abhdehem*, "servants of them," objective genitive, "those who served them"). A complete reversal of fortune is indicated. Those *despoiling* them shall become their *spoil;* those *who served them* shall become their *masters.* The divine result is so that they **might know that the Lord of armies has sent me** (the Servant of the Lord, the Angel of the Lord, the Messiah, for He is still the speaker throughout this context). He alone will bring these glorious promises to fruition by His coming. He alone, who completely did the will of Him who sent Him, will attest His divine commission of salvation and deliverance to the world.

5. *The Earth Will Be Prepared for Full Millennial Blessing* (Zech. 2: 10-13) [2:14-17]. Little wonder in anticipation of the advent of the Messiah into the world and the blessed results accruing from Him, Zechariah following the custom of the former prophets, enjoins the **daughter of Zion,** that is, Jerusalem viewed as a beautiful young woman, to **sing aloud** and **rejoice** (cf. Zech. 9:9; Isa. 12:6; Zeph. 3:14, 15).

This preparation for full millennial blessing will be brought about (1) *by Messiah in the midst of Jerusalem* (vs. 10) [14]; (2) *by the proclamation of the message of salvation to the nations* (vs. 11) [15]; (3) *by specially encouraging promises to Palestine and Jerusalem* (vs. 12) [16]; and (4) *by worldwide judgments upon the nations* (vs. 13) [17].

(1)   *By Messiah in the midst of Jerusalem* (vs. 10) [14]. The reason for the command "to shout aloud and rejoice" is **for** [because] **lo, I come.** This is *not* a reference to the first advent as in Psalm 40:7, 8 [40:8, 9], but to the second. Failure to see these two advents has resulted in the blindness which is upon Jewish hearts today. When He comes the second time in glory, He will dwell in the midst of Jerusalem.

And I will dwell (*shakan*, "settle down, abide, reside") used of God (Exod. 25:8; Num. 5:3; Ezek. 43:9; Joel 3:17, 21 [4:17, 21]). The reference is evidently to the personal, visible presence of the Lord in Jerusalem, the political and religious

capital of the millennial earth.
(2) *By the proclamation of the message of salvation to the nations* (vs. 11) [15]. And many nations shall join themselves unto the Lord in that day and shall become my people; and I will dwell in the midst of thee [repeated from the preceding verse to stress its certainty] and you shall know that the Lord of armies has sent me [the Messiah] unto you.

In that [millennial] day fixes the time of the prophecy. *At that time,* because of Messiah's advent and manifestation, many nations shall be joined [or "join themselves," *nifal,* passive or reflexive] to the Lord. This prophecy predicts the conversion of the Gentiles to a knowledge of salvation. To be joined to the Lord implies union with Him in faith and spiritual experience.

When Leah conceived her third son, she said, "Now this time will my husband *be joined* unto me, because I have borne him three sons: therefore was his name called Levi," i.e., "Joined" (Gen. 29:34). Leah meant that her spouse would be inseparably united to her by the bond of childbirth.

Aaron was instructed that his brothers also of the tribe of "Levi" were to "be joined" (associated with, united in a common calling) with him in the work of the sanctuary (Num. 18:2). Isaiah foretells that "foreigners will *join* them [Israel restored to Palestine] and will cleave to the house of Jacob" (Isa. 14:1). Although Zechariah echoes, as often the former prophets, he gives us the added emphasis that aliens will join Israel, but in doing so actually will be joined to the Lord, for Israel will be converted and draw her converts not to herself, but to her newly found Redeemer, whom she will find so precious in that day (Isa. 2:1-4; 60:1-3; Zech. 8:20-23). Many nations will thus become, as the Lord declares, my people (cf. Isa. 56:3-6; Ps. 102:14-23).

But *before* the nations join themselves to the Lord and are called by Him "My people," "the people of Israel . . . and the people of Judah . . . shall seek the Lord their God. They shall ask the way to Zion, with faces turned toward it, saying, Come, *let us join ourselves to the Lord* in an everlasting covenant that will never be forgotten" (Jer. 50:4, 5).

(3) *By specially encouraging promises to Palestine and Jerusalem* (vs. 12) [16]. Lest the conversion of the millennial nations to the Lord cause any doubt that the original election of the nation Israel has in no sense been abrogated, Zechariah declares that God has not forgotten His choice of Israel as uniquely His own people. And the Lord shall inherit Judah his portion upon [in] the holy land, and shall yet choose Jerusalem.

The Lord has time and again spoken of Israel as His inheritance and portion. "But the Lord has taken you, and brought you forth out of the iron furnace, out of Egypt, *to be a people of his own possession* as at this day" (Deut. 4:20). Moses prayed, "O Lord God, destroy not *thy people and thy heritage,* whom thou hast redeemed through thy greatness, whom thou hast brought up out of Egypt with a mighty hand" (Deut. 9:26). "In that day Israel will be the third with Egypt and Assyria, a blessing in the midst of the earth, whom the Lord of hosts has blessed, saying, Blessed be Egypt my people, and Assyria the work of my hands, and *Israel my heritage*" (Isa. 19:24, 25).

Although the term, "The Holy Land," is widely used today to describe Palestine, it occurs only this once in the Bible. Moreover its present-day usage is highly inappropriate and will not become a suitable designation till the land which has been defiled and polluted above all others, at least in proportion to the light it has received from the ancient prophets and apostles, even Christ Himself, is cleansed of its defilement and sanctified by the presence of

Immanuel and the redeemed and sanctified people who will inherit it. Accordingly, the term, "The Holy Land," is a millennial epithet and is reserved for the time when the Lord will say, "I will remove the iniquity *of that land* in a single day" (Zech. 3:9), *when* Israel is cleansed from her sin and reinstated as a high priestly nation (Zech. 3:1-10), *when* under Messiah-King-Priest she becomes the Light of the World with a copious outpouring of the Spirit for testimony (Zech. 4:1-14), *when* iniquity is summarily punished under Messiah's rod-of-iron rule (Zech. 5:1-4), and when commercial and ecclesiastical Babylon is removed from the land forever (Zech. 5:5-11). *In that day* the land shall be holy *when the people are holy.* "And they shall be called *the holy people, the redeemed of the Lord*" (Isa. 62:12).

The clause, **He will yet** [ʿodh, adverb, "before all is done," "eventually"] **choose Jerusalem**, as Feinberg notes, "does not imply that God must choose Israel afresh, but that now, at long last, He will be able to manifest to the world the immutable character of His original choice and its practical outworking in renewed, restored, and resettled Israel" (*God Remembers*, p. 51). As Baron says, "... Jehovah shall then, by the various acts of lovingkindness to His people and to the land, which are enumerated in this prophecy, *demonstrate* in the sight of the whole world *the fact and the immutability* of His original choice of them" (*The Visions and Prophecies of Zechariah*, p. 80).

(4) *By the personal and visible coming of Messiah and world-wide judgments upon the nations* (vs. 13) [17]. **Be silent, all flesh, before the Lord; for he has aroused himself from his holy habitation.** This majestic verse, panoramic in its prophetic sweep, poetically solemn in its announcement of the great climatic event of all prophecy, the glorious advent of Messiah-Redeemer, *spans the whole period of earth judgments that precede*

the kingdom age, and in concise summary statement includes all the events that are catalogued in the heart of the book of the Revelation (5:1-19:16).

This awe-inspiring verse is introduced by an onomatopoetic interjection calculated to command reverent silence. **Be silent!** (*has*, "hush!" "be still!" Cf. Judg. 3:19; Amos 6:10; Hab. 2:20; Zeph. 1:7). The tumultuously raging nations in that day, roused to commotion in their opposition "against the Lord and against his anointed" (Ps. 2:1-3) will need this interjectional imperative.

Humanity in its entirety is addressed (vocative) as **all flesh** (*kol basar*. Cf. Gen. 7:21; 8:17; 9:11, 15; Isa. 40:6; Jer. 45:5; Joel 2:28 [3:1]). This term not only comprehends the thought of universality, but of the weakness and impermanency of mankind. "All flesh is *grass*" (Isa. 40:6). Before the scorching anger of God's judgments about to be unleashed, man will be burned up as grass before the hot sun.

The reason for the hushed silence of all mankind **before the Lord** (*mippene Yhwh*, "from the face of the Lord," "from before the Lord") is because His presence is about to be revealed in judgment (Zeph. 1:7; Hab. 2:20), and **because** (*kî* introducing a causal clause) **he is awakened out of his holy habitation.** Here is the answer to a question that must have vexed the minds of Zechariah's hearers as well as expectant Jews throughout the weary countries of their calamities and world-wide dispersion. *Why*, in the face of the prophet's visions of hope and future felicity, *is God silent so long?* The figure (and it is only a figure, although a bold one) is that God has been sleeping and "is aroused" out of His slumber. But His sleep is only apparent. "He who keeps you will not slumber. Behold, He who keeps Israel will neither slumber nor sleep" was a truth every believing Israelite knew by heart (Ps. 121:3, 4).

To be **aroused** (passive) or "to arouse oneself" (reflexive) is the *nifal* of the word "to be awakened" (*ne'or*, perfect third masculine singular from *'ur*, "to awake"). The word occurs of Zechariah himself being "wakened [aroused] out of his sleep" (Zech. 4:1). Jeremiah uses it of a "great nation" being "aroused" or *"awakened"* from the farthest parts of the north (Jer. 6:22; 50:41). It is employed in Job of being "roused" out of sleep (Job 14:12).

God is thus seen to be *assuredly* (prophetic perfect) **aroused** or "awakened" out of a figurative sleep *in that future day*, as it were, in response to the distressful cries of His wronged and persecuted people:

"Rouse thyself! Why sleepest thou,
            O Lord?
Awake [*'urah*]! Do not cast us off
      forever" (Ps. 44:23 [24]).

With the opening of "the seven-sealed book" of Revelation 5:1–14, the silence of God is broken. "The Lion of the tribe of Judah" is aroused to unloose the seals (followed by the trumpets and bowls), dispossessing Satan and ungodly man from their usurpation of the control of the earth forfeited by Adam's sin. But the rightful owner by creation and by redemption is the Creator-Redeemer

Himself who as the climax to the proceedings of dispossession, appears in the heavens as "King of kings and Lord of lords" (Rev. 19:16).

Zechariah with synoptic brevity sets forth this grand prophetic panorama which will eventuate in Israel's deliverance and establishment in the kingdom. He styles heaven as **his** [God's] **holy habitation.** The word **habitation** (*ma'on*, "dwelling") is from the root *'un*, "to dwell, inhabit" (Isa. 13:22). The word is used of the "dwelling" (lair) of animals (Jer. 9:11 [10]; 10:22; Nah. 2:11 [12]; God's "habitation" in heaven (Deut. 26:15; II Chron. 30:27; Ps. 68:5 [6]).

We might all **flesh** be hushed into silent awe in the presence of Him who shall come forth to smite the earth in judgment to destroy His enemies as well as to deliver His own people. He is the Holy One, who alone can make Palestine "the *Holy* Land" (Zech. 2:12) when He comes out of His *holy* habitation to execute His *holy* acts.

Not only *now* when "the Lord is in His holy temple," but *then* when He "is aroused out of His holy habitation" to deliver the earth and His own on the earth from the squatting usurpation of wicked men and demons, "let all the earth *keep silence before Him*" (Hab. 2:20).

CHAPTER THREE

RESTORATION OF ISRAEL AS A HIGH-PRIESTLY NATION

(THE FOURTH VISION)

THE CLEANSING OF JOSHUA, THE HIGH PRIEST

(ZECH. 3:1-10)

I. THE VISIONS OF DEFILED AND CONDEMNED ISRAEL UNDER THE FIGURE OF JOSHUA THE HIGH PRIEST (Zech. 3:1-3)

1. Israel (Under the Figure of Joshua) Is Accused as a Criminal (Zech. 3:1, 2)
2. Israel (Under the Figure of Joshua) Appears as One Polluted (Zech. 3:3)

II. THE VISION OF PARDONED AND REPOSITIONED ISRAEL UNDER THE FIGURE OF JOSHUA THE HIGH PRIEST (Zech. 3:4-7)

1. Israel (Under the Figure of Joshua) Is Imperilled by Being Deprived of Priestly Office, But Is Pardoned (Zech. 3:4)

2. Israel (Under the Figure of Joshua) Is Fully Repositioned (Zech. 3:5)
3. The Covenant of the Priesthood Is Renewed with Joshua (Zech. 3:6, 7)

III. THE PREDICTION OF REDEEMED AND RESTORED ISRAEL UNDER THE FIGURE OF MESSIAH, THE BRANCH (Zech. 3:8-10)

1. The Recipients of the Prediction of Redeemed and Restored Israel Under the Figure of Messiah the Branch (Zech. 3:8a)
2. The Declaration of the Prediction of Redeemed and Restored Israel Under the Figure of the Branch and the Stone (Zech. 3:8b-10)

In the preceding visions the marvellous purposes of God's grace toward Israel appear in the judgment of her enemies and the restoration of both the land and of the people. But a crucial question arises: How can an infinitely holy God accomplish such plans with a sinful and besmirched people? How can the wondrous manifestations of divine mercy to them be consistent with God's righteousness? This, the fourth vision in a series of eight, discloses the transformation of the nation from self-righteousness to the righteousness of God "which is by faith in Jesus Christ unto all and upon all them that believe: for there is no difference" (Rom. 3:22).

The present vision is a beautiful typical foreshadowing of the future conversion of the Israelite nation when Messiah the Branch is accepted at His second advent. The Jews' rejection of the Messiah at His first coming and their persistence in self-righteousness, denying the righteousness of God in Christ, blinded them to the presence of the Branch in the midst of the nation in His incarnation and earthly life. As the Apostle explains, "For they being ignorant of God's righteousness, and going about to establish their own righteousness, have not submitted themselves unto the righteousness of God" (Rom. 10:3). The transformation symbolized

1 And he shewed me Joshua the high priest standing before the angel of the Lord, and Satan standing at his right hand to resist him.
2 And the Lord said unto Satan, The Lord rebuke thee, O Satan; even the Lord that hath chosen Jerusalem rebuke thee: is not this a brand plucked out of the fire?

1   And he showed me Joshua the high priest standing before the angel of Jehovah, and Satan standing at his right hand to be his adversary.
2   And Jehovah said unto Satan, Jehovah rebuke thee, O Satan; yea, Jehovah that hath chosen Jerusalem rebuke thee: is not this a brand plucked out of the fire?

in this vision in the person of Joshua the high priest, is a prophetic portrayal of St. Paul's declaration, "For Christ is the end of the law for righteousness to everyone who believes" (Rom. 10:4). The nation in the person of Joshua believes and becomes a recipient of divine cleansing and of divine righteousness imputed to all who exercise faith in Christ.

I. THE VISION OF DEFILED AND CONDEMNED ISRAEL UNDER THE FIGURE OF JOSHUA THE HIGH PRIEST (Zech. 3:1-3)

At first glance this vision appears to relate to Joshua as an individual and to his particular needs. Closer scrutiny, however, reveals that in the person of Joshua the high priest, the sinful state of Israel is exhibited in the nation's *representative*. (1) The representative character of Joshua is seen first in the context of this vision in the larger framework of the other seven night visions, all of which have a broad bearing upon the nation as a whole, seen in panoramic prophetic sweep extending from its failure and judgment to its final restoration in kingdom blessing. It would be more than strange if this vision were an exception, and an individual were signalized only in a personal capacity whose role was not signally significant in any way and important only because he happened to be "the high priest" in Israel at the time. (2) The high priest of Israel in general held a position that was normally peculiarly representative of the nation. This fact saliently appears

in this particular vision in the repeated employment of the full title "the high priest" (vss. 1 and 8). As Leupold says of the high priest, "He represents and practically impersonates Israel in his holy office. For the nation he prays; for it he enters the Holy Place; he bears the nation's guilt. We must, therefore, not refer the issues and implications of this chapter to Joshua as an individual, nor merely to Joshua, the high priest. We must conclude that *his* condition is *Israel's* condition, *his* acquittal a typical way of expressing *theirs;* the words of comfort and assurance given *him* apply with equal validity to *them*" (*Exposition of Zechariah*, Columbus, 1956, p. 64).

(3) The representative character of Joshua further appears in the Lord's double rebuke of Satan on the ground of the *divine choice of Israel*, not His personal choice of Joshua (vs. 2). (4) The fact also focusses into clarity inasmuch as Joshua and his colleagues are specifically declared to be "men of symbolic portent" or sign, i.e., men who in their person symbolize future events for Israel (vs. 8). (5) Moreover, "the iniquity of the land" is said to be removed (vs. 9) and not really that of Joshua (vs. 4), Scripture being completely silent concerning any misdemeanors of the latter.

1. *Israel (Under the Figure of Joshua) Is Accused as a Criminal* (Zech. 3:1, 2). Then he [the interpreting angel] **showed me Joshua the high priest standing before the angel of the Lord, with Satan standing on his right hand to resist him. Thereupon the Lord said unto Satan, The Lord**

rebuke thee, Satan; yes, the Lord who makes choice of Jerusalem rebuke thee. Is not this a brand pulled out of the fire? The recital of the vision continues in the story-telling mould of the others and opens with *waw consecutive* expressing temporal sequence. Then he [the interpreting angel] showed [Hebrew, "caused me to see"] Joshua the high [*gadhol*, "great"] priest. The name is significant, being the same as that of Moses' successor, Joshua the son of Nun (Greek, *Iesous*, "Jesus," Num. 11:28; 13:16; Deut. 1:38) and meaning, "Yahweh is salvation." The name is peculiarly appropriate of Joshua, the son of Jehozadak (Hag. 1:1, 12, 14; 2:2, 4; Zech. 3:1, 6, 8, 9; 6:11) inasmuch as he prefigures what Israel ought to have been *ideally* (a holy high-priestly nation, Exod. 19:5, 6) and what the people will yet be *in reality* by God's electing love (vs. 2) when converted and made a medium of the Lord's salvation to the nations.

Joshua is shown standing before the angel of the Lord, i.e., "*attending upon* Him *in the official capacity of a priestly servant* (ʿomedh liphne, meaning to "wait upon, be or become a servant of" [I Sam. 16:22; I Kings 1:2; 17:1; 18:15; II Kings 3:14; Jer. 15:19]). The expression is specifically used of priests "standing before the Lord to minister" (Deut. 10:8; Judg. 20:28; Ezek. 44:15; II Chron. 29:11), and this is the character in which Joshua appears here. He is attempting to minister before the Lord Himself (for the Angel of the Lord here is none other than deity, the preincarnate Christ) and this challenges the presence of Satan and his opposition to Joshua's ministry, since Joshua's sin (as representative of a sinful people) had given a place of advantage to Satan to attack and hinder the high priest's holy ministrations, illustrating Paul's injunction to the Ephesian believers: "Neither give place to the devil" (Eph. 4:27).

The presence of Satan is stated in a circumstantial clause in Hebrew, sub-ordinate to the main clause: Then he showed me Joshua . . . standing before the Angel of the Lord. This subsidiary action or secondary attendant circumstance is best rendered by a phrase in English, with Satan standing at his [Joshua's] right hand to oppose him. Both the Angel of the Lord and Satan are standing (present active participle), one to serve, the other to resist.

Three personalities stand out in the narrative of the vision – Joshua, the Angel of the Lord, and Satan. Although the Hebrew word *satan* has the article, "the Satan," i.e., "the adversary," it is syntactically to be regarded as a proper noun and the name of the great angelic superhuman adversary of God and man, as in I Chronicles 21:1 (cf. II Sam. 24:1) where Satan (without the article) stands up against Israel as an adversary of David. Likewise in Job Satan (*with* the article) appears as one of the *bene haʾelohim* ("sons of God," i.e., "the angels") to accuse Job (Job 1:6, 7, 12; 2:1, etc.). But Satan appears as a *person* (and not a mere personification or a generalized designation of an individual or national adversary (as in Num. 22:22; II Sam. 19:22; I Kings 5:4; 11:25) on contextual as well as grammatical grounds. It would be highly arbitrary to take Satan in any other sense than the great personal spiritual adversary, so well known in Scripture in general, and perfectly understood in Zechariah's day especially so when he *interacts with obvious persons* (Joshua and the Angel of the Lord) in the context of the vision.

Satan's present activity is one of opposition and resistance to Joshua the high priest because God's servant by his sin has given occasion to Satan to attack, in accordance with a truth emphasized throughout the Bible that sin exposes the sinner to satanic attack not only in the case of unbelievers (Matt. 12:43–45), but believers as well (I Cor. 5:5; I John 5:16). The original is expressive,

With **Satan** standing at his [Joshua's] **right hand to satanize** him — the opposer to oppose him (*hassaṭan lesiṭeno*, a paronomasia, or play upon words having the same root. The right hand where Satan is standing to oppose Joshua is not the favored position of an *accuser* under the law (since Joshua is not on trial), but the *position of advantage* gained by Satan because of Joshua's defection and because the Adversary has gained certain rights over man and creation as a result of man's fall. Commentators like Mitchell (*The International Critical Commentary*, "Zechariah," p. 151), who ignore Scriptural usage and the context and depersonalize Satan making the reproof of the adversary by the Angel of the Lord merely "the triumph" of divine mercy "over divine justice" do not give much aid to the expositor who will not be satisfied with less than exegesis which not only takes grammar, context, and historical backgrounds into consideration, but the overall testimony of Scriptures as well.

Joshua is seen **standing before the Angel of the Lord,** not only in service but as signifying that his intimate character is laid bare before the presence of deity as well as the keenly accusing eye of Satan.

Then the Lord [the Syriac has "the angel of the Lord"] **said unto Satan, The Lord rebuke thee, Satan; yes, the Lord who makes choice of Jerusalem, rebuke thee. Is not this a faggot retrieved from the fire?** But there is no need to emend the Hebrew text in order to solve an imaginary impossibility, reading "the angel of the Lord" for **the Lord.** The more difficult reading of the Hebrew is evidently the correct one. Here "the Angel of the Lord" is identified with the Lord Himself (cf. Zech. 2:11, 12). At times He is distinct, then again identical. The identity of these two divine persons is demonstrated by the fact that each does what God does, the Angel of the Lord being merely the earthly worker or agent of the

other, revealed explicitly in the New Testament in the distinctions in the Persons of the Trinity. Jesus enunciated a similar truth, "My Father worketh hitherto *and I work*" (John 5:17).

It is highly suitable that the Lord Himself should reply to Satan's charges which are in line with his opposition to Israel because God has a plan in His purpose for that people (cf. Rev. 12:3–17) and because that people has sinned, giving the Adversary a hold over them and the right to hinder them. Since Joshua's condition is representative of Israel's condition and since this sinful condition is panoramic and *not* merely applicable to Israel's sins in that day, the Lord's rebuke to the Adversary is panoramic in its sweep, and applies as well to the final consummation of the nation's apostasy and her climactic establishment as a high-priestly nation in full kingdom blessing.

For this reason the rebuke to Satan is *thorough* and the reprimand *final* and *authoritative*. This is indicated by the fact that (1) the Lord Himself administers the rebuke, **Therefore the Lord said unto Satan. . . .** (2) Satan is accosted *directly* with stern pointedness, and not addressed indirectly or through another, **The Lord said unto Satan, The Lord reprimand thee, O Satan** (*hassaṭan*, the vocative of *direct* address being used). (3) The rebuke itself is *repeated* (as well as the name of the *rebuker!*) for emphasis and incisiveness. **The Lord rebuke thee; yes, the Lord who chooses Jerusalem, rebuke thee.** Here, as often, in Hebrew syntax repeating a thing twice accentuates its force or enhances its degree (cf. Gen. 14:10, "bitumen pits, bitumen pits" meaning "full of bitumen pits"; Eccl. 7:24, "deep, deep," meaning "very deep," etc.). (4) In addition, the verb "rebuke" is in the jussive mood (the imperative in the third person), expressing an action of the divine will and not an optative or declarative, as Leupold contends on the basis "that

3 Now Joshua was clothed with filthy garments, and stood before the angel.

3   Now Joshua was clothed with filthy garments, and was standing before the angel.

there is no emphasis on the fact that the rebuke is to be administered at some future time" (*Exposition of Zechariah*, p. 68). But Leupold apparently does not reckon with the full scope of all of these visions.

(5) The *basis* of the rebuke was God's *gracious* choice of Jerusalem, **The Lord . . . the Lord who chooses Jerusalem**, the relative clause modifying the repeated name of Yahweh. That was the real ground of God's gracious interposition for Joshua (and Israel) and nothing in themselves.

(6) The divine rebuke of Satan is further strengthened by the exposé of the unreasonableness of Satan's attack. **Is not this** [*zeh*, i.e., *this* fellow Joshua, with a ring of opprobrium in the masculine singular demonstrative, so used as in II Kings 5:7] **a brand snatched out of the fire?** The **fire** here represents not only the Babylonian captivity from which Joshua has been plucked when the nation was almost reduced to ashes in the seventy-year ordeal, but in accordance with the panoramic prophetic vista of this whole vision (and all the other seven, too), the fire represents *all* the world-wide sufferings of Israel from which she shall be delivered to be established in kingdom blessing at the second advent. How ridiculously unreasonable then are Satan's charges in the face of the faithfulness of Israel's God who will allow the bush to burn, but as He showed Moses in the desert, will not allow it to be "consumed" (Exod. 3:1–8).

2. *Israel (Under the Figure of Joshua) Appears as One Polluted* (Zech. 3:3). **Now Joshua was attired in excrement-bespattered garments, but was standing before the Angel of the Lord.** This verse is in the nature of two circumstantial clauses both subordinate to the main clause of 3:1

("then he showed me Joshua the high priest"), and giving further details of Joshua's state. The second clause is best taken as adversative to the first: *we 'omedh*, **but** [*not* "and"] **he was standing** [i.e., to minister] **before the Angel of the Lord**, *despite* his vile condition.

The participles of the verse, **attired** (*labhush*, "clothed," "dressed") and **standing**, stress a continued state of moral and spiritual filthiness of one who should have been conspicuous for holiness and emphasize how utterly incongruous Joshua's condition was, the longer it lasted. In delineating Joshua's vile attire and thus Israel's sin and culpability, since he is representative of the nation in its priestly role, the Hebrew language could have employed no more trenchant term. The word commonly rendered "filthy" actually means "excrement-covered" and hence not only vilely dirty but offensively smelly. The word appears only here as an adjective in the Old Testament. The noun "excrement" (*tsoah*, from the root *yatsa'*, "to go forth," "be evacuated") appears in Isaiah 4:4; 36:12; II Kings 18:27. (Cf. also Deut. 23 [24]; Ezek. 4:12.)

What are the sins that were so grievous as to be portrayed so graphically by **excrement-soiled garments?** Leupold and others who fail to take in the full panoramic prophetic sweep of the vision vaguely describe these as "the sins that characterized the age of Joshua" (*op. cit.*, p. 67). But much more is meant than this. Represented is the whole gamut of Israel's apostasy and infidelity, notably her miserable self-righteousness in the face of her rejection of the Messiah. Joshua's silence before Satan's accusation is palpable proof of his guilt.

In the light of Joshua's contam-

4 And he answered and spake unto those that stood before him, saying, Take away the filthy garments from him. And unto him he said, Behold, I have caused thine iniquity to pass from thee, and I will clothe thee with change of raiment.

4 And he answered and spake unto those that stood before him, saying, Take the filthy garments from off him. And unto him he said, Behold, I have caused thine iniquity to pass from thee, and I will clothe thee with rich apparel.

inated condition and that of Israel, Satan had reckoned on every score of his power. He forgot, however, that the grace of God that chose Jerusalem and snatched the people out of the fire of world-wide captivity (as well as the Babylonian exile) was far superior to his malignity. If God's gracious purposes toward Israel would not be effective, the people of Israel would never have survived till this hour, nor would they ever be cleansed in that great day when they are reconstituted as a high-priestly nation, turning to Messiah and receiving the cleansing this vision describes and which faith in Him *alone* can bring to them.

II. THE VISION OF PARDONED AND REPOSITIONED ISRAEL UNDER THE FIGURE OF JOSHUA THE HIGH PRIEST (Zech. 3:4-7)

With Joshua and Israel's guilt so evident from the foul, excrement-covered garments with which the high priest as a representative of the nation is clothed, the acute problem arises how an infinitely holy God could bless a people in such a judgment-provoking condition. The answer given in verses 4-7 not only sets forth the way of national deliverance for Israel, but illustrates the principle of justification for *every* lost sinner.

1. *Israel (Under the Figure of Joshua) Is Imperilled by Being Deprived of Priestly Office, But Is Pardoned* (Zech. 3:4). And he [the Lord Himself] answered and said unto those who were standing before him [attending upon Him] as follows: Remove the excrement-bespattered clothes from him [Joshua]. And he [the Lord] said to him [Joshua], See,

I have caused thy iniquity to pass from thee, and I will clothe thee with festive garments. The Lord's answering (*wayya'an*) is in reply to the deplorable and anomalous *situation* of the high priest's filthiness and not to any question or remark that appears in the context, the word "answer" (*'anah*) sometimes having this meaning.

The Lord's reply is addressed to those (doubtlessly angels) who were standing before him, i.e., "attending upon Him" or "acting in the capacity of a servant to Him," as Joshua himself was attempting to do in a priestly role in verse 1. The Lord's answer takes the form of a gracious injunction that releases the divine mercy, already anticipated in verse 2, now manifested in the actual cleansing of Joshua, and hence of Israel. The act performed by the angelic attendants in strict accordance with the Lord's command is symbolic not only of the forgiveness of sin and the justification of the nation Israel in the future day of her conversion, but of the individual sinner who trusts Christ, as Israel then will. Two elements appear: (1) the negative — remove the filthy garments from him — emblematic of the cleansing or taking away of sin (Rom. 3:25; Eph. 1:7); (2) the positive — clothe him with festive garments — portraying the imputation of the righteousness of God in Christ reckoned to the believing sinner (cf. Rom. 1:16, 17; 3:22, 26).

The festive garments with which the cleansed high priest was invested are in striking contrast to the filthy garments from which he was divested. On the one hand appear filthy, smelly, excrement-stained linen; on the other, splendid costly garments (*maḥalatsoth* from the root *ḥalats*, "to put off," deriving from the corresponding Arabic verb having this connotation). Accordingly, fine, beautiful garments, only worn on some special occasion and "put off," like our "Sunday best" for ordinary activity at home, are indicated (Isa. 3:22).

In the high priest's wardrobe these articles of dress were "the holy garments" for glory and beauty (Exod. 28:4, 5; Lev. 8:7-9) made of gold, blue, purple, scarlet, and fine linen and consisting of the "coat" of fine linen (Exod. 28:39), the long garment worn next to the person, and "the robe of the ephod" (Exod. 28:31-35), a seamless piece of blue linen worn over the coat, embroidered with pomegranates, symbols of fruitfulness, alternating at the edge with golden bells (testimony) which tinkled as the high priest went about in his holy ministrations.

The ephod of linen, embroidered with gold, blue, purple and scarlet, set with onyx stones on the shoulder pieces and engraved with the names of the twelve tribes, supported the breastplate (Exod. 28:15-21), a square pouch of linen (Exod. 28:16) containing the Urim and Thummim used oracularly to ascertain the divine will (Num. 27:21; Deut. 33:8). The breastplate also held the oblong gold setting containing twelve precious stones, also engraved with the names of the twelve tribes. The mitre or priestly turban was worn on the high priest's head, supporting upon the front a gold plate engraved with the words, "Holiness to the Lord" (Exod. 28:36, 37).

Added to the above-mentioned garments "for glory and beauty" (Exod. 28:40) were linen trousers (Exod. 28:42), and a linen coat, distinguished from the other more splendid garments of office. On the day of atonement Aaron performed his holy ministrations in the simple "holy linen coat," linen trousers, and linen mitre (Lev. 16:4). Not until he had made full atonement by the elaborate ritual typifying the redemptive work of Christ (Lev. 16:1-22) did he put off the spotless linen garments and put on the garments of glory and beauty (Lev. 16:24) to come forth to minister not now *for* the people before God, as he had previously been doing, but *to* the people *in behalf of* God.

Apparently the filthy garments with which Joshua was clothed were what should have been the holy garments of spotless linen. But in Israel's great future day of atonement when the nation turns to its Redeemer, the people's sin will be gloriously atoned for and cleansed away, so that the spiritually renewed nation shall come forth from the holiest of God's presence in pure linen and go forth in "the garments of glory and beauty" as a high-priestly nation to bless all the nations of the earth in the kingdom age (Rom. 11:26, 27). But apart from God's gracious purposes for Israel in Christ, the people never would have survived, nor would they ever be cleansed and reinstated in blessing as the vision so graphically predicts. In his wonderful exposition of Israel's national election and glorious future in Romans 11, the Apostle summarizes God's unchangeable purpose toward His people with the enunciation of a principle that so beautifully appears here: "For the gifts and *calling* of God are without repentance" (Romans 11:29). Israel's *calling* is to be a high-priestly nation to the nations of the earth and the divine vocation will be realized on the basis of God's faithfulness, not the nation's.

2. *Israel (Under the Figure of Joshua) Is Fully Repositioned* (Zech. 3:5). **Thereupon I** [the prophet] **said, Let them set a clean turban on his head. So they set a clean turban on his head and clothed him with garments, with the Angel of the Lord standing by.** An interesting episode crops out. So

5 And I said, Let them set a fair mitre upon his head. So they set a fair mitre upon his head, and clothed him with garments. And the angel of the Lord stood by.
6 And the angel of the Lord protested unto Joshua, saying,
7 Thus saith the Lord of hosts; If thou wilt walk in my ways, and if thou wilt keep my charge, then thou shalt also judge my house, and shalt also keep my courts, and I will give thee places to walk among these that stand by.

5   And I said, Let them set a clean mitre upon his head. So they set a clean mitre upon his head, and clothed him with garments; and the angel of Jehovah was standing by.
6   And the angel of Jehovah protested unto Joshua, saying,
7   Thus saith Jehovah of hosts: If thou wilt walk in my ways, and if thou wilt keep my charge, then thou also shalt judge my house, and shalt also keep my courts, and I will give thee a place of access among these that stand by.

carried away with enthusiasm by the sight of the cleansing and clothing of the high priest and sensing its vast significance in its bearing upon the future of his people, the prophet with excusable zeal and holy boldness interrupts the proceedings with a personal request for the inclusion of an important item in the priestly "attire" (*begadhim*, from *bagadh*, "to cover, clothe, act fraudulently or covertly" [Prov. 2:22; 11:3, 6; 13:2; Jer. 9:1]; hence "covering," "cloth," "garment," plural "clothes," "garments," usually the outer garment of the Oriental [Gen. 39:12; 41:42; I Kings 22:10] and in the context of this vision denoting the *priestly vestments*).

That the "headdress" of the high priest was included in the term "apparel" or "attire," may easily and naturally be assumed so that the prophet certainly is exonerated from the charge of ignorance as well as presumptuous interference or unseemly zealousness. The ready compliance with the prophet's request is proof enough of this fact. So they set a clean turban [or mitre] upon his head and clothed him with garments (i.e., "with the priestly attire of glory and beauty"). The Septuagint and Latin omission of the reading, Then I said, thus seems unwarranted and the Hebrew is to be followed.

The clean turban is a better rendering than the A.V.'s "fair mitre," since the word clean (*tahar* from root *taher*, "shine, be bright, glisten") means to be "glisteningly clean" "brightly pure," and in a Levitical sense is opposed to "unclean, polluted" (*tame*', Lev. 13:17). The mitre was fair because *shiningly clean* in striking contrast to Joshua's former filthiness.

The turban (*tsanif* from the root "to wind around") was a high skull piece wound around the head of men (Job 29:14), of women (Isa. 3:23) and of the high priest (Lev. 16:4, Zech. 3:5). Its singular significance in being requested to be placed upon the high priest's head by Zechariah is that it signified the *complete reinstatement unto the high-priestly function in deed as well as in truth* for the turban of fine linen bore upon the front of it a gold plate engraved, "Holiness to the Lord" (Exod. 28:36) and indicated that Joshua was morally and spiritually cleansed (as Israel will be) to minister in an office that uniquely demanded this qualification.

Moreover, this cleansing and clothing of Joshua as a mark of complete reinstatement to high and holy priestly office was done in the light of God's unspeakable holiness, suggested by the appended circumstantial clause, giving an incidental sidelight to the whole transaction, And the Angel of the Lord was standing by (vs. 5). It was accordingly done with His full approval and gracious blessing.

3. The Covenant of the Priesthood Is Renewed with Joshua (Zech. 3:6, 7).

Then the Angel of the Lord solemnly testified to Joshua, as follows: **Thus the Lord of armies says, If you will walk in my ways, and keep my charge, then you likewise shall govern [judge] my house, and supervise my courts and I will give you free access among these who are standing here.**

These verses mark the transition from the symbolic vision to the practical application to Joshua. **Then the Angel of the Lord solemnly testified** (wayya'adh, from root "return," "turn back," then "repeat," "do over again," "to say again and again," "to witness," causative, "to bear solemn witness, to solemnly affirm" [Deut. 8:19; 32:46; I Kings 2:42]). That which the Angel of the Lord so solemnly declares to Joshua (the solemnity further accentuated by being followed by the phrase, **Thus says the Lord of armies**) constitutes the conditions of spiritual blessing for the high priest personally. These stipulations are two in number and are introduced by the conditional particle "if" ('im) and form the protasis of a conditional sentence with "the supposition expressing a real contingency of any degree of possibility" (Davidson, *Hebrew Syntax*, p. 176). (1) **If you will walk in my ways** and (2) **if you will keep my charge** (these underscored words are emphatic by position in the Hebrew).

The apodosis of the condition sentence gives the resulting spiritual blessings and privileges that would accrue to Joshua. (1) He shall **rule** God's house. The word "rule" (tadhin) means to "manage," "regulate," in the sense of "govern," by punishing anyone guilty of dereliction (Gen. 15:14; Job 36:31) and defending anyone in the right (Gen. 30:6; Prov. 31:9), as this may come within the province of his priestly duties. (2) He

shall **keep** ("have charge of") God's courts, not incurring demotion or untimely death like Eli (I Sam. 2:27–36) and Abiathar (I Kings 2:26, 27). (3) He shall be given access in spiritual approach to God. The word translated **places to walk** (cf. "place of walking," Ezek. 42:4) in the Authorized Version (mahlekim) denotes "goings" or "comings" in the sense of priestly free access in spiritual approach to God, thus suggesting the official complete reinstatement of the priesthood, showing that Joshua, symbolizing Israel, would have unimpeded ingress and egress in communion with God "among those standing by," i.e., "the angels." Just as these pure, ethereal, unfallen spirits have ready access, so will Joshua, at the moment standing "among" them.

Although Israel in the future kingdom will be fully reinstated nationally to high-priestly fellowship *with God* and high-priestly ministry to the nations *for God*, on the basis of God's gracious purposes and electing love and *not* on any work or merit basis, yet like Joshua, she must not suppose that such manifest mercy to her by any means excuses her from obedience and faithfulness. On the contrary, although *entrance* into that blessing is assured by God's faithfulness, not hers, *continuance* in that blessing *individually* will be conditioned by her faithfulness in receiving and appropriating it. But the same grace that will work in Israel to fit her for receiving her cleansing and reinstatement to priestly ministry to the nations will operate in her to cause her to be faithful in persevering in that grace. Hence the concepts of **walk** and **keep** are prominent in the conditions that are enjoined upon Joshua, and through him to all his priestly colleagues, as well as to the nation Israel as she is prophetically adumbrated by Joshua. The emblazoned insignia on the flashing turban of the high priest, "Holiness to the Lord," is to be a clarion call to present faithfulness on the part of the priest-

8 Hear now, O Joshua the high priest, thou, and thy fellows that sit before thee: for they are men wondered at: for, behold, I will bring forth my servant the BRANCH.

8   Hear now, O Joshua the high priest, thou and thy fellows that sit before thee; for they are men that are a sign: for, behold, I will bring forth my servant the Branch.

hood as well as to future hope on the part of the nation.

III. THE PREDICTION OF REDEEMED AND RESTORED ISRAEL UNDER THE FIGURE OF MESSIAH, THE BRANCH (Zech. 3:8–10)

But the priesthood foreshadowed even more glorious events than those already hinted at in the vision up to this point. Israel, prefigured by Joshua, will be cleansed and converted. The nation will yet fulfill its original priestly call and destiny. Israel shall yet be *"a kingdom of priests and a holy nation"* (Exod. 19:6). However, the question arises, How shall this be brought about? Who will effect this grand transformation? To answer these pivotal questions the vision moves on to its climax in a resplendent burst of Messianic prophecy which is meant to be the cynosure of all eyes opened by faith and all humble hearts attuned to God's plans and purposes for the ages, and particularly for His people Israel.

1. *The Recipients of the Prediction of Redeemed and Restored Israel Under the Figure of Messiah the Branch* (Zech. 3:8a). Hear, if you will, Joshua, high priest, and your colleagues who sit before you, because they are men of prophetic portent. . . . The speaker of these and the remaining pivotal verses of the vision is the *Lord Himself*. Cf. the first person, my Servant (vs. 8b), I set before Joshua (vs. 9), I will remove the iniquity of the land (vs. 9), says the Lord of armies (vs. 10). Moreover, it is highly fitting that words of such tremendous import as these should be uttered by the Lord Himself.

Joshua is addressed directly through the vocative of direct address by an imperative followed by the polite particle *na'* ("if you please," French, *si'l vous plaît*). Hear, if you will, Joshua high priest. The Lord gives the message in a command, for it contains a message of urgency requiring clear apprehension as well as diligent faith. The employment of the term high priest in conjunction with Joshua, shows as in verse 1 that he is not being considered in his own person but as a representative of his people, as throughout the vision. This fact is further confirmed by his colleague priests being included *with him* in the command, Hear if you will, and further by their being styled "men of sign" or men of prophetic portent.

This word sign signifies "a prodigy" or "a supernatural event" (Exod. 4:21; 7:3; 11:9; Ps. 78:43). It also means a "sign" or "proof" (Deut. 28:46; Ps. 71:7). Likewise, it signifies a "sign of a future event," i.e., a "prophetic portent" (Isa. 8:18; 20:3). It is used in this last sense here in the designation men of prophetic portent, men who in their persons shadow forth future events, demonstrating that *both* Joshua the high priest, and his colleagues who sit before him, in official priestly capacity, *symbolize future events for Israel*. These men of portent are to be the recipients of the great Messianic prophecy about to be given, and reflect in their priestly ministries in Israel the priestly ministry of Israel in the future day when the nation is cleansed and converted.

2. *The Declaration of the Prediction of Redeemed and Restored Israel Under the Figure of the Branch and the Stone* (Zech. 3:8b–10). For I assuredly will bring forth my servant, the Branch. For behold, the Stone which I have set before Joshua. Upon [the] one Stone

9 For behold the stone that I have laid before Joshua; upon one stone shall be seven eyes: behold, I will engrave the graving thereof, saith the Lord of hosts, and I will remove the iniquity of that land in one day.

10 In that day, saith the Lord of hosts, shall ye call every man his neighbour under the vine and under the fig tree.

---

9 For, behold, the stone that I have set before Joshua; upon one stone are seven eyes: behold, I will engrave the graving thereof, saith Jehovah of hosts, and I will remove the iniquity of that land in one day.

10 In that day, saith Jehovah of hosts, shall ye invite every man his neighbor under the vine and under the fig-tree.

---

are seven eyes. I will indeed engrave it with its engraving, says the Lord of armies, so that I will remove the iniquity of that land in a single day. In that day, says the Lord of armies, every one of you shall invite his neighbor under vine and under fig tree.

Why are Joshua and his colleague priests **men of prophetic portent,** men who in their official office shadow forth future events? The causal conjunction **for** (*ki*, "because"), introducing a causal clause, presents the reason. **Because I** [the Lord of armies] **will produce my servant, the Branch.** Through Him Israel will be redeemed and restored and constituted a high-priestly nation, which Joshua and his associate priests prefigure.

The Messianic prophecy concerning **my** [the Lord's] **servant the Branch** is graphically couched in a syntactical device known as *future instans* (*hinneni mebhi'*), consisting of the demonstrative interjection *hinneh*, behold, plus the suffixed pronoun I, plus a participle. This lively form in Hebrew "is intended to announce the event as imminent, or at least near at hand (and sure to happen)" (Gesenius-Kautsch, *Hebrew Grammar*, section 116q). Therefore it is to be rendered, "I am about to bring forth," or **I will surely bring forth,** *mebhi'*, the causative of *bo'*, "enter," "come in"; hence "to cause to enter," "lead in," "bring in" (Gen. 43:17; Exod. 6:8; Num. 27:17); here "present," "introduce."

This great Messianic prediction introduces **my servant the Branch.** The Lord's **servant the Branch,** pre-sents Messiah in the aspect of His first advent in humiliation and rejection, obedient unto death (Isa. 52:13–53:12; Phil. 2:5–8), purchasing that redemption on the cross which will be the basis of Israel's future conversion and restoration as a priestly nation at the second advent (Isa. 42:1–7; 49:1–7). The gospel of Mark presents "the Lord's Servant the Branch."

The true Priest who was to come is styled **the Branch,** i.e., "the Shoot" or "Sprout," from the root *tsamah,* "to sprout out," used of growing plants (Gen. 2:5; 41:6), the primary idea apparently being "to shine," as in Syriac and Arabic, and referring to the glistening green of fresh spring verdure. The figure of Messiah is aptly expressive since the noun *tsemah* means "things which sprout or shoot forth" from the earth, i.e., its "verdure, produce, fruit" (Gen. 19:25; Ps. 65:10 [11]; Hos. 8:7; Ezek. 16:7). Although He would "grow up as a *tender* plant and as a *root* out of a dry ground" (Isa. 53:1), and would come in poverty, weakness, and obscurity at His first advent, yet the sprout and the tender plant would manifest remarkable vitality and growth, so that in His second advent the sprig from the stump of David and the shoot (*netser,* "sprout," from Arabic *nadura,* "to shine, be verdant") from his roots (Isa. 11:1) shall be Israel's glorious king (Isa. 11:2–16) and appear as "King of kings and Lord of lords" to set up His kingdom (Rev. 19:16).

Zechariah uses the name **Branch**

(without the article and in apposition to **my servant**) as a proper name, it being a well-known prophetic epithet of the coming Messiah from the days of Isaiah and Jeremiah, and if it had not already become a proper name, Zechariah made it so, as Pusey observes (*The Minor Prophets*, II, p. 356).

Isaiah had presented "the Branch of the Lord" (Isa. 4:2), that is, the "Immanuel" character of Christ (Isa. 7:14), to be fully revealed to converted and restored Israel after His second advent (Matt. 25:31). Jeremiah had introduced the "Branch of David" (Jer. 23:5; 33:15) as the posterity or "off-spring of David according to the flesh" (Rom. 1:3), to be manifest in His kingdom glory as "King of kings and Lord of lords" (Rev. 19:16). Zechariah in addition to presenting the Lord's Servant, the Branch in this passage, in humiliation and death at the first advent also presents the "man whose name is the Branch" (Zech. 6:12, 13), Messiah in His character as the Son of man, "the second [last] Adam" (I Cor. 15:45–47), reigning as King-Priest over the earth in the dominion given to and forfeited by the "first Adam."

What message, it may be asked, did Zechariah's panoramic predictions have for Joshua and his colleague priests? Leupold admirably answers this question by his incisive paraphrase of verse 8: "I shall not let you, Joshua, and your fellow priests be removed from office, nor your office be discontinued, for I have a destiny for you—you are a type of the coming Messiah, who will do My work perfectly ("Servant"), and who will bring the priestly office to undreamed of glory ("Shoot") when He springs forth" (*op. cit., in loc.*).

Not only is Christ presented figuratively as **the Branch** but also as **the Stone** (vs. 9). The former figure, as noted, presents the *first* reason why Joshua and his associate priests were **men of prophetic portent,** men who in their official office foreshadow future

events; namely, because through the Messiah as Servant-Branch Israel's redemption would be wrought out at Calvary at the first advent to furnish the basis for the nation's conversion and restoration as a priestly nation at the second advent. The latter figure of **the Stone** gives the *second* reason for the same symbolism. **For** (*ki,* "because," introducing a second causal clause) **lo the Stone which I** [the Lord of armies] **will set before Joshua. Upon** [that] **one Stone are seven eyes.**

The reason two figures are used, one the **Servant-Branch,** the other the single **Stone,** is because one applies specifically to the first advent and the other centers in the second advent. Leupold, rejecting Luther's correct interpretation of the Stone as Christ, contends there are "two major difficulties" that preclude such an interpretation: (1) "A bewildering variety of figures is employed to describe the Messiah—'Servant, Sprout, Stone'" (*op. cit.,* p. 77). But this is a pointless argument since Zechariah undeniably combines two of them in one "Servant-Sprout" to distinguish other "Sprout" references which refer to the second and not the first advent (e.g., Isa. 4:2; Zech. 6:12, 13) and since the third "the Stone" clearly refers to the second advent and is a *very common* Messianic figure throughout the prophetic Scriptures. (2) Leupold also maintains "a confusion within the figures results: on the one hand the high priest himself together with his companions typifies the coming Messiah (vs. 8), and at the same time the Messiah would be lying before the priest as an object of his care" (*loc. cit.*).

But there is nothing in the Hebrew that would support Leupold's objection. **For behold the Stone which I set** [or "will set" (prophetic perfect)] **before Joshua** does not mean that the Stone was placed at Joshua's feet as his ward. It simply means that "Messiah, the Stone" was held out to Joshua *in prophetic prospect* (cf. "set before," *nathan liphne,* I Kings 9:6) as the Stone cut without hands which will smite the kingdoms of the nations symbolized by Daniel's colossus and become a "great mountain" (the millennial kingdom) to fill "the whole earth" (Dan. 2:34, 35). It is precisely by this destruction of the Satanic world system that the establishment of the kingdom is brought about, which in turn makes possible the restoration of Israel as a high-priestly nation of which Joshua and his priest colleagues are **men of predictive portent.**

Thus **the one Stone,** is the unique One, and is correctly interpreted by Luther and earlier expositors and by Wright, Baron, Pusey, Feinberg, etc., as the Messiah, for this symbol peculiarly relates Christ to Israel, particularly at His second coming when the "stumbling stone and rock of offense" of the first coming (Rom. 9:32; I Cor. 1:23) becomes the "head-stone of the corner" (Zech. 4:7). Inadequate are such views as connect the **Stone** with "the plummet or headstone" (Kimchi), "altar" (Von Orelli), "the kingdom of God" (Hengstenberg), or "the church of God" (Leupold).

Further corroborative evidences that the **Stone** is the Messiah are: (1) **Upon the one Stone are seven eyes,** bespeaking *infinite* intelligence either directed by God on it in loving care (Ezek. 1:18; 10:12) or omniscience, if the eyes are pictured on the Stone itself (cf. Zech. 4:10), as the "Lamb" of the Apocalypse that had been slain had "seven horns *and seven eyes*" which are said to be "the seven spirits of God, sent forth into all the earth" (Rev. 5:6). (2) **The Lord of armies declares, I will engrave the engraving of it** as an "elect precious stone" (Isa. 28:16; I Pet. 2:6). What the engraving of it is, is not explained, but inasmuch as the idiom "to engrave" or "to engrave an engraving" (cf. II Chron. 2:7 [6], 14 [13] for the full idiom) occurs of carving precious stones (Exod. 28:11, 21, 36; 39: 6, 14, 30) and wood of the temple (I Kings 6:29; Ps. 74:6), the reference

is to that in Messiah, the Stone, which was cut in His sinless humanity authenticating Him as the Servant obedient unto the death of the cross; namely, the thorn scars on His brow, the prints of the nails in His hands and feet, the sword wound in His side (John 20:25, 27). These are the divine engravings cut deeply in the precious chosen gem to bring out its beauty and flashing splendor.

(3) That **the Stone** is Messiah is further demonstrated by the *result* that would occur consequent upon the deep cutting the Stone would endure. So that (result, *waw* with perfect) **I** [the Lord of armies] **will remove** [*mashti* from *mush*, "to yield, give away" (Num. 14:44; Josh. 1:8; Isa. 22:25), in causative as here, "to cause to yield or give way," i.e., "remove, take away"] **the iniquity of the land in a single day.** Calvary was the world's antitypical Great Day of Atonement (Lev. 16) when "the Lamb of God" took away "the sin of the world" (John 1:29). But the Jews rejected the Redeemer and His redemption so that their day of atonement was postponed. Now their day has arrived, and **that land** in the context is "Judah's land" and the **one day** is Israel's Great Day of Atonement when they "look upon" him "whom they have pierced... and mourn for him as one mourns for his only son and shall be in bitterness for him, as one that is in bitterness for his first-born" (Zech. 12:10).

The expression **in one day** is always emphatic (cf. Gen. 27:45; I Sam. 2:34; I Kings 20:29; Isa. 9:14; 10:17; 47:9). "Things are crowded into it, which seem too much for *one day*" (Pusey, *in loc.*). Its use in this context in Zechariah is peculiarly fitting and felicitous. The removal of the **iniquity of that land** has as the necessary prelude the removal of the iniquity of its inhabitants, and this shall be the glory of Israel's Great Day of Atonement.

(4) That **the Stone** is Messiah, with emphatic reference to His relation to

Israel at His second advent, is further shown by the millennial figures with which the vision concludes. **In that day** (*bayyom hahu'*, occurring scores of times in Zechariah with reference to the time of the establishment of Israel's kingdom, especially in chapters 12–14) **says the Lord of armies, everyone of you shall invite his neighbor under** [pregnant for "to sit under"] [his] **vine and** [his] **fig tree.** Solomon, whose reign was typical of the millennial reign of the "Greater than Solomon" (Matt. 12:42), "had peace on all sides round about him. And Judah and Israel dwelt safely, *every man under his vine and under his fig tree* from Dan even to Beersheba all the days of Solomon" (I Kings 4:24, 25). It is the prophet Micah who indubitably invests the "vine" and "fig tree" symbolism with millennial connotations. Interwoven in his magnificent description of Israel's future restoration in kingdom prosperity and peace, he writes, "But they *shall sit every man under his vine and under his*

fig tree; and none shall make them afraid, for the mouth of the Lord of hosts hath spoken it" (Mic. 4:4).

Zechariah who echoes the former prophets throughout his entire prophecy was well acquainted with the **vine** and **fig tree** imagery as millennial figures signifying fruitfulness, peace, and prosperity, and fittingly the vision ends with this *terminus ad quem,* which is necessary for the realization of that which is its over-all prediction; namely, the restoration of Israel as a high-priestly nation.

Wonderful is the marvellous grace of God that transforms an excrement-bespattered priest, utterly polluted and taken hold of by Satan, into a holy priest before God, reinstating him in full blessing. It is even more remarkable that all this should typify God's gracious dealing with the nation (through Messiah — Servant-Branch and Messiah — the Stone) through which He has elected in His sovereign grace and love to consummate His specific purposes for the earth in the coming age.

CHAPTER FOUR

ISRAEL AS THE LIGHT
OF THE WORLD
UNDER MESSIAH KING-PRIEST

(THE FIFTH VISION)

THE GOLDEN LAMPSTAND AND THE TWO OLIVE TREES

(ZECH. 4:1–14)

THE purging of Israel from sin and defilement and her restoration as a high priestly nation with the Lord's "Servant the Branch" (3:8) manifested to her in inner salvation, so graphically symbolized in the preceding vision, form a necessary prelude to her millennial ministry of witness as the light of the world under Messiah King-Priest, as set forth in the present vision. The *outward deliverance* from exile and oppression symbolized in the first three visions, while immensely comforting to the people during the long, weary years of their world-wide sufferings, can

1 And the angel that talked with me came again, and waked me, as a man that is wakened out of his sleep.

1   And the angel that talked with me came again, and waked me, as a man that is wakened out of his sleep.

only be brought about effectively to God's glory by their *inner salvation* and their consequent witness to the nations of the world.

This beautiful order of *salvation* followed by *testimony* appears in the fourth and fifth visions. Spiritual regeneration and restoration to priestly access and fellowship with God pave the way for Spirit-anointed witness and effective testimony. If Israel's enemies are to be judged and punished, those who survive of the nations must have the witness of Messiah's salvation brought to them by the redeemed nation, if God is to be truly glorified.

It was God's original purpose for Israel that she should be a lightbearer and witness to the surrounding nations engulfed in the darkness of paganistic idolatry. Moses of old enunciated the strategic spiritual ministry Israel was called to conduct. "When the most High gave to the nations their inheritance, when he separated mankind, he set the boundaries of the peoples according to the number of the children of Israel" (Deut. 32:8). The prophet Ezekiel declared the same thought. "Thus says the Lord God: This is Jerusalem; I have set her *in the center of the nations*, with countries round about her" (Ezek. 5:5). At the same time Ezekiel laments Jerusalem's unfaithfulness in witnessing to the true Creator and Redeemer of mankind. At long last, as this present vision unfolds, the nation is restored to her predestined spiritual role.

I. THE PROPHETIC SYMBOLISM OF THE VISION (Zech. 4:1–5)

Although the imagery of this vision is striking and is easily interpreted in the light of its context in the eight night visions and in the broader framework of Bible prophecy, few interpretative hints are given in the vision itself, which is to a large degree taken up with questions by the prophet. These inquiries do not yield a full response till the concluding verse of the vision.

1. *The Prophet Prepared for the Vision* (Zech. 4:1). **Then** [temporal sequence] **the angel who was speaking to me came back and aroused me** [*hifil* imperfect of '*ur*] **as a man is aroused out of his sleep.** The prophet is made ready for the vision about to be given by the ministry of the interpreting angel, who had been away and now returns to instruct Zechariah and to help him.

The first thing the angel does is to **arouse** or "awaken" Zechariah **as a man** [*one,* purely pronominal] **is awakened** [*nifal* imperfect of '*ur*] **out of his sleep.** The same word occurs in the *nifal* perfect in Zechariah 2:13 [17], (*q.v.*). As Keil notes, "After the prophet had seen four visions one after another, probably with very short intervals, and has heard the marvellous interpretations of them, he is so overpowered by the impression produced by what he has seen and heard that he falls into a state of spiritual exhaustion resembling sleep . . ." (*The Minor Prophets,* Vol. II, p. 262). Daniel, under the spell of overpowering spiritual revelations, had a similar experience. "Then I heard the sound of his words, and when I heard the sound of his [the Lord's] words I fell on my face *in a deep sleep,* with my face to the ground" (Dan. 10:9). Similarly Peter and the disciples on the Mount of Transfiguration "were heavy with sleep . . ." (Luke 9:32). From this state of spiritual lethargy the prophet had to be aroused to a condition of spiritual receptivity.

2 And said unto me, What seest thou? And I said, I have looked, and behold a candlestick all of gold, with a bowl upon the top of it, and his seven lamps thereon, and seven pipes to the seven lamps, which are upon the top thereof:
3 And two olive trees by it, one upon the right side of the bowl, and the other upon the left side thereof.
4 So I answered and spake to the angel that talked with me, saying, What are these, my lord?
5 Then the angel that talked with me answered and said unto me, Knowest thou not what these be? And I said, No, my lord.

---

2   And he said unto me, What seest thou? And I said, I have seen, and' behold, a candlestick all of gold, with its bowl upon the top of it, and its seven lamps thereon; there are seven pipes to each of the lamps, which are upon the top thereof;
3   and two olive-trees by it, one upon the right side of the bowl, and the other upon the left side thereof.
4   And I answered and spake to the angel that talked with me, saying, What are these, my lord?
5   Then the angel that talked with me answered and said unto me, Knowest thou not what these are? And I said, No, my lord.

---

2. *The Prophet Presented with the Vision* (Zech. 4:2, 3). And he said to me, What do you see? Thereupon I replied, I see, and look a lampstand all of gold, and its oil-vessel up above it, and its seven lamps upon it, seven pipes each for the lamps upon the top of it. And two olive trees by it, one on the right of the oil-vessel, and the other on the left of it (vss. 2, 3).

The imagery of the vision presents essentially the seven-branched candlestick of the tabernacle (and temple) with three significant variations. (1) Zechariah's candlestick has its oil-vessel (*gullah*, "basin," "bowl of a lamp," or "oil receptacle," [Eccles. 12:6; I Kings 7:41, 42; II Chron. 4:12, 13] on the top of it, that is *over* the seven lamps, so that the oil flowed by gravity from the elevated oil bowl. This feature was completely lacking from the candlestick of the holy place, the lamps there being filled with oil by the priests.

(2) Zechariah's lampstand has seven pipes (*mutsaqoth*, "tubes or conduits," through which oil is *poured*, from *yatsaq*, "pour, flow, cast" [I Kings 22:35; Job 38:38]). These seven pipes connect with each lamp (forty-nine in all). This is indicated by the

distributive use "seven and seven" (*shibhe'ah weshibhe'ah* in Hebrew idiom meaning seven to each pipe, as the identical idiom is illustrated in II Samuel 21:20 and I Chronicles 20:6). By contrast the tabernacle candlestick had no pipes at all, but only seven branches or arms (*qanim*) to hold the lamps, the latter a self-evident feature of this vision and so not explicitly stated in the imagery.

(3) A third distinguishing feature of the candlestick of Zechariah's vision is the two olive trees on the right and left of the oil vessel (vss. 3, 11), with fruitful branches supplying it with abundant oil transmitted to it through two additional golden pipes (vs. 12). These three unique features of Zechariah's lampstand differentiated it from the tabernacle candlestick and stressed its automatic and spontaneous supply of oil for lighting without human agency.

3. *The Prophet's Inquiry Concerning the Import of the Vision* (Zech. 4:4, 5). After the vision of this extraordinary lampstand had flashed upon his vision, Zechariah asks the meaning of it. Then [temporal sequence] I answered and said to the angel who was speaking with me, What are

these, my lord? Whereupon the angel who was speaking with me answered and said to me, Don't you know what these are?

The clear implication of the interpreting angel to the prophet's query, What are these, my lord? is that the symbolism of the vision was sufficiently plain in its being reminiscent of the tabernacle and temple typology so that the prophet did not need any precise explanation of it, and indeed none is given. Don't you know? (*halo'*, a negative interrogative particle), suggesting a positive "you ought to know." Although no explanation at this point is given, the message for Zerubbabel and the people of that time is indicated fully (vss. 6-10), as well as a hint as to its future fulfilment and meaning in the context of the nation's ultimate eschatological expectations (vss. 11-14).

Since the vision in its essence corresponds to the seven-branched candlestick of the tabernacle, the angel's reply to the prophet's question suggests that the starting point in the comprehension of its meaning is an examination of the typological significance of that important piece of tabernacle furniture.

The "candlestick [lampstand] of pure gold" (Exod. 25:31-40) in the holy place is typical of Christ our Light (John 8:12; Matt. 5:14) manifested in His deity (pure gold) in the plentitude of the power of the sevenfold Spirit (Heb. 1:9; Rev.1: 4), prefigured by the seven lights (fulness and perfection of testimony). But inasmuch as Israel was the *one* nation chosen by God to be the witness to the one true God, the seven-branched lampstand *in the midst* of her (and it was never as a symbol in the midst of any other nation) symbolized *Israel's divine vocation to be a witness and a testimony of God's salvation in Christ to the unbelieving pagan nations around her.* Thus the golden candlestick prefigures Israel in the full fellowship and blessing of God *as she was meant to be* in Messianic faith and expectation in Old Testament times, and *as she will actually be in her millennial restoration.*

However, the nation abysmally failed in her national calling. Although the revelation of the glory of God was granted her for her own enlightenment as well as that she should be a light-bearer to the nations, she persecuted and killed the prophets, disobeyed the Word of God so wonderfully committed to her, lapsed into the disgraceful idolatry of the nations to whom she was to be a light, and finally crucified the divine Redeemer when He came to earth to fulfill her messianic promises. This last and culminating act in the nation's failure as a light-bearer resulted in the removal of her candlestick, *the emblem of her religious and ecclesiastical position,* with the destruction of the temple and the nation's worship. When Jesus died, the whole temple ritual became meaningless as a result of its fulfilment in Him whom the nation crucified, and it was a travesty until destroyed in A.D. 70.

With Israel's candlestick removed, light-bearing testimony passed over to the new people of God, the Church (John 8:12; Matt. 5:14, 15; Eph. 5:8, 9; Phil. 2:15), symbolized *not by one* seven-branched golden candlestick but by *seven* golden candlesticks (lampstands) representing the *one* church of God in every place during this age from Pentecost until the outgathering (Rev. 2:1 – 3:22). God's light-bearing people today, unlike Israel who possessed one earthly center, cannot be represented as an absolute unity (one light-bearing *nation*), but a *spiritual* unity under the headship of Christ (seven), yet all mutually independent in government and external order (*individual* candlesticks).

But the church period will end in spiritual lukewarmness and the lamp of Laodicea is quenched in apostasy, never to be restored. But such is not the case with Israel (Rom. 11:21-29). Not only are her governmental scepter and kingdom to be restored after her long night of dispersion and persecution, but her candlestick of testimony as well will be reinstated after the wearisome centuries of her spiritual darkness and unbelief, to radiate with *a luster never known in the past*. This is the import of Zechariah's vision, and the contrasts of the candlestick of his vision with that of the tabernacle accentuate this glorious fact.

The **bowl** or "receptacle" on the top of the solid gold lampstand emblemizes the full reserve supply of the Holy Spirit, and Hengstenberg is correct in declaring that "oil is one of the most clearly defined symbols in the Bible" (*Christology of the Old Testament*, Vol. III, p. 301), constantly appearing as a type of the Spirit of God, and seen in focal significance in the consecration of prophets, priests, and kings.

The fact of seven pipes or tubes to each of the seven lamps (forty-nine in all) does not constitute a bewildering detail that spoils the chaste simplicity or appearance of the original candlestick of the tabernacle, but is purposely incorporated into the symbolism to accentuate the increased supply of oil, as the kingdom will be inaugurated by a great effusion of the Spirit in *fulfilment* of Joel's prophecy (2:28–32) [3:1–5]. The numerous channels also suggest the meticulously careful and copious conduit of the oil *to each lamp*, so that *all seven* will shine with fullest possible brilliance.

Since the uniquely distinguishing features of Zechariah's candlestick emphasize its automatic and spontaneous supply of oil without human ministration, they show that Israel's candlestick of testimony will not only shine with undiminished purity and radiance in that glad millennial day because of Messiah's manifestation to her and through her and the copious supply of the Holy Spirit vouchsafed to her, but that the witness Israel gives will be spontaneous, without human constraint, and completely the result of the supernatural operation of God in the heart of the redeemed nation.

The tabernacle candlestick by contrast was dependent for its light both upon the people and the priests. The people had to donate the oil. The priests had to trim the wicks, fill the oil vessels, and tend the light morning and evening (Exod. 27:20, 21; 30:7, 8). But in this vision *neither* priests *nor* people appear. *Messiah alone as King-Priest* (prefigured by the two olive trees and branches in vss. 11, 12) in full manifestation to Israel in the plenitude of the Holy Spirit's revelation and operation, is the unfailing and spontaneous source of the light for witness to the nations of the world.

The **two olive trees** (vss. 3, 11) called "sons of oil," i.e., "anointed ones" (vs. 14) through the "two olive *branches*" (vs. 12) are specifically said to empty "gold" (*zahav*, i.e., *golden* oil) by means of two spouts into the oil container on top of the candlestick (vs. 12). Numerous commentators are correct in interpreting the **two olive trees** as the office of king and the office of high priest in Israel. The two olive branches portray their incumbents of that day (Zerubbabel and Joshua). Their responsibility was to direct the nation under God in its civil and spiritual affairs so that it might be a proper and effective witness to the nations of the earth. It is *because* these two representative and responsible ministers of God in their official capacities prefigure the Messiah Jesus Christ, who will reign in the midst of Israel as King-Priest (Zech. 6:13) in the period of the nation's restoration as the light of the world, that they appear in these visions as "men of predictive sign or portent" (Zech. 3:8), that is, as "men who in their persons shadow forth future events" (Isa. 8:18; 20:3; Ezek. 12:6; 24:24).

As Baron says, "It is in *His* [Messiah's] light, and by means of the golden oil of His Spirit, which shall then be shed upon them abundantly, that Israel's candlestick shall yet shine with a sevenfold brilliancy for the illumination of all the nations of the earth" (*op. cit.*, pp. 136, 137).

6 Then he answered and spake unto me, saying, This is the word of the Lord unto Zerubbabel, saying, Not by might, nor by power, but by my spirit, saith the Lord of hosts.

---

6   Then he answered and spake unto me, saying, This is the word of Jehovah unto Zerubbabel, saying, Not by might, nor by power, but by my Spirit, saith Jehovah of hosts.

II. THE EXPOSITION OF THE PURPOSE OF THE VISION (Zech. 4:6-10)

Although the vision in its full sweep is a revelation of the perfect order of government and testimony in the theocracy the Lord will establish in the kingdom age in connection with the exercise of the royal Melchizedek priesthood of Christ (Ps. 110:1-7), nevertheless the small remnant to whom Zechariah prophesied, discouraged and beset by doubts and fears, needed immediate encouragement to lift their drooping spirits.

1. *The Vision Is the Word of the Lord to Zerubbabel* (Zech. 4:6). So [logical result] he answered and said unto me as follows: This is the word of the Lord unto Zerubbabel. The vision as a whole (vss. 2, 3), and not merely part of it, insofar as it conveyed a message to Zerubbabel and his contemporaries, *was the Word of the Lord to them.*

Prophetic Scripture has a message to God's people of every age and not merely to those to whom it is directly addressed or to those upon whom it is fulfilled or to those who may understand it fully. *"All* scripture is given by inspiration of God and is *profitable* for doctrine, for reproof, for correction, for instruction in right-eousness" (II Tim. 3:16). This fact was true in Timothy's day, and it was just as true in Zerubbabel's time. It *is* just as true in our day.

Prophetic teaching that lacks a vital spiritual and practical application and merely ministers to abstract knowledge and intellectual titillation is wrongly directed and suffers a severe deficiency. Zechariah's vision was the word of the Lord, vitally real and effective for the pressing prob-lems of the hour in which it was initially revealed.

Moreover, it is highly doubtful whether either the prophet, Zerubbabel, or the people of that day understood the details or the full prophetic scope of the vision. This is indicated both by the prophet's question concerning the vision in verse 4 and his flat confession of ignorance in verse 5. It is also demonstrated by the fact that the interpreting angel seems to avoid *definite explanation* until after the full message of the word of the Lord proceeding *from the vision* for that day and need was *first* expounded.

All the intricate details of a proph-ecy need not be understood or expounded before spiritual benefit may be derived from it. This truth is not to be misused as an excuse for ignorance in the prophetic Scriptures, but rather as an impetus to study and to read the prophetic oracles as the voice of God to us in our present need. The promise of blessing contained in the climactic book of the canonical prophetic and apocalyptic literature — the Revelation — is not to him who understands, but to him "that *reads,* and they that *hear* the words of this prophecy, and *keep* those things which are written therein . . ." (Rev. 1:3).

2. *The Vision Is Replete with Encouragement to Zerubbabel* (Zech. 4:6b-10). It is amazing that so much of this far-reaching vision should be devoted to what is an immediate and obviously local application. The reason is doubtless because Zerubbabel, the civil head, is featured in this prophecy, whereas in the preceding vision Joshua, the ecclesiastical head, is highlighted. But even in this series

7 Who art thou, O great mountain? before Zerubbabel thou shalt become a plain: and he shall bring forth the headstone thereof with shoutings, crying, Grace, grace unto it.

8 Moreover the word of the Lord came unto me, saying,

9 The hands of Zerubbabel have laid the foundation of this house; his hands shall also finish it; and thou shalt know that the Lord of hosts hath sent me unto you.

10 For who hath despised the day of small things? for they shall rejoice, and shall see the plummet in the hand of Zerubbabel with those seven; they are the eyes of the Lord, which run to and fro through the whole earth.

---

7   Who art thou, O great mountain? before Zerubbabel thou shalt become a plain; and he shall bring forth the top stone with shoutings of Grace, grace unto it.

8   Moreover the word of Jehovah came unto me, saying,

9   The hands of Zerubbabel have laid the foundation of this house; his hands shall also finish it; and thou shalt know that Jehovah of hosts hath sent me unto you.

10   For who hath despised the day of small things? for these seven shall rejoice, and shall see the plummet in the hand of Zerubbabel; these are the eyes of Jehovah, which run to and fro through the whole earth.

---

of immediate and local promises, the far-distant application to the building of the future millennial temple and the execution of God's purposes through Messiah in the kingdom age *are not entirely hidden from view and periodically come to the fore.*

The first promise: The temple will be completed by divine power (vs. 6b). Not by might nor by power, but by my Spirit, says the Lord of armies. The spiritual principle here stated is beautifully illustrated by the imagery of the vision in which the automatic and spontaneous supply of oil for lighting totally apart from human agency prefigures Israel's millennial testimony conducted in the fullness of the outpoured Spirit. But in its context, the promise has direct application to Zerubbabel, then faced with the colossal task of completing the temple.

The promise is unusual syntactically. (1) It is an abbreviated sentence, lacking *both* a subject and a predicate, and containing *only* the adverbial modifier of the predicate. It is thus couched in the form of a slogan for brevity and terse appeal. The full form must be supplied, Not by might nor by power, but by my

Spirit (*will the temple be built* or *will the difficulty be overcome*, etc.). The word order is *predicate modifier*, predicate, subject, giving the predicate modifier the first place of emphasis.

(2) The *negative emphasis* on the complete insufficiency of human strength and resources is striking. Not (the objective negative *lo'* is used) negates, as it stands, the adverbial modifier and thus stresses it, rather than the verb which is omitted in the abbreviated sentence. (3) The repetition of the negative *lo'* heightens the emphasis and correlates it by the conjunction "and" (*waw*) "neither . . . nor*." (4) The *emphatic* positive statement follows the high-lighted negative and is introduced by but (*ki 'im*) — Not by might nor by power but by my Spirit. (5) Use of the words by might and by power (the preposition by is the *beth* of instrument or agency) makes the statement forceful. The word might (Hebrew *hayil*, from root *hul*, "be strong or firm" [Job 20:21; Ps. 10:5]) is a general word for *human* resources, such as "physical *strength*" (I Sam. 2:4; Ps. 84:7 [8]; Eccl. 10:10); "human *ability* or *efficiency*" (Gen. 47:6; Ruth 3:11; Prov. 12:4); "human *wealth*" (Gen. 34:29;

Deut. 33:11); "military *power, force, army*" (Exod. 14:4, 9; I Sam. 17:20). The Ethiopic word denotes an "army," as does the Assyrian *ḫailtu*.

The word "strength" (Hebrew *koaḥ*) is a more general word than *ḥayil* and is used principally of *human strength* (Judg. 16:5; Isa. 44:12); *ability, efficiency* (Deut. 8:18; Isa. 37:3); *power* in contrast to that of God (Amos 2:14; Isa. 10:13); *power* conferred by God (Isa. 40:29; 41:1). But the word is also used of God's *power* (Jer. 10:12; Isa. 50:2) and of angelic *power* (Ps. 103:20). Its usage in Zechariah is, however, that which is most common – denoting merely human strength – physical, mental, material, etc.

(6) This famous passage is given additional force by being appended with the authoritative and exceedingly common formula in the prophets, especially Zechariah: **says the Lord of armies.**

The second promise: Every impediment and obstacle to the work shall be removed (vs. 7a). **Who art thou, O great mountain? Before Zerubbabel** [you shall become] **a plain!** The second promise is, like the first, expressed in lively figurative form: (1) By the *personification* **Who** [not what] **art thou, O great mountain?** (2) By the *apostrophe.* The inanimate "mountain" is addressed directly in dramatic fashion. (3) By the *additional figure* of the mountain standing for a difficulty (Matt. 17:20). (4) By the emphasized greatness of the difficulty or impediment. **Who art thou, O great mountain?** This involves an anomalous point of Hebrew syntax, in which the definite article is omitted before "mountain," but included before the adjective "great," thus accentuating the adjective "great," i.e., "O mountain, the *great* [one]." No matter how colossal the difficulty may be which faces Zerubbabel, it shall disappear before the operation of the Spirit of God working in and through the civil head of the Davidic line.

The promise is also expressed in

lively fashion (5) By the *interrogative form* in which it is placed, introduced by the interrogative pronoun "Who" (*mi*). (6) By *the abbreviated form of the sentence* (**before Zerubbabel – a plain!**), its terseness (the omission of its subject and part of its predicate) giving it the ring of a shout of triumph.

The third promise: The temple shall be successfully and joyfully completed (vss. 7b, 9). . . . . **so that he** [Zerubbabel] **shall bring forth the top-stone amid shoutings, How graceful it is!** The clause expresses the result accruing from the removal of every difficulty declared in the preceding verse. **Who art thou, O great mountain? Before Zerubbabel – a plain! So that he** [Zerubbabel] **shall bring forth the top-stone amid shoutings, How graceful** [lovely] **it is!**

The bringing out of the **top-stone** refers to its being carried "out of the workshop in which it had been cut, to set it in its proper place in the wall" (Keil, *Minor Prophets*, II, p. 270). The top-stone (*ha'ebhen haro'shah*, "the headstone," literally, "the stone, the head," feminine form of *ro'sh*, "head," in apposition to "the stone"), is the finishing or gable stone which marked the completion of the building, and not the foundation stone ('*ebhen pinnah*, Job 38:6, Isa. 28:16; Jer. 51:26). Compare Zechariah 10:4: "From him [Judah] is the Cornerstone" (Messiah, i.e., *pinnah*).

The dedication of the completed edifice is going to be accompanied **with shouts** (*teshu'oth*, adverbial accusative) or "amid shoutings." This is an unusual word denoting "noises," particularly of a storm (*sho'ah*) or devastation (Zeph. 1:15; Ezek. 38:9); "noises" of a city (Isa. 22:2); "rumble" of thunder (Job 36:29). In Zechariah it means the wild tumultuous shoutings and cheers of the people at the completion of the temple.

The slogan the populace will joyfully shout when the temple is finished is literally, **Grace, grace to it. To it** (feminine singular suffix) grammatically refers to "the top-stone," but actually to that which the top-stone merely indicated as finished – the temple itself. The word "grace" (*ḥen*, from the root *ḥanan*, "to show favor," "be gracious," Arabic *ḥanna*, "be favorably inclined towards") denotes "favor," "grace," or "gracefulness (elegance)" in form or appearance (Prov. 11:16; Nah. 3:4; Prov. 17:8). Although Brown, Driver, and Briggs (*Hebrew and English Lexicon of the Old Testament, in loc.*) interpret in the sense of "favor or acceptance" with God, the meaning is probably "loveliness or elegance." The repetition denotes emphasis, and the exclamatory shout in English idiom would be rendered, "*What gracefulness* (beauty, elegance) it has!" or, "*How perfectly beautiful* it is!"

This exultant shout is not at variance with Haggai's plaint, "Who is left among you that saw this house in its former glory? How do you see it now? Is it not in your sight as nothing?" (Hag. 2:3). But Haggai was speaking about the neglected unfinished temple, which he was stirring up the people to complete, not the lovely completed edifice.

The fourth promise: Zerubbabel's hands which began the work shall complete it (vss. 8, 9,a,b). **Then the word of the Lord came to me, as follows: The hands of Zerubbabel have laid the foundation of this house, and his hands will finish it.** This important promise stresses not only the *certainty* of the completion of the temple, but the comparative *immediacy* of that completion. The work is not going to drag on interminably, but *Zerubbabel himself* is going to finish it.

This idea of *certainty* and *immediacy* is shown by: (1) The special emphasis on Zechariah's reception of this prediction by divine revelation. **Then the word of the Lord came to me as follows.** The news was so heartening that some of the discouraged builders might have been tempted to disbelieve it. Therefore, let them know it is *God's word*, not Zechariah's. (2) The special stress on the fact that Zerub-

babel himself (and not someone else at a later time) will complete the task. **The hands of Zerubbabel** [emphatic by position] **have laid the foundation of this house and his very own hands will complete it.** In both *verbal clauses* the *subject* is placed first (instead of the verb as normally in Hebrew idiom), thus high-lighting the subject in each case. (3) The use of the word **will complete** (from root *baṣaʿ*, "to cut off, break off" in *piel* "cut off," "sever" from life [Job 6:9; Isa. 38:12], "finish, consummate, complete," [Isa. 10:12; Zech. 4:9]).

The fifth promise: The Word of God will be fulfilled (vs. 9c). **Then you shall know that the Lord of armies has sent me unto you.** Does the pronoun me, object of the verb "has sent," refer to Zechariah or to "the angel of the Lord"? Since it is the Word of the Lord that came to the prophet, the presumption is that it alludes to the Angel of the Lord, the preincarnate Christ, who in His being sent by the **Lord of armies,** will consummate all God's plans for Israel, including the millennial temple, of which Zerubbabel's edifice was only an adumbration.

The sixth promise: Critics of the work will be silenced (vs. 10a). **For who despises** [present characteristic perfect] **the day of small things? The day of small things** is a period of time when only small things occur (Num. 22:18). It recalls the time when the temple was just begun and was merely in its initial stages of construction, and the work appeared inconsequential (Ezra 3:12); yet it is soon to be finished. But, the passage looks beyond this to that larger prophetic context of all Zechariah's night visions to the establishment of the millennial kingdom as the ultimate in the realization of the future hope of Israel. The verb **despise** (from *buz*, "to contemn, scorn, tread on," Prov. 1:7; 6:30; 13:13; Song of Sol. 8:1) challenges one who would look down upon anything small in which God is glorified. The interrogative pronoun who (*mi*) introduces a rhetorical question, which graphically presents the truth that "Little is much (and will eventually become much) if God is in it." The struggles involved in the construction of the second temple and the temple itself were treated contemptuously by some, but since these things foreshadowed the Messiah, the greater than Zerubbabel, and so were the harbinger of Him who would "grow up as a root out of a dry ground" (Isa. 53:2) in His first coming and in His second coming as "King of kings and Lord of lords" (Rev. 19:16), they were not to be trodden under foot in the estimation of those who were inclined to be critical.

The seventh promise: Well-wishers shall rejoice (vs. 10b). **And they shall rejoicingly see the plummet in Zerubbabel's hand.** The plummet (*'ebhen habbedhil*, "the stone" — apposition — "the lead," i.e., "the lead stone"), is the heavy alloy of tin (Latin *plumbum album* of the Romans) employed on a cord to get perfect right angles for construction. The word "tin" (*bedhil*, from *badhal*, "to separate") originally indicated *that which is separated* from precious metal (Num. 31:22) and means "alloy," "dross," as figurative of evil (Isa. 1:25), of sinful Israel (Ezek. 22:18), and as an article of commerce imported by Tyre (Ezek. 27:12). The alloy was extremely heavy and, like our lead, was used in plumb lines by construction engineers.

The plummet in Zerubbabel's hand was a symbol of his being busy in the superintending and construction of the temple. **And they shall joyfully see** is literally in the Hebrew, *"And they shall rejoice* and they shall see," where the first verb assumes the function of an adverb (Gesenius, *Hebrew Grammar*, 142, 3, a.). Zerubbabel, appearing as a type of the future Zerubbabel (Messiah), who will build the millennial temple of God (Ezek. 40-42), lends additional significance to the rejoicing and the admonition not to despise the day of small things.

The eighth promise: God's wisdom and care will be magnified (vs. 10c). **These seven [are] the eyes of the Lord, which are sweeping through the whole earth.** These seven form the subject of the sentence and **are the eyes of the Lord,** the predicate; or better, the original may be taken as an apposition. "These seven, the eyes of the Lord, are sweeping [ranging] through the whole earth." In any case, **these seven** forms the unit subject, joined by a binder (*maqqeph*) and *cannot* be rendered "these seven eyes." "These seven" (as well known) refer to "the seven eyes" of the preceding vision (Zech. 3:9), which appear as facets on the "one Stone" (Messiah) and speak of the *divine* omniscience which will range continuously through the entire millennial earth.

These words receive their full import only on the supposition that the Angel of the Lord is speaking of the messianic kingdom and the establishment of its millennial worship, for the eyes of the Lord would not need to sweep through the whole earth to ascertain hindrances to the building of Zerubbabel's temple, but simply to guard against Judah's neighboring opponents and the rule of Darius.

The verb "sweep" (*polel* participle from "shut," "to go or rove about") signifies "to go to and fro, eagerly, quickly, searchingly," "range," (Amos 8:12; Dan. 12:4; Jer. 5:1; 49:3; II Chron. 16:9). The participle denotes a continuous activity of the divine omniscience in the kingdom age in the interest and care of the Lord's people.

III. THE PARTICULAR EXPLANATION
OF THE VISION (Zech. 4:11-14)

Despite the full and clear exposition of the purpose of the vision granted Zechariah, the prophet is unsatisfied with a merely general understanding of it, and displays a holy commendable curiosity to know the particulars.

1. *The Prophet's Double Question* (Zech. 4:11, 12). **Then** [temporal sequence] **I answered and said to him** [the interpreting angel], **What are**

11 Then answered I, and said unto him, What are these two olive trees upon the right side of the candlestick and upon the left side thereof?
12 And I answered again, and said unto him, What be these two olive branches which through the two golden pipes empty the golden oil out of themselves?
13 And he answered me and said, Knowest thou not what these be? And I said, No, my lord.

---

11   Then answered I, and said unto him, What are these two olive-trees upon the right side of the candlestick and upon the left side thereof?
12   And I answered the second time, and said unto him, What are these two olive-branches, which are beside the two golden spouts, that empty, the golden oil out of themselves?
13   And he answered me and said, Knowest thou not what these are? And I said, No, my lord.

---

these two olive trees on ['al, "over," "above"] the right of the lampstand and on ['al, "over," "above"] its left? The vision itself (vss. 2, 3) is still clear in the mind of the prophet, but he remains perplexed about some of its imagery. The two olive trees baffle him. They form such an arresting feature of what he had seen and obviously bear such a vital relation to the total import of the vision that the prophet persists in his questioning.

But so eager is Zechariah to know the full meaning of the imagery that he does not wait for the answer. Evidently before his first question is answered, he broaches a second. Then I answered a second time, and said unto him, What are these two branches of the olive trees which are beside the two golden pipes, which are pouring the gold out of themselves? (vs. 12).

Zechariah's second question was more precise than the first and concentrated on a striking feature of the two olive trees; namely, the particularly fruitful "boughs" or branches which were copiously pouring golden oil from themselves into the oil bowl for the supply of the candlestick by means of two spouts. The "bough" or "branch" (shibboleth) actually denotes an "ear" of grain (as in Gen. 41:5, 22; Isa. 17:5; Ruth 2:2; Job 24:24). It is from the root shabal in the causative in Arabic, meaning "to cause to hang down" as

a full ripened ear droops from its weight. The branches of the olive trees are therefore actually "ears of olives," the particular prolific bough of each which struck the prophet's attention being "full of olives, as ears are full of grain" (Kimchi).

These branches [ears] of olives were "close by" (beyad, "at the hand of," "nearby," as in Job 15:23 or instrumentally "by means of which") the two golden pipes. These, according to the Septuagint, Vulgate, and Peshitta, were "channels" or "spouts" and not "oil-presses," as Aben Ezra and others surmise, on the supposition that the olive trees could only furnish their oil when the olives were pressed. The Hebrew word for "channels" (tsanteroth, "conduits") occurs only here, and apparently is related in meaning to tsinnor, "channel," "waterspout." "The sound of Thy (water) spouts" being figurative of the sluices of heaven being open (Brown, Driver, and Briggs).

The two conduits of gold are said to be pouring out, or emptying (causative participle of the root riq, "to be empty") the gold, i.e., the finest purest olive oil that resembles liquid gold. A play upon the word "gold" (paronomasia) is evident, as in chapter 3:1 ("Satan ... satanize"). The spouts of gold pour gold into the oil vessel of the lampstand, which in turn is "all of gold" (vs. 2).

2. The Prophet's Confession of

14 Then said he, These are the two anointed ones, that stand by the Lord of the whole earth.

14   Then said he, These are the two anointed ones, that stand by the Lord of the whole earth.

Ignorance (Zech. 4:13). In reply to Zechariah's double question concerning the meaning of the two olive trees (vs. 11) and the two boughs [ears] of olives (vs. 12), the Angel of the Lord repeats what He had said in verse 4: **Do you not know what these are?** The same honest confession of ignorance on the part of the prophet **(No, my Lord)** prepares the way for the final revelatory declaration of the *meaning of the vision* itself. Up to this point what light has been shed on this question has come in the form of an exposition of the *purpose* of the vision. Now the interpretational hint applies to the vision itself rather than its purpose.

3. *The Interpreting Angel's Definite Answer* (Zech. 4:14). And he [the interpreting angel] said, These are the two anointed ones who are standing by the Lord of the whole earth. The demonstrative pronoun **these** refers directly to the **two branches [ears] of olives** (vs. 12) and indirectly to **the two olive trees** (vs. 11), because these (trees and the branches) are inseparably connected, not only as parts of the tree imagery, but also in their immediate and prophetic significance.

As the golden candlestick symbolizes Israel in full fellowship with God as a light-bearer to the nations as she was divinely intended to be in Old Testament times and as she will actually be in her millennial restoration, so *the two olive trees represent the two offices of the kingship and priesthood* through which the blessing of God was to flow (and will yet do so) to the nation and through the nation in witness to all the nations of the world. Since **the two olive trees** on either side of it (*'al*, "above" or "over," since they rose above the candlestick) represent the royal and priestly office in Israel, **the two [ears] of olives**

portray the two incumbents of these offices in that day, Zerubbabel, the civil prince, featured in chapter 4, and Joshua, the ecclesiastical head, set forth prominently in chapter 3. **These are the two anointed ones** (*bene hayyitsar*), "the sons of oil," "those characterized by oil," i.e., *consecrated* to their office by anointing with oil (Exod. 28:41; Lev. 8:12; I Sam. 15:17; II Sam. 2:4) and *characterized* by the operation of the Spirit in their official capacity as God's representatives of the people (I Chron. 16:22; Lam. 4:20).

Moreover, the word for oil (*yitshar*) denotes *fresh oil*, as the product of the land in an unmanufactured state (Deut. 7:13; Num. 18:12; Hag. 1:11), portraying the need for a fresh anointing in God's service.

But the two offices of king and priest, as well as their incumbents of that day in their official capacity, foreshadow the Messiah, the Lord Jesus Christ, in His millennial role as both King and Priest (Ps. 110:1-7). It is He as "King of kings and Lord of lords" and as "a Priest forever after the order of Melchizedek" (Ps. 110:4) who "will sit and rule [as King-Priest] upon his throne; and *he shall be a priest upon* his throne" (Zech. 6:13).

However, the Messiah's person and dual millennial role of King-Priest seem to focus in the **two golden pipes,** which are seen emptying **the golden oil out of themselves** (vs. 12). This appears in these facts: (1) Messiah in the midst of Israel will be the *medium* of her blessing and the *channel* through which the power of the Holy Spirit (the oil) will flow to her. (2) The blessing of the Holy Spirit to millennial Israel will flow to Israel through Messiah's dual office ("two pipes") of King-Priest. (3) The pipes are "channels *of gold*" speaking of the deity of the King-Priest, as the "lampstand all of gold" (vs. 2) likewise symbolizes the deity of Israel's Source of light. "I am the light of the world" (John 8:12). (4) The pipes are seen continuously emptying (participle) the oil (Holy Spirit) into the "oil cup" (*gullah*), as Messiah will abundantly supply the dynamic for Israel's worldwide testimony. (5) The oil is called "the gold," signifying the exquisite operation of the Holy Spirit as ministered through the medium of deity revealed in fulness and untrammelled blessing to and through Israel in full fellowship with her divine Immanuel as King-Priest.

The two anointed ones are seen **standing by the Lord of the whole earth.** The idiom **standing by** (*ʿomedhim ʿal,* "standing over or above") denotes the position of a servant rising above his seated master (as in I Kings 22:19; Isa. 6:2). Of immense importance to the interpretation of the present vision is the expression, **the Lord of the whole earth.** This is the one *explicit* interpretative lead that unmistakably indicates the millennial scope of this fifth vision (in addition to its position in the context of the eight night visions considered as a whole).

The millennial connotation of the appellative **the Lord of the whole earth** appears from Micah's use of the term in a chapter that magnificently deals with the establishment of the future kingdom over Israel (Micah 4:1–13). The prelude to this universal sovereignty of Messiah is the conquest of Israel's invading enemies destroyed at Armageddon. "Arise and thresh, O daughter of Zion; for I will make thine horn iron, and I will make thy hoofs brass: and thou shalt beat in pieces many peoples: and I will consecrate their gain unto the Lord, and their substance unto the *Lord of the whole earth*" (Mic. 4:13).

The title **Lord of the whole earth** describes Messiah as King-Priest, putting down His enemies and reigning over the *entire* earth during the kingdom age. The book of the Revelation from the opening of the seven-sealed book and the loosing of the terrible seal, trumpet, and bowl judgments (Rev. 4:1–19:16) describes Christ's dispossession of His foes previous to His coming as "King of kings and Lord of lords" (Rev. 19:16) to assume His rightful role (by virtue of creation and redemption) as "the Lord of the whole earth."

The "two witnesses" of the Tribulation period are said to be "the two olive trees and the two candlesticks standing before the God of the earth" (Rev. 11:4) in the sense that in proclaiming the gospel of the coming King and His kingdom, they *witness of Him who is coming to take possession of the entire earth.* Similarly, in the last of the eight night visions portraying the judgment of the nations and the punishment of Israel's enemies previous to the setting up of the kingdom, the symbols of this visitation (the four war chariots) are said to be "the four spirits [angels] which go forth from standing before *the Lord of all the earth* "(Zech. 6:5). As *the Lord of all the earth,* Messiah is seen first destroying the wicked nations which stand in the way of the establishment of kingdom rule and His right of world-wide sovereignty and rule.

When "Melchizedek [type of Christ as King-Priest] king of Salem ... priest of the most high God" met Abram after the patriarch's return from the slaughter of the kings, he blessed "Abram of the most high God, *possessor of heaven and earth*" (Gen. 14:19, 22). This revelation of Christ as King-Priest *of the most high God,* speaks of Messiah in His millennial role exercising the restored dominion of the earth based upon a finished sacrifice, symbolized by the bread and wine which Melchizedek offered, and which as memorials set forth Messiah's right to the title, "the Lord of the whole earth," by virtue of His finished redemption.

Abram caught a vision of this glorious revelation of the absolute authority and ownership of the most high God of the earth so that he at once gave Melchizedek "tithes of all" the spoil of battle in token of the fact and declared: "I have lifted up mine hand unto the Lord, the most high God, the possessor of heaven and earth, that I will not take a thread even to a shoelatchet . . ." from the king of Sodom (Gen. 14:18–23).

Zechariah's vision of the golden lampstand thus portrays Messiah as both Light and Lord of the whole earth in the kingdom age revealed to and through His restored nation Israel so that His elect earthly people shall become a world-wide witness and blessing to all nations in that coming day of national conversion and reinstatement.

Then will Isaiah's prediction of Israel in future glory as the center of illumination and blessing to all the nations of the earth be fulfilled:

"Arise, shine; for your light has come,
  and the glory of the Lord has risen upon you.
For behold, darkness shall cover the earth
  and thick darkness the peoples;
But the Lord will arise upon you,
  and his glory shall be seen upon you.
And nations shall come to your light
  and kings to the brightness of your rising"
  (Isa. 60:1–3).

THE DESTRUCTION OF SINNERS AND THE ROD-OF-IRON RULE OF THE MILLENNIUM

(THE SIXTH VISION)

THE VISION OF THE FLYING ROLL

(ZECH. 5:1-4)

AT this point the series of visions takes a sharp turn from that which heretofore has been comforting, to a stern warning that the Lord (Yahweh) is a holy God and cannot brook evil. If the people continue to sin, they shall be visited with severe punishments. This thought is set forth in the two visions of this present chapter. The prophecy has an application to the restored community, but it goes beyond the immediate context and portrays the unsparing destruction of sinners previous to the establishment of the millennium as well as the rigid judicial and governmental administration of the millennium itself.

The prophet has been apprized of great future blessing for Israel in the preceding prophetic disclosures. In the general context are portrayed the enlargement of Israel, the subjugation of her enemies (chapters 1 and 2), internal cleansing and reconstitution as a priestly nation (chapter 3), and consequent ministry of illumination and witness to the rest of the world (chapter 4). But now that the nation is promised restoration, God must deal with recalcitrant and unrepentant sinners before that period of blessing can dawn, as well as with the outbreak of sin during that period of blessing. Sinners and transgressors will be severely and summarily dealt with. Grace manifested (chapter 3) and rejected will eventuate in judgment and death. Grace accepted but trifled with and resulting in outbroken sin will be handled in the rod-of-iron rule of the millennium.

The application of the vision to

1 Then I turned and lifted up mine eyes, and looked, and behold a flying roll.

1   Then again I lifted up mine eyes, and saw, and, behold, a flying roll.

Zechariah's time constituted a warning of punishment to sinners of that period. Transgressors in the future millennial day are also warned. God's gracious interposition for the nation must not be taken advantage of. The minatory aspect of this vision complements the consolatory nature of the preceding visions.

I. WHAT THE VISION WAS (Zech. 5:1, 2)

Then [temporal sequence] I raised my eyes once more. Hebrew idiom has, "Thereupon I returned and lifted up my eyes," meaning not that the prophet had departed somewhere and came back, but that he again lifted up his eyes as he had already done a number of times previously (cf. 1:18 [2:1]; 2:1 [2:5], where the first finite verb appears adverbially). So absorbed by the visions already seen, Zechariah has been looking down in deep meditation. Once more he looks up.

1. The Prophet Sees a Flying Scroll (Zech. 5:1). And I saw and look a flying scroll! The demonstrative interjection, behold! hinneh, as often, points out or signalizes an object in a lively manner. Here the important item is a scroll or roll (megillah). The kind of material of which the scroll was made, whether papyrus or leather, is not stated. As early as the twenty-sixth century B.C. skins of animals were used as a writing material. Hides of sheep or of goats were suitably prepared for writing upon one side, more rarely as in Zechariah's vision, upon both sides. The skins were cut into sheets and sewed together, end to end, to make rolls of the required length. In the case of papyrus, which was used as early as the Old Kingdom in Egypt (c. 2800-2250 B.C.), the rolls were made of ancient paper (papyrus) by cutting the pith of the papyrus plant which grew along the Nile and pressing two or three layers together crosswise.

The largest single papyrus roll in common use was some 30 feet in length and about 10 inches wide, sufficient for the text of Isaiah or Genesis. The Egyptians, however, in unusual instances, had such huge papyrus scrolls as the Papyrus Horris (133 feet in length and 17 inches wide) and the Book of the Dead (123 feet in length and 19 inches wide).

In either case, whether of leather or papyrus, the roll was wound, being wrapped around a single roll (without a stick) or wound around two sticks, one at each end. When the scroll was read, it was simultaneously wrapped around one stick while being unwound from the other. The codex, a book in which the leaves were sewed together and turned, was a later development from the third century of the Christian era (F. Kenyon, Recent Developments in the Development of the Textual Criticism of the Greek Bible, Oxford, 1933, pp. 53-55).

The scroll of Zechariah's vision was not wound up but unrolled or spread open, like a huge sheet. This fact appears from the circumstance that it is a flying roll (megillah 'aphah), the participle denoting a continuous verbal action of "floating" since the scroll itself was inanimate, but evidently graphically described as animate to symbolize the active energie of the Word of God it represents. "For the Word of God is living and active, sharper than a two-edged sword, piercing to the dividing asunder of soul and spirit, of joints and marrow, and is a discerner of the thoughts and the intentions of the heart" (Heb. 4:12).

That the scroll was unwound also appears from the fact that it was inscribed on both sides, which could only be ascertained if it were unrolled.

2 And he said unto me, What seest thou? And I answered, I see a flying roll; the length thereof is twenty cubits, and the breadth thereof ten cubits. 3 Then said he unto me, This is the curse that goeth forth over the face of the whole earth: for every one that stealeth shall be cut off as on this side according to it; and every one that sweareth shall be cut off as on that side according to it.

---

2 And he said unto me, What seest thou? And I answered, I see a flying roll; the length thereof is twenty cubits, and the breadth thereof ten cubits.
3 Then said he unto me, This is the curse that goeth forth over the face of the whole land: for every one that stealeth shall be cut off on the one side according to it; and every one that sweareth shall be cut off on the other side according to it.

This circumstance is indicated by the expression **on this side and on that** [the other] **side, according to it,** which is repeated twice in verse 3, suggesting that this element in the vision is stressed. The same expression is employed of the two tables of the law to enunciate the fact that they, too, "were written on both sides: *on the one side and on the other* [*mizzeh-u-mizzeh*] were they written "(Exod. 32:15).

2. *The Prophet Is Given Added Details Concerning the Size of the Roll* (Zech. 5:2). This constitutes a third reason why the scroll was unrolled, since the size could not otherwise be clearly computed or seen. **Then he** [the interpreting angel] **said to me, What do you see?** Thereupon, I **responded, I see** [i.e., I am in the act of seeing (with pronoun plus participle)] **a flying** [floating] **scroll, its length being twenty cubits and its width being ten cubits.** The measurements are given in two nominal circumstantial clauses, each adding a secondary or subsidiary thought to the main or principal clause: **I see a flying scroll.** The dimensions of the scroll, although significant, are thus secondary to the flying scroll itself. The cubit (*'ammah,* Assyrian *ammatu*) is probably to be derived from *mater brachii,* i.e., the length of the forearm (Latin *cubitum,* "elbow," Greek *pechus,* the "forearm"). It was an important measure among the Hebrews (Exod. 25:10;

I Kings 7:24; Ezek. 40:5) and other Semites. It was commonly computed as the distance from the elbow to the extremity of the middle finger, about 18 inches, although like Babylonians and Egyptians, the Hebrew had an older smaller cubit (Deut. 3:11) and a larger one a handbreadth longer (Ezek. 40:5; 43:13). The common Hebrew measure was 17.72 inches, the longer 20.67 inches, apparently the same as the Egyptian royal cubit. Zechariah's scroll evidently was measured by the common cubit, approximating one foot and a half. The roll was thus roughly 30 feet long and 15 feet wide, constituting a large rectangle in its unrolled floating state. Since these measurements are the exact size of the tabernacle in the wilderness, as may be computed from the boards used to build it (Exod. 26:15-25), the indication is that the judgments proceeding were in accordance with the holiness of the Lord's habitation in the midst of Israel. Since the measurements are also those of the porch of Solomon's temple, others (cf. Baron, op. cit. p. 147) take the less likely meaning that the judgment threatened would begin at the house of God.

II. WHAT THE VISION MEANS (Zech. 5:3, 4)

1. *The Roll Symbolizes the Curse of God Against Sinners Primarily of Israel, Both before the Establishment of the Kingdom and in the Covenant*

Nation during the Kingdom Age (Zech. 5:3a,b). **Then he** [the interpreting angel] **said to me, This is the curse which is in the process of issuing forth** [participle] **upon the face of all the earth.** Not merely "the land" of Palestine is meant (1) because the curse embraces *all Israelites* — those who will have returned to the Israeli state as well as those still scattered among the nations; (2) because the rooting out and destruction of sinners of Israel previous to the setting up of the kingdom is envisioned, as also the messianic rod-of-iron rule over Israel (as well as the Gentiles) in the *world-wide* kingdom after its establishment. The word *'eretz,* **earth,** has this indisputable meaning in Zechariah 5:9, in the following vision, which is closely akin to this in context. (3) The **flying** motion of the scroll also denotes the world-wide extent of the curse, the participle pointing to the continuous and swift movement of the curse.

Pusey's objection (*in loc.*) to *'eretz* meaning **earth** instead of "land" in this context on the ground that those upon whom the curse was to fall were those who swore falsely by the name of Jehovah, which was true of *Judah* only, is invalid, since the vision in its full sweep comprehends Israelites then still in Babylon, as well as Israelites who would be in world-wide dispersion at the end time.

Keil's objection that in the following vision of the ephah, which is closely connected with this in context, "the land" must be "Judah" because it is contrasted with "the land of Shinar," is also invalid. The scope of this next vision is likewise world-wide, since it comprehends the millennial removal of ecclesiastical and commercial wickedness from the entire earth previous to the establishment of the kingdom over Israel. The satanic world system of which this wickedness forms an integral part is world-wide, as the scope of *all* the eight night visions is.

The **curse,** *'alah,* means the punish-

ment or retribution which falls upon those who affront God's infinite holiness by the infraction of His word and law, symbolized by the scroll. Thus in this case the word denotes a "curse" or judgment from God (Num. 5:23; Deut. 29:18, 19, 20; 30:7; II Chron. 34:24; Isa. 24:6; Jer. 23:10; Dan. 9:11), although it may sometimes comprehend merely "a curse" from men, as in Job 31:31; Psalm 10:7; 59:12 [13]. Ezekiel's *scroll,* which the prophet was told to eat, symbolized a similar curse resulting from the transgression of God's holy word and law (cf. Gal. 3:13). "But you, son of man, hear what I say to you; be not rebellious like that rebellious house; open your mouth and eat what I give you. And when I looked, behold, a hand was stretched out to me, and, lo, *a written scroll* was in it; and he spread it before me and it had writing on the front and on the back and there were written on it words of *lamentation and mourning and woe*" (Ezek. 2:8-10). A similar roll appears in Revelation 5:1-9 and also in 10:1-11, both of which unleash the judgments of God upon age-end transgressors previous to the setting up of the kingdom.

Although the scroll symbolizes the word and law of God to the covenant nation, in this case infracted and entailing a curse, it specifically refers to the terms of the Palestinan covenant (Deut. 30:1-10), which outlined the conditions under which Israel was to enter the Promised Land, as well as the stipulations under which the people were to retain possession of it, and be restored to it when disobedience and the ensuing curse scattered them among the nations.

The Palestinian covenant distinctly warned of: (1) *Dispersion for disobedience to the covenant.* "And it shall come to pass when all these things have come upon thee, *the blessing and the curse* ['alah] which I have set before thee, and thou shalt call them to mind among the nations, *whither the Lord thy God hath driven thee*"

(Deut. 30:1; cf. 28:63-68). (2) *The future repentance of Israel while in the dispersion.* "And shalt *return unto the Lord thy God and shalt obey his voice, according to all that I command thee this day,* thou and thy children, with all thy heart, and with all thy soul" (Deut. 30:2). (3) *Reversal of Israel's fortunes and the return of the Lord.* "Then the Lord thy God will turn thy captivity, and have compassion on thee, and *will return*" (Deut. 30:3). (4) *Final regathering and restoration to Palestine.* " . . . and gather thee whither the Lord thy God hath scattered thee. If any of thine be driven out unto the uttermost parts of heaven, from thence will the Lord thy God gather thee, and from thence he will fetch thee: and the Lord thy God will bring thee into the land which thy fathers possessed, and thou shalt possess it: and he will do thee good, and multiply thee above thy fathers" (Deut. 30:3-5). (5) *National conversion.* "And the Lord thy God will circumcise thine heart and the heart of thy posterity, to love the Lord thy God, with all thine heart and with all thy soul, that thou mayest live" (Deut. 30:6). (6) *The judgment of Israel's enemies.* "And the Lord thy God will put all these curses upon thine enemies, and on all them that hate thee, which persecuted thee" (Deut. 30:7). (7) *Obedience and millennial blessing.* "And thou shalt return and obey the voice of the Lord . . . and the Lord thy God will make thee plenteous in every work of thy hand, in the fruit of thy body, and in the fruit of thy cattle, and in the fruit of thy land, for good: for the Lord will again rejoice over thee for good, as he rejoiced over thy fathers" (Deut. 30:9).

But two elements in "the curse" and "the blessing" entailed in the covenant are to be carefully noted as they pertain to Zechariah's vision. First, "the curse" which is *primarily* upon Israel for disobedience to her covenant with the Lord, also extends *secondarily* upon the Gentile nations,

her oppressors. "And the Lord thy God will put *all these curses* upon thine enemies, and on them that hate thee, who persecuted thee" (Deut. 30:7). Second, the curse which has attended Israel in her present, weary, world-wide dispersion and which will descend upon her in catastrophic severity in the Great Tribulation, the time par excellence of "Jacob's trouble" (Jer. 30:7), to purge out the wicked and unbelieving Jews in preparation for kingdom blessing, will *also be visited upon recalcitrant sinners in Israel after the establishment of millennial conditions.* For such blessing, while guaranteed to the converted nation, will apply only to individual Israelites as they *continue to obey* the covenant. "If thou shalt hearken unto the voice of the Lord thy God, to keep his commandments and his statutes which are written in this book of the law, and if thou turn unto the Lord thy God with all thine heart and with all thy soul" (Deut. 30:10). Otherwise, under the rod-of-iron rule of Messiah, sinners in Israel as well as among the millennial nations shall still be visited *with the curse* of a violated covenant and the broken law of God.

2. *The Subjects of the Curse Are Representative of All Sinners* (Zech. 5:3c). **Because everyone who is stealing shall be cut off on this side, according to it, and everyone swearing shall be cut from the other side, according to it.** The causal clause gives the reason for the flying scroll being a curse; namely, it contains the divine punishment for the particular offenses named.

The two sins cited, *theft* and *perjury,* are representative of both tables of the law and involve the transgression of the Mosaic covenant, which is inextricably bound up with the Palestinian covenant, and transgression of the one necessarily also involves the violation of the other.

Everyone stealing (the articular participle indicating one engaged in the act of stealing, suggesting swift

4 I will bring it forth, saith the Lord of hosts, and it shall enter into the house of the thief, and into the house of him what sweareth falsely by my name: and it shall remain in the midst of his house, and shall consume it with the timber thereof and the stones thereof.

4 I will cause it to go forth, saith Jehovah of hosts, and it shall enter into the house of the thief, and into the house of him that sweareth falsely by my name; and it shall abide in the midst of the house, and shall consume it with the timber thereof and the stones thereof.

and irremedial punishment) violates the eighth commandment, involving the second table dealing with one's duty to one's fellow man. **Everyone swearing** (i.e., "falsely by My [the Lord's] name" as in verse 4) transgresses the third commandment, found in the first table concerning man's duty to God. In both instances the middle commandment from each table is enumerated, pointing to the probability that the two selected are mentioned as "samples and summaries of the whole" (Baron, *op. cit.*, p. 146) and together comprehend the injunction: "Thou shalt love the Lord thy God with all thine heart, and with all thy soul, and with all thy might" (Deut. 6:5; Lev. 19:18; Matt. 22:37-40).

The expression **cut off** (A.V. and R.S.V.) is more accurately "be cleansed out" or "purged from," (Hebrew *niqqah*), a *nifal* prophetic perfect, "shall surely be cleaned out," in a passive sense from the root *naqah*, originally evidently "to empty out," "pour out" as a libation (Assyrian *naku*); hence, "be empty, clean." Both in Aramaic and Phoenician the adjective means "pure," as in Arabic *naqiya*. So the *nifal* here means "be cleaned out," as a plundered city (Isa. 3:26). Just as a nest of robbers or a gang of thieves must "be cleaned out" before the inhabitants of any region can dwell in safety, so these sinners *in the time preceding the kingdom age* (the Tribulation) must be "cleaned out" according to it (*kamoha*) in accordance with the requirements of the flying scroll, as symbolizing the curse of God's infracted law upon

sinners, chiefly among Israelites but also among the Gentiles, as well as sinners within the covenant nation and the nations of the earth during the kingdom age.

Although the kingdom itself will be initiated by a new start with the wicked (both of Israel and the nations) purged out, nevertheless, children born of the righteous of that period will to some extent develop into sinners, or the righteous themselves may lapse into sin. In any case Messiah's throne in the midst of His people will not tolerate wickedness, especially when the revealed blessings of God are so fully manifested to men, with Satan and demon powers imprisoned (Rev. 20:1-3), the Satanic world system destroyed, and Edenic conditions, at least in part, prevailing (Isa. 11:6-9; Rom. 8:19-23). The flying scroll as the unchangeable Word of God in swift operation appears in the act of going forth as the inexorable measure of judgment.

3. *The Enforcement of the Curse Portrays the Severity of the Divine Dealing Previous to the Setting Up of the Kingdom and of Messiah's Administration During the Kingdom* (Zech. 5:4). **I will cause it** [the curse] **to issue forth, says the Lord of armies, and it** [the curse] **shall enter into the house of the thief and into the house of him who swears falsely by my name, and it shall abide in** [Hebrew "in the middle of"] **his house and consume it, both its timbers and its stones.**

He who pronounces the curse in His word and covenant will cause it to be executed upon transgressors. Dramatically the first person is introduced

"*I*, the Lord of the celestial as well as the terrestrial armies, will cause the curse to go forth, with certainty and celerity. With certainty because *I* will send it forth, with celerity because it shall go forth as a *flying* scroll."

None will be able to sin and hide from God in that day. In our present age — uniquely a period of grace and divine long-suffering with the sins of men, while the gospel of salvation is patiently proclaimed and God is for the most part silent to the blasphemies and crimes of ungodly sinners, while the heavens have received the crucified and risen Redeemer "until the times of the restitution of all things, which God hath spoken by the mouth of all his holy prophets since the world began" (Acts 3:21) — criminals, often undetected in their crimes, may prosper.

But in the millennial age to come, and in the tribulation of the day of the Lord that inaugurates it (Rev. 4:1 – 19:16), the unrelenting curse of God will ferret out the sinner to destroy him before the kingdom is established and pursue and overtake the presumptuous sinner that will develop during the kingdom, in spite of all the pressures and ideal conditions spurring men on to righteousness and godliness in that age of the superlative revelation of Christ among men and the blessings of God poured out upon the entire death.

The curse will enter the house of the sinner and *abide* there (*laneh* for *lanah* from *lun*, "to lodge" or "spend the night" [Gen. 32:21 (22); Exod. 23:18; Judg. 19:13; II Sam. 12:16; 17:8]). The curse will do its work rapidly, and will not have to remain long. The sinners in whose house the judgment of God abides are the thief and the perjurer of the preceding verse, with the difference that the former is not described as "the one stealing" (articular participle, as in verse 3, "one in the act of stealing") but is designated in verse 4 as "the professional thief" (gangster), the nominal *piel* form with the doubling

of the middle radical of the root "to steal," *ganabh*, denoting one who practices thievery as a vocation.

The curse abiding in the house of the thief and perjurer "will consume it, both its timbers and stones." Evidently the homes of wealthy sinners are designated, as stone houses of stout timbers were confined to the rich in the economically precarious age of Zechariah (Hag. 1:4–11).

The words **consume it** (*killattu*, assimilated from the full form *killethathu*, from root *kalah*, "be complete, be finished, be at an end," Assyrian *kalu*, "*cease, vanish*") are the *piel* perfect, having an intensive causative meaning, "complete," "finish," "bring to an end," in the sense of "destroy," "exterminate," "consume" *it*, the 3 m.s. pronoun, referring to "the house" of the thief and perjurer (Josh. 24:20; Isa. 10:18; Jer. 5:3; Hos. 11:6). The curse following upon God's broken word shall go into the presumptuous sinner's home and completely destroy or exterminate it, bringing it and its inhabitants to an untimely end. The picture is a lively one, giving a hint of the thorough judgment and punishment of those who, in the full glow of Messianic light and blessing, flaunt the rule of the Messiah.

This whole passage is very valuable as a commentary on the nature of Christ's rule in righteousness in the millennial period as well as the severity of His dealing with sinners once the day of grace is ended and the day of wrath and judgment is ushered in with the opening of the seven-sealed roll of Revelation 5:1–9, loosing the seals, trumpets, and bowl judgments that dispossess Satan, demons, and wicked men from the earth preparatory to the advent of the King of kings and Lord of lords to establish His rule and kingdom.

Then He, whose *right to rule* the earth as its Creator and Redeemer is established before the entire universe, *will rule* and none shall be able to resist His reign. "He will shepherd them [the nations] with a rod of iron; as the vessels of a potter shall they be broken to pieces," and His prerogative for so doing will be, "even as I received of my Father" (Rev. 2:27). He the son, a male child, to whom the woman (Israel) gives birth, is destined "to shepherd all nations with an iron staff" (Rev. 12:5). At His glorious second advent to set up His kingdom, it is declared, "He will shepherd them with an iron staff" (Rev. 19:15). Would that wicked men everywhere would see the wisdom of bowing before Him as Saviour and Lord now, unto whom one day they must bow, but then to their eternal misery and doom.

CHAPTER FIVE

(Continued)

REMOVAL OF ECCLESIASTICAL AND COMMERCIAL WICKEDNESS FROM THE MILLENNIAL EARTH

(THE SEVENTH VISION)

THE WOMAN IN THE EPHAH

(ZECH. 5:5-11)

WHEREAS the preceding vision of the flying scroll symbolizes the removal of *transgressors*, both of Israel and the nations, this vision sets forth the final removal of *iniquity itself*, not only from Palestine (then to become "the Holy Land," cf. 2:12 [16]), but from the millennial earth. In line with the scope of all eight of Zechariah's night visions, the fulfilment of this likewise extends into the millennial kingdom. Nevertheless the immediate application of the vision to the prophet's time and to the conditions then prevailing is plain.

The Jews at that time in the land had recently been in exile in Babylon. Outwardly they had put away paganistic idolatry. However, in the great foreign commercial emporium they had acquired an insatiable greed of gain. Nehemiah in his day scathingly rebuked the nobles and rulers for exacting heavy interest from their impoverished brothers who were to an alarming degree falling into debt, losing their patrimonies, and seeing the tragic spectacle of their children sinking into servitude (Neh. 5:1-13). Severely Nehemiah, the governor, calls upon these selfish interest-exactors to restore the vineyards, olive groves, and houses of their oppressed brothers. Under pressure they promised to restore these alienated properties and to exact nothing.

The prophet Malachi also inveighs

5 Then the angel that talked with me went forth, and said unto me, Lift up now thine eyes, and see what is this that goeth forth.
6 And I said, What is it? And he said, This is an ephah that goeth forth. He said moreover, This is their resemblance through all the earth.

---

5 Then the angel that talked with me went forth, and said unto me, Lift up now thine eyes, and see what is this that goeth forth.
6 And I said, What is it? And he said, This is the ephah that goeth forth. He said moreover, This is their appearance in all the land;

---

against the same ungodly secularism and intense commercial preoccupation that gripped the people at a somewhat later period. "Will a man rob God? Yet ye have robbed me. Yet ye say, Wherein have we robbed thee? In tithes and offerings. Ye are cursed with a curse. Ye have robbed me, even this whole nation" (Mal. 3:8, 9).

Zechariah in this divinely given vision is granted an insight into the intense commercial propensity and spirit of self-centeredness that had been foreign to Israel as a simple shepherd people, but which under the spell of Babylon had taken possession of them. This vision is aimed at correcting this specific evil and setting forth its latter-day complete removal from Palestine, which until that time will never be truly "the Holy Land" (Zech. 2:12 [16]), as well as its purging out of the entire earth in the kingdom age.

I. AN EPHAH IS OBSERVED (Zech. 5:5–7a)

1. *The Prophet's Attention Is Aroused* (Zech. 5:5, 6a). **Then the angel who was conversing [speaking] with me came forward** [i.e., advanced into the foreground] **and said to me, Lift up your eyes and see what this is that is going forth. And I said, What is it?** The *waw* consecutive introducing verse 5 expresses temporal sequence, as frequently in the story-like recital of these eight visions in graphic narrative form. **Then** [thereupon, after that] **the interpreting angel advanced to the foreground.** The angel came forward to speak to the prophet in order to prepare him for the ensuing vision. This he does by a command:

Lift up your eyes, if you will, or in modern idiom, "Look up, please," the polite particle *naʾ* (like French, *s'il vous plaît*, German *bitte*, English "please") softening the imperative with true angelic courtesy. **Look up, please, and see** [another command] **what this that is going forth** [or out] **is.**

The object of the imperative **see** is a noun clause in the form of an indirect question: **What is** [predicate] **this that is going forth** [subject], "this that is in the act of going forth" (graphic participle, presenting the action of the verb as taking place before the eyes of the prophet).

Zechariah's attention now being fully aroused by the ministry of the interpreting angel, resolves the angel's indirect question, **and see what this that is going forth is** into a direct question, **What is it?** So striking was the object that the prophet now sees (like the scroll he had just glimpsed) that he naturally enquires concerning the identity.

2. *The Ephah Is Introduced* (Zech. 5:6b). **Thereupon, he** [the interpreting angel] **replied, This is the ephah that is going forth and this is their appearance in all the earth.** Whether because of dimness of sight, overwhelming spiritual ecstasy because of the other visions, distance from the object, or because he was still occupied with the dreadful curse of God going forth against man's sin, symbolized by the ominous flying scroll of the preceding vision, the prophet did not at once recognize what the ephah was, and is eager to know what it meant.

The interpreting angel, therefore, proceeds to explain the ephah. **This is the ephah that is going forth.** The ephah is a dry measure containing ten omers (Exod. 16:36). It is equivalent to 1.05 bushels American measure, and was employed for such commodities as flour (Judg. 6:19) or barley (Ruth 2:17). It was equal to a bath or one-tenth of a kor (Ezek. 45:11, 14), and contained one Attic metretes or 72 sextaries (Josephus, *Antiquities* VIII, 2, 9; XV, 9, 2). Being somewhat larger than our bushel dry measure, it was capable of accommodating a person of small stature.

As a further word of explanation of the ephah, it is said, **This** [the ephah] **is their appearance** ['*enam*, "their eye," or "aspect"] **in all the earth.** The pronominal suffix **their,** not having an immediate antecedent in this vision, is connected by Keil (*Minor Prophets*, II, p. 283) with "the sinners mentioned before, viz., the thieves and perjurers" of the preceding vision (which he arbitrarily makes one vision). Moreover, Keil takes the word **appearance** in the sense of shape (as in Lev. 13:55; Ezek. 1:4). "The ephah (bushel) is the shape, i.e., represents the figure displayed by the sinners in all the land, after the roll of the curse has gone forth over the land; i.e., shows into what condition they have come through the anathema" (*loc. cit.*). This condition, according to Keil (following Kliefoth), is one of being heaped or collected together "as separate grains" are in a bushel.

But this interpretation, although ancient, following similar ideas of Cyril and Jerome, of the filling up the measure of sins, with Israel's sins heaped together and so filled up, is scarcely correct. The plain simple meaning of the ephah, the thought that would automatically strike anyone who saw it, irrespective of anything or anyone in it, is that it symbolizes trade or commerce. It was the new principle with which the Jews had become imbued in Babylon, and which has exercised such a potent formative influence over them throughout the centuries, and will continue to do so until it is removed

from them at the advent of their Messiah and the establishment of the kingdom.

According to the Septuagint and the Syriac version, which fits the context of the vision exactly, the ephah symbolizes "wickedness." "This is their wickedness," '*awonam* (Gen. 4:13; 15:16; Isa. 43:24; Jer. 5:25; Hos. 4:8), the possessive pronoun evidently referring to the godless rich inhabitants of the earth of the last days, whom James so pointedly upbraids. "Come now, you rich, weep and howl for the miseries that are coming upon you. Your riches have rotted and your garments are moth-eaten. Your gold and silver have rusted, and their rust will be evidence against you and will eat your flesh like fire. You have laid up treasure for the last days [*in the last days,* A.S.V.]. Behold, the wages of the laborers who mowed your fields, which you kept back by fraud, cry out; and the cries of the harvesters have reached the ears of the Lord of hosts. You have lived on the earth in luxury and in pleasure; you have fattened your hearts in a day of slaughter. You have condemned, you have killed the righteous man, he does not resist you. Be patient, therefore, brethren, *until the coming of the Lord*" (James 5:1–7).

The godless commercialism, the inordinate love of gain, and the thorough-going secularism are not only inveighed against by the Apostle James as being prominent in the last days, but form an important aspect of political and commercial Babylon, which the Apostle John in similar apocalyptic vision saw climaxing age-end wickedness and destroyed (with the Satanic world system of which it is an inseparable part) to make way for the establishment of Christ's millennial kingdom (Rev. 18).

But the Babylon John saw in Revelation 18 and which Zechariah glimpsed in the **ephah** is not a city but a system. Zechariah saw the ephah *as the symbol of the evil system*

7 And, behold, there was lifted up a talent of lead: and this is a woman that sitteth in the midst of the ephah.

7 (and, behold, there was lifted up a talent of lead;) and this is a woman sitting in the midst of the ephah.

(and the ephah is evil, whether one follows the Masoretic reading, This is their appearance, or the Syriac and the Septuagint, "This is their iniquity").

Although Zechariah in the symbol of the ephah only glimpsed the *emblem* of the Satanic world system in its godless *commercial* and *economic* aspects, the Bible as a whole presents a full-orbed view of this wicked system in all its ramifications — educational, cultural, scientific, governmental, religious, and social. The system comprises the whole mass of unregenerate mankind, alienated from God, hostile to Christ, and organized as a system or federation under Satan. In more than thirty important New Testament passages, a full revelation of the Satanic world system is presented. Satan is revealed as its directing head (John 12:31; 14:30; 16:11; I John 5:19; Rev. 2:13). The system is revealed to be wholly evil, as God evaluates it (Gal. 1:4; Col. 1:13; II Peter 2:20; James 4:4; I John 4:3). It is shown to be limited and temporary (I John 4:4), doomed to destruction at Christ's second advent, (I John 2:17; Rev. 19:11-16; Rev. 20:1-3), characterized by pride, greed, and war (James 4:1-4), and perpetually perilous to the child of God (I John 2:16).

As in the preceding vision, the earth (*ha'arets*) designates not merely Palestine, although this is the primary reference, and the removal of godless commercialism is first and foremost from "the land," which will then be in reality "the Holy Land" (Zech. 2:12 [16]); but more broadly the term points to the entire millennial earth. The reason is simple. The Satanic world with its evil component of godless commercialism is world-wide, and hence its removal must be world-wide. There could be no kingdom over Israel established (cf. Acts 1:6) without the removal of the ephah of godless commercialism both from the millennial nations as well as from Israel herself.

3. *The Ephah Is Associated with a Talent of Lead* (Zech. 5:7a). And look! a talent of lead is being lifted up. The interjectional adverb, look! behold! (*hinneh*), as frequently in animated Hebrew style, graphically points out an object of unusual interest or striking significance. Here the talent of lead has such import. The talent, like the ephah, is transparently a symbol of business and commerce, being a weight employed both for ordinary items of trade and for precious metals weighed as a medium of exchange. It was the largest weight among the Hebrews where 20 gerahs were equal to 1 shekel, 50 shekels to 1 maneh, and 60 manehs to one talent. Reckoning the shekel of Palestine at 176.85 grains, a talent would weigh 75.793 pounds avoirdupois or 92.109 pounds troy. Thus the talent of lead was heavy enough to confine a human occupant in the ephah, Brown, Driver, and Briggs calculating its weight according to later Babylonian reckoning at 108.29 pounds.

The word talent, "a circle," "something round" (II Sam. 12:30), here means a "round weight" (from its shape), serving as a cover to a bushel basket. As a unit of weight of silver or gold, "talent" occurs in II Samuel 12:30; I Kings 9:14; 20:39; II Kings 5:5, as well as of iron in I Chronicles 29:7 and bronze in Exodus 38:29. It also occurs in the meaning of a "loaf of bread" (from its round shape) in I Samuel 2:36, Proverbs 6:26, and Jeremiah 37:21.

The talent is thus the largest measure of weight and it was made of

8 And he said, This is wickedness. And he cast it into the midst of the ephah; and he cast the weight of lead upon the mouth thereof.

8 And he said, This is Wickedness: and he cast her down into the midst of the ephah; and he cast the weight of lead upon the mouth thereof.

lead as the most common heavy metal which was employed in all commercial transactions for weighing out money. In the Song of Moses the heaviness of lead is referred to when Israel's enemies are said to have sunk "as lead in the mighty waters" (Exod. 15:10). This metal among others was taken as spoil by the Israelites from the Midianites (Num. 31:22). Jeremiah refers to smelting it (Jer. 6:29), and Ezekiel lists it as imported from Tarshish (Ezek. 27:12). The Sinaitic Peninsula also furnished large quantities of the metal, and it was found in Egypt, too.

The prophet sees a talent of lead being lifted up (*nifal* feminine singular participle from *nasa'*), that is, from its position as cover (vs. 8) on the ephah.

II. A WOMAN IS INTRODUCED (Zech. 5:7b, 8a)

1. *The Woman Is Described as Sitting in the Ephah* (Zech. 5:7b). And this [the new element introduced into the vision] is a woman [*one* woman] sitting in the middle of the ephah. Probably because the woman at first sight was sitting contentedly in the ephah, and hence not plainly or fully visible, the demonstrative pronoun is employed, this is one woman, i.e., not the indefinite "a woman," but "*one* woman," in distinction from more than one. The participle sitting, *yosheveth*, from *yashav*, "to sit down, dwell, remain," Assyrian *ashabu* (I Sam. 20:25; Isa. 40:22; 47:1; Jonah 3:6), carries with it in this context the idea of sitting quietly, contentedly, and remaining in a relaxed position, or "dwelling" in a place (Gen. 4:16; 13:7; 19:29; Deut. 1:4; Josh. 20:6; II Sam. 7:6). The woman has surrounded herself with the ephah and sits or dwells in

it, apparently enjoying the luxury and wealth the commercialism symbolized by it affords her. She evidently flourishes in the center of (*bethokh*, "in the middle of") godless commercialism and mammon-worship. Her "sitting or dwelling in the midst of the ephah" denotes the woman's intimate contact with worldly wealth and commerce, by which she is supported and in which she delights.

2. *The Woman Is Defined as to Her Character* (Zech. 5:8a). Then he [the interpreting angel to incite the prophet's careful attention] said, This is the wickedness [Septuagint, *anomia*, "lawlessness," the very embodiment of evil itself]. Such a vital part of the meaning of the vision demands the prophet's keenest attention, and the interpreting angel knows how to secure it.

Various unsatisfactory views prevail concerning the identity of the woman, among which are the following: (1) She symbolizes the Jewish people, with iniquity full, and hence carried away into captivity (Jerome, Rosenmuller, etc.). But such a view in requiring a retrospective interpretation violates the scope and context of all the other night visions, all of which are prospective and relate to the future. (2) She symbolizes the Jewish people with a prospective captivity in mind. But again this destroys the scope and purpose of the two visions of chapter 5, which are *not* intended to portray *the judgment of Israel* but her cleansing as a restored people with wickedness itself purged from her in preparation for kingdom blessing. (3) She is a collective symbolism of individual sinners massed together as grain in an ephah for judgment (Kliefoth, Keil). But this too violates the scope of both this and the immediately preceding vision.

The **woman** represents *ecclesiastical Babylon* and, as *personified religious wickedness*, is the same (although in a simpler stage of development) as the evil woman of Revelation 17, "Babylon, the great, mother of harlots, and of the abominations [idolatries] of the earth" (Rev. 17:5). As such this *"one* woman" represents *all* apostate religious movements from their inception in ancient Babylon of Nimrod (Gen. 10:8-10), the seat of the first departure from God eventuating in the judgment of the confusion of tongues (Gen. 11:1-9), to their terrible consummation in Romanism, apostate Protestantism, demon-controlled Judaism (Matt. 12:43-45), paganism, and other evil religious forces of the last days.

This **woman** does not represent an unusual figure in Scripture. Frequently the Bible symbolizes that which is not in its proper place spiritually or religiously as a woman. The woman in Matthew 13:33 hid *leaven* (an unvarying symbol of evil in Scripture) in three measures of meal till the whole "was leavened." In the church at Thyatira "that woman Jezebel, who calls herself a prophetess" taught God's servants deceitfully to practice unchastity and to partake of idol offerings (Rev. 2:20). The woman of Revelation 17:3-17 likewise is evil, and graphically portrays in brilliant symbolism composite ecclesiastical and religious Babylon, that aspect of the Satanic world system that has always been the quintessence of its wickedness.

John the Revelator envisioned the woman *"sitting* upon a scarlet-colored beast" (representing political Babylon), "full of the names of blasphemy, having seven heads and ten horns," the last form of Gentile world power (Rev. 17:3). Thus latter-day ecclesiastical Babylon rides into power and prestige by a church-state union, in which the ecclesiastical power employs political power for its own selfish pleasure and ends. Zechariah, on the other hand, sees the woman *sitting,*

not upon a scarlet-colored beast (the political power), but in an ephah (the commercial and business aspects of the governments of the Satanic world system). And is this not highly significant? More and more, as the governmental and political aspects of the Satanic world system develop toward their final climactic form before Christ's coming, their inextricable connections with economic and financial interests become increasingly evident.

If the **woman** in the ephah is to enjoy the wealth and luxury which are hers, she must court the favor of the kings of the earth, commit spiritual fornication with them, and intoxicate them with "the wine of her fornication" (Rev. 17:2); for only by her worldly compromising position astride the scarlet-colored beast can she as a base harlot be "arrayed in purple, and scarlet color, and be ornamented with gold and precious stones and pearls" (Rev. 17:4). Moreover, the woman not only makes her illicit lovers drunk "with the wine of her fornication," but even more horribly she herself is "drunk with the blood of the saints [of the Old Testament] and with the blood of the martyrs of Jesus" [New Testament saints]. (Rev. 17:6).

III. THE FATE OF THE WOMAN IS
      INDICATED (Zech. 5:8b-11)

1. *The Woman Is Imprisoned in the Ephah* (Zech. 5:8b). Having announced concerning the woman, **This is wickedness, thereupon he** [the interpreting angel] **cast her** [the woman] **into the middle of the ephah and cast the lead stone** [weight] **upon its mouth** [opening].

Several observations must be made concerning the status of the woman. As already observed, she initially appears "sitting" or "dwelling" in the ephah, indicating a settled-down condition with some sense of satisfaction and showing her delight in, and contentment with, the ungodly commercialism which supports her and maintains her worldly compromising position. Then, too, it is to be noted that the woman had to be cast back into the ephah and *kept* there under restraint by means of a lead covering.

The question naturally arises, How then can the woman be sitting contentedly in the ephah and yet wishing to escape? The answer is she has been all along sitting or dwelling in the ephah, contentedly, but now that the time has come for commercial Babylon to be removed, to be destroyed, the woman tries to escape from it, because *she does not want to be removed with it,* and so share its inevitable fate. Therefore, she tries to escape.

It must be carefully held in mind, however, that the removal of the ephah to Babylon *is for its destruction* (Rev. 18). Although this latter feature is *not* revealed in this particular vision, the woman evidently knows it and does all she can to avoid the judgment of her complicity with the wickedness of political and commercial Babylon. The angel's hurling her back into the center of the ephah and restraining her there with a lead weight demonstrates the principle that "His own iniquities shall snare the wicked, and he shall be caught in the toils of his sin" (Prov. 5:22), demonstrating that the sins of the wicked become the means of their undoing and destruction.

John the Revelator saw this tragic ending, "The waters which thou sawest, where the harlot sits, are peoples, and multitudes, and nations, and tongues. And the ten horns which thou sawest upon the beast [the political power which the harlot uses to ride into prestige], these shall hate the harlot, and shall make her desolate and naked, and shall eat her flesh, and burn her with fire" (Rev. 17:15, 16).

Zechariah glimpses the symbolism of the satanic world system at the juncture when it is *about to be removed* from God's holy land (and earth) and from His people Israel (and necessarily from *all* the inhabitants of the earth)

who survive the divine judgments upon Babylon — political and commercial, as well as religious and ecclesiastical.

The interpreting angel with such crucial emphasis brands the woman so incisively as **the wickedness** or "the lawlessness" because of the preeminent position she is to play in the final age-end apostasy and in the role she performs in connection with the full revelation of "the mystery of iniquity" (II Thess. 2:7) and "the lawless one" (the antichrist) whom "the Lord Jesus will slay with the breath of his mouth and destroy by his appearing and coming" (II Thess. 2:8). As he, the "lawless one," is destroyed, so she, "the lawlessness," shall likewise be exterminated, but not until she, as an apostate system, has deluded many with the same Satanic cunning that characterizes the climactic career of the man of sin "with all power and signs and deceiving wonders, and with all wicked deception for those who are to perish because they refused to love the truth that they might be saved. And for this cause God shall send them strong delusion that they might believe *the lie,* that they all might be condemned who believe not the truth, but had pleasure in unrighteousness" (II Thess. 2:9–12).

2. *The Ephah Is Lifted Up Between Earth and Heaven* (Zech. 5:9). **Afterwards** [temporal sequence with *waw* consecutive] **I raised my eyes and looked** [saw], **and, lo, two women were advancing with wind in their wings.** The interjectional adverb, **look! lo! behold!** (*hinneh*) occurs for the second time in this vision to point out graphically a detail of arresting significance. In the first instance it was "a talent of lead being lifted up" to confine the woman in the ephah. Here it is "two women in the act of advancing forward" (active participle). A circumstantial clause appended adds a subordinate detail to the **two women,** namely, **and wind was in their wings,** i.e., in English

9 Then lifted I up mine eyes, and looked, and, behold, there came out two women, and the wind was in their wings; for they had wings like the wings of a stork: and they lifted up the ephah between the earth and the heaven.
10 Then said I to the angel that talked with me, Whither do these bear the ephah?
11 And he said unto me, To build it an house in the land of Shinar: and it shall be established, and set there upon her own base.

---

9 Then lifted I up mine eyes, and saw, and, behold, there came forth two women, and the wind was in their wings; now they had wings like the wings of a stork; and they lifted up the ephah between earth and heaven.
10 Then said I to the angel that talked with me, Whither do these bear the ephah?
11 And he said unto me, To build her a house in the land of Shinar: and when it is prepared, she shall be set there in her own place.

---

idiom, "with wind in their wings."

The prophet hastens to explain what he has already anticipated in the circumstantial clause above-mentioned, by a second circumstantial clause, and the women possessed wings as the wings of the stork, i.e., large, broad pinions capable of supporting their own weight in the air as well as that of the woman in the ephah.

And they [the two-winged women] lifted up the ephah between the earth and the heavens.

Who are these two stork-winged women? Obviously they are symbolic, like the ephah and the one woman in it, for women do not have "wings," stork-like or otherwise. While this particular symbolism is meaningful, as is the symbolism in all the night visions, undue dogmatism as to its significance is to be avoided, as well as the opposite extreme of laxity of interpretation that summarily dismisses such items in the vision as background drapery, that merely gives distinctness to the main prophetic picture, as Hengstenberg, Keil, Bredenkamp, and a number of other expositors hold.

That the women are agents of evil, apparently suggesting demonic forces, is indicated by the following considerations: (1) They *are* women in symbol and *are associated* with "the *one* woman" who personifies in herself "the wickedness" (lawlessness) of

apostate world religionism. (2) Their association is a *protective relationship*, because for a time they shelter the woman from the divine judgment which is about to overtake her. (3) They transport the lawless woman *to the land of Shinar*, which has evil connotations as the seat of the first great apostasy and its consequent punishment (Gen. 10:8-10; 11:1-9). (4) They build an abode for the ephah and establish it in Babylonia showing their complicity with the evil personified. (5) They have stork-like wings, which belong to an unclean bird (Lev. 11:19; Deut. 14:18). (6) As the "one woman" symbolizes the final form of religious and ecclesiastical apostasy, this is notably the sphere in which evil spirits operate to corrupt sound doctrine (I Tim. 4:1-5; I John 4:1-6), issuing in the apostasy of the church (Rev. 3:14-22) and the more terrible and awful declension of the tribulation period (Rev. 9:1-21; 16:13-16).

3. *The Ephah Is Carried Away to Babylon* (Zech. 5:10, 11). And I [Zechariah] said to the angel who was speaking with me, Where are they [the stork-winged women] taking the ephah? Thereupon he replied to me, To build a house for it [the ephah] in the land of Shinar, and when it [the house] is established, it [the ephah] shall be caused to rest there upon its [the ephah's] own base.

The significant fact is to be observed that the final verses of this vision (vss. 9–11) are concerned with the removal of the *ephah* (godless commercialism of the satanic world system) from Palestine (and the entire earth) and *not* the woman, *except* as the latter has been associated with the ephah in her iniquitous career and confined in the ephah to share its eventual fate. The cleansing of the land, however, must invoke both the ephah and the woman and both *are* involved as being inseparable in their sin.

It is plain that this vision occupies itself with the removal of "wickedness" (commercial and religious) from God's land and God's people without concerning itself with its final destiny in the land to which it is transported by evil powers. The destruction of ecclesiastical and commercial Babylon (here symbolized by the term **the land of Shinar** in Babylonia) *after* its removal from the earth is a revelation vouchsafed to the apocalyptic seer of Patmos (Rev. 17 and 18). With the second advent of Christ and the establishment of the kingdom over Israel the satanic world system will be destroyed, Satan will be bound in the bottomless pit (Rev. 20:1–3), and evidently the demons also; and that system of organized godlessness, which has dominated society from Nimrod's day on, will collapse.

This is what John saw when he heard the angelic voice cry, "Babylon the great is fallen, is fallen, and is become the habitation of demons, and the hold of every foul spirit, and a cage of every unclean and hateful bird. For all nations have drunk of the wine of the wrath of her fornication, and the kings of the earth have committed fornication with her, and the merchants of the earth have grown rich through the abundance of her delicacies. . . . Come out of her, my people. . . . For her sins have reached unto heaven, and God hath remembered her iniquities" (Rev. 18:1–5).

"And a mighty angel took up a stone like a great millstone, and cast it into the sea, saying, Thus with violence shall that great city Babylon be thrown down, and shall be found no more at all. . . . And in her was found the blood of the prophets, and of saints, and of all [showing she is a system] that were slain upon the earth" (Rev. 18:21–24).

Not until this evil system is removed from Palestine will it become "the holy land," and not until it is rooted out of the whole earth in its entirety will God's kingdom come and God's will be done in earth as it is in heaven.

CHAPTER SIX

THE JUDGMENT OF THE NATIONS PREPARATORY TO THE ESTABLISHMENT OF MESSIAH'S KINGDOM

(THE EIGHTH VISION)

THE VISION OF THE FOUR CHARIOTS

(ZECH. 6:1-8)

I. THE VISION OF THE JUDGMENT OF THE NATIONS PRESENTED (Zech. 6:1-3)

1. *The Four Chariots Are Set Forth Issuing from Between Two Mountains of Brass* (Zech. 6:1)
2. *The Chariots Are Pictured with Their Horses* (Zech. 6:2, 3)

II. THE VISION OF THE JUDGMENT OF THE NATIONS EXPLAINED (Zech. 6:4-8)

1. *The Explanation Is Prefaced by a Question* (Zech. 6:4)
2. *The Explanation Is Made Possible by a Key* (Zech. 6:5)
3. *The Explanation of the Vision Is Concerned with Judgment* (Zech. 6:6, 7)
4. *The Vision Concludes with a Message of Hope to the People of the Prophet's Day* (Zech. 6:8)

THIS vision completes the cycle in the series of eight night visions and connects with the first of the series. In the first prophetic disclosure horse-riders were dispatched to reconnoitre among the nations of earth to ascertain their condition relative to Israel's restoration and final blessing. The nations were found to be in a state of ease and rest far removed from the trouble and ferment in which they were prophesied to be thrown, before the Lord would restore His chosen people to millennial blessing (Hag. 2:6, 7, 20, 21).

In this concluding night vision that which has been determined by God through the report and the findings of horse-riders of the first vision is executed through the war chariots.

In the two visions of chapter five God visits judgment primarily with reference to His own people Israel. In the vision of Chapter 6 judgment is visited upon the Gentile nations who have oppressed God's people. Both the judgments upon Israel and upon the nations constitute a necessary prelude to the establishment of God's people in millennial blessing.

I. THE VISION OF THE JUDGMENT OF THE NATIONS PRESENTED (Zech. 6:1-3)

1. *The Four Chariots Are Set Forth Issuing from Between Two Mountains of Brass* (Zech. 6:1). **Afterwards** [*waw* consecutive expressing temporal sequence] **I once again raised my eyes and saw** [in vision] **and look! four war**

1 And I turned, and lifted up mine eyes, and looked, and, behold, there came four chariots out from between two mountains; and the mountains were mountains of brass.

1 And again I lifted up mine eyes, and saw, and, behold, there came four chariots out from between two mountains; and the mountains were mountains of brass.

chariots in the act of going forth [*qal* active participle] from between the two mountains, and the mountains were mountains of brass [bronze].

The story-like narrative of the recital of the night visions, draws to a conclusion with this, the last one in sequence. "Afterward" or, then once again I looked up (Hebrew, "then *I returned* and raised my eyes," where the first finite verb with *waw* consecutive is used adverbially, "Then *once more* I raised my eyes"). When Zechariah looks up again (having been weighed down by such numerous overpowering visions), he again saw and look! four war chariots! The exclamatory interjection *hinneh* (lo! look!) fastens particular attention upon the four war chariots, for these are the vehicles of the divine judgment upon the nations and the significant symbols in this vision. Graphically these chariots are seen advancing from between two mountains. The expression two mountains is actually in the Hebrew, "*the* two mountains," describing two well-known or definite mountains.

Although T. W. Chambers (*The Book of Zechariah*, 1899, in J. P. Lange, *A Commentary on the Holy Scriptures, in loc.*) does not attach any specific definiteness to this article, yet the case is plain that two particular mountains in the vicinity of Jerusalem are indicated, especially as verse 5 associates them with the "presence" or "dwelling place" of "the Lord of the whole earth," as Baron notes (*The Visions and Prophecies of Zechariah*, p. 173). Very likely Mount Zion and Mount Olivet are intended (so Keil, Baron, Pusey, Wright, Feinberg, Von Orelli, etc.), since the valley between these two hills is elsewhere

set forth as the theatre of divine judgment (Zech. 14:4; Joel 3:2 [4:2]). This is a fitting place for the war chariots of judgment to go forth on their divine commission. Judgment upon the nations oppressing Israel will proceed from the heart and capital of the Jewish homeland.

Having mentioned the two mountains from which the chariots of judgment are seen issuing, the Hebrew adds a circumstantial clause, giving a secondary detail concerning them. And the mountains were mountains of brass [bronze].

Brass is an alloy of copper and zinc and is a comparatively modern discovery. Bronze, an alloy of copper and tin, is the ancient counterpart (Hebrew *nehosheth*). In the Old Testament copper is apparently sometimes meant (Gen. 4:22) and was smelted from ore dug from the ground (Deut. 8:9; Job 28:2). In Edom and Lebanon traces of very ancient copper works remain; and Egyptians smelted copper in the Sinai Peninsula as early as 5000 B.C.

From bronze (copper and its alloys) various utensils were made for tabernacle use; such as, pots, shovels, pans, spoons, basins, snuffers (Exod. 38:3; Lev. 6:28; Num. 16:39). In Scripture bronze is commonly used as a symbol of divine judgment upon sin. The bronze serpent set up in the wilderness (Num. 21:9) prefigures Christ crucified as a sin offering and symbolizes sin judged. "As Moses lifted up the serpent in the wilderness, so also must the Son of man be lifted up" (John 3:14). The brazen (bronze) altar in the tabernacle, which is a type of the cross of Christ upon which our Lord as a whole burnt offering presented Himself without spot unto God (Exod. 27:2) also pictures judg-

2 In the first chariot w er e red horses; and in the second chariot black horses;
3 And in the third chariot white horses; and in the fourth chariot grisled and bay horses.

---

2 In the first chariot were red horses; and in the second chariot black horses;
3 and in the third chariot white horses; and in the fourth chariot grizzled strong horses.

---

ment. In John 12:31–33 "the judgment of the world" (the Satanic world system) is referred to in connection with the cross of Christ. "Now is *the judgment* of this world. . . . And I, if I be lifted up from the earth, will draw all men unto me." These various Bible references fix the symbolic meaning of bronze as *divine manifestation in judgment.*

Thus the divine judgment upon the nations of the earth proceeds from Jerusalem in the vicinity of Mount Zion and Mount Olivet, symbolized by the two mountains . . . of bronze. At least as early as the time of Eusebius in the fourth century after Christ, the Valley of Jehoshaphat (meaning "Jehovah judges") has been identified with the Valley of Kidron, so that Jews, Christians, and Moslems fix the scene of the "last" judgment there. This identification is also suggested by the topographical changes in this locality prophesied to be effected by a great earthquake in this locality just before the advent of the Lord (Zech. 14:4). So far as evidence goes, however, no valley in antiquity actually bore the name of Jehoshaphat. The term, accordingly, is undoubtedly a symbolic designation chosen by the prophet Joel and appropriate for the grand event of the judgment of the nations at the end of the age (Joel 3:2 [4:2]).

2. *The Chariots Are Pictured with Their Horses* (Zech. 6:2, 3). In [that is, harnessed to] the first chariot w er e red horses, and in [harnessed to] the second chariot were black horses. And in [harnessed to] the third chariot were white horses, and in [harnessed to] the fourth chariot were dappled strong horses. In the case of each of the four horsed

chariots a nominal clause presents the statement of fact, and in each instance the *predicate* comes before the subject, giving it the emphasis in the word order. Thus *the fact that the horses were hitched to each of the four chariots in immediate readiness to execute the divine judgment universally in world-wide fashion upon all the nations is stressed,* rather than *the horses themselves or their colors.* The universality of the judgment is indicated by the number *four.* Cf. "the *four corners of the earth*" (Isa. 11:12), "the four winds of heaven" (Zech. 6:5; Jer. 49:36).

However, this truth does not at all deny the significance of the varicolored horses, which undoubtedly connect with the so-called "four horsemen of the Apocalypse" (Rev. 6:1–8). The horses of the Revelation appear in the same context of judgment, riding forth in vengeance upon the nations of the earth as a result of the opening of the seven-sealed book, the divine legal document of the Lamb, which He opens to dispossess wicked men from their squattership on the earth by virtue of His prerogatives as Creator and risen Redeemer (Rev. 5:1–14).

The red horses harnessed to the first chariot symbolize war and bloodshed. "And there went out another *horse that was red*, and power was given unto him that sat thereon to take peace from the earth, and that they should kill one another. And there was given to him a great sword" (Rev. 6:4).

The black horses harnessed to the second chariot symbolize famine and death. "And I saw, and behold *a black horse* and he that sat on him had a pair of balances in his hand. And I

4 Then I answered and said unto the angel that talked with me, What are these, my lord?

5 And the angel answered and said unto me, These are the four spirits of the heavens, which go forth from standing before the Lord of all the earth.

4   Then I answered and said unto the angel that talked with me, What are these, my lord?

5   And the angel answered and said unto me, These are the four winds of heaven, which go forth from standing before the Lord of all the earth.

heard a voice in the midst of the four living creatures say, A measure of wheat for a penny, and three measures of barley for a penny..." (Rev. 6:5, 6).

The **white horses** harnessed to the third chariot symbolize victory and triumph. "And I saw, and behold *a white horse,* and its rider had a bow, and a crown was given to him, and he went out conquering and to conquer" (Rev. 6:2).

The **dappled** [*beruddim,* "hail-spotted," as if sprinkled with hail (Gen. 31:10, 12); cf. *barad,* "hail"], **strong** horses harnessed to the fourth chariot symbolize death, evidently not alone by famine following war as in the black horse, but death by more direct divine plagues and judgments. "And I looked, and behold a *pale* horse [as the color of a sick person]: and his name that sat on him was Death, and Hell followed him. And power was given unto them over the fourth part of the earth, to kill with sword, and with hunger, and with death, and with the beasts of the earth" (Rev. 6:8).

II. THE VISION OF THE JUDGMENT OF THE NATIONS EXPLAINED (Zech. 6:4–8)

1. *The Explanation Is Prefaced by a Question* (Zech. 6:4). **Then I answered and said to the angel who was talking with me, What are these, my lord?** The prophet's desire to know the meaning of this, the last vision, is aroused. He is concerned particularly about the significance of the **chariots,** as is shown by the emphasis upon this phase of the vision as presented in verses 2 and 3 (see the

syntactical comments made there demonstrating this fact). The question Zechariah asks the angel is, accordingly, **What are these** [horsed chariots], **my lord?** — not, "What are these horses?"

2. *The Explanation Is Made Possible by a Key* (Zech. 6:5). **Then the angel replied and said to me, These** [chariots] **are the four winds** [spirits] **of the heavens going forth** [participle] **from standing before the Lord of all the earth.** The four chariots are accordingly declared to be **the four winds** (*ruhoth,* singular *ruah,* "breath," "wind," "spirit," from root "breathe," "blow," Arabic *rihun,* "breath," "wind," "spirit," *ruhun,* "soul," "spirit," Aramaic *ruha'* [Gen. 8:1; Jer. 49:36]) "of the heavens." But Pusey sensibly observes, "They cannot be literal winds: for **spirits,** not winds, **stand before God,** as His servants; as in Job, "*the sons* of God came to present themselves [the same idiom *hithyatstsev 'al* (Job 1:6; 2:1)] *before the Lord*" (*The Minor Prophets,* II, p. 370).

Micaiah, the prophet, similarly "saw the Lord sitting on his throne, and all the host of heaven [angels] *standing beside* him on his right hand and on his left" (I Kings 22:19). Daniel in beatific vision saw "a stream of fire" issuing from before the returning Messiah, and declares "a thousand thousands served him and ten thousand *stood before him* ..." (Dan. 7:10). The angel who appeared to Zechariah with a message of the birth of John the Baptist announced: "I am Gabriel, who *stands* in the presence of God" (Luke 1:19).

Baron is thus amply justified in

regarding these four chariots as "*angelic beings* or *heavenly powers*" — those invisible and ethereal "messengers" of God "who excel in strength, and who ever stand in his presence, hearkening unto the voice of his word," and then issue forth in glad service, as fleet as "winds" (Ps. 103:20, 21; 104:4) to do the divine will (*op. cit.*, p. 175). This view is better than construing them as mere personifications of the providential acts of God, or impersonally as "divine judicial powers exerted in judgment, carrying out the purposes of God" (Feinberg, *op. cit.*, p. 98).

Chambers' arguments against the interpretation that the chariots in being called *ruhoth* cannot refer to "angelic beings" are singularly weak. (1) His contention that the plural is not employed to denote angels, citing Psalm 104:4, certainly overlooks the fact that Hebrews 1:7 specifically applies this verse to "the angels." (2) His assertion that if angels are meant (rather than "winds"), the modifying phrase **of the heavens** would in that case have no suitable meaning, ignores the fact that the words "heaven" or "heavens" are constantly used in connection with angelic ministries (cf. Luke 2:15; Rev. 12:7; 14:6; 15:1; 20:1). (3) His statement that Scripture reveals nothing of *four* pre-eminent angels forgets that the book of the Revelation dealing with the identical period envisioned by Zechariah (Rev. 5:1 — 19:16) mentions angels and angelic ministry in connection with eschatological events no less than fifty-eight times, and speaks of "the *four* angels" (7:1, 2) as well as the "the *seven* angels" (8:2; 15:6, 7, 8) and numerous other prominent angels (10:1, 5; 14:6; 20:1). Moreover, the book of Daniel (3:28; 6:22; 10:13; 12:1) dealing with the same period has a prominent angelology.

There is every reason to believe these chariots represent "personal beings," that is, angelic messengers, rather than mere impersonal forces.

These **four spirits of the heavens** are said to **go forth** [present active participle, expressing action in process] **from standing before the Lord of the whole earth** (vs. 5).

That the designation **the Lord of the whole earth** *is millennial and describes the universal rule of Messiah over the earth in the kingdom age* appears from the following considerations: (1) The use of the term in Micah 4:13 in a magnificent millennial context (Mic. 4:1–12). (2) Its use in a similar kingdom context in Zechariah 4:14 (see comments on this passage *in loc.*) where Israel, under Messiah King-Priest, is set forth as the light of the millennial earth. (3) The implication of the epithet itself — **Lord** ['*adhon*, *master*, Josh. 3:11, 13; Ps. 97:5; Mic. 4:13; Zech. 4:14] **of the entire earth,** suggesting Messiah's subjugation of His enemies and His rule over the *whole* earth, as set forth in full eschatological sweep in the Apocalypse (Rev. 4:1 — 19:16), culminating in the revelation of the "King of kings and Lord of lords" (Rev. 19:16) to assume the hegemony of the earth, which is His *now* by virtue of creation and redemption, but which shall *then actually* be His by conquest and active appropriation. (4) The use of the epithet in the great millennial Psalm 97 (vs. 5). (5) Its adumbrative use of Israel's great Deliverer as the people's victorious march into Canaan followed "the ark of the covenant of the Lord of the whole earth" (Josh. 3:11, 13), and the nation was given a sample of the conquest Messiah would win over their enemies and in behalf of their establishment in the future kingdom of universal righteousness and peace.

(6) The reference to the "two witnesses" of the great tribulation as "the two olive trees and the two candlesticks standing before *the God of the earth*" (Rev. 11:4) not only connects with Zechariah's vision of Israel as the light of the millennial earth under Messiah King-Priest, but also with the "two witnesses" of the

6 The black horses which are therein go forth into the north country; and the white go forth after them; and the grisled go forth toward the south country.

7 And the bay went forth, and sought to go that they might walk to and fro through the earth: and he said, Get you hence, walk to and fro through the earth. So they walked to and fro through the earth.

---

6   The chariot wherein are the black horses goeth forth toward the north country; and the white went forth after them; and the grizzled went forth toward the south country.

7   And the strong went forth, and sought to go that they might walk to and fro through the earth: and he said, Get you hence, walk to and fro through the earth. So they walked to and fro through the earth.

Apocalypse or heralds of the coming King and the establishment of His universal kingdom, which involves the King's taking possession of the *entire earth*. (7) Similarly, Zechariah's use of the title in this last of the eight night visions is very significant, inasmuch as the judgment of the nations, Israel's oppressors, is in view, which is an indispensable prerequisite to the setting up of the kingdom.

(8) The reference to "the most high God, *possessor of heaven and earth*" (Gen. 14:19, 22) in connection with Melchizedek (type of Messiah as King-Priest) reveals Christ in His Messianic role exercising power over the restored dominion of the earth, as a result of a complete redemption, symbolized by the bread and wine "the king of Salem" offered (after victory), which elements memorialize Messiah's right to the title, **the Lord of the whole earth.**

3. *The Explanation of the Vision Is Concerned with Judgment* (Zech. 6:6, 7). **That** [chariot] **in which the black horses are** [i.e., hitched] **are going forth** [i.e., the horses] **to the land of the north. And the white went forth after them, and the dappled went forth to the land of the south, even the strong went forth** [unto the land of the south], **and they** [i.e., all the horses] **were restive to go to and fro in the earth. Then he** [i.e., the angel speaking with me] **said, Go, walk to and fro in the earth** (vss. 6, 7).

The **horses,** as noted above, symbolize earth judgments, and the **chariots** angelic spirits. *The chariots*

and their horses thus portray *divine judgments upon earth-dwellers as administered by angels,* as often in the same eschatological context in the Apocalypse. Compare the seven-trumpet angels (Rev. 8:2, 7, 8, 10, 12; 9:1, 13; 11:15) and the seven-bowl angels (Rev. 15:1; 16:2, 3, 4, 8, 10, 12, 17).

The black horses (famine and death), followed by **the white horses** (victory and conquest), are seen issuing forth to the **north country** whence Israel's most terrifying and terrible enemies (the Assyrians, Babylonians, Seleucids, and Romans) came to invade Palestine.

The **dappled** ["spotted, as if sprinkled with hail"] **went forth to the land of south,** toward Israel's ancient enemy Egypt. Following the Greek of the Codex Sinaiticus, the **strong** horses also went forth *to the land of the south.* In fact, the **dappled** horses which are linked with the **strong** horses in verse 3, to form one category "dappled-strong," are apparently also *identified* as one category (not two) in verses 7 and 8, although most expositors contend that they are "clearly distinguished" (cf. Feinberg, *op. cit.,* p. 97) in these latter verses.

However, it is possible the Codex Sinaiticus reading is original and that the **strong** (*'amuṣṣim,* "powerful") of verse 7 are epexegetical of the **dappled** (*beruddim*) of verse 6. Thus the *"dappled-strong"* horses go to the south in the direction of Egypt, just as the **black** horses followed by the **white** horses (two categories, of course, in contrast to the one category of "dappled-strong") went to the north.

Nothing is said in the Masoretic Text of horses going east and west because the Great Sea (the Mediterranean) bordered Israel's land on the west and the Arabian desert on the east. The millennial scope of this and of all eight of the night visions necessitates a world-wide sally of the horses (denoted by the number four) with their chariots, as in the first vision in the case of the horsed riders presented there (Zech. 1:7-17). Only a north-south departure could indicate such a world-wide unleashing of judgment upon the nations.

But since *all* the horsed chariots are headed for a world-engirdling trip *after* judgment is visited specifically upon the north and south country, Zechariah adds, **And they** [evidently *all* the horses] **sought to go to walk to and fro in the earth** (vs. 7). The word "seek" (*yebhaqeshu*) "to strive after, be zealous" (Exod. 2:15; 4:24; I Sam. 19:2) portrays the horses as restively eager to go forth *in every direction* to unloose judgment upon the earth preparatory to the establishment of Messiah as King-Priest (Zech. 6:9-15) over His *universal* kingdom.

A singular difficulty to be noted in the vision is that the **red horses** (war and bloodshed) mentioned at the beginning of this vision are apparently ignored in the rest of the vision where they would normally be expected to be alluded to in the sending-out of the same horsed chariots. Some commentators suggest the possibility that the omission is due to a copyist's error, on the ground that the Syriac and Aquila in verse 7 have the red horses rushing forth to seek a field of action for themselves.

Rignell (*Die Nachtgesichte des Sacharja*, Lund, 1950) equates **strong** (*'amcts*) with **red**, following Calvin and others. Leupold (*Exposition of Zechariah*, p. 116) sees five chariots in all with only four of the five going out. "One remains behind," he contends,

"—the red one." Chambers (*in loc.*) wisely suggests that although "the various colors of the horses had some significance, yet that this was not a matter of very great importance, else the distinctions stated would have been more accurately observed."

However, the immediate context of the vision itself and its larger setting in the framework of the seven preceding visions make the general sense of the vision clear, irrespective of the view adapted as to the variations in the description. The scope is world-wide and *all* the horsed chariots go out in every direction *after* the black horses and the white horses have executed judgment in the north country and the dappled-strong have done likewise in the south country. Apparently the red horses are reserved and held in check until the black horses and the white have finished their special work in the north and the spotted-strong horses have completed their task in the south. Then as symbolic of war and bloodshed these join the others (latter part of verse 7) in carrying out the world-encircling sweep of judgment that this vision presents in line with the scope of all the other night visions, especially as this is the capstone and conclusion to all the rest, especially the first.

In the first vision the Lord sent forth the red, speckled, and white horses "to walk to and fro," i.e., "in every direction" throughout the whole "*earth*," since the reconnoitering or scouting expedition there was surveying the condition of the various nations with reference to Israel's age-end trouble (Jer. 30:7) and subsequent restoration (Zech. 1:7-17). In this concluding vision the Lord again sends out the *horsed war chariots* to traverse the same unlimited territory to execute the divine judgment upon the nations in accordance with the report and condition ascertained in the first vision. **And he** [the Lord of the whole earth] **said, Go forth, walk in every direction in the earth. So** [*waw* consecutive, expressing logical result]

8 Then cried he upon me, and spake unto me, saying, Behold, these that go toward the north country have quieted my spirit in the north country.

8 Then cried he to me, and spake unto me, saying, Behold, they that go toward the north country have quieted my spirit in the north country.

they walked in every direction in the earth (vs. 7b).

The person who speaks and gives the double command for the chariots to issue forth on their world-wide mission is **the Lord of the whole earth,** who (vs. 5) causes the chariots to go forth and thus executes the predetermined judgment upon Israel's enemies. With this authoritative voice issuing the double imperative, the logical result is the going forth of the chariots of judgment in every direction in the earth, interestingly enough with the Hebrew verb agreeing grammatically with the chariots, stressing these, rather than the horses drawing the chariots.

4. *The Vision Concludes with a Message of Hope to the People of the Prophet's Day* (Zech. 6:8). **Then he called out loudly to me and said, See, those who are going forth into the land of the north have caused my Spirit to be quiet in the land of the north.** The speaker in this concluding verse is evidently the interpreting angel, as Chambers correctly notes, since it is a question of intermediation and instructive help. But it is the interpreting angel speaking *directly* for "the Lord of the whole earth" since the first person is indicated by the suffix on spirit (i.e., "*My* Spirit").

The interpreting angel cries out enthusiastically and with gusto to Zechariah to encourage him and his generation with a word of cheer. The verb employed, **Then he called out loudly** (*wayyaz'eq* is the causative of *za'aq*), is used for "calling out" for military service (Judg. 4:10, 13; II Sam. 20:4, 5), "having a proclamation made" (Jonah 3:7) or "calling out to one spiritedly," as here. Such good news that God had not forgotten His people who were so pitilessly overrun by enemies from the north,

notably the Assyrians and the Chaldeans, but that He would deal with Israel's foes from that quarter in particular and preserve His people for further blessing, was a heartening message of hope for that day that demanded enthusiastic announcement.

The message of the interpreting angel was, **See, those** [the black and the white horsed chariots] **who are going forth into the land of the north have quieted my Spirit in the land of the north.** The idiom "to quiet God's Spirit," as Leupold (*op. cit.*, p. 117) correctly notes, means "they have caused God's anger to cease. . . ."

As a result of the report of the reconnoitering patrol in the first vision, the Lord has announced His burning love for Israel and His violent anger against the nations persecuting her (Zech. 1:15, 16). This love was on the basis of His unchangeable purposes of grace for His covenant people as reflected against the background of His infinite holiness outraged by the crimes of the nations against His own. His Spirit thus disturbed and made restless by unjudged atrocities is here "quieted" in the sense of "appeased" by judgment. Henderson (*The Book of the Twelve Minor Prophets*, London, 1845) rightly observes "that among other significations *ruaḥ* has that of *anger* (see Judg. 8:3; Eccl. 10:4; Isa. 33:11)." Accordingly, the phrase, "cause one's spirit to rest," is equivalent to "cause one's anger to cease," as in Ezekiel 5:13; 16:42; 24:13; in the sense of "satisfy, pacify."

Baron (*op. cit.*, p. 182), also interpreting "spirit" (*ruaḥ*) as "anger," construes the expression as "cause to rest" (*heniaḥ*, *hifil* from *nuaḥ*, "to rest," Assyrian *naḥu*, "relax," Arabic 4, "make a camel recline") in the sense of "set down" or "deposit" (Josh. 4:3, 8; I Sam. 6:18). According to this view the company of the invisible host (angels of judgment), symbolized by the chariots whose mission was toward the north, have caused God's anger to rest *on* the north country, in the sense of having carried it there and deposited it, making it remain *upon* the kingdom as its abode. But this interpretation is scarcely necessary. The simple meaning of the expression used in this passage is to "cause to rest" with the significance "to give rest to" (as in Exod. 17:11; Ezek. 5:13; 16:42; 24:13). The thought is therefore of pacifying God's anger *in* the north country rather than causing the divine anger to rest or remain in the north country.

Leupold (*op. cit.*, p. 118), following Pusey (*in loc.*), apparently adopts this composite idea that God's Spirit could have no rest till it had vented its displeasure on the offender by *remaining* there, and with Rignell (*in loc.*) posits a saving and blessing ministry "for when God's Spirit is brought to a place . . ., He at the same time does a constructive work. . . ." But this is reading something into the scope of the vision that is foreign to it. The thought of the last vision is judgment, not blessing, upon the nations which are Israel's enemies. Until these nations are judged, Israel cannot enter into the kingdom blessing with Messiah's throne established in the midst of her,

nor realize her predestined goal toward which human history is moving.

But the concluding night vision not only ends with a panoramic prophetic vista comprehending judgment upon Israel's foes previous to the nation's restoration in kingdom blessing, but it contains a note of cheer to the prophet's contemporaries as well. The specific prophetic application had to do with the kingdom of Babylon on the north (Jer. 1:14, 15; 25:9) and Israel's ancient foe Egypt on the south. Between these two formidable nations God would preserve "His feeble flock, checkmating every effort to destroy them till Messiah should Himself appear" (H. A. Ironside, *Notes on the Minor Prophets*, p. 372).

But upon Babylon (vss. 6, 8) would His special punishment be vented, not only because Israel suffered so terribly from that nation, but because from the land of Shinar the wicked commercial, political, and religious system developed (Zech. 5:5-11) which became so inextricably interwoven with the nations and so polluting and contaminating in their career that both they and the system (Rev. 17 and 18) must face the inexorable judgment of God before the restoration of Israel can be effected. Zechariah 5:5-11 presents the destruction of the Babylonian system and Zechariah 6:1-8 delineates the judgment of the nations defiled by the system and, as inveterate enemies of Israel throughout the centuries, finally judged.

CHAPTER SIX

(Continued)

RESTORED ISRAEL UNDER MESSIAH KING-PRIEST

THE CORONATION OF JOSHUA

(ZECH. 6 :9–15)

IMMEDIATELY following the overthrow of Gentile world power by the earth judgments symbolized by the horse chariots (Zech. 6:1–8) occurs the manifestation of Christ in His kingdom glory (Zech. 6:9–15) typified by the crowning of Joshua the high priest. This is the usual prophetic order: first, the judgments of the day of the Lord; then full kingdom blessing (Ps. 2:5, cf. Ps. 2:6; Isa. 3:24–26, cf. 4:2–6; 10:33, 34, cf. 11:1–10; Rev. 19: 19–21, cf. 20:4–6).

The eight night visions have ended, but the coronation of Joshua is closely connected with these revelations which extend in scope from Zechariah's day to the full establishment of Israel in blessing. The crowning of King-Priest Messiah is thus set forth symbolically by the coronation of Joshua, which is not a vision, but an actual historical act, which evidently took place the day following the night of visions.

The last thing the prophet saw was

109

9 And the word of the Lord came unto me, saying,
10 Take of them of the captivity, even of Heldai, of Tobijah, and of Jedaiah, which are come from Babylon, and come thou the same day, and go into the house of Josiah the son of Zephaniah;

---

9   And the word of Jehovah came unto me, saying,
10   Take of them of the captivity, even of Heldai, of Tobijah, and of Jedaiah; and come thou the same day, and go into the house of Josiah the son of Zephaniah, whither they are come from Babylon;

---

the horses galloping away with their war chariots. And in Jerusalem, what a sight meets his eyes, to demonstrate that the truth contained in his visions was already coming to pass!

I. THE HISTORICAL EVENT AND THE PROPHETIC SYMBOLISM (Zech. 6: 9–11)

1. *The Arrival of the Deputies from Babylon with Gifts for the Temple* (Zech. 6:9, 10a). Then the word of the Lord came to me, saying, Receive [accept a gift] from the returned exiles, namely, from Heldai, from Tobijah. and from Jedaiah. . . . The eight night visions having been given, Zechariah reverts to the usual prophetic formula authenticating what is to be said and done as by the Spirit of God and not from the prophet himself. Then [i.e., *after* the conclusion of the night visions 1:7 – 6:8] the word of the Lord came to me, saying (*le'mor,* "in the following manner"). Now the word of God is not to come in a vision, but by means of an interesting event that was to furnish the basis of a meaningful prophetic symbolism (cf. Zech. 4:8; 7:4; 8:1, 18).

The word of the Lord which came to the prophet was a command "to *receive* the donation brought by the returned exiles" (pregnant construction). Receive or "accept" (the gift). The infinitive absolute *laqoah* is used for the imperative, as in Jeremiah 32:14 (cf. Gesenius, *Hebrew Grammar,* sect. 113, 4). The verb *laqah,* "to take," in this passage has the meaning of "receive" or "accept," especially a gift, a bribe, etc., as in Ethiopic and

Aramaic. In Genesis 4:11 it is used of the earth opening "her mouth *to receive* Abel's blood." In I Samuel 8:3 and Amos 5:12 it is employed of *receiving* or *accepting* bribes. Isaiah uses the verb concerning Jerusalem *receiving* chastisement (Isa. 40:2). In Joshua 13:8 and 18:7 it is employed of Reubenites and Gadites *receiving* their tribal inheritance.

The idiom, "to receive anything *from* anyone" (*me'eth*), is illustrated by Exodus 30:16, "And ye shall *take* [accept, receive] the redemption money *from* [*me'eth*] the children of Israel," and by Exodus 25:2: "Speak unto the children of Israel that they bring me an offering. *From* [*me'eth*] every one who giveth it willingly [and] with his heart *ye shall take* [*tiqehu,* "receive," "accept"] my offering." The same idiom appears also in Exodus 35:5 and Leviticus 7:34.

The gift was to be received (and not scorned or refused) from the returned exiles (*golah*). This word is from the root *galah,* "uncover, remove, depart," which in Arabic (*jala*) means "to go forth, emigrate"; cf. *jaliyatun,* "a company of exiles." Although the Hebrew word is often employed in the abstract, "exile" or "captivity" (Jer. 48:11; Ezek. 12:11; Ezra 6:21; 9:4; 10:6), it is often used collectively of "exiles" (Esther 2:6; Jer. 29:1; Ezek. 1:1). The word is used here by Zechariah in the sense of returned exiles, that is, "those who have visited or returned to Jerusalem from the place of exile, Babylon."

The names of the returned captives (*golah*) are given as Heldai, Tobijah, and Jedaiah, God-honoring names displaying faith – Heldai (apparently, "the Lord's world") Tobijah ("good is Yah"), Jedaiah ("Yah [i.e., Yahweh] knows"). These three men were doubtlessly characterized by spirituality and liberality among the Jewish captives in Babylon, which explains their selection by their Babylonian brothers for the arduous task assigned them and their willingness to undertake such a devoted and unselfish mission.

2. *The Command to Zechariah to Meet the Babylonian Delegation* (Zech. 6:10b). **And come thou the same day, and go into the house of Josiah the son of Zephaniah.** The great importance and urgency of Zechariah's present task is indicated. **Come** [or go] **thou** (*ubha'thah 'attah*, i.e., "thou *thyself*," thou and no other). No one else will do because no one but Zechariah has been divinely prepared for the momentous event to follow. His eight night visions are introductory and preparatory to what he is now enjoined to do, and will form a fitting climax to the revelations he has received and give meaning to them.

Go thou thyself that same day (*bayyom hahu'*). The impact of the visions must not be dissipated by time. The arrival of the Babylonian delegation was divinely timed, so were Zechariah's visions, and so must be his response. Divine providences dovetail, and human response that is immediate and timely must fit into them.

Zechariah is specifically enjoined to **go to the house of Josiah the son of Zephaniah, where they** [i.e., the delegation] **have arrived from Babylon.** The returned exiles who were bringing donations for the construction of the temple were evidently being entertained at Josiah's house. Whether or not their being put up at this particular place had anything to do with their doubt about whether their gifts would be received or not (as Pusey suggests, *op. cit.*, p. 372) is not stated, and can scarcely be implied. There was, of course, the possibility that their

generosity might be refused since they had preferred to remain in Babylon. But the urgency of the command to Zechariah and the divine leading in the whole affair were to obviate any doubt in anyone's mind.

The name of the delegation's host, **Josiah** ["the Lord supports"] **the son of Zephaniah** ("the Lord conceals" or "hides"), occurs only here in the Old Testament, except for the name of Israel's famous king. His other name "Hen" ("graciousness"), given in verse 14, suggests his cordial hospitality displayed on this occasion in his opening his home to the pilgrims from Babylon. Both he and they, as well as the prophet, were to be recipients of a great common blessing, as each was obedient to the leading of the Lord.

Josiah's house is described as **where** ['*asher* used as a relative adverb, as in Gen. 35:13; Num. 13:27; Deut. 1:31; I Kings 8:9; Isa. 55:11 rather than a relative pronoun] **they** [the delegation] **have come from Babylon.** Kimchi's rendering "*who* have come from Babylon," expressly including Josiah, is manifestly impossible.

How encouraging must have been this delegation to Zechariah and his countrymen, but especially to the prophet who was so wonderfully prepared for the deeper prophetic meaning that lay behind the event! With the whole grand panorama of Israel's future glory as portrayed so vividly in the eight night visions still vibrant in his consciousness, the prophet was now to see an event enacted that would summarize the grand scope of all those visions – Messiah crowned as King-Priest in the future kingdom. Moreover, the visitors from far-off Babylon with princely gifts for the temple were a precursor of the vast numbers of Gentiles in the millennial age who would bring their homage to the King and their wealth to build His temple in that glad future day which the prophet envisioned. Just so the handful of Greeks who came seeking to "see Jesus" (John

11 Then take silver and gold, and make crowns, and set them upon the head of Joshua the son of Josedech, the high priest;
12 And speak unto him, saying, Thus speaketh the Lord of hosts, saying, Behold the man whose name is The BRANCH; and he shall grow up out of his place, and he shall build the temple of the Lord:

---

11   yea, take of them silver and gold, and make crowns, and set them upon the head of Joshua the son of Jehozadak, the high priest;
12   and speak unto him, saying, Thus speaketh Jehovah of hosts, saying, Behold, the man whose name is the Branch: and he shall grow up out of his place; and he shall build the temple of Jehovah;

12:20–24) were a harbinger of the multitudes of Gentiles who would be brought into the church consequent upon the death and resurrection of the Lord.

3. *The Instruction of Zechariah to Make a Crown and Coronate Joshua the High Priest* (Zech. 6:11). **And take silver and gold and make a crown and place it on the head of Joshua the son of Jehozadak the high priest.** Although the Hebrew is pointed plural '*ataroth* (thus "crowns" and not "crown"), the meaning both contextually and lexically is here singular, **crown,** and here and in verse 14 should be pointed '*atereth* (singular) following the Septuagint. Even if the plural were followed, it would indicate not two crowns but *one composite crown* of two or more parts, an ornate majestic crown, like that of the returning Messiah in Revelation 19:12. Care must be taken to note that no crown was placed upon the head of Zerubbabel. To have crowned him an heir of the Davidic dynasty would have been misleading, pointing to a re-establishment of the Davidic kingdom, which was not the divine purpose at that moment.

The whole import of this incident lies in the fact that this crown was placed upon the head of Joshua *only* and *by no means* upon the head of Zerubbabel. In the Old Testament the kingly and priestly offices were kept rigidly distinct. The office of king pertained alone to the house of David (II Sam. 7; Ps. 89) while the priestly office was confined to the Levite tribe.

Uzziah's intrusion into the priestly office was warning enough of God's irrevocable separation between these two functions (II Chron. 26:16–21). The fact that the high priest Joshua, who could not wear a crown, here does so, proves that the act is typical, delineating the future *priestly kingship* of Christ according to Hebrews 7:1–3 and Psalm 110:4. Joshua the high priest had the kingly dignity added to him typically. Christ's priestly work for us on the cross and afterward at the right hand of the Father is the precursor to His future kingly ministry over Israel and the nations.

II. THE MESSIANIC SIGNIFICANCE OF THE PROPHETIC SYMBOLISM (Zech. 6:12, 13, 15)

This symbolic act, springing out of the preceding eight night visions, meaningfully sets forth the Person of the promised Redeemer, graphically portraying the offices He is to fulfill and the mission He is to accomplish. The act itself is a brief one but is far-reaching in its ramifications and is worthy as a climactic résumé of the events predicted in the series of eight night visions. As Pusey correctly says, this symbolic act "points to and sums up and interprets the preceding visions" (*The Minor Prophets,* II, p. 372).

1. *Messiah, the Branch, Shall Appear as Joshua's Antitype* (Zech. 6: 12a, b). Zechariah was directed to speak unto Joshua, saying, **Thus speaketh the Lord of hosts, Behold the man.** Pontius Pilate was echoing

13 Even he shall build the temple of the Lord; and he shall bear the glory, and shall sit and rule upon his throne; and he shall be a priest upon his throne: and the counsel of peace shall be between them both.

13   even he shall build the temple of Jehovah; and he shall bear the glory, and shall sit and rule upon his throne; and he shall be a priest upon his throne; and the counsel of peace shall be between them both.

prophecy when he uttered these words before the yelling, murderous mob at Jesus' trial (John 19:5). If the assembled Jews had not been demoniacally blinded by hatred and unbelief, they would have recalled the prophetic usage in Zechariah. It was as a man that Messiah wore a crown of thorns in rejection when He was made an offering for sin. Once again the cry, "Behold the man" will sound forth in glory when He comes in the clouds of heaven crowned then, not with thorns, but with a diadem of glory (Rev. 19:12). His eyes shall be like a flame of fire, and on His head shall be many crowns (diadems).

Behold the Man, the Branch [the Shoot]! How wonderfully does Joshua here prefigure Christ, whose kingship (Ps. 2:6) and priesthood (Ps. 110:4) he symbolizes. "And he shall grow up out of his place." From poverty and obscurity He grew up before God as a tender plant (Isa. 53:2). "I will cause the Branch of Righteousness to grow up unto David" (Jer. 33:15). "Except a grain of wheat fall into the ground and die, it abideth alone; but if it die, it bringeth forth much fruit" (John 12:24). Messiah sprouted out of the fallen trunk of David, from His own land and nation, a true scion of the native stock (Isa. 11:1).

2. *Messiah, the Branch, Shall Build the Millennial Temple* (Zech. 6:12c, 13a). "The sprout ... will sprout" (paronomasia). This One who is to grow out of poverty and obscurity will **build the temple ... even he shall build** [*hu' yivneh*] **the temple.** The repetition is very vivid and emphatic. **Even he,** notwithstanding His lowliness, shall accomplish the work. The reference here is not to the

earthly temple which was then in process of construction, for this was to be finished by Zerubbabel (Zech. 4:9), but the millennial temple is meant (Ezek. 40–42; Isa. 2:2 .).

3. *Messiah, the Branch, Shall Bear the Glory* (Zech. 6:13b). The Hebrew is emphatic, **he himself shall bear the glory** [*hodh*]. This Hebrew word denotes "majesty, honor, beauty." It is used almost exclusively of the divine splendor. "Who has set thy *glory* above the heaven" (Ps. 8:1 [2]). "Gird on thy sword with thy *glory* and thy majesty." (Ps. 45:3 [4]). "His *glory* is above the earth and heaven" (Ps. 148:13). "His *glory* covered the heavens" (Hab. 3:3). "And he hath on his vesture and on his thigh a name written, King of kings and Lord of lords" (Rev. 19:16).

4. *Messiah, the Branch, Shall Be a King-Priest* (Zech. 6:13c, d). **He shall sit and rule as a king upon his throne** (vs. 13c). **he shall be a priest upon his throne** (vs. 13d). He, the Creator-Redeemer, has now taken possession of His inheritance (Rev. 5:1 – 19:16). The heart of the book of the Revelation prefigures the dispossession of Satan, demons, and wicked men who have taken possession of the blood-bought inheritance. Now the rightful owner as King-Priest comes into possession of the earth (Gen. 14:19, 22).

How wonderfully does the name of Christ, the Branch, appear. The designation **the man whose name is the Branch** (Zech. 6:12) sets Him forth in His character as Son of man, the "last Adam," the "second man" (I Cor. 15:45–47). This characterization presents Him as a Priest-King over the earth in the dominion given to Him and forfeited by the first Adam. As the "second man," the "last Adam," Jesus regains full control of the earth, as is here set forth in Zechariah.

Already Zechariah had presented "the Servant, the Branch" (Zech. 3:8), setting forth Messiah's humiliation and obedience unto death in His pouring out of His life unto death (Phil. 2:5–8) in fulfillment of Isaiah 52:13 – 53:12. Isaiah portrays Him as "the Branch of Jehovah" (Isa. 4:2), in His Immanuel character to be fully manifested to restored Israel at His second advent (Matt. 25:31). He is also elsewhere presented as "the Branch of David" (Isa. 11:1; Jer. 23:5; 33:15). In this prophecy He is seen as the posterity of David (Rom. 1:3), set forth in earthly splendor as "King of kings and Lord of lords."

5. *Messiah, the Branch, Shall Combine in Perfect Concord the Two Offices of King and Priest* (Zech. 6:13e). **And the counsel of peace shall be between the two of them.** Counsel (from the root *ya'ats*, "to advise, counsel") comprehends "mutual advice or consultation." The word is frequently used of political "consultation" (II Sam. 17:7; I Kings 1:12; Isa. 8:10; Ezek. 11:2). **Counsel of peace** denotes "mutual advice or consultation" which eventuates in "peace" (*shalom*, that is, "concord" or "agreement"). This "discussion or consultation issuing in concord or agreement" is said to be **between the two of them** (*shenehem*, literally, "their two"). *Neither* the substantival numeral "two" *nor* the pronominal suffix masculine plural "them," is connected grammatically with a definitely stated antecedent in the Hebrew. Consequently the interpreter must carefully determine (1) by implication and (2) by context what the meaning of the expression, **the two of them,** is.

Fortunately this is not too difficult a task since Messiah has just been said (1) to **sit and rule on his throne** (a clear reference to the "kingship") and (2) to **be a priest** [a transparent

reference to the "priesthood"] **upon his throne** (an obvious reference to the *combination of the two offices in one person*). Therefore the declaration **the counsel of peace shall be between them** means "the discussion and consultation" eventuating in concord and agreement shall be the result of *the kingship and the priesthood being united in one person,* thus in the kingdom age precluding all disagreement and discord that had so often arisen in Israel, where these offices had been rigidly kept distinct and held by fallible men, who often made serious mistakes. Messiah as King-Priest will thus produce peace because He will become in His glorious omniscient and all-righteous person not only all administrative and judicial functions but all ecclesiastical and spiritual ones as well.

He who now "is our peace" (Eph. 2:14) and who made peace by the blood of His cross (Eph. 2:15) will act in the same capacity to Israel and the nations in the kingdom age. He who is a "Wonder of a Counsellor, the Mighty God, the Eternally Existing One" will manifest Himself preeminently as "the Prince of Peace" (Isa. 9:6). But as Zechariah sees Him in this passage it is His being "a Wonder of a Counsellor" that eventuates in His being "the Prince of Peace." No disagreement or discord shall mar the millennial administration of Him in whose glorious person "righteousness and peace" shall kiss each other (Ps. 85:10 [11]).

Barnes in considering the immediate historical circumstances of this prophetic act suggests a possible rift between the kingship and the priesthood of that day in a disagreement between Zerubbabel, the civil governor, and Joshua, the high priest (*Cambridge Bible*, p. 55). If this is true, and if it did happen upon occasion in Old Testament times, it will not occur in the future.

6. *Messiah, the Branch, Shall Bind Together in Unity Both Jew and Gentile* (Zech. 6:15a). **And they that**

15 And they that are far off shall come and build in the temple of the Lord, and ye shall know that the Lord of hosts hath sent me unto you. And this shall come to pass, if ye will diligently obey the voice of the Lord your God.

---

15   And they that are far off shall come and build in the temple of Jehovah; and ye shall know that Jehovah of hosts hath sent me unto you. And this shall come to pass, if ye will diligently obey the voice of Jehovah your God.

---

are afar off shall build in the temple of the Lord. The deputation from far-away Babylon bringing an offering of silver and gold for the temple, which was then in the process of construction, was the occasion for Zechariah's prediction of a future glorious temple to be established in Jerusalem as a House of Prayer for all nations, and to which even the Gentile peoples from afar shall flow, bringing their worship and their gifts.

Isaiah had envisioned the same wonderful truth. "And it shall be in the last days that *the mountain of the Lord's house* shall be established in the top of the mountains, and shall be exalted above the hills; and *all nations shall flow unto it*. And many people shall go and say, Come ye, and let us go up to the mountain of the Lord, *to the house of the God of Jacob*; and he will teach us his ways, and we will walk in his paths: for out of Zion shall go forth the law, and the word of the Lord from Jerusalem" (Isa. 2:2, 3).

"Arise, shine, for thy light is come, and the glory of the Lord is risen upon thee. For, behold, darkness shall cover the earth and gross darkness the people. But the Lord shall arise upon thee, and his glory shall be seen upon thee. And the Gentiles shall come to thy light and kings to the brightness of thy rising. Lift up thine eyes round about and see. All they gather themselves together, they come to thee. Thy sons shall come from afar and thy daughters shall be nursed at thy side . . . the abundance of the sea shall be converted unto thee, the *resources of the nations shall come unto thee* . . . multitudes of camels . . . dromedaries . . . gold and incense, and

they shall show forth the praises of the Lord. All the flocks of Kedar . . ., the rams of Nebaioth *shall minister unto thee: they shall come up with acceptance on mine altar, and I will glorify the house of my glory*" (Isa. 60:1-7). Compare Micah 4:1, 2.

Whereas the nations **shall build in the temple of the Lord** (*yivneh behekal yahweh*), the Lord Himself shall *build the temple*. "Behold, the man whose name is the Branch . . . he shall build the temple of the Lord: *Even he* shall build the temple of the Lord" (Zech. 6:12, 13). The nations shall build *in* the temple in the sense of bringing their wealth into it, but only the Lord will *build it*, for it will be *His* house, under His direction and according to His plan and for His glory alone. "Except the *Lord build* the house, they labor in vain that build it" (Ps. 127:1).

Again Isaiah says, "Also the *foreigners* who unite themselves to the Lord to serve him and to love the name of the Lord, to be his servants, . . . even them will I bring to my holy mountain, and make them joyful *in my house of prayer*. Their burnt offerings and their sacrifices shall be accepted *upon my altar, for my house shall be called a House of Prayer* for all people" (Isa. 56:6, 7).

7. *Messiah the Branch Will Corroborate and Establish the Truth of God's Word* (Zech. 6:15b). **And ye shall know that the Lord of armies has sent me unto you.** The question in this passage is, To whom does the personal pronoun "me" refer: (1) to Zechariah (Baron and others), or (2) to the Angel of the Lord, i.e., Messiah (Keil, etc.)? Since only the prophet Zechariah and not the Angel of the Lord appears

in the immediate context as acting
and speaking, it would at first blush
seem that the divine authentication of
the message centers in the human
messenger. However, Keil's view is
probably correct which argues that
the meaning is to be ascertained in the
larger context of the eight night
visions and that "we must not change
the 'sending' into 'speaking' here,
or understand the formula or expression, used in any other sense here than
in chapter 2:8-11 and in 4:9" (Keil,
in loc.). Under this assumption therefore it is taken that Zechariah's
utterance passes imperceptibly into
the Lord's utterance and that Messiah
the Branch Himself will establish the
truth of the Word of God here declared.

It is noteworthy however that
whether the authentication of this
prophecy centers in the prophet or in
Messiah, the Spirit of God anticipated
the adamant unbelief of our day,
which if it does not deny the fact of a
future millennium for Israel, staunchly
denies the building of a literal millennial temple as a "House of Prayer
for all people" (Isa. 56:7). The divine
corroboration of this aspect of prophecy, so widely denied, is therefore
highly significant at this particular
point. God must and will demonstrate
in these matters the certain fulfilment
of His Word. The divine covenants
and promises made to Israel in the
Old Testament will be most assuredly
fulfilled.

8. *Messiah, the Branch, Will Demand Unflinching Obedience* (Zech.
6:15c). **And this shall come to pass,
if you will diligently obey the voice of
the Lord your God.** As Baron correctly
says, "Not that the fulfilment of the
prophecy will be conditional on their
obedience — that is in the *will and
unchangeable purpose of God alone* —
but *their participation in it* depends
on their faith and obedience (*op. cit.*,
p. 205).

Some commentators would make
this passage an aposiopesis that
abruptly breaks off in an incomplete
sentence. Thus, "And it shall come

to pass, if you will diligently obey the
voice of the Lord your God, . . ."
This would give the protasis of a
conditional sentence with its apodosis
omitted or broken off in silence. But
such an assumption is unnecessary
and meaningless as H. C. Leupold
(*Exposition of Zechariah*, pp. 126f.)
correctly points out.

The stress upon complete and
diligent obedience in order to enter
into God's blessings is indicated by
the infinitive absolute followed by the
finite verb, in which the infinitival
verb accentuates the verbal idea of
the finite construction. **If you will
diligently or thoroughly listen to**
[i.e., obey] **the voice of the Lord your
God.** Zechariah echoes Deuteronomy
28:1. "And it shall come to pass, if
thou shalt hearken diligently unto the
voice of the Lord thy God, to observe
and to do all his commandments
which I command thee this day, that
the Lord thy God will set thee on high
above all the nations of the earth."
This is to be viewed as a partial
quotation by Zechariah from the book
of Deuteronomy, and not an accidental
interpolation in a corrupt text, as
some critics maintain. Since Deuteronomy, chapter 28, gives *the conditions*
of blessings in the land where Israel
will then be, the quotation is relevant
and highly significant.

III. THE PROVISION FOR A PERMANENT
MEMORIAL (Zech. 6:14)

Leupold maintains that "whether
Zechariah ever attempted to carry out
the letter of this command and
actually made or had others make a
crown and then set it upon Joshua's
head must remain an open question"
(*op. cit.*, p. 127). This perhaps is true.
But is it credible to imagine that the
prophet who was graced with such
far-reaching visions of Israel's grand
future, and then to top it all, was
especially favored with the dovetailing
event of the arrival of the delegation
from Babylon with princely gifts for
the temple, so rich in Messianic
significance, would have been so

14 And the crowns shall be to Helem, and to Tobijah, and to Jedaiah, and to Hen the son of Zephaniah, for a memorial in the temple of the Lord.

14 And the crowns shall be to Helem, and to Tobijah, and to Jedaiah, and to Hen the son of Zephaniah, for a memorial in the temple of Jehovah.

grossly dilatory to duty, as to have failed to make the crown and to have memorialized the event, as well as its vast prophetic and typical significance? Certainly the crown was made as directed.

1. *The Crown Made Was Not to Be Given to Joshua* (Zech. 6:14a). And the crown shall be for Helem and for Tobijah and for Jedaiah and for Hen the son of Zephaniah, for a memorial in the temple of the Lord. Joshua's crowning was merely a brief and transitory typical act. The important thing is that a memorial of this crucially significant typical event be preserved by the members of the Babylonian delegation and their Hebrew host, Josiah.

The variations in the form of the proper names in this verse from their occurrence in Zechariah 6:10 are interesting. "Heldai" there occurs here as "Helem" and "Josiah" appears here as "Hen." The identity of the latter is vouched for by the father's name being the same in both cases. It was common in antiquity for people to have two names. Uzziah was also called Azariah; Ahaz was styled Jehoahaz by the Assyrians; Simon was surnamed Peter; Saul was latter called Paul.

In our own day nicknames are common, the latter being not the real name, but a sobriquet arising out of some character or physical trait of the person to whom it is applied; cf. "Fatty," "Slim," "Shorty," etc., and such common nicknames as Bill for William and Bob for Robert. "Hen" ("graciousness") is apparently a nickname for Josiah to describe his hospitality and liberality, which here show up in his entertaining the delegates from Babylon, although the precise connection between Heldai and Helem (if any) is obscure.

Moreover, that some such explanation is probable in the case of Josiah is indicated by the witness of the ancient versions which attest the correctness of the text. All except the Syriac, which repeats the names of verse 6:10, have or imply the names Helem (not Heldai) and Hen (not Josiah).

2. *The Crown was to Be Kept as a Memorial in the Temple* (Zech. 6:14b). And the crown shall be . . . a memorial in the temple of the Lord. The word "memorial" (*zikkaron*, from the root *zakar*, "to remember") denotes a "reminder," here employed of "an object designed to recall an event." The word is common in the Old Testament in this sense. The two stones "upon the shoulders of the ephod" engraved with the names of the children of Israel were for the purpose that Aaron might "bear their names before the Lord upon his two shoulders *for a memorial*" (Exod. 28:12, 22; 39:7). Similarly Aaron bore the names of the Israelites "in the breastplate of judgment . . . *for a memorial* before the Lord continually" (Exod. 28:29). The "atonement money" was to be appointed "for the service of the tabernacle . . . that it may be a *memorial* unto the children of Israel before the Lord" (Exod. 30:16). The custom of monthly trumpet-blowing over burnt offerings and peace offerings was "for a *memorial*" before the Lord (Num. 10:10). The stones set up in the Jordan River were such a "memorial" or reminder of God's undertaking (Josh. 4:7).

According to Jewish tradition preserved in the Middot, "the crowns" (taken as plural) "were hung in windows in the height of the temple." Moreover, there is no reason to doubt Jewish tradition here. Certainly the "memorial" was made and placed in the temple and had a long and fruitful ministry of reminding the people of the important typical and prophetic event it portrayed, not only retrospectively in looking back to Zechariah's visions culminating in Joshua's coronation, but also prospectively in looking forward to the fruition of these visions in the eventual crowning of Messiah as millennial King-Priest in the period of the consummation of Jewish hopes and aspirations. Zecha-riah ("whom the Lord *remembers*") as the prophet of hope is given a permanent "memorial" to keep alive the memory of God's promised grace. As the Lord's supper is a memorial "to show forth the Lord's death [retrospective] till He come" [prospective], so the crown in the temple in looking backward and forward had a similar function in preserving the memory of the Person and Work of Him in whom both Christian and Jewish hopes and expectations center.

CHAPTER SEVEN

RITUALISM VERSUS SPIRITUAL REALITY

THE QUESTION OF THE FASTS

(ZECH. 7:1–14)

APPROXIMATELY two years have elapsed since the night visions have been given describing the whole future of the nation Israel, including the subjugation of her enemies, her regathering to the land of Palestine, her cleansing, restoration to high priestly witness, and establishment as a theocracy. The result of these apocalyptic visions was that the people gave heed to the warnings and encouragements of Zechariah's prophecies and Haggai's teaching, and had begun to build the temple, which was probably already more than half completed.

It is now 518 B.C. As the edifice arose before the people's eyes, with every obstacle removed to the completion of the structure by the decree of Darius confirming the original decree of Cyrus (Ezra 6:1–14), the situation looked promising. Although the walls of Jerusalem were still in ruins and some quarters of the town still in utter desolation, the city began to take on a prosperous look as private homes began to be erected and some fine residences completed (Hag. 1:4). With this new upsurge of prosperity, the question pressed to the fore whether it was necessary or not to observe the solemn seasons of mourning by which the people had commemorated the calamitous events of their former history, especially the anniversary of the burning of the city and the temple by the Babylonians on the tenth day of the fifth month. Accordingly a message of inquiry was sent to the priests and the prophets at Jerusalem to which the Lord through Zechariah granted a full and satisfying answer.

1 And it came to pass in the fourth year of king Darius, that the word of the Lord came unto Zechariah in the fourth day of the ninth month, even in Chisleu;
2 When they had sent unto the house of God Sherezer and Regemmelech, and their men, to pray before the Lord,

1   And it came to pass in the fourth year of king Darius, that the word of Jehovah came unto Zechariah in the fourth day of the ninth month, even in Chislev.
2   Now they of Beth-el had sent Sharezer and Regem-melech, and their men, to entreat the favor of Jehovah,

I. THE QUESTION OF THE FAST BROACHED (Zech. 7:1-3)

The occasion of the great prophecies given by inspiration to Zechariah in chapters 7 and 8 is plainly set forth in the first three verses of chapter 7. These far-reaching predictive utterances, although they stand separate from the disclosures in the eight night visions (1:7−6:8) and the climaxing typical event of the crowning of Joshua (6:9-15), nevertheless set forth the same general prophetic truths symbolized and typified in them but in terms of simple literal language, and not couched in apocalyptic visions and typical occurrences.

1. *Zechariah Receives a Revelation Anticipating the Question of the Fasts* (Zech. 7:1). Then it happened in the fourth year of Darius the king that the word of the Lord came unto Zechariah in the fourth day of the ninth month, in [the month] Chislev. Again as in the case of the dating of Zechariah's opening sermon (Zech. 1:1) and the series of eight night visions (Zech. 1:7), the time notation has an *emphatic* position in the word order of the sentence, showing the importance of the fact that the events underlying this prophecy occurred in the fourth year of Darius, who by his decree so signally aided the construction of the temple. But the time notation in Zechariah 7:1 is interestingly different from that in Zechariah 1:1, 7. There the *complete* notation is stressed by emphatic word position, here *only part* of the notation, in the fourth year of Darius. After the year is first stated, a separating clause is inserted the

word of the Lord came unto Zechariah, demonstrating that this fact of the prophet's inspiration is very significant in relation to Darius' fourth year. The day and the month (unlike 1:1, 7) are not here featured with the year. Chislev corresponds to the month December.

The enunciation of the fact of the prophet's inspiration, already occurring here in 7:1, is anticipatory since this fact is repeated in 7:4. It is given before the recital of the event that called forth the question, for the answer of which the prophet needed special divine revelation.

2. *The City of Bethel Sends a Delegation of Inquiry* (Zech. 7:2). Now [the people of] Bethel sent Sharezer and Regemmelech and their men to entreat the favor of the Lord. The name Bethel ("house of God") does not refer to the temple then under construction at Jerusalem, as the A.V., Kimchi, Hengstenberg, and others assert, but to the well-known city located some dozen miles north of Jerusalem, and which had been an important religious center of the Ten Tribes from the time of Jeroboam I's setting up of the golden calves there till the fall of the Northern Kingdom (I Kings 12:28; 13:1; Amos 7:13).

Baron, Wright, Keil, Pusey, Feinberg, Leupold, and others are correct in construing Bethel in the nominative case and the subject of the sentence. Bethel [i.e., "the people of Bethel," a personification] sent. Making the word "Bethel" an adverbial accusative and referring it to "the house of God" (the temple), so that the idea

3 And to speak unto the priests which were in the house of the Lord of hosts, and to the prophets, saying, Should I weep in the fifth month, separating myself, as I have done these so many years?

3 and to speak unto the priests of the house of Jehovah of hosts, and to the prophets, saying, Should I weep in the fifth month, separating myself, as I have done these so many years?

is that "Sharezer and Regemmelech sent to the house of God" is an untenable rendering, inasmuch as the proper term for the temple, then about halfway finished, is *Beth Yahweh* ("the house of the Lord"), employed in this very context (7:3) and over 250 times in the Old Testament. *Beth 'Elohim* or *Beth ha'elohim*, "the house of God," occurs about 50 times, but *Beth 'el* does *not occur once*. The ancient versions also agree in making the reference to the city of Bethel, and the position of the word in its sentence grammatically supports it as nominative case, subject of the verb, and not as an adverbial accusative. Moreover, the city "Bethel" is used by metonymy for "the people of the city."

The name **Sharezer** is regarded as a Babylonian name, *sharuṣur*, "protect the king!" apparently meaning Bel or Nergal. It was therefore a name given to its possessor in the land of exile, as Daniel and his Hebrew colleagues were given foreign names in Babylon (Dan. 1:7). Sharezer interestingly was the name of one of Sennacherib's sons (II Kings 19:37; Isa. 37:38, cf. Nergal-sharezer, Jer. 39:3).

Regem-melech perhaps means "king's friend," (*regem*, "friend," Arabic *rajmun*, "friend" [cf. I Chron. 2:47] and *melek*, "king"). Both Sharezer and Regem-melech were important leaders at Bethel because they had a following which was dispatched by the people to accompany them on this particular mission to Jerusalem.

The purpose of the embassy is clearly stated. These Bethelites came in the first instance to **entreat the favor of the Lord** at Jerusalem (*leḥalloth 'eth peney Yhwh*, "to make sweet or pleasant the face of the Lord" from *ḥalah* [Arabic and Aramaic, "be sweet or pleasant"]). Thus the idiom means "to mollify, appease, entreat the favor of" (I Sam. 13:12; Prov. 19:6; Job 11:19; Zech. 8:21, 22).

This reference makes it plain that Bethel certainly did not supersede Jerusalem as the religious capital of the restoration community after the captivity. It is well known, moreover, that Bethelites returned with the remnant from Babylon (Ezra 2:28; Neh. 7:32; 11:31). The town was subsequently rebuilt. For the inhabitants to send a deputation of inquiry to Jerusalem at this time, as here indicated, would be a most natural thing.

3. *The Subject of the Inquiry Is Explained* (Zech. 7:3). **To say unto the priests who were of the house of the Lord of armies and unto the prophets, as follows: Shall I weep in the fifth month separating myself as I have done these so many years?** It is patent that Bethel acknowledged Jerusalem as the ecclesiastical center and owned the priests *associated with* (*'asher le*, "to belong to") the temple and the prophets Haggai and Zechariah and perhaps others as the *authenticated spokesmen* for the Lord on spiritual matters. Therefore, the city, through its representatives in the delegation, addresses its inquiry to them. Correctly they refer to the temple, then in process of construction, as *beth Yhwh* and not "house of God" (*beth 'el*). Compare verse 1.

The reason the first person is employed is because Bethel is personified, and speaks as *one man*, showing how universal in the city was the concern about the inquiry made, extending to *each* individual. **And**

Bethel sent . . . to say, Shall I weep . . . separating myself as I have done these so many years? The city speaks through its representatives and does so as a single individual. The question here graphically expresses an optative idea. "Would that I might be free of these customs."

Shall I weep? The verb "weep," *bakhah* (Arabic *bakā*, Assyrian *bakû*, "cry, bewail") is employed of shedding tears and showing other evidences of humiliation, joy, or grief (Gen. 42:24; Exod. 2:6; Isa. 30:19; Lam. 1:2). In this context the word is used of showing emotion expressing grief or humiliation commemorating a past national calamity. But it seemed foolish to continue to mourn over a past tragedy when present prosperity and progress were being enjoyed. Why should they go on grieving when their calamities had apparently passed away?

When the people apostatized from the Lord, incurring His chastisement, God had periodically issued a call for a national period of fasting (cf. Joel 1:13, 14). But such exercises were not meant to become set mechanical seasons of humiliation or annual fasts. The only injunction in the Mosaic law actually enjoining mourning was in connection with the day of atonement, and then only by implication. "Ye shall afflict your souls" (Lev. 23:27). These fasts, accordingly, were not God-ordained in their establishment, hence not divinely required, nor God-honoring, except as heart and life were expressing themselves in true spirituality by their observance.

But this emphatically was not the case with the inquiry from the city of Bethel. It is plain the question propounded was concerned with religious externalism instead of heartfelt reality. The Bethelites were exercised about a merely human institution. They were weary of what had become a meaningless ritualism which was occasioned by no evidence of true faith. The use of the expression, **so many years** (*zeh kammeh shanim*, an

adverbial accusative expressing duration of time) betrays their weariness of the ritualistic ceremony and their desire to be freed from its load, but with a good conscience.

The mourning **in the fifth month,** accompanied with fasting, to which they referred, marked the destruction of Jerusalem by the Babylonian army. From the seventh to the tenth day of the fifth month (August) Jerusalem was in flames when Nebuchadnezzar's army burned "the house of the Lord and the king's house, and all the houses of Jerusalem, and every great man's house with fire" (II Kings 25:9; Jer. 52:13). This was the first and foremost national calamity and had precedence over the other fasts, hence constituting a test case.

In Zechariah 8:19 other fasts are mentioned and added to this foremost one; namely, the fasts of the fourth, seventh, and tenth months, that of the seventh month alone being added to the list in Zechariah 7:5. The fast of the seventh month marked the anniversary of the murder of Gedaliah (Jer. 41:1–18; II Kings 25:22–26), whom the king of Babylon had made governor over the land after the captivity.

The fast of the fourth month (Tammuz) commemorated the breaching of the walls of Jerusalem during the final siege by the Babylonians (II Kings 25:3; Jer. 39:2–4). The fast of the tenth month (Tebeth) memorialized the beginning of the siege of Jerusalem (II Kings 25:1; Jer. 39:1).

The ritual observed in these days of grief and humiliation included "weeping" and "separating one's self" (*hinnazer*, an infinitive absolute taking the place of the finite verb, from the root *nazar*, "to consecrate, dedicate, separate" in a religious and ceremonial sense, Arabic *nadhara*, "make a vow"). In the *nifal*, as here, the word means "to dedicate oneself," for example, "to shame" (i.e., Baal, Hos. 9:10); "hold oneself sacredly aloof from (*min*) apostasy" (Ezek. 14:7); from "the holy things of Israel" (Lev.

4 Then came the word of the Lord of hosts unto me, saying,
5 Speak unto all the people of the land, and to the priests, saying, When ye fasted and mourned in the fifth and seventh month, even those seventy years, did ye at all fast unto me, even to me?
6 And when ye did eat, and when ye did drink, did not ye eat for yourselves, and drink for yourselves?

---

4 Then came the word of Jehovah of hosts unto me, saying,
5 Speak unto all the people of the land, and to the priests, saying, When ye fasted and mourned in the fifth and in the seventh month, even these seventy years, did ye at all fast unto me, even to me?
6 And when ye eat, and when ye drink, do not ye eat for yourselves, and drink for yourselves?

22:2). In the present passage the word means "consecrate [separate] oneself by fasting." Thus a Nazarite (*nazîr*) is "one consecrated or devoted to the Lord by a vow involving abstinence from intoxicants, from touching a corpse, and from cutting his hair (Judg. 13:5; 16:17; Num. 6:2; Amos 2:11, 12). Since the Bethelites had utterly lost the sense of voluntary dedication to the Lord in the matter of fasting, their legalistic observance of the rite was devoid of any glory to God or spiritual benefit to themselves.

II. THE SELFISHNESS BEHIND THE QUESTION IS EXPOSED (Zech. 7: 4–7)

The visit of the delegation from Bethel with its perplexity about continuing a ritualistic period of mourning offered the prophet Zechariah not only an occasion for important spiritual instruction to the people of that day, but gave rise to circumstances that were to form the basis for far-reaching prophecies dealing with the nation's future. In fact, the prophetic aspects of chapters 7 and 8 constitute the same basic predictions as were comprehended in the eight night visions, but spring out of a historical circumstance and are couched in plain, unabstruse language, rather than conveyed in apocalyptic symbols, as in the case of the visions.

1. *The Rebuke of Meaningless Ritualism* (Zech. 7:4–6). **Then the word**

of the Lord of armies came to me, saying: (5) Speak to all the people of the land and to the priests as follows: When you fasted and mourned in the fifth and in the seventh [months] these past seventy years, did you really fast to me? (6) And when you were eating and when you were drinking, was it not you yourselves who were eating and you yourselves who were drinking?

These words constitute a well-deserved rebuke not only to the questioners from Bethel, but also to the priests and people of the land in general. But the prophet is extremely cautious to make plain the fact that the rebuke is the Lord's and not his in any sense. Accordingly, although the thought of the prophet's receiving a special divine communication for the occasion had already been announced in 7:1, it is here repeated. God's servants must be careful to administer rebuke where rebuke is needed, but must always be certain that it is by divine direction and not the result of personal pique or selfish animosity.

Moreover, emphasis on the special revelation of God's word to the prophet in this instance is required by the apparent unfitness of the priests (to whom the Bethelites initially addressed their problem) to give a satisfactory answer since they themselves were affected by the empty ritualism. The rebuke is administered not only (1) to **all the people of the land,** i.e., the rank and file of the population of the country, but (2) primarily to them as **the priests.** These two categories comprised the entire nation, and this division of the populace is employed because the priests were the particular class who ought to have had the answer. They were therefore the persons from whom advice was sought. Because they did not possess the answer, the prophet receives a divine communication, and that is why this feature is emphatically stressed in the account. Zechariah's reply was to the effect that **the priests** and **the people of the land** needed a word of correction, as well as the people of Bethel, who raised the question.

It is to be carefully noted, however, that the actual question the Bethelites broached was not the significant issue. The problem of observing or not observing man-made seasons of humiliation and self-abnegation was in itself a very minor matter. But the episode was far-reaching in its ramifications in that it was symptomatic of a deeper problem of attitude and the barometer of a serious evil that was infesting the nation. The matter of the fast and the desire to be freed of its burden merely pointed out the evil itself. This, in turn, is the reason why the inquiry of the Bethelite delegation is not answered directly throughout chapters 7 and 8, and why the question of whether they henceforth kept or did not keep the fasts in question is inconsequential, and accordingly left unsettled by Zechariah's account.

The sinful attitude revealed by the question of the fast was that it was not observed for God's glory (vs. 5), but purely for self (vs. 6). It was therefore mechanically formalistic and external. It was of a piece with the empty ritualism powerfully denounced by Isaiah in his day (Isa. 1:10-15). This was true despite the fact that the practice had been going on **these past seventy years** (cf. "these so many years" of 7:3). This latter expression points to the fact that a considerable span of years had passed. The former

notice gives the exact time span. Since it was the fourth year of Darius (518 B.C.) and the fourth day of the ninth month, and since Jerusalem had been destroyed in 587 B.C., more than sixty-nine of the seventy years of Jeremiah's prophecy (Jer. 25:11) had already been completed. By the time the next fast lamenting Jerusalem's destruction came around, the full seventy years would be consummated.

During these seventy years the Lord could ask, **Did you really fast to me?** Several grammatical considerations accentuate the incisiveness of this query: (1) The fact the Lord Himself through the prophet posits the question (vss. 4, 5). (2) Introduction of the question itself by the interrogative particle *ha*. (3) The use of the *first* personal suffixed pronoun *tsamtuni*, **Did you fast to me?** (4) The emphasis on this personal element, **Did you fast to me — even me** (*'ani*), where the pronominal suffix is reinforced by the separate pronoun following it appositionally to intensify its force. (5) By the use of the infinitive absolute to intensify the finite verb "fast," *tsom tsamtuni*, **Did you really fast?** Was there any self-denial in the practice or any thought of God's glory in their ritual? (6) The use of the perfect *tsamtuni* (completed action), moreover, indicates that the defect exposed had its beginning from the time they started the fast, and hence was of long standing.

Fasting *to the Lord* would have been an exercise of self-humiliation, not for self-interest, but for God's glory, not a legalistic asceticism, but an act of loving service to render the body more susceptible to the higher interests of the soul. It could have been a healthful reminder of the deserved affliction suffered at the hands of the Lord, and a token of genuine and continual repentance in the light of God's chastisement. Such self-humiliation would have been highly profitable and would have been consonant with the general principle of conduct laid down

7 Should ye not hear the words which the Lord hath cried by the former prophets, when Jerusalem was inhabited and in prosperity, and the cities thereof round about her, when men inhabited the south and the plain?

7 Should ye not hear the words which Jehovah cried by the former prophets, when Jerusalem was inhabited and in prosperity, and the cities thereof round about her, and the South and the lowland were inhabited?

in the New Testament. "Whether you eat or drink, or whatever you do, do all to the glory of God" (I Cor. 10:31).

Instead of their observance being on a high plane of action, the Lord through the prophet lays His finger upon the root of their failure. They were all along doing or not doing (imperfect tense expressing incomplete action in past time) what they did for selfish reasons. And when you were eating and when you were drinking, was it not you yourselves ['attem, subject of a nominal clause] who were the ones who were eating [ha'okelim, articular participle, predicate of a nominal clause] and you yourselves ['attem, subject] the ones who were drinking [hashshothim, predicate]? The negative interrogative halo' dramatically sets forth their sin in a rhetorical question, implying the answer "yes" as a confession of guilt. "Yes, it was you, who were doing the eating and the drinking! God had no adequate place in your mechanical and external ritual!"

Incisively the Hebrew focuses attention upon the complete self-centeredness of the people's fasting and "mourning." Sapodh is an infinitive absolute used in lively fashion to continue what was begun by the finite verb, the root saphadh meaning "to lament, wail" (Assyrian sapâdu, "mourn," Amharic noun form signifying "a dirge"). Orientals, being demonstrative, "wail," "lament" with profuse tears, loud crying, and energetic smitings on the breast (Gen. 23:2; I Kings 13:29; Jer. 16:5; Isa. 32:12; Eccl. 12:5; Mic. 1:8; Zech. 12:10, 12).

2. The Exhortation to Heed the Word of God (Zech. 7:7). [Should you not obey] the words which the Lord proclaimed through the former prophets, when Jerusalem was peacefully inhabited and prosperous and her towns round about her with the Negeb and the Shepelah peacefully inhabited? The prophet's initial reply to the questioners is here couched in a very forceful question, the incisiveness of which is enhanced by its being elliptical. The verb is presupposed ("Should you not obey"), since the words ('eth haddevarim) constitute the definite objective accusative, indicated in Hebrew by the sign of such an accusative 'eth, which is not translatable.

Zechariah would say, "The important thing is 'the words!' Should you not obey them?" Moreover the words which they are challenged to obey are not new, but the old words "which the former prophets proclaimed." Isaiah and Jeremiah, in particular, are meant, but also included are Joel, Amos, Micah, and others. All through his prophecies Zechariah echoes and features these words of the former prophets. Now he would enjoin the necessity of obeying these injunctions upon his interrogators, concerned as they were with an empty ritual. The all-important matter is heeding the voice and the word of God. Without this no religious observance, no matter how punctiliously observed, is of any value. These words long ago constituted the answer to this and every question of the Bethelites or anyone else. Compare I Samuel 15:22, 23; Deuteronomy 10:12, 13; Isaiah 58: 3–12.

The prophet would remind the people too of the happy and prosperous condition of Judah and Jerusalem in the days when the Lord was blessing them with His words through the

8 And the word of the Lord came unto Zechariah, saying,
9 Thus speaketh the Lord of hosts, saying, Execute true judgment, and shew mercy and compassions every man to his brother:
10 And oppress not the widow, nor the fatherless, the stranger, nor the poor; and let none of you imagine evil against his brother in your heart.

---

8   And the word of Jehovah came unto Zechariah, saying,
9   Thus hath Jehovah of hosts spoken, saying, Execute true judgment, and show kindness and compassion, every man to his brother;
10   and oppress not the widow, nor the fatherless, the sojourner, nor the poor and let none of you devise evil against his brother in your heart.

---

prophets (*beyad*, "by the agency or instrumentality" of the prophets). Compare *beyad* in Judges 6:36; I Samuel 11:7; 16:20, especially as it is used of the Lord's speaking *by the agency of* the prophets (Exod. 9:35; Lev. 8:36; 10:11; Num. 4:37; 10:13; II Kings 9:36; II Chron. 1:17; Neh. 8:14).

The prophet draws his illustration of the need of obeying God's word in terms of what the restoration community, poor and struggling as it was, was most acutely sensitive; namely, the poverty and desolation of their city and country. They must be impressed that all this calamity had been the result of their disobedience to God's Word. Let them contrast this wretched state of affairs with their former blessedness when Jerusalem *was* (1) peacefully **inhabited** (*yosheveth*, participle denoting a continuous unbroken condition; cf. Zech. 2:4 [8]; 9:5; 12:6; 14:10, 11); (2) and **prosperous** (*shelewah*, feminine adjective, "quiet, at ease," referring to persons; "prosperous," used of a city; cf. Job 16:12; Jer. 49:31; I Chron. 4:40); (3) when she had **her towns round about her,** as a city of her rank and importance deserved; (4) when **the Negeb** [*hannegev*, i.e., the Southland south of the central Judaean highland beyond Beersheba] was **peacefully inhabited;** (5) as well as the **Shepelah,** where the Judaean highlands on the west of Judah sloped down to the Palestine Plain (see G. E. Wright and F. Filson, *The Westminster Historical Atlas to the Bible,* plate 1).

In the light of this picture of the former extent and prosperity of Judah when the Lord was honored, the prophet would remind the people that their restoration was still very incomplete as compared with their former happy condition. If concern was to be exercised over a dead ritual rather than over spiritual reality, the people might well despair as they faced the Herculean tasks of reconstruction ahead.

III. THE CALL TO REPENTANCE IS ANNOUNCED (Zech. 7:8-14)

This section has a twofold emphasis. It connects with the past and it ties in with the present. The basic mistake of the pre-exilic nation had been its failure to obey the word of the Lord, with the resultant captivity. The same fundamental blunder, the prophet asserts (vss. 4-7), is being made by the restoration community. It was lapsing into the same sin that wrought the ruin of their fathers.

1. *The Divine Command to Put the Word of the Lord into Practice* (Zech. 7:8-10). **Then the word of the Lord came unto Zechariah as follows.** (9) **Thus the Lord of armies says, Render a judicial decision based on truth and practice kindness and compassion one toward another.** (10) **Neither oppress the widow nor the orphan, the transient nor the poor, and do not let any of you devise a wrong in your heart against another.**

Once again Zechariah in words renewed to himself by the direct inspiration of God's Spirit gives the gist of the message of the former prophets. Once again, as in 7:4, **Thus says the Lord** forms the introduction to his authoritative declaration. If the wayward people and priests are to obey the word of God, they must hear it plainly and unequivocally. Hence the stress on inspiration (vs. 8) and divine authority (vs. 9).

It is noteworthy that man's duties to man are stressed. The reason for this is that such duties not only presuppose man's duties toward God, but constitute the concrete and visible proof of the reality of the man-to-God relationship. The man-to-God relationship is thus demonstrated practically by the man-to-man relationship. Therefore, these practical virtues from the second table of the law are featured.

Leupold (*Exposition of Zechariah*, p. 136), Henderson (*The Minor Prophets*, p. 400), Chambers, (*Zechariah* in J. P. Lange's *Commentary*, Vol. 14, p. 56) construe the perfect *'amar* in a past sense. Says Leupold (*loc. cit.*), the prophet "is referring to a speaking of God in the past, namely, prior to the Exile, as comparison with verses 11, 12 shows." While this is a possible interpretation, the tense is better to be taken in a *present completed* sense, as in the A.V. and R.S.V. **Thus says the Lord.** . . . (1) Since the formula occurs over and over in this sense in Zechariah, it is unlikely that an exception is to be noted here. (2) Moreover, the moral principles enunciated have an omnitemporal application, equally valid for Zechariah's hearers, as for the pre-exilic sinners. (3) This interpretation does not clash with the reference to the pre-exilic offenders made in verses 11, 12. It includes them, but embraces more than them, comprehending the sinners in the restored community as well, in fact, *primarily*. (4) It would not be necessary to lay the unusual emphasis upon special revelation and consequent authority in verses 8 and 9 if the prophet were merely recapitulating what the former prophets had said to an earlier generation and not

enforcing the validity of these words *for his own time*. (5) In verses 11–14 the prophet is merely recounting the disaster that overtook the former generation in their disobedience to the word as a warning of a similar fate for disobedience *to the same* word now enjoined upon the new generation.

The command involves four important injunctions as a practical test of spiritual reality and genuine practical godliness of life: (1) Render a judicial decision based on truth. (2) Practice kindness and compassion in general conduct. (3) Do not oppress the helpless — the widow, orphan, transient, or the poor. (4) Do not cogitate evil in the heart against a fellow human being.

The first injunction is literally, "judge," *shephoṭu*, (imperative) a "judgment of truth," *mishpaṭ 'emeth*. This means a judicial decision *characterized by truth*, i.e., based upon objective evidence, utter impartiality, and the entire absence of falsehood or dishonesty (Ezek. 18:8). In the verbal clause the object (*mishpaṭ 'emeth*) comes first in the sentence, before the verb, thus stressing it. **Render a true decision** (in contrast to a false one).

The second command, **practice** [literally "do" or "work" (imperative)] **kindness** [graciousness, *hesedh*] **and compassion** [*raḥamim*, intensive plural with singular meaning] **one with another,** also emphasizes the object which, as in the first clause, also comes first in this verbal clause. **Practice kindness and compassion one with another.** Compare Micah 6:8. The word **compassion,** *raḥamim*, seems to be from *reḥem*, "womb," and is apparently a denominative originally referring to the "brotherly feeling" characterizing those born from the same womb (Gen. 43:14; I Kings 8:50; Amos 1:11; Prov. 12:10). This comes very near the "love" described in I Corinthians 13.

The third injunction is a negative

11 But they refused to hearken, and pulled away the shoulder and stopped their ears, that they should not hear.

12 Yea, they made their hearts as an adamant stone, lest they should hear the law, and the words which the Lord of hosts hath sent in his spirit by the former prophets: therefore came a great wrath from the Lord of hosts.

11   But they refused to hearken, and pulled away the shoulder, and stopped their ears, that they might not hear.

12   Yea, they made their hearts as an adamant stone, lest they should hear the law, and the words which Jehovah of hosts had sent by his Spirit by the former prophets: therefore there came great wrath from Jehovah of hosts.

command (jussive) like the first two, stressing the object, **Do not oppress the widow or the orphan, the transient or the poor.** Each of these represent a helpless member of society, particularly exposed to the unscrupulosity of godless men (Exod. 22:22; 23:6–9; Lev. 19:15–18; Deut. 10:18, 19; 24:14; Jer. 7:6), and each is therefore signalled out as not to be taken advantage of in their helplessness. Those who do so plainly manifest their hypocrisy and godlessness.

The last injunction goes deeper than the first three and searches out the sin that lies at the basis of them, but which is much more subtly hidden and undiscernible. **Let none of you devise evil against one another in your heart** (W. H. Lowe, *Zechariah*, p. 70). The Hebrew phrase, *'ish 'aḥiv*, is the objective genitive (Lowe) in construct relation with *ra 'ath*, and so the entire construction means "evil against one another." This whole expression as the object stands first in the verbal sentence, and is accordingly *emphatic* by position.

2. *The Refusal of the Pre-exilic People to Obey the Word* (Zech. 7:11, 12). **But they refused to give heed and offered a stubborn shoulder and made their ears dull that they might not hear. (12) And they made their heart adamant so as not to hear the law and the words which the Lord of armies had sent by his Spirit through the agency of the former prophets, so that there was great wrath from the Lord of armies.**

With penetrating sharpness the prophet depicts the rejection of the Word of God by pre-exilic Israel. "A variety of expressions is used to convey the thought of obstinate rebellion: the rebellious shoulder, the heavy ears, and the adamant heart" (Feinberg, *God Remembers*, p. 124). The figure **offered a rebellious shoulder** is taken "from the conduct of an ox or heifer refusing the yoke" (Chambers, *op. cit.*, p. 57), as in Hosea 4:16 and Nehemiah 9:29. The term **stubborn** or "recusant," *sorareth*, is a feminine participle from *sarar*, "be stubborn" or "rebellious," Assyrian *sararu* (Deut. 21:18; Isa. 30:1; 65:2; Jer. 5:23). The idea is an animal intractably refusing to be bound by the constraint of a yoke and continually rebelling against any imposed authority. So pre-exilic Israel refused to give heed to God's word, being recalcitrant against its control and authority over the life.

The figure **they made their ears heavy** suggests that they deliberately refused to listen to God and accordingly were responsible for their auditory senses becoming "dull" and "unresponsive" (cf. Isa. 6:10), although the hardening process was actually the judicial judgment of God upon them. The idea of their refusing God's word was that **they might not hear**, *mishshemoa'*, the infinitive prefixed by a *min* of separation (Gesenius Kautzsch, 119:3d) expressing negative purpose (cf. vs. 12 for the identical construction).

The third figure is metaphorical. **They made their hearts adamant.** The comparison to an impenetrably hard

13 Therefore it is come to pass, that as he cried, and they would not hear; so they cried, and I would not hear, saith the Lord of hosts;
14 But I scattered them with a whirlwind among all the nations whom they knew not. Thus the land was desolate after them, that no man passed through nor returned: for they laid the pleasant land desolate.

13   And it is come to pass that, as he cried, and they would not hear, so they shall cry, and I will not hear, said Jehovah of hosts;
14   but I will scatter them with a whirlwind among all the nations which they have not known. Thus the land was desolate after them, so that no man passed through nor returned; for they laid the pleasant land desolate.

substance ("emery" or "diamond," Akkadian *ashmur*), is a metaphor and not a simile, "*as* adamant." The rendering adamant, *shamir*, is better than "diamond" because it suggests "only that point for which the term is introduced, namely, its impenetrable hardness" (Chambers, *op. cit.*, p. 57). Jeremiah (17:1) refers to the "sin of Judah" being "written with a pen of iron with the point of adamant" (A.V. "diamond"). Ezekiel speaks of "adamant harder than flint" (Ezek. 3:9). The substance referred to was so hard "it would cut rocks; it could not be graven itself, or receive the characters of God" (Pusey, *Minor Prophets*, II, p. 381). This is how the pre-exilic Israelites "made" their hearts (*samu* from *sim*, "make, constitute, set, place" with two accusatives; cf. I Sam. 8:1; II Kings 10:8; Neh. 9:7).

The word hearts is actually singular (*lebh*, "heart") and has reference to "the inner man" or the soul, comprising mind, affections, and will (Deut. 4:29; 6:5; 10:12; Josh. 22:5; I Kings 2:4; 14:8; Ps. 86:11). When these rejecters of the word made their *heart* adamant, they constituted their *minds* and *wills* hard and impervious to God's voice. The Hebrew word order emphasizes the object, Their heart [object] they made adamant (second accusative).

The aggravated wickedness of the fathers appears in the fact that "not through infirmity, but of set purpose, they hardened themselves" (Pusey, *in loc.*). Their avowed aim was not to

hear (*mishshemoa'*, same construction as in verse 11, *q.v.*) the law and the words which the Lord of armies sent by his Spirit through the former prophets. The Holy Spirit was the chief agent, by his Spirit (*beruḥo*, the preposition *beth* indicating primary agency). The inspired prophets were the human or secondary instruments (*beyadh*, "by the hand of," as in Zechariah 7:7, i.e., "through the human instrumentality of," Exod. 9:35; Lev. 8:36; II Chron. 1:17; Neh. 8:14; 9:14).

The law, *torah*, recalls Moses, one of the greatest of the prophets, and must be included in this reference, both as mediated by the great lawgiver and as consistently enjoined by all the prophets. The passage (vss. 11, 12), also suggests a progressive spiritual deterioration. (1) They wilfully refused to heed the Word of God. (2) They offered a recusant shoulder, rebelling like an untamed animal to the yoke, and stubbornly turned away from the inner motions of God's Spirit or by general chastisements when God would have brought them to the yoke of obedience. (3) They lapsed into complete obduracy, when their adamantine hearts could not be impressed with promises or threats. Accordingly, there was no other divine recourse but the visitation of judgment. Therefore, came great wrath from the Lord of armies, the prophet returning to that stern note of warning of God's wrath (1:7) which his introductory sermon contained and which prepared the way for his visions of future mercy. There it was "wrath" (*qetseph*), here it is **great wrath** (*qetseph gadhol*).

3. *The Results of the Refusal of the Pre-exilic People to Obey the Word* (Zech. 7:13, 14). **Therefore it came to pass just as he called, but they did not hear, so they will call and I will not hear, says the Lord of armies, (14) and I will scatter them among all the nations, which they have not known. And the land was made desolate after them, so that no one passed through or returned, and they made the pleasant land a desolation.**

Besides the general result of God's chastening wrath coming upon the pre-exilic fathers (vs. 12) Zechariah names several other resultant calamities that overtook that disobedient generation. They were cursed with powerlessness in prayer (vs. 13). They were scattered among the nations like the whirlwind (vs. 14). Their pleasant land became desolate (vs. 14).

Therefore it came to pass [the *waw consecutive* is that of logical result] **just as** he called **but they did not heed, so they will call but I will not heed, says the Lord of armies** (vs. 13). The *inevitable result* of their disobedience was powerlessness in prayer. The **just as**, *ka'asher*, introduces the protasis, in which the prophet is the speaker. The **so**, *ken*, however, introduces the apodosis, which consists of the Lord's words, **Just as he cried, and they did not hear, So they call and I will not hear, says the Lord of armies.** Thus, as Chambers notes, "the writer passes from narration, and cites the *ipsissima verba* of Jehovah" (*op. cit.*, p. 56).

As Zechariah continues to describe how the captivity came about as the result of the failure to hear the Word of the Lord, he describes it as a merited retaliation in terms of the *ius talionis, as the crime so the punishment* (Leupold, *op. cit.*, p. 139). The **great wrath** of the Lord was manifested toward them in essence for seventy years when He turned a deaf ear to their cries, as they had previously turned

a deaf ear to Him when He called.

Jeremiah had forewarned of this awful fate. "Therefore thus saith Jehovah, Behold, I will bring evil upon them, which they shall not be able to escape; and they *shall cry unto me, but I will not hearken unto them*" (Jer. 11:11; cf. 11:14; 14:12). Isaiah, likewise, cried out, "When you spread forth your hands, I will hide my eyes from you; yea, *when you make many prayers, I will not hear;* your hands are full of blood" (Isa. 1:15). Solomon also had warned, "When your fear cometh as a storm, and your calamity cometh as a whirlwind, when distress and anguish come upon you. Then will they call upon me, but *I will not answer;* they will seek me diligently, but they shall not find me" (Prov. 1:27, 28).

Besides the curse of ineffectiveness in prayer, the people were to be scattered like the whirlwind among the nations which they had not known (vs. 14a). The Lord, introduced as the speaker in the preceding verse, **So they shall cry, and I will not hear . . .** continues in this verse, **But I will scatter them among all the nations which they have not known.**

The verb **scatter** is from the root, "to storm, to rage" (Assyrian *sharu*, "wind," Arabic *sa'ara*, "excite, inflame, be mad, insane"). The noun *sa'ar* means "a tempest" (Amos 1:14; Jer. 23:19; Jonah 1:4). The verb as used by Zechariah in the *piel* signifies, "I [the Lord] will *whirl* or *storm* them away [i.e., *hurl* them by a storm-wind] upon the nations." The expression accordingly is very strong, and denotes a violent scattering, like a mighty hurricane or tornado would scatter objects. The Masoretic Text points this verb with *simple waw (we'esa-'arem)*. "And I *will hurl* them." If this pointing is original, it "summarizes what God had threatened before it came" (Leupold, *op. cit.*, p. 140). However, numerous sources (Marti, *Das Dodekapropheton,* p. 424), point with *waw consecutive,* "And I *scattered* them," making it a narrative account of what happened, instead of a warning of what would happen.

The clause describing where the Lord scattered His disobedient people can be rendered in two ways because of the ambiguous peculiarity of the Hebrew relative 'asher, "who, which, what." (1) "I will scatter them among the nations who did not know them," where 'asher is a pure relative (not prefixed in this case). (2) "I will scatter them among the nations whom they did not know" (where the 'asher is a nota bene sign giving relative significance to the pronominal element following it). This latter interpretation is preferred. What made the captivity so unbearable was to be hurled out among nations who were complete strangers to Israel (Deut. 28:36; Jer. 16:13).

After the direct words of the Lord, the description of the complete desolation of the land follows. **And the land** [Palestine] **was made desolate** [nashammah] **after them.** The verb is nifal (passive) from the root shamem, "be desolate, deserted, empty," used of roads (Lev. 26:22); lands (Jer. 12:11; Ezek. 29:12; 30:7); cities (Isa. 54:3).

A further detail of the desolation of the land is given in the expression, **from one passing out** [participles] **and coming back in,** where the preposition min, "from," is used as a negative particle (privative), in the sense of negative result — "so that [there will be] no one going out and coming in." This is a picture of complete emptiness and desolation. The same peculiar expression is used of Alexander's conquest (Zech. 9:8), and is one of the internal evidences binding together the first part of the prophecy (chapters 1–8) with the last part (chapters 9–14).

The concluding passage of this chapter apparently lays the guilt of the whole desolation of the land upon the disobedient fathers themselves, who are evidently the subject of the sentence. **They made** [yasimu] **the pleasant land a desolation.** It is possible, however, that **they** is the third

masculine plural indefinite, and the meaning is simply "the pleasant land was made a desolation." But the context and the stronger meaning favor the first rendering, inasmuch as it was really the fathers' sins that caused the captivity and the desolation of their land.

The land of Canaan in its beauty and prosperity is graphically named **the pleasant land** ('erets ḥemdah, i.e., "land of desire, delight," from root ḥamadh, "desire, delight in, take pleasure in"). This designation of Palestine in its desirability is reflected in Jeremiah 3:19: "I sought how I could set you among my sons, and give you a pleasant land ['erets ḥemdah], a heritage most beauteous of all nations." The Psalmist also employs this designation. "Then they despised the pleasant land ['erets ḥemdah], they believed not his word" (Ps. 106:24). Daniel uses a different but similar term when he calls Palestine "the glorious land" ['erets hatstsevi], "land of beauty" (Dan. 11:16, 41).

But what about the delegation from Bethel? Did they have their question concerning observing the fast answered? In one sense, "yes." In another, "no." Actually their original question was left unanswered. But by diverting their minds from the comparatively insignificant point it comprehended to issues of far greater moment, their question was really answered indirectly in the matter with which they were so forcefully brought face to face; namely, the issue of indifference and disobedience to the Word of God in the midst of them. In being concerned about observing or not observing a lifeless ritual, are they thereby giving evidence that they were beginning to react to the Word of God in the same way their fathers did? Let them take heed. Observing fast days was an unimportant matter. Obeying the Word of God was the all-important question that faced them. This larger issue, if faced honestly, would automatically answer the smaller problem.

CHAPTER EIGHT

WHEN THE FASTS BECOME JOYFUL FEASTS

ISRAEL'S EVENTUAL RESTORATION TO FULL MILLENNIAL BLESSING

(ZECH. 8:1-23)

I. THE PRESENT PARTIAL RESTORA-
TION THE HARBINGER OF AN
EVENTUAL FULL RESTORATION OF
ISRAEL (Zech. 8:1-8)

1. *The Future Full Restoration
Assured by the Word of God
and the Love of God* (Zech.
8:1, 2)
2. *The Results of the Full Restoration of Israel* (Zech. 8:3-6)
   (1) The Lord's return (vs. 3a)
   (2) The permanent divine
   presence (vs. 3b)
   (3) The exaltation of Jerusalem (vs. 3c)
   (4) The great increase of the
   peace and security of Jerusalem (vss. 4, 5)
   (5) The exemplification of divine power (vs. 6)
3. *The Promise of Future Regathering and Full Restoration
Is Repeated* (Zech. 8:7, 8)

II. THE ENCOURAGEMENT AMID THE
WOES OF THE PRESENT PARTIAL
RESTORATION (Zech. 8:9-17)

1. *The Subjects of the Encouragement* (Zech. 8:9)
2. *The Reasons for the People's
Discouragement* (Zech. 8:10)
3. *Details of the People's Encouragement* (Zech. 8:11-15)
   (1) God terminates His controversy with them (vs. 11)

(2) God promises them prosperity (vs. 12)
(3) God reverses their fortunes (vs. 13)
(4) The Lord Himself determines to do them good
(vss. 14, 15)
4. *The Use the People Are to
Make of Their Encouragement*
(Zech. 8:16, 17)
   (1) They are to deal strictly in
   truth (vs. 16a)
   (2) They are to render fair
   and peace-producing judicial decisions (vs. 16b)
   (3) They are not to meditate
   evil against each other
   (vs. 17a)
   (4) They are not to tolerate
   perjury (vs. 17b)
   (5) They are to bear in mind
   the reason for avoiding
   these sins (vs. 17c)

III. FULL FUTURE RESTORATION TO
MILLENNIAL JOY AND DIVINE
FAVOR (Zech. 8:18-23)

1. *Jewish Fasts Will One Day
Give Way to Millennial Feasts*
(Zech. 8:18, 19)
2. *Gentiles Will Eagerly Seek the
Lord in the Kingdom Era*
(Zech. 8:20-22)
3. *The Jew Millennially Restored
Will Enjoy Special Divine
Favor* (Zech. 8:23)

CHAPTERS 7 and 8 of Zechariah's
prophecy form a unit. Chapter 7 gives
the negative part of the answer to the
question of the national fasts. Chapter
8 presents the positive reply. Chapter

8 is a continuation of the preceding
chapter. Chapter 7 is actually a call
to repentance, reminding the people
that their sorrows and calamities were
the direct results of their transgres-

132

1 Again the word of the Lord of hosts came to me, saying,
2 Thus saith the Lord of hosts; I was jealous for Zion with great jealousy, and I was jealous for her with great fury.

---

1   And the word of Jehovah of hosts came to me, saying,
2   Thus saith Jehovah of hosts: I am jealous for Zion with great jealousy, and I am jealous for her with great wrath.

---

sions. This negative part of the answer is in an important sense preparatory to the positive portion. In chapter 8 the prophet proceeds to reveal the glorious fact that in the future Israel's fasts shall change into feasts, and the people shall enjoy the good things promised to them by the Lord, but they must give earnest heed to the Word of God spoken through the prophets. The nation's restoration to full kingdom blessing is assured by God's redemptive purposes, but there must be the spiritual renovation of the nation to enter into and enjoy these divinely predetermined favors. But God who will give them, will by His sovereign grace and power effect the spiritual change in the nation.

Lest anyone should stagger at the promises of God through unbelief, the series of panoramic promises in this chapter are appended by, **Thus saith the Lord of armies.** Over ten times in this section this expression is met with. Compare verses 2, 3, 4, 6, 7, 14, 19, 20, 23. Some twenty-two times occurs the name of the Lord (Yahweh). So wonderful are these promises, so outstanding are the blessings prophesied to Israel, that the unbelief of man will not accept them. The very repetition of the divine promise in this section emphasizes the certainty of their fulfillment and would rebuke man's unbelief.

In the blessed assurances of the bright future of Jerusalem and the people of Israel, the question concerning the fasts is answered in a larger and more glowing way than the petitioners in chapter 7 had ever dreamed. God's strange work is judgment. His delight is to bless His people. The judgments have been

predicted, and now the time for blessing has come, and the love of God overflows for Israel, His people.

I. THE PRESENT PARTIAL RESTORATION THE HARBINGER OF AN EVENTUAL FULL RESTORATION OF ISRAEL (Zech. 8:1–8)

As chapter 7, particularly verses 8–14, looks back into the past and applies the lessons taught by history to the contemporary scene of its day, so chapter 8 envisions the future, but applies the lessons taught by prophecy to the contemporary scene of the prophet's own day. Chapter 8 blends the near and the far. It surveys the present partial restoration of the nation, although accompanied with much trial, poverty, and hardship, as the precursor of the grand final reestablishment of Israel in kingdom blessing. Moreover, it employs the magnificent far-distant millennial hope as the basis for the immediate inspiration and encouragement of the people of that day affected as they were by the exigencies of the restored community. Thus the chapter teaches the important lesson that the prophetic Scriptures should always be expounded with a moral and spiritual appeal and challenge to present-day auditors or readers.

1. *Future Full Restoration Assured by the Word of God and the Love of God* (Zech. 8:1, 2). **Then the word of the Lord of armies came, saying, The Lord of armies says thus: I am acutely jealous for Zion and with intense passionate heat I am jealous for her.**

This passage dramatically and cogently sets forth God's undying love for Israel in the following ways: (1) *By divine revelation.* **Then the word of the Lord of armies came.** (2) *By*

3 Thus saith the Lord; I am returned unto Zion, and will dwell in the midst of Jerusalem: and Jerusalem shall be called a city of truth; and the mountain of the Lord of hosts the holy mountain.
4 Thus saith the Lord of hosts; There shall yet old men and old women dwell in the streets of Jerusalem, and every man with his staff in his hand for very age.
5 And the streets of the city shall be full of boys and girls playing in the streets thereof.
6 Thus saith the Lord of hosts; If it be marvellous in the eyes of the remnant of this people in these days, should it also be marvellous in mine eyes? saith the Lord of hosts.

---

3   Thus saith Jehovah: I am returned unto Zion, and will dwell in the midst of Jerusalem: and Jerusalem shall be called The city of truth; and the mountain of Jehovah of hosts, The holy mountain.
4   Thus saith Jehovah of hosts: There shall yet old men and old women dwell in the streets of Jerusalem, every man with his staff in his hand for very age.
5   And the streets of the city shall be full of boys and girls playing in the streets thereof.
6   Thus saith Jehovah of hosts: If it be marvellous in the eyes of the remnant of this people in those days, should it also be marvellous in mine eyes? saith Jehovah of hosts.

---

divine inspiration. Zechariah is the human agent. (3) *By consequent authority.* The word of the Lord of armies . . . the Lord of armies says thus. The *repetition* of this divine appellation The Lord of armies buttresses the divine assurance behind the assertion. The name itself presents "Yahweh Sebaoth, God of the battled array of Israel" (I Sam. 17:45), and who, as the Marshaller both of the armies of the terrestrial and celestial spheres, fights for Israel against her enemies, notably in the great final deliverance (Zech. 12:1-9; 14:1-7; Rev. 19:11-17). (4) *By extremely emphatic assertion.* I am jealous, a characteristic present perfect, *qinne'thi*, being emphatically first in its clause, and being itself a strong word, denoting arduous, zealous passion, "from color produced in the face by deep emotion" (Brown, Driver, and Briggs), Arabic root "become intensely red," Aramaic, Ethiopic "be zealous, jealous." Compare "the jealous God" (*'el qanna'*), as the one punishing those who hate Him or His people (Exod. 20:5; Deut. 5:9), which is evidently the thought in Zechariah

8:2. As "the jealous God" He also demands exclusive worship and service (Exod. 34:14; Deut. 4:23, 24; 6:14, 15). The English word "jealous" goes back to the Latin *zelus*, "zeal."

Emphatic assertion of God's love for Israel is further declared (5) *by the use of the cognate accusative,* I am jealous (*qinne'thi . . . qine'ah*) with jealousy, in English idiom, "I am *very* jealous"; and still further accentuated (6) *by the use of the adjective "great" with the cognate accusative,* I am jealous . . . with great jealousy (*qine'ah gedholah*), i.e., "I am *acutely* or *keenly* jealous."

But the vehemence of God's jealous love for Israel is still more accentuated (7) *by the uncognate accusative strengthened,* as the cognate form, by the adjective great (*hemah gedholah*) "with great heat," i.e., "anger" or "wrath" (Gen. 27:44; Deut. 29:27; Jer. 7:20; Cf. Zech. 1:14, 15, from the root *hamam,* "be or become warm," Arabic *hamma,* "become hot," as water. (8) *By the repetition of the verb* jealous. I am jealous with great jealousy . . . with great heat [emphatic by position] I am jealous for her. (9) *By the further repetition and emphasis on the object of the fierce love.* **I am jealous for her . . . I am jealous for Zion.** (Cf. Zech. 1:14.)

Thus in the warp and woof of the syntax of this verse is interwoven God's great passion for His elect people Israel. This burning emotion is seen manifesting itself in various ways in the succeeding verses.

2. *The Results of the Future Full Restoration of Israel* (Zech. 8:3–6). **The Lord of armies says thus: I will assuredly return to Zion and will dwell in the midst of Jerusalem. Then Jerusalem shall be called the City of Truth, the Mountain of the Lord of armies, the Holy Mountain. (4) The Lord of armies says thus: Aged men and women shall yet dwell in the streets of Jerusalem, each one with his cane in his hand because of advanced age. (5) Moreover, the streets of the city shall be filled with boys and girls playing in its streets. Thus the Lord of armies says, If it is marvelous in the eyes of the remnant of this people in those days, shall it also be marvelous in my eyes, says the Lord of armies?**

Since the full restoration of Israel is assured by the Word and love of God (vss. 1, 2), the results of the full restoration (with application and encouragement to those participating in the partial restoration) are started. The first result is *the Lord's return.* **The Lord of armies says thus: I will return [*shavti*] to Zion** (vs. 3; cf. 1:16). Although the verb *shavti* may, of course, be a past historical perfect and embrace the fact that the divine Shekinah presence had left the city when it was given up to its foes (Ezek. 11:23) but now in grace the Lord may be thought of as having returned in favor, yet the expression, by virtue of the context and scope of the prediction, *must* be construed as a prophetic perfect. This is the case the more so since the Shekinah presence never returned at the restoration from Babylon, and Israel to this day has remained in the Ichabod period of her history. The verb, accordingly, de-

clares the certainty of the second advent of Christ in glory. Only as Messiah returns in triumph over His enemies will these age-penetrating prophecies be fulfilled, and will Israel once again have the glory of God in the midst of her (Ezek. 43:2–5).

Hosea clearly foresaw this same return, and the Lord speaks through the prophet: "I will go and return to my place till they acknowledge their offence and seek my face: in their affliction they shall seek me early" (Hosea 5:15). Then the Lord will return to His people Israel with mercies and "His going forth" will be "prepared as the morning" and He will come to His people "as the latter and the former rain to the earth" (Hosea 6:3). To Jerusalem which rejected Him in His day our Lord Himself warned, "Ye shall not see me henceforth, till you shall say, Blessed is he that cometh in the name of the Lord" (Matt. 23:39).

The second result of Israel's full future restoration is the *permanent divine presence.* **I will assuredly return to Zion and will dwell in the midst of Jerusalem.** The verb **dwell,** *shakhan,* means "to settle down, abide, remain, reside" and is used elsewhere of God, as here (Gen. 9:27; Exod. 25:8; 29:46; Num. 5:3; I Kings 8:12; Isa. 33:5; 57:15). The "tabernacle" or "dwelling of Yahweh" hence is called the *mishkan,* i.e., "place of dwelling" or "residing" (Exod. 25:9; 40:34, 35, etc.). Accordingly, the Lord in the person of the returned Messiah **will dwell in the midst of Jerusalem.**

Feinberg is correct in linking the two declarations **I will return to Zion** and **I will dwell in the midst of Jerusalem** "as cause and effect" and in insisting that they "transpire in the same Messianic era" (*God Remembers,* p. 129), against C. H. H. Wright who maintains all the promises of chapters 7 and 8 have been fulfilled in the interval between Zerubbabel and Christ (*Zechariah and His Prophecies,* p. 180). But such an interpretation as Wright's necessitates a drastic watering-down of the plain meaning of these chapters, besides throwing them completely out of line with the eight night visions of 1:7–6:8 and the typical event of Joshua's coronation (6:9–15), all of which involve Israel's Messiah's second advent.

The third result of Israel's full future restoration will be *the exaltation of Jerusalem*. The Lord's personal return to Zion and permanent dwelling in Jerusalem will be that the city, then become the governmental and religious capital of the millennial earth, will be known by a threefold designation: (1) **The City of Truth** (2) **The Mountain of the Lord of Armies** and (3) **The Holy Mountain**. (Cf. Isa. 1:26; 60:14; 62:12).

Jerusalem will be **the City of Truth** (*'ir ha'emeth*) because it will be the abode of the "God of truth," *El ha'emeth*, and because the converted remnant inhabiting the millennial city will no "longer work iniquity nor speak lies" (Zeph. 3:13), but be famous for their fidelity to truth. It will be styled **the Mountain of the Lord of armies . . . the Holy Mountain** because "out of Zion shall go forth the law and the word of the Lord from Jerusalem" (Isa. 2:3). The Holy One of Israel shall return and take up His residence in the city and sanctify it, as well as its inhabitants by His presence. "Holiness unto the Lord," once inscribed on the golden plate adorning the headdress of Israel's high priest, shall then be inscribed upon Jerusalem and its inhabitants, as well as upon the commonest objects in the city (Zech. 14:20, 21). Then the whole city, restored to the Lord, will at last enter into the high-priestly role which was originally God's intent for the nation from the beginning of its career (Zech. 3:1–10).

The fourth result of Israel's full future restoration will be *the great increase of the peace and security of Jerusalem*. Because the city has so desperately suffered from wars and sieges through the centuries, the reiterated Word of the Lord gives assurance of eventual undisturbed tranquillity. **Thus the Lord of armies says, Yet** [*'odh*, emphatic by first position in its clause] **aged men and aged women shall dwell in the streets of Jerusalem, each one with his cane in his hand because of advanced age.** Intermittent wars throughout the centuries have been merciless on these older people as well as helpless children. At long last such enduring peace will come to Jerusalem that both these segments of society on opposite extremes of the age-scale shall find complete security. The very advanced in age, so weak and tottering as to require a staff or cane to walk, will be proof of long-standing freedom from war, as well as the children with carefree abandon **playing** (graphic participle denoting continuous action, from the root *sahaq*, "to laugh"). The picture is that of youngsters laughingly engaged in childish sports, the *piel* verb being used of the Philistines calling for Samson "to make sport" for them (Judg. 16:25), of the women who sang to one another and *played* (including dancing and instrumental music) while they chanted "Saul has slain his thousands and David his ten thousands" (I Sam. 18:7). Compare the use of the word in the sense of "making merry" (Jer. 15:17; 30:19; 31:4).

Theodore Cuyler Speers interprets Zechariah's reference to the oldsters and youngsters as presenting "a novel criterion for an ideal city," namely, "one in which old people and children are obviously happy and contented" (*The Interpreter's Bible*, "Zechariah," Vol. 6, p. 1085). But the prophet is scarcely suggesting an "ideal city" or that we "measure our cities by their effect upon two groups easily overlooked — the old and the young" (Speers, *in loc.*), but is merely using these two groups graphically to portray the well-established peace of the millennial city. Neither does the reference apply primarily at least, to the return from Babylon after the seventy-year captivity when "the old and the young would be among the last to return, when the work of reconstruction had progressed to the point where they could enjoy some safety and comfort" (Speers, *in loc.*). The prophet focuses his gaze upon a far-distant future involving Israel's full restoration, but he does so as an encouragement to his own countrymen.

The fifth result of Israel's full restoration will be *the exemplification of divine power.* **Thus the Lord of armies says, If it is marvelous in the eyes of the remnant of this people in those days, should it also be marvelous in my eyes? the Lord of armies says. The remnant of this people in those days** (*bayyamim hahem,* incorrectly rendered "in these days" in the A.V.) constitutes *not* the generation of the prophet's day nor any generation of Jews in the past, but the still-future remnant of the last days, who surviving the final "time of Jacob's trouble" (Jer. 30:7) will be converted and established by God's power in full millennial blessing. The question involved in verse 6 regarding the manifestation of divine power is interestingly buttressed before and behind by **Thus the Lord of armies says** and by "the oracle of the Lord of armies." Thus it receives a double guarantee.

The protasis of the conditional sentence introduced by if (*kî*), contains an interesting verb. **If it be marvelous** (*yippale'*) actually means "if it be difficult to do," or "if it be beyond one's power." The root *pala'* denotes "to be *separate* or *distinguished* from that which is ordinary or usual," and in the *nifal,* as here, comprehends the idea of being insuperably difficult or beyond the reach of human ability, and so when accomplished, "extraordinary" or "marvelous" (II Sam. 13:2). Accordingly, the word is used in the divine reply to Abraham concerning Sarah's laughing incredulity at the promise of the birth of a son to her in her advanced age. "Is

anything *too hard* [*yippale'*] for the Lord?" This constituted the ringing divine challenge to human unbelief. No matter how difficult, God's power could effect it.

The same word is used in Jeremiah's prayer when the prophet, as an expression of faith in the Word of God and the promise of restoration, bought a field in Anathoth from his cousin at a time when such a business transaction seemed utter folly with the Chaldeans besieging Jerusalem and the captivity imminent. "Ah! Lord God! It is thou who hast made the heavens and the earth by thy great power and by thy outstretched arm! Nothing is too hard [*yippale'*] for thee" (Jer. 32:17). The Lord was able to do the seemingly impossible in bringing both His people to inhabit the land again and make Jeremiah's investment a wise one. So the Word of the Lord encourages the prophet with the same thought Jeremiah had enunciated in his prayer: "Behold, I am the Lord, the God of all flesh; is anything *too hard* [*yippale'*] for me?" (Jer. 32:27).

If the remnant of the nation in that future day will scarcely be able to comprehend how such miraculous things just promised could become a reality, the divine reply is, "Because they seem difficult to you, must they also seem hard to Me?" The apodosis of the conditional sentence is thus patently a question, although the interrogative force is indicated only by the context. The interrogative particle *ha* is sometimes omitted, as is the case here, when the context makes the interrogative force obvious, or something more than a question is intended, as the expressing of strong feeling or something incredible to imagine, namely, that anything should be *even thought of* as being hard for God to accomplish.

3. *The Promise of Future Regathering and Full Restoration Is Repeated* (Zech. 8:7, 8). **The Lord of armies thus declares, I will save my people from the land of the East and from**

7 Thus saith the Lord of hosts; Behold, I will save my people from the east country, and from the west country;
8 And I will bring them, and they shall dwell in the midst of Jerusalem: and they shall be my people, and I will be their God, in truth and in righteousness.

---

7   Thus saith Jehovah of hosts: Behold, I will save my people from the east country, and from the west country;
8   and I will bring them, and they shall dwell in the midst of Jerusalem; and they shall be my people, and I will be their God, in truth and in righteousness.

---

the land of the West (8) **And I will bring them back, and they shall dwell in the midst of Jerusalem, and they shall become my people, and I myself will become their God in reality and in righteousness.** That this great promise does not refer to the partial restoration from Babylon of the prophet's own day, but to a still-future, world-wide regathering of Israel is patent from several considerations. (1) The partial restoration from Babylon was only from one direction; namely, from "the east" more commonly spoken of as from "the north" since Babylonian and Persian armies and caravans entered Palestine from the north via the Fertile Crescent, inasmuch as the deserts in the east barred travel. Few if any Jews in that era had migrated westward. Actually the prophecy is couched in language that embraces *all parts of the earth.* The terminology is "from the land of the rising of the sun [*me'erets mizraḥ*] and from the land of the going down of the sun [*me'erets mebho' hashshamesh*]." Compare the similar idiom in Psalm 50:1; 113:3 and Malachi 1:11 where the terminology patently signifies the entire earth. (2) The context of this passage also suggests its future final application. It is on a par with the comprehensive promises of Zechariah 8:1-6, which have not yet actually been fulfilled. The chief phase of the restoration from Babylon had already occurred, and this promise is obviously something entirely future from Zechariah's point of view. (3) Only after the fall of Jerusalem in A.D. 70 did the Jewish dispersion really become world-wide

and mainly in the countries west of Palestine. (4) Zechariah's prophecy is in the same category with many similar promises of Israel's *final* pre-kingdom regathering to be found in the former prophets, and in fact is a condensed summary of them. For example, Isaiah 11:11, 12, "The Lord shall set his hand again the second time to recover the remnant of his people . . . and shall assemble the outcasts of Israel and gather together the dispersed of Judah from the four corners of the earth." Compare also Isaiah 43:5, 6: "Fear not, for I am with thee: I will bring thy posterity from the east and gather thee from the west: I will say to the north, Give up; and to the south, Keep not back. Bring my sons from far and my daughters *from the ends of the earth.*"

(5) The regathering, moreover, is still future because it involves Israel's national conversion, which is still an unfulfilled event. **And they shall become my people, and I will become their God in reality [truth] and righteousness.**

Israel's *becoming* (*hayah le*, "become," not "be") My (i.e., God's) people represents the nation's passing out of the long *lo-'ammi* ("Not-My-people") period of its history, separated from God and abandoned to its enemies into the new phase of its national blessing in which the Lord shall restore them spiritually as *'ammi,* "My people." This will mean also that the Lord will become their God **in reality [i.e., "truth") and righteousness.** All through the *lo-'ammi* period the Lord *has* in a sense *been* their God, for they lay claim to a rigid mono-

9 Thus saith the Lord of hosts; Let your hands be strong, ye that hear in these days these words by the mouth of the prophets, which w e r e in the day t h a t the foundation of the house of the Lord of hosts was laid, that the temple might be built.

9   Thus saith Jehovah of hosts: Let your hands be strong, ye that hear in these days these words from the mouth of the prophets that were in the day that the foundation of the house of Jehovah of hosts was laid, even the temple, that it might be built.

theism but not "in truth" for they have rejected Him who is "the Truth" (John 14:6), and not "in righteousness" for "they being ignorant of God's righteousness and going about to establish their own righteousness, have not submitted themselves unto the righteousness of God" (Rom. 10:3). But in that day He who was their God shall *become* their God in reality. Religion shall then be exchanged for salvation. The long-interrupted covenant relationship and communion between them and their God shall be resumed. Wonderful will be their regathering. More wonderful yet will be their spiritual regeneration and restoration.

Numerous commentators (Wright, Keil, Pusey, Leupold, Laetsch, etc.) deny a literal restoration of Israel in these verses, as well as oppose a literal interpretation of the declaration **and they** [the restored Israelites] **will dwell in the midst of Jerusalem.** Says Leupold, "For at none of these times could all Jews have dwelt in the one city. The word Jerusalem represents the true church of God" (*Exposition of Zechariah*, p. 148).

Against this erroneous objection the following may be said: (1) The Jerusalem is the same literal city that shall enjoy *very great expansion* as the religious and governmental center of the millennial earth (Zech. 2:2–4 [2:6–8]; 14:10, 11). (2) The expression **in the midst of Jerusalem,** as even Wright, who opposes any future fulfilment of this prediction in a literal Israel, declares: "The allusion is evidently to Jerusalem, not so much as the actual residence of all the people, but as the place where Israel

should worship Jehovah" (*op. cit.* p. 184). (3) By metonymy the city here stands for the land, because it will be the center and focal point of the land where the glory of the true Messiah will be fully manifested. (4) As Baron says, "Even in times past the tribes from all parts of the land went up during the three great festivals, there to appear before God, being thus taught to regard the place where His honor dwelt, and His glory was specially manifested, as their true home (*op. cit.*, p. 241). Compare Psalm 90:1, "Lord, thou hast been *our dwelling* place in all generations." Psalm 91:1, "He that *dwelleth* in the secret place of the most High shall *abide* under the shadow of the Almighty."

II. THE ENCOURAGEMENT AMID THE WOES OF THE PRESENT PARTIAL RESTORATION (Zech. 8:9–17)

Although the preceding glorious prophecies will only find their fulfilment eschatologically in Israel's final period of consummating history in the coming millennial age, nevertheless the prophet does make an application, as he had done in the eight night visions (Cf., e.g., 3:8–10; 4:6–10) to the needs of his own age and generation in these grand unfulfilled predictions. From them he draws the elixir of consolation and encouragement for his impoverished and hard-pressed countrymen. Out of future hopes he distills inspiration for the trials and tribulations the struggling restored community was facing. This encouragement is given in the application of the prophecies to the local situation in verses 9–17.

10 For before these days there was no hire for man, nor any hire for beast; neither was there any peace to him that went out or came in because of the affliction: for I set all men every one against his neighbour.

10   For before those days there was no hire for man, nor any hire for beast; neither was there any peace to him that went out or came in, because of the adversary: for I set all men every one against his neighbor.

1. *The Subjects of the Encouragement* (Zech. 8:9). In this manner the Lord of armies speaks. Let your hands be strong, you who in these days have been hearing these words from the mouth of the prophets since the day the foundation of the house of the Lord of armies was laid that the temple might be built. The people exhorted by the Lord Himself through the prophet are described as those **who in these days** [i.e., in the prophet's own time, specifically Darius' fourth year, 518 B.C.] **have been hearing** [*hashshome'im*, the articular participle denoting a continuous hearing of *the Word of God*, described as] **these words from the mouth of the prophets.** Whoever else may be meant, certainly Haggai and Zechariah himself are intended (Ezra 5:1, 2). These postexilic prophets exercised their ministry since the foundation of the temple had been laid some twenty years previously (Ezra 3:8–13), and the good effects of their preaching were to be seen in the present progress toward the completion of the edifice.

The fulfilment of what Haggai and Zechariah had then spoken in the name of the Lord was a reason "why their hands should be strong, now and thereafter, for every work which God gave or should give them to do" (Pusey, *Minor Prophets*, II, p. 387). **Let your hands be strong** (*tehezaqnah yedhekhem*, jussive issuing a lively injunction in the third person) means to "be of good courage" (Judg. 7:11; II Sam. 16:21). Those who hear the Word of God and heed it may well be encouraged as they see its results. Zechariah urges his hearers to survey what has been accomplished and how God has blessed since they undertook to obey God's voice and proceed to

complete the temple, since resumption of the work two years previously.

2. *The Reasons for the People's Discouragement* (Zech. 8:10). **For previous to those days there was no hire for man nor did hire for beast exist. Moreover, there was no safety to him who went out or came in because of the adversary, and I set everyone against another.** This verse presents a contrast of the present, when they had begun to obey the Word of God, with the past, when they did not. The **for** (*kî*, "because") gives the reason for their former woes. **Before** ["previous" to] **those days** describes the era before work on the temple had been resumed (536–520 B.C.).

The first element in the people's discouragement was the fact that *trade had been dead.* The severe economic depression in the years previous to 520 B.C. had been a chastisement from the Lord for their selfishness and sin manifested in their failure to complete the temple, while they had expended their resources on themselves. That period is graphically described by Haggai: "Thus says the Lord of armies: This people say the time has not yet come to rebuild the house of the Lord. Then the word of the Lord came by Haggai the prophet, Is it time for you yourselves to dwell in your paneled houses, while this house lies in ruins? Now therefore . . . Consider how you have fared. You have sown much and harvested little; you eat, but you never have enough; you drink, but you never have your fill; you clothe yourselves, but no one is warm; and he who earns wages earns wages to put them into a bag with holes" (Hag. 1:2–6).

"Thus says the Lord of armies: Consider how you have fared. Go up

11 But now I will not be unto the residue of this people as in the former days, saith the Lord of hosts.

12 For the seed shall be prosperous; the vine shall give her fruit, and the ground shall give her increase, and the heavens shall give their dew; and I will cause the remnant of this people to possess all these things.

13 And it shall come to pass, that as ye were a curse among the heathen, O house of Judah, and house of Israel; so will I save you, and ye shall be a blessing: fear not, but let your hands be strong.

14 For thus saith the Lord of hosts; As I thought to punish you, when your fathers provoked me to wrath, saith the Lord of hosts, and I repented not:

15 So again have I thought in these days to do well unto Jerusalem and to the house of Judah: fear ye not.

---

11   But now I will not be unto the remnant of this people as in the former days, saith Jehovah of hosts.

12   For there shall be the seed of peace; the vine shall give its fruit, and the ground shall give its increase, and the heavens shall give their dew; and I will cause the remnant of this people to inherit all these things.

13   And it shall come to pass that, as ye were a curse among the nations, O house of Judah and house of Israel, so will I save you, and ye shall be a blessing. Fear not, but let your hands be strong.

14   For thus saith Jehovah of hosts: As I thought to do evil unto you, when your fathers provoked me to wrath, saith Jehovah of hosts, and I repented not;

15   so again have I thought in these days to do good unto Jerusalem and to the house of Judah: fear ye not.

---

to the hills and bring wood and build the house. ... You have looked for much, and, lo, it came to little; and when you brought it home, I blew it away. Why? says the Lord of armies. Because of my house that lies in ruins, while you busy yourselves each with his own house. Therefore the heavens above you have withheld the dew and the earth has withheld its produce. And I have called for a drought ... upon men and cattle and upon all their labors" (Hag. 1:7–11).

Unemployment affected both man and beast. Jobs were scarce and pay was so paltry that it amounted to practically nothing. Animals stood idle because there was no work for them to do in the economic standstill. In addition, *travel had been dangerous.* "There was no safety" (*shalom*, "peace," from *shalem*, "to be complete, sound"); "completeness, soundness" in the sense of "peace, quiet, safety, tranquillity, security" (I Kings 2:5; Isa. 57:2; Jer. 12:5; 25:37). Added to this, *social relationships had*

been strained. This insecurity was "because of [causal *min*] the oppressor," who was not only numbered among the Gentile overlords, but among the Jews themselves, since each "was arrayed" against his neighbor," i.e., "against one another" in civil and internecine strife among their own kith and kin, because they had not put God and His house first.

3. *Details of the People's Encouragement* (Zech. 8:11–15). **But now I will not be to the remnant of this people as in the former days, says the Lord of armies. (12) For there shall be peaceful sowing. The grapevine shall yield its fruit, and the countryside shall yield its produce, and the heavens shall yield their dew. And I will cause the remnant of this people to come into possession of all these things. (13) And it shall be just as you were a curse among the nations, O house of Judah and house of Israel, so I will deliver you, and you will become a blessing. Do not be afraid. Let your hands be strong. (14) For the Lord of armies**

declares, Just as I purposed to punish you when your forefathers angered me, the Lord of armies declares, and I did not alter my mind, (15) so I have once more purposed in these days to do good to Jerusalem and the house of Judah. Do not be afraid.

The first detail in their encouragement is that *God terminates His controversy with His people* (vs. 11). **But now not as in the former days** [emphatic by word position] **will I be.** The divine Word includes stress on the drastic change taking place in God's attitude toward them. The expression, *we'attah,* **but now** (adversative *waw* plus the temporal adverb "at the time, now," which describes a *present* state "as things are" as in I Samuel 8:5; 9:6; 13:12; 14:30; Job 14:16; 16:7) contrasts with the *past* time indicated in the expression "in the former days." Brown, Driver, and Briggs (*Hebrew and English Lexicon,* p. 254), however, construe the *we'attah* as expressing "an informal inference, or consequence, *so, then . . . now, therefore.*"

The remnant of this people constitutes the group which will experience the Lord's changed dealings. God promises to end His disciplinary and chastening activity and to bless His people.

A second detail of the people's encouragement is that *the Lord promises them prosperity* (vs. 12). Drought, scarcity, and economic depression in general will give way to the increased productivity and fruitfulness of their agricultural economy, which was central in their whole financial fabric. **For there shall be a peaceful sowing,** literally "the seed [sowing] of peace," a construct chain in which the genitive "of peace" is that of nearer definition. The term "seed" is here used in the sense of "sowing" or "time of sowing," as in Gen. 8:22; 47:24; Num. 20:5; Lev. 26:5. Hence the thought is not "the seed of peace," namely, the vine (Wright, Baron, Keil, Koehler, Leupold), but "sowing" or "time of sowing (seedtime) characterized by

peace" (as opposed to war). In the latter case newly planted crops are either destroyed if planted, or never planted at all, because of the exigencies of military campaigning.

The sowing of peace is thus "seedtime marked by the absence of war when crops can not only be planted but permitted to grow and come to successful harvest." But peace permitting sowing of seed and planting of crops is only one agricultural blessing. There will be the natural fruitfulness of the crops themselves under divine blessing. **The grapevine shall yield its fruit, the earth** [countryside] **shall yield its produce, and the heavens shall yield their dew.** That this happy condition is the Lord's doing is indicated by the direct divine statement: **And I will cause the remnant of this people to inherit all these things** (*hinhalti,* "give them as an inheritance," causative of the denominative verb "to get" or "take as a possession").

The third detail in the people's encouragement is that *the Lord reverses their fortunes* (vs. 13). The Lord declares that **just as** [*ka'asher,* comparative conjunction] **you** [His people] **were a curse among the nations . . . so** [*ka'asher* equated with *ken,* adverb "so," as in Num. 2:17; Isa. 31:4] says **the Lord, I will save** [deliver] **you and you shall be a blessing.** The blessing will be in contrast to the curse. The recipients of the blessing, namely the **house of Judah and the house of Israel** are dramatically addressed directly in the vocative case. Both Judah and Israel are included because both were represented in the return from exile in Babylon, and both will be represented and take part in the final age-end conversion and regathering to Palestine for kingdom blessing (Cf. Ezek. 37:11, 15-26).

The transformation from **a curse** to **a blessing** will be on the basis of experiencing God's redemption manifested in the Messiah. It is He who says, **I will save you** (*'oshia' 'ethekhem*). This prominent Old Testament word for salvation has the idea of "deliver, save, liberate" in the sense of "giving width and breadth to" (causative) from the root "be wide or spacious," Arabic *wasi'a*. It is used prominently of God *delivering* His people from evils and troubles, both internal and external, spiritual and temporal (Deut. 20:4; Josh. 22:22; Judg. 3:9; II Kings 14:27; Isa. 35:4; 49:25; Jer. 31:7; Heb. 1:2; Zeph. 3:17; Zech. 10:6; 12:7). In the future eschatological sense included here it will embrace not only Israel's rescue from outward enemies and evils, but the inner spiritual and moral regeneration of the people releasing them from their unbelief and Christ-rejection. This alone will convert them from a curse into a blessing.

The word curse, *qelalah* from the root *qalal*, "to be slight, trifling, contemptible" in the *piel* means "to curse," i.e., properly "to make contemptible" (Gen. 12:3; Exod. 21:17; Lev. 19:14). The noun "curse" signifies the infliction of great evil and calamities upon one so as to make him contemptible in the eyes of those who know him (Gen. 27:12; Judg. 9:57, Deut. 28:15, 45). Zechariah uses the term concerning Israel as the *object of God's curse* in a twofold sense, both negatively in the divine withdrawing of blessing, and positively in the infliction of punishments and contempt. This curse was predicted as the result of apostasy and sin (Deut. 28:15–62) and was to eventuate in the punishment of a world-wide dispersion (Deut. 28:63–68). The full reach of Zechariah's words extends to the sufferings and persecutions of this final diaspora, sweeping the entire span of the *lo-'ammi* period when their national election has been set aside (Rom. 11:1–12) and the Lord through Jeremiah declares: "I will give them up to be tossed to and fro among all the kingdoms of the earth for evil; to be a reproach and a proverb, a taunt and a curse in all places wherein I shall drive them" (Jer. 24:9).

Whereas the full sweep of Zechariah's prophecy concerning Israel's being a curse among the nations covers the entire *lo-'ammi* period still in progress and not terminated till the nation "looks unto" Him whom they pierced and "the spirit of grace and supplications" is poured out upon them (Zech. 12:10–14), the complete scope of the prophet's prediction concerning the nation's salvation and its becoming "a blessing" likewise embraces their final age-end restoration as well as the full gamut of the *'ammi* period. This is the reason for the *ka'asher ... ken* equation—just as ... so. Moreover, just as Israel's becoming a curse is the nation's becoming *the object of God's wrath* (i.e., an illustration and an example as well as a warning to the nations of the inevitable tragedy defection from God brings in its wake), so Israel's becoming a blessing is the nation's becoming *the object of God's grace* (i.e., an illustration and example of the benefits that follow in the wake of fellowship with, and devotion to, the living God). In addition, there is correspondence between the protracted severity of the curse and the perpetuity and sublimity of the blessing of Israel's final restoration (Gen. 12:1–3; Isa. 19:24; Ezek. 34:26).

This prophetic prospect is so grand and inspiring that Zechariah, whom Theodore Laetsch aptly styles, "The prophet of hope and encouragement in troublous times" (*Bible Commentary, The Minor Prophets*, St. Louis, 1956, p. 403), employs it in direct ministry to the faltering and discouraged people of his time, some of whom were more concerned about external ritual than spiritual reality. Do not fear, let your hands be strong, the negative command (jussive), preceding and preparing for the positive injunction repeated from verse 9, accentuates its force. "Do not fear, *be encouraged!* Let a panoramic glimpse of God's purposes of grace for His people calm your spirit and lift up your soul!"

The fourth detail of the people's encouragement is that *the Lord Himself determines to do them good* (vss. 14, 15). After this manner the Lord of armies speaks. **Just as I purposed to do evil to you, when your ancestors provoked me to anger, the Lord of armies speaks, and I did not relent; (15) So again I have purposed to do good to Jerusalem and to the house of Judah; do not be afraid.**

It is noteworthy that the Lord's declaration that He did not relent of His purposes to do evil to the remnant's ancestors when they provoked Him to anger by their apostasies is doubly strengthened by the repetition of the formula, **the Lord of armies speaks** (cf. Zech. 1:3, 4 for a similar accent upon the authority of the Word of God). **I purposed,** *zamamti,* "devised," is a word employed particularly of the divine purpose in punishment (Jer. 4:28; 51:12; Lam. 2:17; Zech. 1:6) "and therefore manifests God's work both for evil in the past and for good in the future as the result of a deliberate, purposive planning" (Leupold, *Exposition of Zechariah,* p. 153). The trials of the captivity, the woes and punishments of wayward Israel, were not mere accidents or unexplainable calamities. They were according to the unerring purpose of an unchanging God, who does not (*lo'*) "repent," *nihamti.* "I did not relent," that is "be sorry or repent of my own doings" (Exod. 13:17; Jer. 20:16; Joel 2:14, Jonah 3:9; Ezek. 24:14). The unchangeable God *never* violates the infinite holiness of His character at the expense of His love and pity. When His holiness is outraged by man's sin, He is said anthropopathically "to be angered" (*hiqtsif,* causative of *qatsaf,* "be angry"), and determines man's punishment. Therefore, that punishment is purposeful and certain, and when unleashed, is as resistless as an avalanche (Jer. 4:28). **As I thought** [devised, determined] **to punish you** is literally *hara',* "to do evil," causative of *ra'a',* "be evil or bad," apparently from the idea

"to break or break in pieces" (Jer. 11:16; Isa. 24:19; Prov. 25:19; Ps. 2:9; Job 34:24). God's planning "to do evil" is, therefore, *not* moral or spiritual evil, but merely temporal or physical disaster strictly in the sense of "punishing" or "afflicting" the disobedient or sinful in allowing calamities to overtake them according to His all-wise purpose in chastening them or in punishing them according to His just judgment.

With the same contrast between Israel being made a "curse" and subsequently a "blessing" (vs. 13) is presented God's former purpose to punish them in the light of His present intention to do them good. The same comparative conjunction **just as** (*ka'asher*) equated with the same adverb **so** (*ken*) is also employed, with similar practical exhortation closing the contrast — **Do not fear,** repeated from verse 14.

So I have again [adverbial use of the finite verb *shavti,* see Gesenius-Kautzsch, *Hebrew Grammar* 120, 2b) **determined to do good to Jerusalem and to the house of Judah.** To do good," *hetiv,* is the opposite of "to do evil," *hara'.* As the latter means "to afflict or punish" for sin or disobedience, so the former signifies "to bless" for faith and obedience. The root is from *yatav,* "to be good," in the causative stem meaning *"to do good to* or *deal well with* a person" (Exod. 1:20; Num. 10:29; Judg. 17:13; I Sam. 25:31; Mic. 2:7).

In verse 13 the recipients of the warning and promised blessings are styled **the house of Judah and the house of Israel.** Here the objects of the same warning and exhortation are designated **Jerusalem and the house of Judah.** These terms are meant to comprehend the *nation as a whole* represented in the remnant returned from Babylon and its subsequent history through the centuries.

These glorious eschatological promises illuminating the future of the Jews and setting before them their future national hope also came as an il-

16 These are the things that ye shall do; Speak ye every man the truth to his neighbour; execute the judgment of truth and peace in your gates:
17 And let none of you imagine evil in your hearts against his neighbour; and love no false oath: for all these are things that I hate, saith the Lord.

16   These are the things that ye shall do: Speak ye every man the truth with his neighbor; execute the judgment of truth and peace in your gates;
17   and let none of you devise evil in your hearts against his neighbor and love no false oath: for all these are things that I hate, saith Jehovah.

lustration to them of the blessing God had in store for them at that time. To describe this the prophet uses the expression in these days (vs. 15). But the benefits that were immediate *did not exhaust the full scope* of these sweeping prophetic previews.

The Lord's reversing their fortunes and transforming them from a curse into a blessing still awaits realization. Yet how realistic has been Israel's curse among the nations down through the centuries being cast out of their own land and plagued with unbelief in Messiah the Redeemer. Like Jonah out of God's will they have caused a storm among the Gentiles. Yet in a future day, after their great tribulation, like Jonah's experience in the fish, they shall be restored to faith and obedience to minister to the nations of the millennium, as Jonah did to the Ninevites.

4. *The Use the People Are to Make of Their Encouragement* (Zech. 8:16, 17). **These are the things which you shall do. Speak truth one with another. Render truth in your gates and judicial decision that eventuates in peace. (17) Do not devise evil in your hearts against one another, and do not love a false oath, for all these things I detest, is the oracle of the Lord.**

The prophet points out incisively that the remnant's encouragement by illustrative glimpses into the nation's glorious future, both immediate and far-distant, is to be met with a practical response in spirituality and corresponding worthy moral conduct. The moral injunctions here set forth have already been presented once by the prophet (Zech. 7:9, 10), and their

repetition at this juncture demonstrates that the prophet's purpose is to challenge his hearers and especially the inquirers from Bethel (who were exercised by mere outward ritualism) to faith and obedience, especially as the prophetic disclosures had made them cognizant of the good things the Lord was to bring to pass because of His sovereign purposes of grace toward His people.

These are the things which you shall do. They are to be "*doers* of the word, and not hearers only" (Ja. 1:22). God's purposes of grace toward them are to draw out their love for Him. But despite the importance of their *doing* as a practical proof of the reality of their *believing*, the emphasis is on *what they are to do*. This is expressed by a noun clause in the emphatic position, *both* the subject and predicate of which point out **these things** and resume their stress by a relative clause, the antecedent of whose relative pronoun is the highlighted clause. **These things** (four in number), all enjoined so forcefully in the original upon the people, are listed. The first two are positive, the last two are negative.

First, *they are to deal strictly in truth.* **Speak truth** (vs. 16a) **one with another**; literally, "a person [man, *'ish*] with his neighbor," *'eth re'ehu*, where the generic substantives are to be pronominalized to fit English idiom. Compare the injunction, "execute judgment of truth," i.e., "judicial decision based on truth" in Zechariah 7:9. **Truth,** *'emeth,* is to control not only their *lips,* but also their hearts, "for out of the abundance of the heart the mouth speaks" (Matt. 12:34), and their *actions* as well, as the next injunction also shows.

Second, *they are to render fair and peace-producing judicial decisions* (vs. 16b). **Render** [judge, *shiphetu*] **truth and judicial decision of peace** (*mishpat shalom*, literally "judgment of peace"), namely, court verdicts that result in peace "because they are decidedly fair" (Leupold, *op. cit.*, p. 154) and so obviously meticulous with regard to truth and honesty that both litigants are satisfied and silenced. Again the Hebrew stress is on the object in the verbal clause, which is placed *before* the verb and subject, literally "*truth and judgment of peace judge.*" The pivotal thing is *how* they judge, not the act, since they are going to continue judging, either honestly or dishonestly. The phrase **in your gates** describes the space inside the city wall near the entrance where public court was frequently held and where elders, judges, kings, and other officials sat to administer justice and deliberate on matters of moment (Deut. 21:19; 22:15; II Sam. 18:24; 19:9 [8]; I Kings 22:10; Prov. 24:7; Job 5:4; Ruth 4:1; Amos 5:12; Isa. 29:21).

Third, *they are not to meditate evil against each other* (vs. 17a). **Do not devise evil in your hearts one against another.** The prohibition is expressed by the subjective negative *'al* with the normal jussive form of the verb *tahshevu* from the root *hashav*, "to think" (Isa. 10:7; Mal. 3:16), then "devise," "plan," "imagine" as *evil against each other* (vs. 17a). **Do not** 48:2; Dan. 11:25; Esther 8:3; 9:25; Neh. 6:2). The prohibition is directed against evil being cogitated or hatched up *in the mind*, i.e., *bilevavekhem*, literally "in your heart" (singular, with specific reference to the "mind" or "intellect," i.e., "the frontal lobe of the brain" in modern psychological terminology [Num. 16:28; 24:13; Jer. 5:21; Hos. 7:11; Prov. 6:32; 7:7; 9:4; Eccl. 10:3; Job 36:5]).

This injunction, as frequently in Hebrew, stresses both the singular (*the individual*) and the plural (*the people as a whole*). The Hebrew is: "*A man* [singular dangling subject] do not *you* [real plural subject] devise evil against his neighbor" (literally, "*evil of his neighbor*, construct relation containing an *objective* genitive, "*against* his neighbor," i.e., "against *one another*," pronominalized to conform to English idiom). Moreover, the original stresses *the object* of the verb by word order: "*Evil one against another* do not cogitate in your heart." Hence the prohibition is directed not against the "devising" but *the evil* devised or imagined in the mind.

Fourth, *they are not to tolerate perjury* (vs. 17b). Literally, **and an oath of falsehood do not love,** the object again being highlighted by its primary position in the clause in place of the finite verb. The abhorrent sin of coddling "an oath *of falsehood*," i.e., characterized by *sheqer*, "deception, untruth, lying," that is, "what deceives, betrays, and falsifies, and so ends up in bitter disappointment," from the root *shaqar*, "to deceive"; Aramaic *sheqar* "deceive"; Syriac, *pael*, "falsify"; Assyrian *tashkirtu*, "a lie." The word in the Old Testament has particular applicability to destructive *falsehood* in court testimony (Exod. 20:16; Deut. 19:18; Prov. 6:19; 14:5; Jer. 5:2; Mic. 6:12; Isa. 32:7; Job 13:4).

The practice of lying while under a solemn affirmation by appeal to God to speak only truth is a crime of great severity both in the ancient and modern world and cannot for a moment be countenanced by anyone who would profess to know God or follow God's commandments. It has already been alluded to by the prophet (5:4).

Fifth, *they are to bear in mind the reason for avoiding these particular sins* (vs. 17c). **For** [*kî*, "because"] **all these things** [are those] **which I detest, is the oracle of the Lord.** The object (very emphatic by position and structure) is actually an abbreviated nom-

18 And the word of the Lord of hosts came unto me, saying,
19 Thus saith the Lord of hosts; The fast of the fourth month, and the fast of the fifth, and the fast of the seventh, and the fast of the tenth, shall be to the house of Judah joy and gladness, and cheerful feasts; therefore love the truth and peace.

18   And the word of Jehovah of hosts came unto me, saying,
19   Thus saith Jehovah of hosts: The fast of the fourth month, and the fast of the fifth, and the fast of the seventh, and the fast of the tenth, shall be to the house of Judah joy and gladness, and cheerful feasts; therefore love truth and peace.

inal clause, with predicate implied, used as the objective antecedent of the compound relative pronoun 'asher, which itself is actually the object in its own clause. Hence the employment of the abbreviated clause as an object, which in the full form is actually subject, with an implied predicate nominative, together with a following relative also objective, greatly accentuates the object which God declares I hate, sane'thi, "detest," from root sane', "hate," as in Arabic, shaniya, Aramaic, sena', as well as Syriac and Ethiopic (Amos 6:8; Hos. 9:15; Jer. 12:8; Isa. 1:14; 61:8; Mal. 2:16). What God hates, His people who expect to enjoy His promised blessings, are likewise to detest, especially those sins that are emphatically signalled out as particular objects of His detestation.

III.   FULL FUTURE RESTORATION TO MILLENNIAL JOY AND DIVINE FAVOR (Zech. 8:18–23)

Having demonstrated to the people the mere externalism and empty ritualism of their observance of the fasts as well as pointing out to them the sins and transgressions that caused their sufferings and calamities (Zech. 7:1–7), and having given them warning in particular against certain sins which were common (7:8–14), Zechariah had been free to announce the divine blessing to be realized in part at that time and in full in a future millennial day (8:1–17).

1. Jewish Fasts Will One Day Give Way to Millennial Feasts (Zech. 8:18, 19). The way is now open for the

prophet to answer the initial inquiry first presented by the deputation from the city of Bethel. The question was: "Shall I weep in the fifth month separating myself as I have done so many years?" (Zech. 7:3). Zechariah now gives a pointed and plain answer. And the word of Jehovah of hosts came unto me, saying, In this manner the Lord of armies speaks: The fast of the fourth month and the fast of the fifth, and the fast of the seventh, and the fast of the tenth shall become to the house of Judah joy and gladness and pleasant feasts; but love truth and peace (8:18, 19).

Only the fasts of the fifth and seventh months had been included in the original inquiry of the embassy. In the final divine answer to Zechariah, however, the whole gamut of fasts is included. The fast of the fourth month lamented the opening of the city of Jerusalem to Nebuchadnezzar as a result of the extremity of famine within the walls, during Zedekiah's eleventh year (Jer. 39:2, 3; 52:6, 7). The fast of the tenth month marked the beginning of the siege by Nebuchadnezzar in his ninth year (II Kings 25:1; Jer. 39:1; 52:4). These fasts, together with those of the fifth month and the seventh month, are to become a joyful season and times of great happiness (cf. Zech. 7:3, 5).

Whereas Amos saw the exact opposite when Israel's feasts would be turned into fasts and her "songs into lamentations" (Amos 8:10), Isaiah envisions this same period as Zechariah when he saw at last their fasts

20 Thus saith the Lord of hosts; It shall yet come to pass, that there shall come people, and the inhabitants of many cities:

21 And the inhabitants of one city shall go to another, saying, Let us go speedily to pray before the Lord, and to seek the Lord of hosts: I will go also.

22 Yea, many people and strong nations shall come to seek the Lord of hosts in Jerusalem, and to pray before the Lord.

---

20   Thus saith Jehovah of hosts: It shall yet come to pass, that there shall come peoples, and the inhabitants of many cities;

21   and the inhabitants of one city shall go to another, saying, Let us go speedily to entreat the favor of Jehovah, and to seek Jehovah of hosts: I will go also.

22   Yea, many peoples and strong nations shall come to seek Jehovah of hosts in Jerusalem, and to entreat the favor of Jehovah.

===

turned into feasts. "To comfort all that mourn, to appoint unto them that mourn in Zion, to give unto them beauty for ashes, the oil of joy for mourning, the garment of praise for the spirit of heaviness that they might be called the trees of righteousness, the planting of the Lord that he might be glorified" (Isa. 61:2, 3). Isaiah again envisions this period and says, "I will rejoice in Jerusalem, and joy in my people, and the voice of weeping shall be no more heard in her, nor the voice of crying" (Isa. 65:19).

The manifestation of the kingdom will be attended by such a fulness of salvation that Judah will forget to commemorate the former mournful events and will only have occasion to rejoice in the benefits of grace bestowed by God. But even in this exalted prediction of God's favor, they are commanded to love truth and peace. The Hebrew word order is very emphatic. **But truth and peace, love.** The emphasis is on the object which is in this case placed first in the Hebrew verbal sentence. Enjoyment of the highest spiritual and temporal blessings always carries a warning against apostasy and declension.

2. *Gentiles Will Eagerly Seek the Lord in the Kingdom Era* (Zech. 8:20-22). But in the manifestation of full millennial joy, the Jewish national fasts will not only give way to feasts. Gentiles shall seek God. This great promise is also preceded by **Thus saith the Lord of armies.** So grandly glo-

rious is this and the other prophecies of blessing in this chapter that only God's Word backing up the promise with His certainty will cause it to penetrate the unbelief of skeptical men. **It shall yet be that peoples** [*'ammim*, the non-Jewish nations as in Zech. 11:10; 12:2, 3; 14:12] **shall come and the inhabitants of many cities. And the inhabitants of one** [city] **will go to another and say, We will go** [or, cohortative, "Let us go," *nelekhah halakh*, "Let us get on our way immediately," the infinitive absolute intensifying the urgency of the verb] **to entreat the favor of the Lord and to seek the Lord of armies.**

Then some straggler or doubter, realizing the attractive power of the Jew in contact with God's blessing, will say, **I too will go!** or "Let *me* go too!" (*'elekhah gam 'ani*). The fire will catch. The zeal will spread. Israel, filled with God's blessing, will be like a magnet attracting peoples and nations to her and dispensing to them the real knowledge of God. **And many peoples** [as in verse 20], **and strong nations shall come to seek the Lord of armies in Jerusalem and to seek the Lord's favor** (vs. 22).

Here is a remarkable picture, not of world conversion in this age, but of the restoration of the Jew to the center of God's favor. With the Davidic kingdom established, Israel will be a medium of blessing to the entire globe.

The prophet Isaiah gives us a

23 Thus saith the Lord of hosts; In those days it shall come to pass, that ten men shall take hold out of all languages of the nations, even shall take hold of the skirt of him that is a Jew, saying, We will go with you: for we have heard that God is with you.

---

23   Thus saith Jehovah of hosts: In those days it shall come to pass, that ten men shall take hold, out of all the languages of the nations, they shall take hold of the skirt of him that is a Jew, saying, We will go with you, for we have heard that God is with you.

---

beautiful picture of this time when Jerusalem will be the capital of the millennial earth and the center of millennial worship with delegations like that which came from Bethel to Jerusalem in Zechariah's day flowing from all the nations to the temple of the Lord established in the capital city. "And it shall come to pass in the last days that the mountain of the Lord's house shall be established in the top of the mountain and shall be exalted above the hills and all nations shall flow into it. And many people shall go and say, Come ye, and let us go up to the mountain of the Lord, to the house of the God of Jacob. And he will teach us of his ways and we will walk in his paths. For out of Zion shall go forth the law and the word of the Lord from Jerusalem" (Isa. 2:2, 3). Then restored and rehabilitated Israel will exhort one another with the words, "O house of Jacob, come ye and let us walk in the light of the Lord" (Isa. 2:5). Then there will be the world-wide realization of Psalm 122:

I was glad when they said to me,
Let us go to the house of the Lord!
Our feet are standing
Within thy gates, O Jerusalem.

Jerusalem, thou art builded
As a city that is compact together.
Whither the tribes go up, even the tribes
of the Lord,
For an ordinance for Israel,
To give thanks unto the name of the Lord
For there are set thrones for judgment,
The thrones of the house of David.

Pray for the peace of Jerusalem!
They shall prosper that love thee.
Peace be within thy walls,
And prosperity within thy palaces.
For my brethren and companions' sake

I will now say, Peace be within thee,
For the sake of the house of the Lord our
God
I will seek thy good.

In this gloriously radiant atmosphere of happiness there will be no place for fasts or mourning. Israel's calamities will have passed. "The time of Jacob's trouble" (Jer. 30:7) will be over.

It shall yet be that (vs. 20). These great predictions made by Isaiah, the Psalmist, and other prophets have not yet been fulfilled, despite the fact that the Jews at that time were only a handful of people and the temple was still unfinished, its very completion contingent upon the whims of their heathen overlords. The rival worship of Samaria was prospering and inviting coalition. As Pusey says concerning Zechariah's great prophecy, "appearances and experiences were against it" (op. cit., p. 390).

But no matter what difficulties may lie in the way, it shall yet be that the Word of God will be fulfilled. The nations shall yet flow into Jerusalem. Jerusalem shall yet be the center of the earth. God's Word and God's promises and covenants shall yet be fulfilled. From Washington, London, Paris, Berlin, and the capitals of the world shall yet come innumerable delegations (such as that from Bethel to Jerusalem) to seek the God of Israel and the blessing that will be administered world-wide through the Israelite nation in the coming age.

3. *The Jew Millennially Restored Will Enjoy Special Divine Favor* (Zech. 8:23). The last verse of this chapter is an amazing one. Not only will fasts give way to feasts in the

millennium and the Gentiles seek after God, through God-blessed Israel, but the *special divine favor* upon the Jew of that age is here delineated (vs. 23). **Thus says the Lord of hosts, In those days ten men from the nations of every language shall take hold of the robe of a Jew, saying, Let us go with you. We have heard that God is with you.** The specific time indicated in the fulfillment of this prophecy is given by the expression **in those days** (*bayyamim hahemmah*). This means in millennial times when the fasts shall give way to feasts and when the Gentiles shall be attracted to Israel because of God's blessing upon her.

The number **ten** is doubtless representative of all (Lev. 26:26; cf. Gen. 31:7). Says Pusey, "*Ten* is a symbol of a whole, all the numbers meeting in it and starting again from it" (*op. cit., in loc.*). The verb **lay hold of,** *yaḥaziqu,* from root "be firm, grow strong" in the causative means "to take firm hold of, seize, catch" (Gen. 19:16; Exod. 4:4; Judg. 7:20; Isa. 4:1). It is a graphic word and means "to grab." Being repeated, it has a double emphasis. This expression indicates the zeal of those who would seek after the Jew (*'ish yehudhi*), literally "a man, a Jew." The zealous cry of Gentile converts will be, **We will** [determination] **go with thee** or, possibly, "Let us (earnest entreaty) go with thee." The reason is given by a causal clause, **because we have heard God is with you.**

God in the midst of millennial Israel will be the great attractive force to draw the nations unto the Jew. Then the reborn nation, and each member of it, like the Apostle Paul who was as "one whose birth was abortive" (I Cor. 15:8), will be a great and powerful missionary agency, as was the Apostle to the Gentiles.

Nowhere in the prophetic word is there a more striking section on God's future blessing for Israel. Nowhere in predictive prophecy is the reinstatement of God's covenant people more emphatically asserted. This section offers a grand climax to the first part of the prophecy, summing up all the apocalyptic visions and giving a grand finale to the answer of the question of the fasts. Zechariah's visions span the centuries and look at the sunlight of God's favor behind the dark clouds of the present storm that has involved unbelieving Israel. For them a day of glory will dawn. God has a future for His ancient people. The concluding age of human history, which will prelude eternity, will prove this revealed truth.

CHAPTER NINE
HUMAN WORLD CONQUEROR AND DIVINE PRINCE OF PEACE

(ZECH. 9:1–17)

I. THE SUDDEN RISE OF THE PROUD WORLD CONQUEROR, ALEXANDER THE GREAT (Zech. 9:1–8)
   1. The Prophecy Against the Land of Hadrach (Zech. 9:1, 2a)
   2. The Prophecy Against Tyre and Sidon (Zech. 9:2b–4)
   3. The Prophecy Against the Philistine Cities (Zech. 9:5–7)
   4. The Prophecy of Jerusalem's Escape from Alexander the Harbinger of a Future Complete Deliverance Under Messiah (Zech. 9:8)

II. THE FIRST ADVENT OF ISRAEL'S HUMBLE KING AND SAVIOR (Zech. 9:9)
   1. The Joyful Announcement of the Coming of Israel's King and Savior (Zech. 9:9a)
   2. A Featured Account of the Character and Condition of Israel's King and Savior (Zech. 9:9b)

(1) He is just and righteous (vs. 9b)
(2) He shows Himself a Savior (vs. 9b)
(3) He is lowly (vs. 9b)

III. THE SECOND ADVENT OF ISRAEL'S GLORIOUS KING AS ESTABLISHER OF A WORLD-WIDE KINGDOM OF PEACE (Zech. 9:10–17)
   1. Zion's King Establishes Peace at His Second Advent (Zech. 9:10)
   2. The Lord Encourages Suffering Israelites in View of the Nation's Future Hope (Zech. 9:11, 12)
   3. The Maccabean Struggle with Godless Paganism, an Adumbration of Israel's Final Conflict before Kingdom Blessing (Zech. 9:13–15)
   4. Israel's Final End-Time Deliverance before Kingdom Blessing (Zech. 9:16)
   5. Israel's Realization of Full Kingdom Blessing (Zech. 9:17)

THE scope of the second part of Zechariah (chapters 9–14) is the same as the first part (chapters 1–8). The series of eight night visions (1:7 – 6:8) extend from Zechariah's time to the establishment of the kingdom over Israel in blessing (cf. Acts 1:6). The symbolic crowning of the high priest Joshua (6:9–15) is a climactic act illustrating, as an event in history, the setting of the King-Priest, Messiah, over the established kingdom. The answer to the question of the fasts (chapters 7–8) also leads in its final explanation to the time when the fasts will become feasts in full millennial blessing.

Chapters 9–14 cover the same prophetic time period and involve the overthrow of Gentile world powers and the establishment of Messiah's kingdom. This great prophecy of the Messianic future involves two prophetic oracles or "burdens." The first oracle embraces the first advent and rejection of Messiah, the Shepherd-King (chapters 9–11), and the second oracle deals with the second advent and acceptance of Messiah, Shepherd-King (chapters 12–14). The marvelous unity and scope of Zechariah's prophecy bind these two main sections of the book (chapters 1–8 and 9–14) together and argue against a "second or third Zechariah."

The first prophetic oracle (chapters

1   The burden of the word of the Lord in the land of Hadrach, and Damascus shall be the rest thereof: when the eyes of man, as of all the tribes
of Israel, shall be toward the Lord.
2   And Hamath also shall border thereby; Tyrus, and Zidon, though it be
very wise.

1   The burden of the word of Jehovah upon the land of Hadrach, and
    Damascus shall be its resting place (for the eye of man and of all the
    tribes of Israel is toward Jehovah;)
2   and Hamath, also, which bordereth thereon; Tyre and Sidon, because
    they are very wise.

9-11) delineates the judgment through which Gentile world power over Israel is finally destroyed and Israel comes into full blessing with strength to overcome all her enemies. The second oracle (chapters 12-14) deals with the divine purging through which Israel herself is sifted and purified in the final great struggle with the nations and changed into a holy, priestly nation.

I. THE SUDDEN RISE OF THE PROUD WORLD CONQUEROR, ALEXANDER THE GREAT (Zech. 9:1-8)

The prophet envisions the glorious prophecy of the first advent of Israel's Messiah and Savior against the preparatory background of the conquests of Alexander the Great. The form of the vision takes the mode of a burden (*massa'*). This word, from the root *nasa'* ("to lift up") means a prediction of a threatening act and one which is admonitory in character. It is an oracle that is heavy, freighted with woe or judgment. The force of the word is therefore not an *utterance* but rather a "burdensome message" of the Lord (cf. Hengstenberg, *Christology of the Old Testament*, Vol. 3, pp. 339-343).

1. *The Prophecy Against the Land of Hadrach* (Zech. 9:1, 2a). The prediction of the rise of Alexander the Great commences: A burden — The word of the Lord is in the land of Hadrach, with Damascus as its resting place. For the eye of man as well as of all the tribes of Israel is toward the Lord. Here the heavy, burdensome prophecy (cf. Isa. 13:1; 15:1; 17:1; 19:1; 21:11; 22:1, etc.) begins in

the hinterland of Syria across the Lebanon mountains at Damascus, which is said to be the **resting place** of the minatory prediction. The word **resting place,** *menuhah,* is from the root *nuah,* "to rest," Ugaritic *nh,* Akkadian *nahu,* "rest," Arabic 4th conjugation, "to cause a camel to lie down on its breast" and the substantive *munahun* designating "the resting place of a camel." The weighty prophetic burden thus settles down in the sense of remaining or abiding *on* or *at* Damascus until its prediction is completely fulfilled. (For the use of the word *menuhah* in the sense of a "resting place" or "the place of abode or settling down," see Num. 10:33; Deut. 12:9; Isa. 32:18; Mic. 2:10.)

Although Damascus is said to be the **resting place** or protracted abode of the prophetic burden, the idea is not that of a beneficent, quiet, peaceful resting, indicating the conversion of the people of Damascus. This concept is entirely erroneous, clashing with the context. The reference is rather to be understood as God's wrath falling and resting (remaining) in Damascus, because this city state in the fertile and prosperous *Gutah* or Damascene plain was, for several centuries (900-721 B.C.), one of the most terrifying and formidable of Israel's enemies.

The reference to Damascus occurs in a circumstantial clause, which gives a detail or secondary thought subordinated to the main clause, which is nominal. A burden — the word of the Lord [subject] is in the land of Hadrach [predicate], and Damascus is

its resting place [circumstantial clause] rendered as a phrase in English idiom, "The word of the Lord is in the land of Hadrach *with Damascus as its resting place.*" Thus, although the prophetic oracle rests in Damascus, the chief thought of the passage is "A burden – the word of the Lord is in the land of Hadrach," designating the more general region of Damascus.

The proper name **Hadrach** occurs only here in the Old Testament. Older, fanciful interpretations of this *hapax legomenon* can now be completely abandoned, including Leupold's more recent view, who building upon the old traditional Jewish idea of a figurative compound name *ḥad* ("sharp") and *rakh* ("soft"), refers it not to Messiah (with Jarchi and Kimchi), but scarcely less tenably to "the land Sharp-soft," as an imagined symbolical appellation of the Persian Empire, to describe its twin moral strength and weakness, and at the same moment to hide any open criticism of this world power "at a time when neighbors were trying to prove Israel traitorous" (*Exposition of Zechariah*, pp. 164–165; cf. also Henderson, *The Minor Prophets*, p. 407).

Theodore Laetsch is correct in noting that "Hadrach, for centuries a puzzling historical problem, has now been definitely identified with Hatarika mentioned in the annals of Assyrian kings as an Aramaean country near Damascus and Hamath, against which Assyria campaigned in 772, 755, and 733 B.C." (*The Minor Prophets*, Saint Louis, 1956, p. 450). So also Robert C. Dentan, "Zechariah" in *The Interpreter's Bible*, 6, p. 1093) who says, "While the name does not occur in post-exilic times, its appearance here may be an example of popular survival or of conscious archaism."

The only difficulty is whether the well-attested city is located north of Hamath on the Orontes River southwest of Aleppo (Merrill F. Unger, *Israel and the Aramaeans of Damascus*, London, 1957, p. 166, note 12) or

between Hamath and Homs, just south of Qarqar (James Montgomery, *Journal of Bib. Lit.* 28:69). The reference to Hadrach on the eighth-century B.C. stele of King Zakar of Hamath under the name "Hazrek" attests its power and influence in that day (Unger, *op. cit.*, pp. 85–87), and explains its survival in popular memory as a name for the entire hinterland region of Phoenicia, beyond the Antilebanon mountains from Damascus and South Syria to North Syria in the region of Arpad (E. Kraeling, *Rand-McNally Bible Atlas*, map XI, p. 245).

At the battle of Issus in southeastern Asia Minor (October, 333 B.C.) Alexander the Great inflicted a defeat upon Darius and the Persians which immediately threw open Syria and Palestine to his lightning-like conquests, and exposed Egypt to his victorious armies. The prophet envisions the defeat of the historic enemies of Judaism: first Damascus, Hamath, and the cities of the Syrian interior, then the cities along the Mediterranean coast that stood in the conqueror's way in his victorious sweep into Egypt.

After a detachment of Alexander's forces had subjugated **the land of Hadrach,** taking the key towns, Damascus and Hamath, the prophet pictures **the eye of man** [*'en 'adham,* "the eye of *mankind,*" *'adham* used collectively of human beings in general, as in Gen. 1:26; 9:5; Deut. 4:32; Num. 5:6 as well as the eye (gaze, attention)] **of all the tribes of Israel** fixed upon the Lord. What is meant is that when all civilized men at that time, as well as all the tribes of Israel, were fastening their gaze intently upon Alexander the Great and his phenomenal conquests, they were *actually fastening their eyes upon the Lord.* Alexander was simply God's servant of judgment and chastisement (cf. vs. 4 where the Lord Himself is said to have dispossessed Tyre, when Alexander is known to have done so). Hamath is also mentioned as being "in the land of Hadrach," bordering

3 And Tyrus did build herself a strong hold, and heaped up silver as the dust, and fine gold as the mire of the streets.
4 Behold, the Lord will cast her out, and he will smite her power in the sea; and she shall be devoured with fire.

3   And Tyre did build herself a stronghold, and heaped up silver as the dust, and fine gold as the mire of the streets.
4   Behold, the Lord will dispossess her, and he will smite her power in the sea; and she shall be devoured with fire.

on the region of Damascus. This great ancient city (modern Hama) on the Orontes, north of Damascus, is now well known from archaeology.

2. *The Prophecy Against Tyre and Sidon* (Zech. 9:2b–4). Next **Tyre with Sidon** is pictured, for **she is exceedingly wise** (vs. 2). **Tyre** is singled out for special mention in this prophecy. Her prosperity and worldly wisdom constituted a standing moral difficulty to the Jews. Why should this city, devoted so unscrupulously to the pursuit of wealth, go unharmed, while God's people were afflicted with one calamity after another? Ezekiel had delineated the perverted wisdom and pride of the island city as manifested through its "prince":

Because your heart is proud
  and you have said, I am a god,
I sit in the seat of the gods,
  in the heart of the seas.
Yet you are but a man, and no god,
  though you consider yourself
    wise as a god—
. . . .
By your wisdom and your understanding
  you have gotten wealth for yourself,
and have gathered gold and silver
  into your treasuries;
by your great wisdom in trade
  you have increased your wealth
  and your heart has become proud
    in your wealth;
therefore, thus says the Lord God:
  Because you consider yourself
    as wise as a god,
therefore, behold, I will bring
  foreigners upon you,
  the most terrible of the nations.
. . . .
They shall thrust you down into the pit
  and you shall die the death of the slain
  in the heart of the seas (Ezek. 28:2, 4–8).

So corrupted, God-opposing, and overweaningly proud was Tyre that Ezekiel expands his prophecy con-

cerning the proud opulent city to embrace (under the figure of the Tyrian king) the pre-fall career of Satan (Ezek. 28:11–19). Many critics who fail to see the close identification of Satan with the Satanic world-system, so splendidly represented by the Tyrian king, deny this larger perspective of this prophecy. But the identification is extraordinarily apt in the light of the full, Biblical revelation concerning the Satanic world system and its relation to human government. For the precise connection of Satan and demonic agencies with world governments, see Merrill F. Unger, *Biblical Demonology*, pp. 181–200.

Zechariah says, **Tyre** [*tsor*, probably "rock"] **built for herself a bulwark** (*matsor*, "citadel"). The usage constitutes an intentional pun (paronomasia) or similarity of sound and meaning to play upon the great strength and impregnable position of the insular city. C. H. H. Wright (*Zechariah and His Prophecies*, p. 211) suggests the English rendering to capture the word play, "*Tyre* built for herself a *tower*." The Hebrew word *matsor*, however, from the root *tsur*, "to besiege," "beleaguer," as in Aramaic (II Sam. 11:1; I Kings 15:27) has a wider use than a "military tower" and denotes "siege-works or entrenchments" or "a siege" itself (Ezek. 4:2; Jer. 10:17; Nah. 3:14; Deut. 20:20). Zechariah uses it in the sense of "rampart."

But Tyre was likely so named because of her naturally strong position as a "rocky stronghold," since the Greek name *Turos* (cf. the A.V. rendering "Tyrus") is from the Aramaic form *tura'*, "rock." This was

5 Ashkelon shall see it, and fear; Gaza also shall see it, and be very sorrowful, and Ekron; for her expectation shall be ashamed; and the king shall perish from Gaza, and Ashkelon shall not be inhabited.
6 And a bastard shall dwell in Ashdod, and I will cut off the pride of the Philistines.
7 And I will take away his blood out of his mouth, and his abominations from between his teeth: but he that remaineth, even he, shall be for our God, and he shall be as a governor in Judah, and Ekron as a Jebusite.

---

5 Ashkelon shall see it, and fear; Gaza also, and shall be sore pained; and Ekron, for her expectation shall be put to shame; and the king shall perish from Gaza, and Ashkelon shall not be inhabited.
6 And a bastard shall dwell in Ashdod, and I will cut off the pride of the Philistines.
7 And I will take away his blood out of his mouth, and his abominations from between his teeth; and he also shall be a remnant for our God; and he shall be as a chieftain in Judah, and Ekron as a Jebusite.

---

new Tyre, built some distance (700 paces) from the mainland. Isaiah calls the fortress "the stronghold of the sea" (Isa. 23:4).

Emphasizing Tyre's proverbial wealth and consequent power, Zechariah uses two very descriptive similes. The city is said to have heaped up silver as dust and gold [ḥaruts "shining," a poetical name of gold] as the mire of the streets. The word heaped up, tiṣbor, is from ṣabhar, "to pile up" in great quantities, Arabic ḍabara, "collect, bind together"; of amassing grain (Gen. 41:35, 49); dead frogs (Exod. 8:10); dust (Hab. 1:10). Dust and mire are apt figures to which to compare Tyre's phenomenal opulence. Both dust (when the weather was dry) and mud (when the weather was wet) were familiar sights and nuisances in the unpaved streets of ancient oriental cities.

Although insular Tyre had a comparatively small area, it was surrounded by a wall 150 feet high. It was such a stalwart bastion that the Assyrian Shalmaneser besieged it for five years unsuccessfully. Nebuchadnezzar, the Babylonian monarch, tried to take it for thirteen years, but in vain. Ancient historians speak of the pride and self-security of the Tyrians. Tyre's wealth, commerce, and apparent impregnability were famous.

No prophecy of the Old Testament was more dramatically fulfilled. Look! hinneh, is an interjectional adverb fastening attention upon the dramatic fall of the city. Look, the Lord shall dispossess her and smite her military power in the sea. And she [hi', emphatic] shall be burned with fire. All this was meticulously fulfilled in history. When the city resisted Alexander, he besieged it for seven months and, by building a mole out to it, directed new siege engines against it. He also amassed a great navy from nearby city states. He took the proud metropolis after a siege of seven months, doing what no one else had ever done.

Clearly Alexander was aided by supernatural strength and wisdom. Amazingly this is indicated in the prophecy of Zechariah. Behold the Lord shall disposses her. Not, "Alexander shall dispossess her," but divine power, characterizing the world-conqueror as an instrument of the divine punishment, through whose conquests the earth would be prepared for the coming Messiah, the true world conqueror. The word dispossess is from root yarash, "take possession of," "inherit," Arabic waritha, "inherit" in the causative stem "to cause to inherit," then generally "to dispossess," as someone is dispossessed when another is made to inherit (Josh.

13:13; 16:10; Judg. 1:29, hence being employed of "driving out" the Canaanites).

3. The Prophecy Against the Philistine Cities (Zech. 9:5–7). But the prophetic burden travels south with Alexander's advance. In verses 5 and 6 a prophecy is indicated against the Philistine cities. **Let Ashkelon see and be afraid** [jussives]. **And let Gaza** [also see it and be afraid] **and be severely distressed** [*taḥil meʾodh*, "pained like a woman in travail"] **and Ekron, for her expectation** [her hope] **shall be ashamed. And the king shall perish from Gaza, and Ashkelon shall not be inhabited. Moreover, a person of blemished birth shall dwell in Ashdod, and I will cut off the pride of the Philistines.**

Only four of the five capital cities (Pentapolis) of Philistia are mentioned. Gath is omitted, probably because at that time it had been incorporated into Judah. In the annals of Alexander's advance there is no record made of Ashkelon, Ekron, or Ashdod. However, the fate of Gaza is fully recorded. This stout impregnable fortress, like Tyre in its natural strength, ventured to defy the great conqueror in spite of Tyre's fate. This city held out for five months against Alexander. Its king was slain, for the Persians had permitted its own local ruler to reign as a sub-king, the Persian monarch himself being termed "king of kings."

After the surrender of Gaza, ten thousand of its inhabitants were slaughtered and the remainder sold into bondage. The king, Batis, was bound to a chariot with thongs and dragged to death through the streets of the city. The Syriac, Septuagint, Targum, and Vulgate render the term *mamzer*, "a foreigner." Hengstenberg construes the word to denote "a rabble." Apparently a person of blemished birth is meant, although a collective idea may be indicated, as the Revised Standard Version translates the passage: "*A mongrel people shall dwell in Ashdod.*"

These calamities are said to result in "*the pride* of the Philistines" being destroyed. The term "pride" (*gaʾon*, from the root *gaʾah*, "be proud, boastful") refers to the *exaltation* and magnificence of nations in their outward splendor, *e.g.*, Chaldeans (Isa. 13:11), Egypt (Ezek. 32:12); Israel (Hos. 5:5). Often it is tinged with the thought of "pride" in a bad sense, as doubtless here (Isa. 16:6; Zeph. 2:10; Ezek. 7:20). Philistine arrogance in their independence, their nationality, and their prowess was proverbial. But Zechariah sees a good result of the judgment of the people of Philistia. They are going to be delivered from their idolatrous abominations and incorporated as a remnant into the people of God. **And I will take away his blood and his abominations from between his teeth, and he** [*gam huʾ*, "even he"] **shall be left as a remnant** [*nishʾar*, "be left over" (Exod. 8:27)] **for our God. And he shall be as a chiliarch in Judah, and Ekron shall be as a Jebusite.**

The Philistine nation here is individualized as a man, spoken of in the singular. The **blood** alluded to is that of idolatrous sacrifices. The **abominations** are the polluting foods and other practices of idolatry. These paganistic customs shall be purged away. They are referred to as "detested things" (*shiqqutsim* from the *piel* denominative verb *shiqqets*, "detest, abhor, render detestable"). The term often refers to idolatry as that which is utterly abominable and horrible (Dan. 11:31; 12:11; Jer. 4:1; 7:30; II Kings 23:24; Isa. 66:3). As uncircumcised idol-worshippers, the practices of the Philistines were particularly abominable to pious Israelites. The Philistines, however, shall become like "a clan" (*ʾalluph*, "a chiliarch," evidently derived from *ʾeleph*, meaning "a thousand") and shall be as important as a man having political authority over a thousand people among God's own in Judah, or like the clan of a thousand people itself. **And Ekron shall be as the Jebusite,**

8 And I will encamp about mine house because of the army, because of him that passeth by, and because of him that returneth: and no oppressor shall pass through them any more: for now have I seen with mine eyes.

8   And I will encamp about my house against the army, that none pass through or return; and no oppressor shall pass through them any more: for now have I seen with mine eyes.

(vs. 7), that is like the ancient Jebusites, who inhabited Zion when David took the city. These idolatry-delivered Philistines shall be amalgamated with the people of God like Araunah, the Jebusite, who lived in the midst of God's people as a distinguished citizen and the friend of David (II Sam. 24:15-25; I Chron. 21:18-29).

Judgment will not only fall on the neighboring nations who have been Israel's ancient enemies, and a remnant of them be converted, but the Lord will carefully protect and preserve His own people for the coming of Messiah their Savior and eventual World Conqueror. This thought is now taken up.

4. *The Prophecy of Jerusalem's Escape from Alexander the Harbinger of a Future Complete Deliverance Under Messiah* (Zech. 9:8). Then I will encamp about my house against an army passing through and returning, neither will an oppressor any more overrun them, for now I see with my eyes.

The first part of this verse had an amazing and precise fulfillment in the advance of Alexander against Palestine. According to Josephus (*Antiquities of the Jews*, XI, 8:3), Alexander demanded of the Jewish high priest Jaddua the payment of tribute which the Jews had customarily paid to the king of Persia. The high priest refused to break his agreement of loyalty with Darius. Alexander, in a rage, threatened to inflict a severe punishment on Jerusalem as soon as Tyre had fallen and he had reduced the Philistine strongholds.

Having taken Gaza, Alexander planned to go to Jerusalem. The high priest ordered the Jerusalem popula-

tion to make sacrifices to God and pray for deliverance. God gave the high priest a dream, instructing him that he should take courage and go out of the city to welcome Alexander.

When Alexander was not far from the city, the high priest led a venerable procession to meet the Macedonian. When the conqueror saw the Jewish high priest arrayed in purple and scarlet with his mitre on his head, having a golden plate with the name of God engraved upon it, and attended by priests in white robes, he adored the name of Jehovah and saluted the high priest. Alexander said he had seen such a person in a dream at Dios in Macedonia. As a result of this experience, Alexander treated the Jews kindly. The city, the temple, and the people were granted a marvelous deliverance according to this prophecy of Zechariah, as its contextual relations in this chapter show.

It is noteworthy that the Lord Himself through the prophet announces His direct interposition in this remarkable undertaking. **Then will I encamp about my house because of an army.** The word "encamp," *hanah*, is a military term from the root "decline," "bend down," Arabic *hanā*, "bend down." It is employed of a day *declining to its close* (Judg. 19:9), and in the sense of "encamp" has the notion of the *settling down* of an army at the day's end or in conquered territory. Accordingly it is used of Israel conquering Canaan (Josh. 4:19; 5:10) and of the Philistine army (I Sam. 4:1; 13:16). It is employed metaphorically of the Lord's encamping "at" or "by," preposition *l*, as here, *levethi*, "at" or "by my house," in the sense of *saviv le*, "round about" (Num. 2:34; Exod. 18:5;

I Sam. 26:5; Ps. 34:7, 8), so Marti (*Das Dodekapropheton*, p. 429).

The expression **my house** by metonymy stands for God's land or His people Israel among whom He has taken up His residence in the temple at Jerusalem (as in Jer. 12:7; Hos. 8:1; 9:15) as Henderson, Chambers, Leupold, etc., show (Leupold, *op. cit.*, p. 170; Henderson, *The Minor Prophets*, p. 409). It is obvious, moreover, that the protection of God's house is closely associated with the protection of His people. The *reason* the Lord will encamp about His house (and people) is **because of an army**, *mitstsava'*. The preposition *min*, commonly here taken causally "by reason of," as in Exodus 2:23; 6:9; Deuteronomy 7:7; I Kings 14:4; Isaiah 53:5, is rather to be construed with Chambers in a secondary sense "against," that is, "I will encamp *against* an army" (Lange's *Commentary*, vol. 14, p. 67), which suits the context admirably, although the common causal use of *min* is also satisfactory.

The *keri* reading, **because of** [or "against"] **an army**, *mitstsava'*, is evidently correct, rather than the *kethiv*, *matstsavah*, which the R.S.V. follows: "I will encamp at my house *as a guard*" (adverbial accusative). Compare also Marti, *op. cit.*, who cites I Samuel 14:12, where however, the word is *matstsavah* (from *natsav*, "to take one's stand, guard") for *matstsav*, "a garrison, guard." Accordingly Kuenen, Stade, and Marti's reading, adopted also by Leupold (*Exposition of Zechariah*, p. 171) and unsoundly followed by the R.S.V., is as Brown, Driver, and Briggs say "probably non-existent" (*Hebrew and English Lexicon*, p. 663). Laetsch (*The Minor Prophets*, p. 450) more acceptably follows the *keri* reading, "army."

The army referred to being that of Alexander of Macedon, the promise maintains that the Jews were not to be molested either on the army's march to or from Egypt. **And I will encamp about my house against the army passing through and re-** turning. The Hebrew has "against [it] passing through [*me'over*] and against [it] returning," *mishshav*. The same phrases occur in Zechariah 7:14, but with a different contextual meaning. The participles present a continuous action and, modifying "army" (*tsava'*), give the resultant meaning: "And I will encamp about my house *against* the army *when it is passing through and returning*." The repetition of the preposition *min*, "against," *three* times, once before the substantive and twice before the modifying participles, is a grammatical device to emphasize the Lord's complete protection in a time of supreme crisis. Although the Jews were in a very precarious situation because of their declared loyalty to Persia, and although Alexander severely punished the Samaritans, he showed great favor to the Jews, as Zechariah's prophecy had intimated.

Although most scholars construe "army" as definite **the army,** the word is without the article in the Hebrew and is more strictly "an army." In prophetic vision Zechariah simply envisioned "an army," which to him though formidable and phenomenally successful, yet was indefinite as he glimpsed it. Fulfilment of the passage historically gives the context a definiteness that the broad prophecy when uttered did not possess.

At this point prophecy, as is so often the case, like a tornado funnel, leaves the ground and lifts to a higher altitude. In setting forth the past judgment of the kingdoms contiguous to Israel and the signal deliverance of God's people in the case of Alexander the Great, the world conqueror, the prophecy now portrays the future punishment that awaits the enemies of God's people, Israel, who will be dwelling in the lands adjacent to Palestine at the end of the age. Zechariah's prophecy is intended not only to instruct the people of that age, in regard to the first advent of Christ, but to give a broader eschatological context in describing the destruction of the Gentile world powers preceding the second advent of Christ and the establishment of the millennial kingdom. The contrast is between *two world-conquerors*, Alexander and the Messiah in His second advent. The prophecy of the one being the occasion of the long-range prediction of the other, and the long-range view of the latter embracing (vs. 9) also the shorter-range view. For the prophet well knew Messiah could not come as World-Conqueror, King of kings and Lord of lords (Rev. 19:16) at His second advent until He first appeared as rejected King and lowly Savior at His first coming.

Thus verse 8 *bridges the centuries* between the deliverance of Israel under Alexander, the human world-conqueror **(then will I encamp about my house against an army passing through and returning)** and the nation's *final* deliverance under Messiah, the divine World Conqueror at His second advent **(neither will an oppressor any more overrun them, for now I see with my eyes).**

No oppressor such as Egypt, Assyria, Babylon, Persia, or Alexander, the world conqueror, will again overrun the Lord's people, Israel. **Oppressor,** *noges*, is a participle, by its form indicating the continuousness of the cruel oppression so frequently endured from foreign tyrants. The root *nages* has the notion of "driving fiercely," Arabic *najasha*, "rouse and drive game," Assyrian *nagashu*, "throw down, overthrow." In Ethiopic it means "to exercise royal power, reign as a king." The Hebrew participle means a "taskmaster," that is, "a slave driver," "oppressor" (Exod. 3:7; 5:6, 10, 13, 14), "foreign tyrant or oppressor" (Isa. 9:3; 14:2, 4) and this is the use in Zechariah 9:8, as well as in Zechariah 10:4 (*q.v.*).

Since the adverb "again" (*'odh*, "yet," "still") expressing "continuance" or "persistence" from the root *'udh*, "repeat," "do again," limits the verbal action to a single occurrence and is negative, the thought is "*not*

again" (cf. Gen. 4:25; 9:11; 18:29; Hos. 12:10; Jer. 31:4). **An oppressor will not overrun** [emphatic by position] **them again.** This can *only* be applied to the period initiated by the second advent of Messiah and not the first advent, as Henderson erroneously imagines, who must confess, however, that the Jews "were indeed subject to much suffering, both from the Egyptian and Syrian kings, especially from Antiochus Epiphanes, but their nationality was not destroyed, and the evils to which they were exposed only paved the way for the Maccabean victories, and the Asmonean dynasty" (*op. cit.*, pp. 409, 410).

But this prophecy embraces much more than the mere survival of the Jewish nationality until the coming of Israel's king at His first advent. It says **an oppressor shall not again overrun them,** which was cruelly true both of the Seleucids and later the Romans. Under the latter's tyranny, the most terrible and relentless of all, Messiah was born.

The reference can only be to the second coming of Messiah, the true World Conqueror and Establisher of the kingdom over Israel and through Israel over the nations of the millennial earth. His victorious and all-righteous reign alone will insure that **an oppressor shall not again pass over against** [*ya'avor 'al*, "hostilely overrun" (cf. I Sam. 14:4), *'alehem*] **them,** *i.e.*, the Lord's people Israel, by metonymy, "My house," (see vs. 8a) standing for "My people" and furnishing the antecedent for the pronoun "them."

The Lord appends this age-spanning prophecy with a declaration that explains its magnificent panoramic sweep from the rise of Alexander the conqueror to Christ the coming King of kings and Lord of lords, and gives the reason for the Israelite nation's hope (and Zechariah *is the prophet of hope*) in ultimate *complete* deliverance from every tyrant. For [*kî*, "because"] **now I see with my eyes** (*i.e.*, now *I see quite plainly*), is an expressive anthropopathism very graphically ac-

9 Rejoice greatly, O daughter of Zion; shout, O daughter of Jerusalem: behold, thy King cometh unto thee: he is just, and having salvation; lowly, and riding upon an ass, and upon a colt the foal of an ass.

9   Rejoice greatly, O daughter of Zion; shout, O daughter of Jerusalem: behold, thy king cometh unto thee; he is just, and having salvation; lowly, and riding upon an ass, even upon a colt the foal of an ass.

centuating the fact that for their preservation at the time of Alexander and for their future deliverance from every oppressor, Israel is indebted to the providence of God which watched over them for good. **I see with my eyes** is tantamount to "I am with omniscient perspicacity exercising My providential interposition." God always "sees," but "sees plainly" when *openly* and *visibly* He undertakes for His own, as He will when Messiah returns to put down His enemies and establish His kingdom of righteousness and peace over Israel (Acts 1:6; Ps. 2:1–12).

It is as if the Lord were declaring: "Now at last I see the affliction and distress of My people and the time will come when I will grant *full* deliverance to them." The words are meaningfully reminiscent of Israel's affliction at the hands of their Egyptian "taskmasters" (same word *noges* as in Zech. 9:8 in plural) and their rescue from Egypt which are typical in prophecy of Israel's future national deliverance, with the overthrow of her enemies foreshadowed by the destruction of the Egyptian army in the Red Sea. "I have surely seen the affliction of my people which are in Egypt, and have heard their cry by reason of their *taskmasters* [*nogesaw*], for I know their sorrows" (Exod. 3:7).

Messiah's first advent (vs. 9) was to be the earnest of the proof that now at length the Lord had seen the afflictions of His people and would undertake for them. But it was only the earnest. Although Messiah died to make atonement for human sin (including Israel's), His own people rejected Him and refused His salvation and Lordship. Not until He comes as the divine true World Conqueror of

whom Alexander was the human contrast will the full meaning of "Now I see with My eyes" dawn upon Israel, for not until then will they accept Him and the glorious deliverance He purchased for them by His Cross.

II. THE FIRST ADVENT OF ISRAEL'S HUMBLE KING AND SAVIOR (Zech. 9:9)

Against the background of the invincibly marching armies of Alexander, however, envisioned as only a tool in the hand of God, emerges a strikingly contrasting figure of another great King and Deliverer, not a human conqueror, but a divine Prince of Peace; not one who inspires fear and dread, but one whose coming calls forth paeans of lilting joy; not a foreign tyrant, but Israel's *own* King, not cruel and oppressive, but infinitely righteous; not slaying His foes, but providing salvation; not rich and powerful, but poor and meek; not astride a prancing steed, but riding upon a humble ass, an animal of peace.

1. *The Joyful Announcement of the Coming of Israel's King and Savior* (Zech. 9:9a). **Exult exceedingly, O daughter of Zion! Shout aloud, O daughter of Jerusalem. Lo, your King comes to you....** The advent of Israel's King is heralded in stirring imperatives enjoining intense joy and lively vocatives, addressing Jerusalem directly and challengingly in poetic personification with synonymous parallelism (the second line repeating precisely the thought of the first line and thus reinforcing it):

Exult exceedingly, O daughter of Zion! Shout aloud, O daughter of Jerusalem!

The third line gives the reason for the joyful ecstasy here so graphically enjoined in the first two lines:

Lo, your King comes!

The style of this great prophetic passage is joyfully animated. The prophet employs stirring language as if he were actually viewing the animated scene before his eyes. *The high pitch of ecstatic rejoicing* portrayed by the passage is achieved in the following ways: (1) Its being flashed so brightly and suddenly against the somber backdrop of the fear engendered by Alexander the Great's world conquests. (2) Its repetition (for emphasis) of the command to rejoice in *two* imperatives, both enjoining ecstatic joy. **Rejoice** (*gili,* second feminine singular from *gil,* Arabic *jala,* "go round and round," "be ecstatically joyous" (Isa. 35:1; 49:13; Ps. 2:11). It is reinforced by the adverb *meʾodh,* "exceedingly" or "greatly." The second imperative is **shout,** *hariʿi,* also second feminine singular agreeing with the feminine **daughter,** used in the causative stem in the sense of "raising a shout" or "giving a blast" on a horn. The word is used also of *shouting an alarm* for battle (Josh. 6:10; Judg. 7:21); *shouting triumphantly* over foes (Jer. 50:15); *shouting in approbation* (I Sam. 10:24) and with religious impulse (I Sam. 4:5; Ezra 3:11). Zechariah uses it in the sense *"to shout" in applause and joyful approbation.*

The high pitch of joy of Zechariah 9:9 is also achieved (3) by the lively vocatives of *direct address,* **O daughter of Zion!** ... **O daughter of Jerusalem.** (4) By the personification of *Zion* (Ṣiyyon), originally the Jebusite stronghold taken by David (II Sam. 5:7; I Chron. 11:5) on the southern part of the east hill of Jerusalem south of the Temple (I Kings 8:1). The old city is personified by poet and prophet to denote Jerusalem's inhabitants from a political point of view. Both Zion and Jerusalem are personified as beautiful young women, as was customary (cf. "Daughter of Babylon," that is "Babylon" Zech. 2:7 [11]). (5) By the parallelism (see above). (6) By the dramatic fashion in which the *reason* for the commands

to rejoice is introduced. The employment of the interjectional adverb **Lo,** [*hinneh*] **behold thy King!** centering attention upon the person of the King! (7) By employing the pronominal suffix, *"thy King," malkekh.* (8) With the good news of His advent — **the King comes!** (9) With the added note of joy, **comes to you,** i.e., "for your benefit and good."

This is the occasion of immense spiritual significance demanding energetic and intense expressions of joyful emotion, to which Orientals are accustomed, aptly set forth to announce the coming of the long-awaited One and to welcome Him with the joyous acclaim His Person and mission import.

2. *A Featured Account of the Character and Condition of Israel's King and Savior Is Given* (Zech. 9:9b). **Righteous and dispensing salvation is he, lowly and riding on an ass, on a colt the foal of an ass.** Having announced the joyful advent of the King, a featured description of His character and condition is given in synthetic parallelism (the progressive flow of thought in which the second, or following lines, add something to the first ("Lo, thy King comes to you"):

"Righteous and dispensing salvation is He,
humble and riding on an ass,
on a colt the foal of an ass."

Four features of Zion's King are presented, each in striking contrast to the great Greek conqueror, against whose worldly brilliant career His divine portrait is flashed. First, **He is righteous** or "just." This Alexander was not, often being capriciously and violently unjust, especially against those who offended his towering ego. The adjective *tsaddiq* is from the verb *tsadeq,* "be just, righteous" in conduct and character (Job 10:15; 15:14; 22:3). The adjective is used of God (Deut. 32:4; Ps. 119:137; 129:4; Job 34:17) and especially of the Servant of the Lord, the Messiah, as justified and vindicated by the Lord (Isa. 53:11), as well as His people justified by Him (Isa. 60:21).

Messiah is "just" or "righteous" in government, which is the chief virtue of a king (Isa. 11:3–5; Ps. 45:6, 7 [7, 8]). Of Messiah as a future reigning Davidic King the prophecy is:

A ruler shall rise over men, who is *righteous*, who holds his dominion through reverence for God (II Sam. 23:3).

Jeremiah prophesied: "See, the days are coming, says the Lord, when I will raise up to David a *righteous* Branch, and He shall reign as king, deal wisely, and *execute judgment* and *righteousness* in the land. In his days Judah shall be saved, and Israel shall dwell securely; and this is his name whereby he shall be called: THE LORD OUR RIGHTEOUSNESS" (Jer. 23:5, 6).

He alone who would come as "the posterity *of the woman*" (Gen. 3:15), who alone would be "a child born" (His humanity) as well as "a son given" (His deity) (Isa. 9:6 [5]) could be *truly righteous*. As the sinless One supernaturally born of a virgin (Isa. 7:14; Matt. 1:23), He alone could be the Sinless One and righteous in an absolute sense. He had Himself to be "infinitely just" (righteous) in order to be "the justifier" of the sinner who would believe on Him (Rom. 3:26). This is first and foremost in the character and Person of Him who came to "seek and to save that which was lost" (Luke 19:10).

The R.S.V. rendering of *tsaddiq* by "triumphant," following such critics as Marti (*op. cit.*, p. 429) and Wildeboer (*Zeitschrift für Alttestamentliche Wissenschaft*, 1902, pp. 167–169) is arbitrary, contrary to the context, and oblivious of the plain normal meaning of the adjective.

A second feature of Israel's King is given. **He shows himself a Savior,** i.e., *"saves"* (*nosha'*). This is a *nifal* participle with a normal *reflexive* (not a passive) meaning. It thus means "showing Himself a Savior." This Alexander in diametrical contrast was not, butchering, slaughtering thousands, as at Tyre and Gaza, and selling other countless thousands into slavery. "The Son of man came not to

destroy men's lives, but to save them" (Luke 9:56, margin).

That the correct meaning of *nosha'* is "showing Himself a Savior" is shown from the following considerations. (1) The reflexive is a *normal idiomatic* use of the *nifal*, especially with verbs not used in the *qal*. For example, *sha'an*, "support"; *nish'an*, "support oneself," "lean" (Num. 21:15; Isa. 10:20); *shava'*, probably "count seven"; *nishba'*, "bind oneself by seven things, adjure oneself," i.e., "swear" (Gen. 24:7, 9; Deut. 6:13); *'adar*, "be great, noble"; *ne'dar*, *nifal* participle, "displaying oneself glorious" (Exod. 15:11). (2) The passive sense "saved," despite Calvin, Cocceius, Chambers, Leupold, Laetsch ("One Delivered"), and most modern writers, is scarcely satisfactory in the context. If it were said, *"the people were saved,"* this sense would be acceptable, but to speak of a King who came to save others as "saved" or "delivered" without any intimation of previous danger or suffering is scarcely admissible. Leupold does the most that can be done with this interpretation, showing that the "God-man, as a man," needed help and received it in prayer, etc." (*op. cit.*, p. 174). Actually, however, rather than being "delivered," the Savior was delivered up to suffering and death at the hands of His enemies in order to deliver or save others.

(3) Something much more radical and fundamental than the passive idea "saved" is indicated here by the close association of the participle *nosha'* with the preceding adjective, "righteous," *tsaddiq*. Our Lord's "showing Himself a Savior" for others was a unique proof of His possession of that infinite righteousness which was an indispensable prerequisite for the justification of guilty sinners (I Cor. 1:30; Phil. 3:8, 9; Rom. 3:26; II Cor. 5:21; I John 2:1). In the structure of this great Messianic prophecy, the adjective *tsaddiq* ("righteous") bears the same relationship to the participle *nosha'*,

"showing Himself a Savior," as *'ani* ("lowly") bears to the participle *rokhev* ("riding"). In either case the participle expresses the proof or manifestation of that characteristic of Messiah which the adjective denotes. As His being "righteous" was demonstrated in His "showing Himself a Savior," so His being "lowly" was manifested in his "riding upon an ass."

(4) The fact that all the ancient versions render *nosha'* actively favors the reflexive rendering of the *nifal*, not the passive. It is plain this active sense is the result *not* of ignoring the *nifal* form of the participle but of the active meaning that easily springs out of the germane *reflexive* idea. "Showing Himself a Savior" is precisely the same as "dispensing salvation" or the Septuagint *sōzōn* ("saving") or the Vulgate *Salvator* ("a Savior"), since participles have a pronounced substantival quality. The R.S.V. completely misses the real meaning of this vital Messianic passage not only in translating *tsaddiq* "triumphant," but still more lamentably in rendering *nosha'* "victorious." Not only is the context violated, but the real purpose and mission of the Messiah at His first advent are lost sight of.

The third characteristic of Israel's King is that **He is lowly.** The connotation here is "humble" (Ps. 18:27 [28]; II Sam. 22:28). Again what a contrast to the proud, dashing Greek world conqueror, Alexander. But the adjective *'ani* (from the root *'anah*, "be afflicted, bowed down," Arabic *'ana*, "be lowly, submissive") has wider ramifications in Messiah's life than His merely being "humble" or "lowly." The adjective comprehends the full outworking of this basic attitude of His mind (Phil. 2:5–7). The word also embraces the meaning "poor, needy" in an economic sense (Deut. 15:11; 24:14; Prov. 31:20; Lev. 19:10; 23:27) which our Lord was (Matt. 8:20; Luke 9:58). It also comprehends the meaning of a pious person "afflicted" by evil men (Isa. 14:32; Hab. 3:14). Hengstenberg,

Keil, Baron, and others correctly view this word in its larger connotation as epitomizing "the whole of the lowly, miserable, suffering condition" of the righteous Servant of the Lord so graphically delineated in Isaiah 52:13 – 53:12 (Baron, *The Visions and Prophecies of Zechariah*, pp. 308f.). How naturally with the sinlessness and the Saviorhood of the Messiah set forth in Zechariah 9:9 should follow the thought of His rejection, suffering, and atoning death. Zechariah, thoroughly conversant with the former prophets, and quoting and echoing them throughout his entire prophecy, apparently features this important aspect of Messiah's earthly career.

An illustration of Messiah's lowliness is the fact that He would appear **riding upon an ass.** Again what a contrast to the proud and impetuous world conqueror Alexander astride the finest horse procurable in the ancient world. The ass after the time of Solomon was regarded as a very lowly animal ridden only by persons who possessed no rank or worldly position. Israel's King riding on this modest animal indicates Him to be without station or prestige.

Although the ass was a respectable beast which even nobility rode in early Israel (Judg. 5:10; 10:4; 12:14; II Sam. 17:23; 19:26), the wide introduction of horses after David's reign (I Kings 10:25–29; II Kings 9:18, 19) completely changed the situation. Thereafter people of wealth and importance, especially kings and warriors, rode horses, and the ass was considered a menial burden-bearer, utterly unsuited to the dignity of princes. Archaeology has resurrected mementoes of Solomon's traffic in horses and chariots (I Kings 10:25–29), especially the numerous stables at the monarch's chariot city of Megiddo in the plain of Esdraelon.

Jeremiah speaks of kings and princes "riding in chariots and on horses, they and their princes, the men of Judah and the inhabitants of Jerusalem" (Jer. 17:25). Although the humility

10 And I will cut off the chariot from Ephraim, and the horse from Jerusalem, and the battle bow shall be cut off: and he shall speak peace unto the heathen: and his dominion shall be from sea even to sea, and from the river even to the ends of the earth.

10   And I will cut off the chariot from Ephraim, and the horse from Jerusalem; and the battle bow shall be cut off; and he shall speak peace unto the nations: and his dominion shall be from sea to sea, and from the River to the ends of the earth.

and lowliness of Messiah are those features of character which come into focus in Messiah's riding upon an ass, the thought of His peaceful career is not necessarily excluded, since the ass is a common burden-bearer and points to a time of peace. But the thought of humble station is the salient idea, and is stressed in the following phrase, **and upon a colt, the foal of an ass.** The conjunction **and** (*waw*) is conjunctive. Israel's King is not only **riding upon an ass,** the animal is accompanied by a young colt, cf. Matt. 21:1, 2.

Christ's Triumphal Entry into Jerusalem (Matt. 21:4, 5; John 12:14, 15) attests its Messianic connotation of this great prophecy, but this far-reaching prediction was not intended to depict in the main the Triumphal Procession. It rather had in mind the entire scope of the Savior's life, the complete order of events which transpired at His first advent. The Triumphal Entry simply brought into focus this panoramic view of Messiah's Person and character.

In the matter of quoting this passage there is a blending of both Zechariah 9:9 and Isaiah 62:11. Both of these wonderful Old Testament prophecies coalesce to cast their light of fulfilment on the New Testament incidents. Modern criticism would judge these quotations word by word, but the Holy Spirit through the sacred writers elicits the sense of these great passages and presents a composite sketch of the character of Messiah which comes into clearest view in the events of the Triumphal Entry of the King into Jerusalem.

III.   THE SECOND ADVENT OF ISRAEL'S GLORIOUS KING AS ESTABLISHER OF A WORLD-WIDE KINGDOM OF PEACE (Zech. 9:10-17)

From the deep humiliation and affliction of Messiah at His first advent (vs. 9) the prophet is now directed to the glory that should follow and the blessed events connected with the second coming of Israel's Redeemer-King, not only as these are related to Jerusalem and Israel, but to the whole earth. Messiah's coming as the Son of man in glory will alone bring the fulfilment of these far-reaching words.

1.   *Zion's King Establishes Peace at His Second Advent* (Zech. 9:10). **And he** [following the Septuagint] **will cut off the chariotry from Ephraim and the cavalry from Jerusalem, and the battle bow shall be cut off.** The rule and reign of Messiah's kingdom are here described. The King will extend His sway by peaceful methods. Having conquered evil men, He will effectually remove all the instruments of war from His people. **The chariot, the horse,** and **the battle bow** stand for the whole class of offensive weapons to be destroyed (cf. Mic. 5:10, 11 [9, 10]).

As Messiah will bring salvation not by means of human weapons of war, so His Kingdom of righteousness shall not be established on the principles of world power nor will the subjects of the millennial kingdom rely upon armaments any more. As the Lord says through Hosea, "I will, however, still show pity for the house of Judah, and I will deliver them through the Lord their God; but I will not deliver them by bow, or sword, or war, or

11 As for thee also, by the blood of thy covenant I have sent forth thy prisoners out of the pit wherein is no water.

12 Turn you to the strong hold, ye prisoners of hope: even to day do I declare that I will render double unto thee;

---

11   As for thee also, because of the blood of thy covenant I have set free thy prisoners from the pit wherein is no water.

12   Turn you to the stronghold, ye prisoners of hope: even today do I declare that I will render double unto thee.

---

horses, or horsemen" (1:7). At last there will be total world disarmament. At last permanent world peace, which statesmen have worked so hard and so futilely to attain in this age, will be a reality.

Israel's King comes to **speak peace** (*dabber shalom*). This does not mean to command peace, but it does imply that there is effectiveness and authority in the word which He shall speak to bring about peace both externally and internally. Messiah will publish peace. As He speaks "peace to his people and to his saints" (Ps. 85:8 [9]), so He will announce peace and the removal of all hostility. Moreover, His spoken word will be efficacious.

In describing the extent of Messiah's kingly reign it is interesting that Zechariah quotes from Psalm 72, which gives a complete vision of the Messianic kingdom. "And his dominion shall be from sea to sea and from the river to the ends of the earth" (Ps. 72:8). All David's prayers will find their answer in the Kingdom (Ps. 72:20; II Sam. 23:1–7). The phrase "from sea to sea" (Heb. *miyyam 'adh yam*) cannot be circumscribed. It has its full earth-wide connotation in this kingdom context. The Euphrates, mentioned as the easternmost boundary of the promised land (Gen. 15:18; Exod. 23:31) is perhaps indicated as the starting point. But whatever the *terminus a quo*, the dominion indicated is world-wide. Palestine, which will then have its greatest limits promised to the patriarchs, will be the focal point of the kingdom-rule which will extend from it to the ends of the earth.

What a contrasting Messianic pic- ture is offered in Zechariah 9:9, 10. In verse 9 is presented the view of Messiah at His first advent – righteous, showing Himself a Savior, poor, afflicted, rejected, riding upon a lowly ass! In verse 10 is pictured His second advent in power and glory, cutting off the instruments of war, speaking peace to the nations, with His dominion extending to the uttermost confines of the earth. Such is the blended picture of the first and second advents of Messiah everywhere evident in Old Testament prophecy.

2. *The Lord Encourages Suffering Israelites in View of the Nation's Future Hope* (Zech. 9:11, 12). Having presented Israel's King in His first and second advents, the prophet now devotes his attention to encouraging the godly sufferers in Israel in prospect of the blessings of peace to come to Zion and the world in the establishment of Messiah's kingdom. Zion is personally addressed. **As for thee also, because of the blood of thy covenant I have sent forth thy prisoners from the pit** [*bor*, Prov. 28:17] **in which there is no water** (vs. 11). The words as for thee also stand out because of their dangling position. Zion is emphatically addressed. Paraphrased, the expression runs thus: "Even though *you*, Zion, are in such a desperate situation, taken captive and in dire straits, yet I have grace in store for *you*."

This grace is based upon **the blood of the covenant**. Probably as Chambers, Baron, Laetsch, and others observe, what is referred to is the blood of the Mosaic covenant (Exod. 24:8), although one would expect either the Palestinian (Deut. 30:1–10) or Davidic covenant (II Sam. 7:4–17) to be meant. At any rate, the shedding of blood sealed the covenant, and the death of Jesus Christ is the badge of fulfilment of *any* of the covenants and promises to Israel as well as any promise made to saved Gentiles.

Thy prisoners [O Zion], **are going to be rescued from the pit in which there is no water.** This is an apparent allusion to Joseph's forlorn condition (Gen. 37:24). In antiquity prisoners were often kept in a cistern or a dry well. While this section of the prophecy doubtless refers to the time of Israel's trouble during the great tribulation just preceding the coming of her King, yet the near and far view blend. The struggles of the Maccabean period loom in the background and as that was a *religious* war, so this portrays prophetically that Armageddon and the final windup of wars preceding the advent of the Prince of Peace will have a *religious* nature.

Anti-Semitism, energized by diabolical hatred of Israel because of God's plan and purpose for her in the earth, will characterize in part the war of the last days, just as the Maccabean struggle was a contest between the religious life of Judaism and the crass paganism of Greek Hellenism. This is the reason why the Maccabean contest with Antiochus Epiphanes looms in the background.

The brave stalwarts of the Maccabean age are told to return to the **fortress** because they are **prisoners of the hope** (vs. 12). This doubtless refers to the hope of all the ages, the hope centered in Messiah. The promise of deliverance is clear. **Yea, this very day I am declaring** [participle] **that I will recompense to you double** (vs. 12).

It was fortunate for Joseph that there was no water in the pit, otherwise it would have spelled his death. So Israel, in the pit of captivity and affliction, is nevertheless not suffered to be utterly destroyed. God will bring the nation out of affliction and into the kingdom. Like Joseph they shall be lifted from the dungeon and

the pit to the throne (Ps. 40:2, 3 [3, 4]). The **stronghold** to which the people are to return is best taken as God Himself (Joel 3:16 [4:16]).

The reference to God's restored people receiving a **double portion** (Heb. *mishneh*) has in mind Israel as the first-born among the nations (Exod. 4:22). As the first-born son received a double portion (Deut. 21:15–17), so as a principle of God's dealing with His own people, His restored nation shall receive "double" in blessing, the law stipulating that the first-born son should inherit a double portion of his father's property as compared with other members of the family. Personal unfitness or transgression could forfeit this privilege.

But the idea of "double" can indicate not only reception of blessing but of punishment. Israel, as God's first-born among the nations, had a corresponding responsibility. If she failed to realize her double blessing by obedience, she would receive a double punishment. This is the significance of Isaiah 40:2 and Jeremiah 16:18.

The phrase **prisoners of hope** shows that Israel's disobedience and resultant chastisements are not to be perpetual. "For their shame they shall have double [*mishneh*]; and instead of confusion they shall rejoice in their portion. Therefore, in their land they shall inherit the double portion [*mishneh*]. Everlasting joy shall be theirs" (Isa. 61:7).

3. *The Maccabean Struggle with Godless Paganism, in Adumbration of Israel's Final Conflict Before Kingdom Blessing* (Zech. 9:13–15). **For I will bend Judah for me as a bow. I will fill it with Ephraim. And I will stir up your sons, O Zion, against your sons, O Greece. Then will I make you as the sword of a hero** (vs. 13). As Laetsch says, "In bold metaphor the Lord compares Himself to a warrior using Judah as His bow, Ephraim as His arrow" (*Minor Prophets*, p. 458). Moreover, how beautifully does the

13 When I have bent Judah for me, filled the bow with Ephraim, and raised up thy sons, O Zion, against thy sons, O Greece, and made thee as the sword of a mighty man.
14 And the Lord shall be seen over them, and his arrow shall go forth as the lightning: and the Lord God shall blow the trumpet, and shall go with whirlwinds of the south.
15 The Lord of hosts shall defend them; and they shall devour, and subdue with sling stones; and they shall drink, and make a noise as through wine; and they shall be filled like bowls, and as the corners of the altar.

13   For I have bent Judah for me, I have filled the bow with Ephraim; and I will stir up thy sons, O Zion, against thy sons, O Greece, and will make thee as the sword of a mighty man.
14   And Jehovah shall be seen over them; and his arrow shall go forth as the lightning; and the Lord Jehovah will blow the trumpet, and will go with whirlwinds of the south.
15   Jehovah of hosts will defend them; and they shall devour, and shall tread down the sling-stones; and they shall drink, and make a noise as through wine; and they shall be filled like bowls, like the corners of the altar.

Lord signify His identification with His people Israel in their woes and His fighting for them. Ephraim is the "arrow" because used to fill the bow, Judah. As a warrior how wonderfully the Lord manipulated these instruments of war, causing His people to triumph so gloriously over overwhelming odds in the heroic Maccabean struggles. Zion itself in the same valorous conflict was made as a sword [*ḥerev*] of a hero (*gibbor*, adjective, "*strong*," *puissant* from *gavar*, "be powerful," then a "strong, valiant man" ([Josh. 10:2; I Sam. 2:4; I Kings 1:8]). The Lord is pictured as "bending" or "stretching His bow" (Judah), i.e., by "treading," or "stepping" with His weight on it (*darak*, "tread," i.e., bend the large composite bow [Jer. 51:3; Lam. 2:4; 3:12; I Chron. 5:18; 8:40; Isa. 21:15]). How signally does God show how able *He* is to conquer all His people's enemies, bringing about the ultimate full realization of their hope in Messiah.
The sons of Zion (*bene Ṣiyyon*) are "citizens of Zion," i.e., "Zionites" and the sons of Greece (*bene yawan*) are citizens of Ionia or Greece, i.e., Greeks. Javan (Assyrian *Iamanu*) is called a "son" of Japheth (Gen. 10:2). In Ezekiel 27:13 Javan refers to

Ionians as traders and in Isaiah 66:19 as a distant country. The declaration of the Lord, Then I will stir up your sons, O Zion, against your sons, O Greece, demonstrates what the spiritual dynamic was that so signalized the Jews in their heroism in the Maccabean era. The verb stir up (*'orarti*) is from the stem *'ur*, "awake, rouse oneself," which in the *polel* means to "rouse, excite" with the preposition *'al*, "to incite hostilely against anyone" (Isa. 13:17; Jer. 50:9; Ezek. 23:22).
The reference to "the Zionites" and "the Greeks" (vs. 13) envisions the mighty delivering hand of the Lord *in the war* of the Maccabees in a later and most critical period of Jewish history (175–163 B.C.); just as in the earlier part of this prophecy, there was a divine deliverance *without war* against Alexander the Great's invasion.
Verse 14 *portrays the Lord protecting His people under the figure of a storm*, as He had just described His deliverance of His people under the metaphor of their being bow, arrow, and sword in His omnipotent hand. And the Lord [emphatic by first position in a verbal sentence] over them [*'alehem*, "above them," *His distressed people*, secondary emphasis] shall appear [*yera'eh*, "be seen or show

Himself," *nifal* passive or reflexive]. The symbolism reminds one of Assur, the national god of Assyria, hovering protectingly over the embattled armies of his people, as appears on Assyrian reliefs. The Lord will appear "over" His people because He fights from heaven on their behalf.

Then shall his arrow [*hitstso*] **issue forth as the lightning** [*baraq*] **and the Lord God** [A.V.—*'adonai Yhwh*—literally, "*My Lordship, Yahweh,* emphatic by position] **shall blow with the trumpet.** The *shophar* is the curved horn of the ram or cow used as an instrument for alarm (Exod. 19:16; Judg. 7:22). It was a martial instrument, used chiefly in war, but was also employed in sacred ceremonies (Lev. 25:9; Ps. 47:5 [6]; 81:3 [4]; 150:3). The idiom *taqaʿ bashshophar* means to "give a loud blast with the ram's horn" (Judg. 3:27; 6:34; Josh. 6:4; I Sam. 13:3; I Kings 1:34, as here in Zech. 9:14) to arouse to danger or war or to announce some important event.

As the protector of His people the **lightning** becomes the Lord's **arrow,** the thunderblast the blowing of His **trumpet,** while He Himself *marches* (*halak,* "walks, goes") as a divine general **in the storms of the south.** The **tempest** was "a violent storm wind" (*seʿarah,* from *saʿar,* "to storm or rage," often as the vehicle of divine wrath [Isa. 29:6; 40:24; 41:16; Jer. 23:19; 30:23; Ezek. 13:11, 13]), used of the storm wind of Elijah's translation (II Kings 2:1, 11) and in connection with Ezekiel's beautific vision (Ezek. 1:4).

The storms of the south were always the most violent and destructive as they swept in unimpeded from the desert. The term **south,** *teman,* is from the root *yaman* (which although ambiguous in its origin has to do with the right hand; cf. adjective *yemani,* "right hand," as one faces east, hence "south.") In Isaiah 43:6 and Zechariah 6:6 it is employed as opposite to the "north" or "country of the north" and in Joshua 15:1 it is used

to describe the farthest southern part of the land.

Verse 15. The Lord *is presented again* (cf. vs. 14) *as hovering defensively over His people.* **The Lord of armies** [emphatic by position] **shall defend them.** The expression *yagen* (from *ganan,* "cover protectingly, defend, surround," Arabic *janna* [Isa. 31:5; Zech. 12:8]) means to *defend* by throwing a completely protective cover *around* and *over* (*ʿal*) anyone. The Lord of both the celestial as well as terrestrial armies will cover His people's heads, as well as their entire persons, in the day of battle.

The divine interposition having been described, now the results in human activity are graphically outlined. **And they** [the Lord's people] **shall devour** (*weʾakhelu*). Although the word is the ordinary one, "to eat" (Assyrian *ʾakalu,* Arbaic *ʾakala*) used of human beings (Gen. 3:11; Exod. 12:43), of the sword devouring or slaying (Deut. 32:42; II Sam. 2:26) and as a figure of oppression (Prov. 30:14; Hab. 3:14), the word is frequently found in connection with wild beasts *devouring* their prey, of Israel under the figure of a lion devouring others (Ezek. 19:3, 6) or the nations as lions devouring Israel (Jer. 50:7, 17; 51:34). In Hosea 13:8 the Lord pictures Himself as a lion devouring the wicked. Zechariah evidently here has the figure of the Lord's people devouring their oppressors like lions. What a picture of the plight of those who fight against God's people! Balaam saw Israel thus victorious. "Surely the people arise as a lioness, even as a lion they exert themselves; it does not rest till it eats its prey, nor till it drinks the blood of the slain" (Num. 23:24).

Not only will the Lord's people aided by Him victoriously devour their enemies like lions, but they will trample them under their feet like **sling stones** (*ʾavne qelaʿ*), that is, stones that have missed their mark and have fallen into the mire to be trodden down contemptuously by the

16 And the Lord their God shall save them in that day as the flock of his people: for **they shall be as** the stones of a crown, lifted up as an ensign upon his land.

16   And Jehovah their God will save them in that day as the flock of his people; for **they shall be as** the stones of a crown, lifted on high over his land.

marching victorious armies of the Lord. The Lord's people are also described as those who drink (i.e., blood) and make a noise, hilariously celebrating their triumph. **And they shall drink and be noisy** [*ḥamu*, "be turbulent," or "boisterous," (Prov. 7:11; 9:13; 20:1)] **as through wine and be full like a sacrificial bowl, as the corners of the altar.** These figures, as Chambers notes, "are priestly and intimate, a holy war and victory" (Lange's *Commentary*, 14, p. 74), as the Maccabean struggle was and as end-time Armageddon will be (Ps. 2:1-12).

The **sacrificial bowl** (*mizraq*) is a "basin." i.e., "a vessel for throwing or tossing a liquid" from *zaraq*, "to sprinkle or toss, scatter profusely," Aramaic "disperse," Assyrian *zaraku*, Arabic *zaraqa*, "throw at." It is the "basin" or "bowl" in which the priests caught the sacrificial blood of victims and from which they scattered it upon the altar (Exod. 27:3; 38:3; Num. 4:14; I Kings 7:40, 45; Jer. 52:18; Zech. 14:20). Once Amos uses the word for a "wine bowl" (Amos 6:6), and doubtless Zechariah had this allusion also in mind in the present reference.

The words **as the corners of the altar** (*mizbeaḥ*, "altar of burnt offering") presents a second striking simile. Not only will God's victors drink *full* of the blood of their vanquished enemies and be **like the sacrificial bowls** filled with blood to be sprinkled upon the sides of the altar and its horns, but they shall come through gory triumph bespattered with blood like the **corners of the altar,** itself (cf. Lev. 1:5, 11).

4. *Israel's Final End-Time Deliverance Before Kingdom Blessing* (Zech. 9:16). **And the Lord their God will deliver** [save] **them in that day as the**

flock of his people, for like the jewels of a crown will they be sparkling over his land. The faithful in Israel tasted of this victory after the terrible trials of the Maccabean wars, but the prophecy broadens out at this point and in chapter 10, which proceeds without a break, to present Israel's final time of trouble and deliverance prior to kingdom status. This fact is indicated by the time phrase **in that day,** which always in chapters 9-14 embraces the final eschatological era of Israel's future reinstatement and deliverance.

The Lord's delivering and "saving" them will be because of "the covenants" and "promises" made to His ancient elect people, which must yet be fulfilled by a faithful, covenant-keeping God (Rom. 9:4, 5). His "saving" them, therefore, will be more than help against their enemies and will involve true spiritual regeneration (Zech. 12:10-14), as well as restoration to their national election, in which position they have been temporarily set aside during this present period of their Christ-rejection and during the present age of the election of grace (Rom. 11:1-25). Afterwards, however, they will be reinstated in their *election as a nation* and saved (Rom. 11:26-36). This is the meaning of Zechariah's prophecy, **And the Lord their God shall save them in that day as the flock of his people.** Now the nation is *lo-ʿammi* ("not My people" in their unbelief). Then it will be *ʿammi*, "My people" in their belief, when they become *the flock* of the Lord's people.

The term **flock** (*tsoʾn*) involves Israel's status as "sheep" under the Good Shepherd of Israel, and the figure represents the nation restored in covenant relation and spiritual blessing, when the Lord will do for them, and be to them *all that a shepherd does and is to his flock.* This means not only seeking, delivering, gathering them, but tending them in all the full connotation of the Hebrew word shepherd (*ro'eh*), one who continually tends the sheep. Then Psalm 23, the beloved Shepherd Song, will be the testimony of the entire converted and restored nation.

Then Psalm 100 will be the song of their national thank offering:

Make a joyful sound to the Lord, all ye lands!
Serve the Lord with gladness!
Come into his presence with singing.
Acknowledge that the Lord is God!
It is he who made us and we belong to him.
We are his people and *the sheep of his pasture.*
Enter into his gates with thanksgiving
And into his courts with praise.
Give thanks to him, bless his name!
For the Lord is good,
His lovingkindness shall continue forever,
His faithfulness throughout all generations.

Isaiah had Israel's glorious Shepherd in view also when he combined the figure of Messiah in a second-advent context. "Look! the Lord God will come in power with his arm exerting dominion for him. Look! His reward is with him and his recompense before him. He shall feed *his flock like a shepherd.* He shall gather the lambs in his arm and carry them in his bosom. He shall gently lead on those that are with young" (Isa. 40:10, 11). Restored as sheep of God's pasture, what tender and loving care will Israel enjoy from the hand of the great Good Shepherd, whom so long they have rejected.

Not only does restored Israel enter into the enjoyment of the great Good Shepherd's tender care, but another aspect of the salvation the Lord shall bestow upon them is set forth. **For they shall be as the gems of a crown sparkling over his** [the Lord's] **land** (vs. 16b). The saved remnant who have come out of Israel's end-time tribulations will become attractive in the beauties and graces of salvation so copiously bestowed upon them. This is the reason for the magnetic and dynamic drawing power of saved Israel, already mentioned by Zechariah. "Thus says the Lord of armies; In those days ten men from nations of varied languages shall take hold of a Jew's robe, hold on to it, and say, Let us go with you, for we have heard that God is with you" (Zech. 8:23).

In apparent antithesis to Israel's enemies as *sling-stones* trodden in the mire in the preceding verse, Zechariah compares Zion's victorious sons (the saved remnant) to *precious stones* of a crown which sparkle over the Lord's land. The figure is evidently of the reward of the faithful martyrs and valiant saints of Israel who enter the kingdom of Messiah. "They shall be mine, saith the Lord of armies, in the day when I make up my jewels" (Mal. 3:17; cf. Heb. 11:36–39).

The **crown** (*nezer*, from the root *nazar*, "to separate," in a religious sense "dedicate," "consecrate") is properly that which distinguishes or separates from people at large, and is a sign or symbol of consideration to a task or cause. The word is used of the "crown" of a king (II Sam. 1:10; II Kings 11:12) and of the golden crown of holiness of the high priest (Exod. 29:6; 39:30; Lev. 8:9). The symbol is peculiarly fitted for Israel who will be restored as a high-priestly nation (Zech. 3:1–10) in full fellowship with Messiah, sharing His regal glory and utterly separated to Him and completely His in that day.

The participle modifying **the crown jewels,** *mithnosesoth,* has been variously rendered: (1) "The stones of a crown *lifted up as an ensign*" (A.V. – taken as a denominative from *nes*, "an ensign." (2) From *nasas*, "raise," lift up," "The stones of a crown *lifted on high* (R.V. – marginal reading, "glittering on high"). (3) "Like the jewels of a crown *they shall shine*" (R.S.V.) (4) "The stones of a crown *brilliant*" (Berkeley). It is best, perhaps, to construe the participle in the sense of "*glittering, shining*" (following Ewald, Maurer, Köhler, Fürst, Cham-

17 For how great is his goodness, and how great is his beauty! corn shall make the young men cheerful, and new wine the maids.

17 For how great is his goodness, and how great is his beauty! grain shall make the young men flourish, and new wine the virgins.

bers, etc.) or more clearly, "sparkling." The saved remnant of Israel, with the beauty of the Lord their God upon them will "sparkle" or "glitter" over the Lord's land (Palestine) and wherever they go as world-wide ambassadors and missionaries for Messiah, their Redeemer and King.

5. *Israel's Realization of Full Kingdom Blessing* (Zech. 9:17). For how great is his goodness and how great is his beauty! Grain shall make the young men flourish and new wine the maidens. The testimony of the victorious and saved remnant of Israel, the Lord's triumphant heroes in that day, who shall "sparkle" or "glitter" like crown jewels over the Lord's land ("the Holy Land," Zech. 2:12 [16]) will be, How great is his [the Lord's] goodness! How great is his beauty!

That the pronouns in this verse refer to the Lord (and as such are correctly construed by Ewald, Hengstenberg, Pressel, Chambers, Laetsch, Leupold, etc., as against Köhler, Marti, Nowack, etc., who mutilate the passage, as does the R.S.V.) is shown by the following considerations: (1) On *strict grammatical grounds*, for the contextual pronoun "His land" and "His people" (vs. 16) refer to the land. (2) On *the basis of usage*. Both goodness and beauty are properly applied to the Messiah. "Goodness" is freely applied to God in the Old Testament. How great *is thy goodness*, which thou hast reserved for those who revere thee" (Ps. 31:19 [20]); "They will pour forth a recital of *thy great goodness* and sing aloud of thy righteousness" (Ps. 145:7). While beauty (*yaphi*), it is true, is not predicated of God in the Old Testament, *it is* predicated of Messiah, of which this passage speaks, and so objections by Köhler and other scholars on this score are pointless. "Your

eyes shall see the king in his beauty," *yaphyo* (Isa. 33:17), using the same word as Zechariah. "Thou [Messiah] art fairer [*yophyaphitha*, same root meaning "more beautiful"] than the children of men, graciousness is poured upon thy lips, therefore God hath blessed thee forever" (Ps. 45:2 [3]). (3) *On a theological basis*. Both goodness and beauty are properly ascribed to the Lord, and eminently so by Israel's saved and ecstatically praiseful remnant. (4) Neither is it necessary to tone down the meaning with Henderson (*op. cit.*, p. 414) who rightly attributing the pronominal suffixes to the Lord, yet insists the meaning is merely the goodness and beauty which the Lord "bestows." Why this dodging of the issue when Psalm 45 plainly foretells that in the millennial era Messiah's beauty will be freely confessed and testified to?

Grain [emphatic subject] shall make the young men [emphatic object] flourish and new wine the young women (also emphatic object). The sentence is abbreviated, one verb is made to serve both clauses. The grain and the new wine here symbolize prosperity (Deut. 33:28; Ps. 4:7 [8]) and yet *not merely* the prosperity that ensued after the Maccabean conquest, but in full scope, the *millennial prosperity under Messiah*. The grain and wine are said to make the young men and maidens flourish (from the root *nuv*, "to bear fruit," Aramaic *nova'*, "fruit"). The millennial prosperity will cause the youth of that day to flourish both in temporal prosperity and spiritual blessing. Then the universal testimony will be, How great is his [Messiah's] goodness! How wonderful is his [our King's] beauty! Extolling and praising the Lord is ever the beginning of true spirituality and joy in any age.

CHAPTER TEN

DIVINE PRINCE OF PEACE, DELIVERER OF HIS PEOPLE

(ZECH. 10:1–12)

I. THE SECOND ADVENT OF ISRAEL'S SAVIOR-KING AND THE CURE OF THE NATION'S DECEPTION (Zech. 10:2–4)

1. *The Types of Israel's Deception* (Zech. 10:2a, b)
2. *The Results of Israel's Deception* (Zech. 10:2c, 3)
   (1) The people have gone astray like sheep (vs. 2c)
   (2) They are being severely afflicted (vs. 2c)
   (3) The nation's oppressors are punished (vs. 3a)
   (4) The nation's eventual restoration and victory over oppressors (vs. 3b)
3. *The Cure of Israel's Deception* (Zech. 10:4)
   (1) Messiah the Cornerstone (vs. 4a)
   (2) Messiah the Tent-Peg (vs. 4b)
   (3) Messiah the Battle Bow (vs. 4c)

II. THE SECOND ADVENT OF ISRAEL'S SAVIOR-KING AND THE NATION'S TRIUMPH OVER ITS FOES (Zech. 10:5–7)

1. *The Lord Promises to Be with His People* (Zech. 10:5)
2. *The Lord Promises to Empower and Restore His People* (Zech. 10:6, 7)

III. THE SECOND ADVENT OF ISRAEL'S SAVIOR-KING AND THE FULL RESTORATION OF THE NATION (Zech. 10:8–12)

1. *The Lord Will Gather Israel out of Its World-wide Dispersion* (Zech. 10:8, 9)
2. *The Lord Will Bring Israel Back into Its Own Land* (Zech. 10:10)
3. *The Lord Will Remove Every Impediment in the Way of Israel's Full Restoration and Deliverance* (Zech. 10:11)
4. *The Lord Will Effect Israel's Complete Spiritual Renovation* (Zech. 10:12)

CHAPTER 10 of Zechariah's prophecy, giving further blessings in store for God's people as a result of Messiah's second advent, is very closely connected with the preceding section, and some scholars think it ought not to have been separated from it. It is indeed true that the first verses of this present chapter are linked to the preceding and form a continuation of the description of the prosperous and happy condition that will result in a restored and converted Israel under the leadership of King-Messiah.

The section 9:17 – 10:1 continues the thought of Zion's returned King bestowing blessings upon nature. "Grain shall make the young men thrive and new wine the maidens" (9:17) is further expanded in chap. 10:1: **Ask rain from the Lord in the time of the latter rain** [spring showers], **from the Lord who makes the storm clouds. And he will give them showers of rain, to everyone vegetation in the field.** This is doubtless meant to be understood as literal rain. But the promise goes on to embrace also spiritual blessing inasmuch as in God's dealing with the nation Israel, rain in due season to insure the productivity of the land was promised as a direct reward of the obedience of the nation to its covenant relationship with the Lord (Lev. 26:3, 4; Deut. 11:13–15; 28:1–12). Jeremiah taught that only God can give rain in contrast to the impotence of the idols (Jer. 14:22). It was necessary, therefore, for the nation to obey God and wait upon Him in faithful trust.

The withholding of rain from Palestine, whatever the secondary causes to be taken into consideration, is one of the conspicuous factors in the prophesied desolation of the land during the many centuries the people have been exiled from it on account of their unbelief and sin. Here the nation returns to faith in its Messiah and obedience to God's Word. Consequent physical and spiritual blessing is the result. Scarcity of rain and terrible drought are one of the curses of the tribulation period (Rev. 11:6). Hosea echoes the voice of the remnant in the last days:

Come, let us return to the Lord;
for he has torn, and he will heal us,
He has smitten, but he will bind us up;
After two days he will revive us.
On the third day he will raise us up,
And we will live before him,
Let us know, let us press on to know the Lord;
His going forth is sure as the morning;
He will come to us as the showers [geshem]
as the latter rain [malqosh] that waters the earth (Hosea 6:1–3).

Here "the latter rain" is typical of spiritual refreshment. The great outpouring of the Spirit upon all flesh (Joel 2:28 [3:1]) in answer to prayer (Zech. 10:1) from the lips of the Jewish saints is the realization of it. Make request of the Lord for rain [matar] at the time of the latter rain [malqosh]. Make request of the Lord who creates storm clouds, and he will give to them plentiful rain [matar-geshem], to everyone herbage in the field. Herbage, ᶜesev, Assyrian esheba, "bear fruit," Arabic ᶜushbun, "tender herbage," includes all verdure, grass, vegetables, and fruit (Exod. 9:22; Amos 7:2; II Kings 19:26).

The latter rain or "spring rain" is a term for the showers that fall in Palestine in March and April which are so indispensable to the maturing of crops and grain. The Hebrew term is malqosh, from the root laqash, Aramaic "be late, do late," Arabic laqasa, "be late" (Hos. 6:3; Jer. 5:24; Job 29:23; Joel 2:23). Ask from the Lord rain [matar] at the time of the latter [or spring] rain (malqosh). The term rain, matar, (Assyrian metru, Aramaic miṭraʾ) is a general word for falling moisture itself as watering the earth, especially Canaan (Deut. 11:11) and withheld by the Lord for disobedience (Deut. 11:14). It has in mind gentle, ample showers of normal rainfall, and so it is necessary that it fall at the time [ᶜeth, "period"] of the latter [or spring] rain.

The result of the asking for rain (matar) at the time of the spring rain (malqosh) is copious showers (meṭar geshem), literally "rain of a (heavy) shower," an ample rain, having a normal gentle quality (matar) but not a destructive violent downpour, which geshem alone might be, apparently from the Arabic root jasuma, "be massive, heavy, or bulky" (Gen. 7:12; I Kings 18:41).

This verse is a beautiful instruction concerning answered prayer although the imperative ask is more rhetorical than an actual command. The request is answered abundantly with heavy showers and with thunderheads and lightnings as the precursors of copious downpours. The storm clouds (R.S.V.), "lightnings" (A.V.), is a translation of the Hebrew ḥazizim, perhaps "thunderheads"; compare Aramaic ḥazizaʾ, "a shining cloud," the better meaning, "rain-laden clouds."

I. THE SECOND ADVENT OF ISRAEL'S SAVIOR-KING AND THE CURE OF THE NATION'S DECEPTION (Zech. 10: 2–4)

In verse 1 prayer to God which brings blessing is contrasted with trust in idols which brings sorrow (vs. 2). The second advent of Messiah

1 Ask ye of the Lord rain in the time of the latter rain: so the Lord shall make bright clouds, and give them showers of rain, to every one grass in the field.
2 For the idols have spoken vanity, and the diviners have seen a lie, and have told false dreams: they comfort in vain: therefore they went their way as a flock, they were troubled, because there was no shepherd.

1   Ask ye of Jehovah rain in the time of the latter rain, even of Jehovah that maketh lightnings; and he will give them showers of rain, to every one grass in the field.
2   For the teraphim have spoken vanity, and the diviners have seen a lie; and they have told false dreams, they comfort in vain: therefore they go their way like sheep, they are afflicted, because there is no shepherd.

will demonstrate to His people that He alone is the source of Israel's help. He will demonstrate that in their past experience their disaster has been the result of their turning to idols and their implication in pagan occultism. Verse 1 furnishes a bright picture contrasting with the somber note of verse 2, where the apostasy and idolatry of the nation are exposed. The types of deception are enumerated as teraphim and diviners.

1. *The Types of Israel's Deception* (Zech. 10:2a, b). For the teraphim utter wickedness, and the diviners envision lies; dreams of vanity they will speak and will comfort emptily. The call to prayer in verse 1 is sustained by a reference to the misery caused by Israel's former dependence upon idols and diviners. This is the force of the for (*ki*, "because," introducing a causal clause). The teraphim speak wickedness, *'awen*, that is the "iniquity" connected with the evil power (demonism) of idolatry (cf. Pederson, *Israel* I-II, 1926, p. 431). It is frequently something said — uncanny words bordering on magic words (Koehler and Baumgartner, *Lexicon in Veteris Testamenti Libros*, 1951, p. 20).

The teraphim were small household oracular divinities (Ezek. 21:21 [26]; Judg. 17:5; Hos. 3:4). Although paganistic in connotation and inconsistent with the true worship of the Lord, the teraphim are encountered repeatedly in Israel's history (Gen. 31:19, 34; I Sam. 15:23; II Kings 23:24). They are expressly forbidden by the Lord (I Sam. 15:23; II Kings 23:24).

Modern archaeology has shed much light on the teraphim. From the site of ancient Nuzu, southeast of Nineveh and not far from modern Kirkuk, have come the Nuzu documents in excavations between 1925-1941. These tablets illustrate customs behind the patriarchal narratives of Genesis, particularly Rachel's theft of Laban's teraphim (Gen. 31:34). Nuzu evidence shows that possession of these household gods implied leadership of the family, and in the case of a married daughter assured her husband the right of her father's property (Cyrus Gordon, *Revue Biblique* XLIV [1935], pp. 35f.). Since Laban had sons of his own when Jacob fled to Canaan, they alone had right to their father's teraphim. Rachel's stealing them was therefore a serious matter (Gen. 31:19, 30, 35), aimed at preserving for her husband the chief title to Laban's estate (cf. Jack Finegan, *Light from the Ancient Past* [1946], p. 55).

Besides the teraphim, the second medium of Israel's deception mentioned is the diviners. And the diviners envision falsehood. The "diviner" (*qosem*, a *qal* active participle from *qasam*, a denominative verb "to practice divination," *qesem* [Num. 23:23; Deut. 18:10; II Kings 17:17]) is one who practices divination or the art of obtaining secret or illegitimate knowledge of the future by methods employed in paganistic religions and which are at variance with the holiness of God revealed in Scripture.

3 Mine anger was kindled against the shepherds, and I punished the goats: for the Lord of hosts hath visited his flock the house of Judah, and hath made them as his goodly horse in the battle.

---

3   Mine anger is kindled against the shepherds, and I will punish the he-goats; for Jehovah of hosts hath visited his flock, the house of Judah, and will make them as his goodly horse in the battle.

Divination is the occult heathen imitation of Biblical prophecy. The primary idea of the Hebrew term seems to be to "cut" or "divide," Arabic *qasama*, "divide, distribute," with the general idea of dividing or separating various omens or to cut up and scrutinize the liver of an animal in a very common form of ancient divination called hepatoscopy (Ezek. 21:21 [26]). The theory seems to be that the god to whom the animal was sacrificed revealed his will by the manner in which he fashioned the organ, considered to be the seat of the victim's life (See Merrill F. Unger, *Biblical Demonology*, 4th ed., pp. 119–142).

Scripture refers to diviners of the nations, such as Balaam (Josh. 13:22), diviners of the Philistines (I Sam. 6:2), of Babylon (Isa. 44:25; Ezek. 21:21 [26]) and the false prophets of Israel (Jer. 27:9; 29:8; Mic. 3:6; Ezek. 13:23; Deut. 18:10). Zechariah sees the diviners as *envisioning* falsehood. The term *hazah* denotes to see "either by the Spirit of God or by demonic inspiration, occasionally by the natural senses" (Isa. 1:1 2:1; Ezek. 13:8). "Falsehood" (*sheqer*), denotes "deception" and is from the Semitic root "deceive," so Aramaic, Syriac in *pael*, and Arabic. Compare Assyrian *tashkirtu*, "a lie."

The first part of verse 2 describes the *characteristic habitual operation* of the teraphim and the diviners (characteristic perfect of the verb). The next part of the verse couched in imperfects sees their operation as a *future incomplete action*, in the time of the nation's gross deception and apostasy (John 5:43; 12:43–45) in the great time of trouble (Dan. 12:1, 2; Matt. 24:15–25) preceding Mes-siah's advent. And dreams of vanity [i.e., vain, empty dreams] they will be speaking and emptily [*hevel*, "with air, mere breath"] they will be comforting. In the first clause the object dreams of vanity is emphatic by position in the sentence as is the adverbial accusative with air shall they be comforting. This passage closely connects with the latter-day idolatry of Israel, as also does Zechariah 13:1–8. In both cases the future deception of the people is couched in terms of their past history of idolatrous complicity.

2. *The Results of Israel's Deception* (Zech. 10:2c, 3). Therefore the people have gone their way as a flock, they are afflicted, for there is no seer. My anger shall blaze against the shepherds and I will punish the he-goats. Because the Lord of armies will visit his flock, the house of Judah, and make them as his splendid steed in the battle.

The first result (*'al ken*, therefore, adverb of consequence) of Israel's deception in the matter of the nation's recourse to pagan media for foretelling the future is that *the people have gone their own way like sheep* (vs. 2c). They [i.e., the people] have gone away (*nase'u*, "set out, pull up stakes, journey," Arabic *naza'a*, "pull up," Assyrian *nisu*, "set out"). The figure is of pulling up tent-pegs, folding up the tent, and journeying on (Gen. 35:5; Num. 12:15; Jer. 4:7), the word denoting "a deliberate departure from one place to another as on a march or journey" (H. G. Mitchell, *Int. Crit. Commentary*, "Zechariah," p. 299). Since the context compares the action of the deceived people "to sheep," *kemo tso'n*, "like *small cattle*," i.e., a flock of sheep and goats (Exod. 10:9), W. Nowack in *Die kleinen*

Propheten (*Handkommentar*, 1903, *in loc.*) suggests *naʿu*, "they wandered," from *nuaʿ*, "go astray," "wander," following J. Wellhausen (*Die kleinen Propheten*, 1898, *in loc.*). But the Masoretic Text would suggest a deliberate departure "from the Lord," like sheep will go their own wilful way if not continually restrained by a faithful shepherd. This is the idea of the A.V. rendering which is faithful to the Masoretic Text. **Therefore the people went their way as a flock.**

The second result of Israel's deception is that *the people are being severely afflicted* (vs. 2). The rendering **troubled** of A.V. is too mild. The verb *ʿanah* means "to be bowed down," "sorely afflicted," Assyrian *enu*, "do violence to, thwart, frustrate" (Ps. 116:10; 119:67). *Yaʿaneh*, the imperfect tense, of course, denotes incompleteness and implies that the condition still exists, and will exist until the second advent of their Messiah forever cures them of apostasy and complicity with demon-energized religion and paganistic occultism. These **are severely afflicted because** [*ki*] **there is no shepherd.** Not until their great good Shepherd appears will this situation be remedied. The sinful people forfeited the tender care of the true divine Shepherd and His earthly representative, their temporal king.

The third result of Israel's apostasy is *the punishment of the nation's oppressors* (vs. 3a). **Against the shepherds** [emphatic by word position] **my anger is kindled** (characteristic present perfect *harah*), literally, "burn," the *pael* in Aramaic meaning "to cause fire to burn" (Gen. 39:19; Num. 22:27; Exod. 32:19; Judg. 9:30), the Arabic substantive *harwatun* denoting "a burning sensation in the throat from rage" (cf. Koehler and Baumgartner, *Lexicon*, p. 331). **The shepherds** are evidently the leaders of the nations oppressing Israel, since concerning Israel it was just declared that **there was no shepherd existing,** *ʾen roʿeh*, the nominal negative denying

existence, and the same word for **shepherd** being used in each case.

As Chambers correctly comments, "Israel having lost its native rulers, fell under the power of the heathen governors, here styled shepherds and *he-goats*" (Lange's *Commentary, Minor Prophets*, 14, p. 78). **And against the he-goats** [emphatic also by word position] **I will visit punishment.** The word **he-goats** (*ʿattudhim*, Arabic *ʿatûdun*, Assyrian *attudû*, "a young male goat") occurs in Isaiah 14:9 to describe "the chief ones of the earth," that is, princes and rulers of the earth. In Ezekiel 34:17 the "he-goats" are trenchantly distinguished by the Lord from His "sheep," and are designated as *leaders* (Jer. 50:8). The bellwether, or sheep that leads the flock with a bell on his neck, is an apt figure of a leader.

Baron, contrary to the normal interpretation of this passage, refers both **the shepherds** and **the he-goats** to Israel's own faithless princes, priests, and prophets, "those of their own nation who should have led them but only misled them" (*Visions and Prophecies of Zechariah*, p. 344). This view, however, can scarcely be correct in the light of the immediately preceding (see above) and succeeding context where the Lord returns in blessing to His flock and punishes its oppressors.

The fourth result of Israel's apostasy will be *their eventual restoration and victory over their oppressors* (vs. 3b). **For** [because, the reason for His punishing the shepherds and he-goats] **the Lord of armies will visit his flock and make them as his splendid steed in the battle.** This comprehends the final phase of the last-day Armageddon and "His flock's" (Israel's) ultimate triumph over its Gentile oppressors (Zech. 12:1–9; 14:1–8).

In the final great conflict **the Lord will make** [*sam*, "set, place, constitute"] . . . **them as his magnificent horse.** The expression is *sus hodho*, "the horse of His majesty," i.e., a splendid, magnificent steed suitable in

4 Out of him came forth the corner, out of him the nail, out of him the battle bow, out of him every oppressor together.

4 From him shall come forth the corner-stone, from him the nail, from him the battle bow, from him every ruler together.

every way for the Lord of *divine glory* to ride upon (cf. Rev. 19:11) in battle to execute His judgments upon the oppressors and foes of His people. The word *hodh* is used almost entirely of kingly and divine glory (Ps. 8:1 [2]; 45:4; Zech. 6:13) or of the splendor of Israel under the Lord's blessing (Hos. 14:7), or of the majesty of Moses (Num. 27:20) under God's direct tutelage and authority.

In the passage there is paronomasia (play upon the word *paqadh*, "to visit *to punish*" Israel's foes [Exod. 20:5; Amos 3:2; Deut. 5:9] and "to visit *to bless*" His own people (Gen. 21:1; 50:24; Isa. 23:17; Jer. 15:15).

3. *The Cure of Israel's Deception* (Zech. 10:4). The different types of deception with their results are now followed with the cure of Israel's deception (vs. 4). This will be Messiah's advent, first as the **cornerstone**, secondly as the **tent-pin**, thirdly as the **war-bow**. This verse constitutes one of the most far-reaching and meaningful Messianic prophecies in the Old Testament in which the seer summarizes a number of declarations by the former prophet, setting forth the character and ministry of Israel's Redeemer-King.

(1) *Messiah the Cornerstone* (vs. 4a). Literally, **From him** [Judah] **shall be the cornerstone** (*pinnah*, vs. 4). Although *pinnah* is without the article like *tsemah*, "Branch" (Zech. 3:8; 6:12), the expression constitutes a Messianic title and accordingly is definite *per se*. In alluding to the cornerstone in the context of Israel's cure of deception, the prophet has Isaiah 28:16 in mind: "Behold I lay in Zion for a foundation a stone, a tried stone, a precious cornerstone, a sure foundation. He that believeth shall not make haste." This is the warning from Isaiah to those who "have made lies their

refuge and under falsehood have hid themselves" (Isa. 28:15).

Rejected in His first advent as "the Way, the Truth, and the Life" (John 14:6), Christ as the cornerstone became to the Jews "a stumbling stone" (Rom. 9:32, 33; I Cor. 1:23) and a "rock of offense." They refused to see Him crucified as a Rock, struck that the Spirit of life might flow from Him to all who will drink (Exod. 17:6; I Cor. 10:4). To the people of God in this age Christ is "the foundation" and "chief cornerstone" (Eph. 2:20). To converted Israel, at His second appearing, He will become the "headstone of the corner" (Zech. 4:7). As Daniel's supernatural "stone cut without hands" (Dan. 2:34), He will destroy Gentile world power as a smiting Rock at His glorious appearing. After the decimation of Gentile world power He will be the Stone that will grow and fill the whole earth in the millennial kingdom. To all unbelievers He is the crushing Stone of judgment (Matt. 21:44).

But Zechariah in this context pictures Him as a Stone, who in His revelation to Israel will be their support and the foundation of truth that will stabilize them and forever banish the deception and blindness brought about by their unbelief and rejection of Him and their consequent contamination with paganistic influences and demon deceptions.

The cornerstone is that which lies at the corner of two walls and unites them. It is thus viewed as the principal stone which forms the corner or foundation of an edifice. As such it points to something fundamental and of primary importance. Used figuratively by Zechariah, the cornerstone points to the importance of Messiah as a leader who will head up the restored nation as the cornerstone on a sloping incline supports a building.

The Old Testament repeatedly refers to great leaders who conduct a nation, as a cornerstone holding up an edifice. "And the chiefs [*pinnoth*, rulers] of all the people, even all the tribes of Israel, presented themselves in the assembly of the people of God" (Judg. 20:2). "And Saul said, Draw near, all you chiefs of the people [*pinnoth ha'am*]; and know and see wherein this sin hath been this day" (I Sam. 14:38). "The princes of Zoan have become fools, the princes of Memphis are deceived, they have caused Egypt to go astray, that are the *cornerstone* (*pinnath*) of her tribes" (Isa. 19:13). Messiah as the Chief and Ruler of His people Israel will be their foundation for truth, the support of their restored theocracy, and their defense against error.

(2) *Messiah the Tent-Peg* (vs. 4b). . . . **from him** [Judah] **shall be the tent-peg.** This is another lovely and expressive figure of Messiah, which apparently presents a many-sided view of Him, since the Hebrew word *yathed* denotes not only **the tent-pin** or "stake" driven into the ground to which the ropes of the tent were fastened to support it (Exod. 27:19; 35:18; 39:40) but also the stout peg inside the tent or built into the wall for hanging up items of value for display (Ezek. 15:3).

Accordingly, by the figure of the **tent nail** or "stake" Zechariah doubtless symbolizes Messiah in the capacity of a ruler as "the support of the state" (Brown, Driver, and Briggs), who in contrast to the unfaithful shepherds and oppressive leaders **(he-goats)** of the preceding verse, will, after His return, not only "rebuild the tabernacle of David, which has fallen" but set it up and gloriously support it in His millennial reign (Acts 15:16).

But Zechariah's primary allusion to the **tent-peg** as a Messianic figure is confessedly not to the pin supporting the tent from without but to the strong nail driven into the tent pole

within or built into the wall of an oriental house. This fact appears from Isaiah's prophecy concerning the ousting of the ambitious and unworthy Shebna, steward over the house of David, and the installation of Eliakim, the son of Hilkiah, into his high place of authority and administration in the house of David (Isa. 22: 5-25).

The Lord declares: "And I will place on his [Eliakim's] shoulder the key of the house of David. He shall open, and none shall shut; and he shall shut, and none shall open" (Isa. 22:22). That this verse and this entire passage is Messianic is shown by the claim of the risen Christ in allusion to the promise made to Eliakim that He was the possessor of the key to the house of David. "These things says he who is holy, he who is true, he who has the key of David, he who opens and no one shall shut, and who shuts and no one opens" (Rev. 3:7).

It is accordingly plain that Isaiah's prophecy, though given primarily to *a* son of David (Eliakim), transcends the local application and extends to *the* Son of David, the Messiah. "And I will fasten him *like a peg in a sure place*, and he will become a throne of honor to his father's house. And they will hang on him all the glory of his father's house, the offspring and issue, every small vessel, from the cups to the flagons" (Isa. 22:23, 24).

Zechariah's reference to Messiah as **the tent peg** obviously has in mind Isaiah's allusion to Eliakim as "a peg in a sure place" upon which was to be hung "all the glory of his father's house." Only in Messiah will all the promises vouchsafed to the house of David find their focal point and their ultimate fulfilment. He alone will "become a throne of honor to his father's house." Only on Him will "all the glory of His Father's house" suspend.

The figure sets forth an oriental tent or house where a large part of the wealth of the occupant was hung on pegs for ornamentation and for the admiration of those who entered. The truth set forth by the figure is that God plans to do a similar thing with Christ. When He "shall bear the glory and sit and rule upon his throne" (Zech. 6:13) in full millennial splendor, then "they shall hang upon him all the glory of his Father's house." His own elect nation Israel, restored and converted, shall give to Him the wholehearted allegiance and render to Him the complete yieldedness of themselves and their possessions to which He is entitled as the true Lord of the Kingdom and rightful heir of the house of David.

When the Lord sends the rod of His strength out of Zion and rules in the midst of His enemies, His people shall be free-will offerings in the day of His power, "in the beauties of holiness from the womb of the morning" (Ps. 110:2, 3). In that day upon the divine "Peg fastened in a sure place" will hang *all the glory of the Davidic House.*

Isaiah's figure of the **tent peg,** however, presents another facet of Messiah's theocratic rule – its permanency. Whereas Eliakim, God's faithful servant and the successor of the faithless Shebna, was to be fastened "like a peg in a sure place" yet "in that day, says the Lord of hosts, *the peg that was fastened in a sure place* will give way, and it will be cut down and fall, and the burden that was upon it will be cut off, for the Lord has spoken" (Isa. 22:25).

Even the most faithful governor and administrator of the house of David, like Eliakim, will not exercise authority permanently. By sickness, incapacity, old age, or death he will be cut down and fall. But the true Scion of the Davidic House, the God-man, the dependable Tent-Peg, will not only have all the glory of the Father's house entrusted to Him, but "the burden" as well (*hammassaʾ* "the heavy weight," i.e., the onerous duty and responsibility of government). But unlike all other members of the House of David, He will not fail. His

rule shall be permanent ,His authority imperishable (Isa. 9:7).

(3) *Messiah the Battle Bow* (vs. 4c) ...from him [Judah] **will be the battle-bow.** Again Messiah is metaphorically denoted. In this third figure He appears as Warrior and Conqueror *par excellence.* As the **battle-bow,** He is the divine archer, who at His second advent directs His "sharp arrows" into the hearts of His enemies so that "the peoples fall" under Him (Ps. 45:5 [6]). John the Revelator envisioned His coming through the opened heavens astride a white horse righteously judging and *making war* (Rev. 19:11). David glimpsed Him shattering kings "in the day of His wrath," executing "judgment among the nations" and filling many places with corpses as He wounds "the heads over many countries" (Ps. 110:5–7; cf. also Ps. 2:1–12).

The revelation of Messiah in the threefold character of **Cornerstone, Tent-Peg** and **Battle-Bow** will not only cure Israel's blindness and deception spiritually but forever put an end to their oppression politically and governmentally. **From him** [Judah] **shall go forth every oppressor together.**

That the reference is not to Messiah (contrary to Baron, *op. cit.,* p. 355) but to oppressive rulers and tyrants is proved from several considerations. First, from the meaning of *noges* which invariably has a bad connotation, as a "task-master" or "slave-driver" (Exod. 3:7), "an exactor of tribute" (Dan. 11:20); an "oppressive ruler" or "tyrant" (Isa. 3:12; 14:2; 60:17; Zech. 9:8). Secondly, the finite verb, "go out, go forth" (*yeṣeʾ*), has the connotation of "going out from" anything when it is implied something was *in* anything and *was a part of it* (Exod. 12:42; Judg. 21:21; Jer. 17:9). This construction occurs with the preposition "from" (*min*) prefixed to the place from which anyone goes out (Gen. 8:19; Job 3:11), or as here the sphere. **From him** [Judah] **shall go out** [depart] **every oppressor.** Third, as

5 And they shall be as mighty men, which tread down their enemies in the mire of the streets in the battle: and they shall fight, because the Lord is with them, and the riders on horses shall be confounded.

6 And I will strengthen the house of Judah, and I will save the house of Joseph, and I will bring them again to place them; for I have mercy upon them: and they shall be as though I had not cast them off: for I am the Lord their God, and will hear them.

7 And they of Ephraim shall be like a mighty man, and their heart shall rejoice as through wine: yea, their children shall see it, and be glad; their heart shall rejoice in the Lord.

---

5   And they shall be as mighty men, treading down their enemies in the mire of the streets in the battle; and they shall fight, because Jehovah is with them; and the riders on horses shall be confounded.

6   And I will strengthen the house of Judah, and I will save the house of Joseph, and I will bring them back; for I have mercy upon them: and they shall be as though I had not cast them off: for I am Jehovah their God, and I will hear them.

7   And they of Ephraim shall be like a mighty man, and their heart shall rejoice as through wine; yea, their children shall see it, and rejoice; their heart shall be glad in Jehovah.

Feinberg notes (*God Remembers*, p. 188), "the reference cannot possibly be to the Messiah because *yahdaw* ("together") proves definitely that more than one oppressor will go forth." Through Messiah's activity all oppressors, everyone of them *together*, will depart from Israel.

II. THE SECOND ADVENT OF ISRAEL'S SAVIOR-KING AND THE NATION'S TRIUMPH OVER ITS FOES (Zech. 10:5–7)

In this passage the prophet instructs the people in the future glorious deliverance the nation will experience in the final time of trouble. This theme looms large on the stage of Jewish eschatology not only in Zechariah, but also in the pre-exilic prophets (cf. Isa. 9:4–7 [3–6]; 11:4; 63:1–6; Ps. 2:1–12; Jer. 30:7, 8; Mic. 4:13; Zeph. 3:8), which "the prophet of hope" so often echoes.

1. *The Lord Promises to Be with His People* (Zech. 10:5). **And they** [Israel] **shall be as valiant heroes in battle, trampling the foe in the mud of the streets.** The simile is a lively one – like **mighty men** [*gibborim*, "strong ones who prevail" from the root *gavar*, "be strong, prevail"]

treading down (*bosim*, participle expressing lively moving action from *bus*, "to trample under foot," denoting thorough subjugation [Jer. 12:10; Isa. 63:18]). Although a different word is employed, the figure recalls Zechariah 9:15, where the Lord's victorious warriors "tread down" (*kaveshu* from *kavash*), "subjugate, tread down in washing [Exod. 19:10] slingstones" (*q.v.*).

The scene is that of the *strengthening* of the Jews in Palestine at the time of the invasion from the North under "the beast" (Dan. 7:8) in conjunction with the events of Armageddon (Rev. 16:14; 19:17–20). This idea of divine empowering appears in the clause, **they shall fight** [successfully] **for the Lord is with them** and also in the designation **mighty men** (vs. 5), **mighty man** (vs. 7), the same root *gabhar* in the *piel* **I will strengthen** (vs. 6), and again **I will strenghten them in the Lord** (vs. 12). Although Israel's ultimate deliverance will be consummated by the glorious coming of the Messiah, their coming Deliverer, nevertheless He empowers His people before this climactic event, fighting not only *for* them but *in* and *through* them, so that they trample their

8 I will hiss for them, and gather them; for I have redeemed them: and they shall increase as they have increased.

9 And I will sow them among the people: and they shall remember me in far countries; and they shall live with their children, and turn again.

---

8 I will hiss for them, and gather them; for I have redeemed them; and they shall increase as they have increased.

9 And I will sow them among the peoples; and they shall remember me in far countries; and they shall live with their children, and shall return.

---

enemies as mud in the streets and "confound" the riders on horses (the cavalry which was the chief arm of strength of ancient oriental rulers and in which Israel was weak). The expression **confound** (*hobhishu*, for *hebhishu*) is expressive, being the causative of *bosh*, "be ashamed," and so in the causative stem "to put to shame or confusion," especially because of frustrated endeavors. The corresponding Arabic word *bahutha* means "to be surprised" or "amazed."

2. *The Lord Promises to Empower and to Repatriate His People* (Zech. 10:6, 7). I will make the house of Judah strong and save the house of Joseph, and I will bring them back to place them for I will have mercy upon them. Moreover they shall be as though I had not rejected them, because I am the Lord their God, and I will answer them.

The difficult form is the verb "cause them to dwell," *hoshevothim*. Ancient Jewish thought conceives it as a composite form in the causative stem combining both *shuv*, "return," and *yashav*, "to dwell," and meaning both to "return to" and "reinstate" in Palestine (so Aben Ezra in the 12th century, Abarbanel [16th], Kimchi [13th] and followed by J. Drusius [17th], Rosenmüller and Pusey [19th]). Numbers of scholars prefer the *hifil* of *yashar* ("cause to dwell"), but if the writer had intended to use this form, he would have added a phrase telling how or where they were to dwell. Mitchell takes the form as *hifil* of *shuv*, "to cause to return" (*I.C.C.* "Zechariah," p. 300).

Zechariah employs the terms **house of Judah** and the **house of Joseph** or "Ephraim" (vss. 6, 7) to designate the whole nation, which will share in the joyful victory and blessing promised in the restored kingdom. Previous to the captivity the people of Israel had for centuries been divided into two frequently hostile nations. However, since the partial restoration from Babylon, they have been regarded as one nation with one hope and destiny. **Ephraim shall be like a mighty man** and shall rejoice jubilantly (vs. 7) as Judah, demonstrating that the great body of the people belonging to the Northern Kingdom, although still in dispersion, contrary to all appearances would one day share in the grand restoration repeatedly foretold by the former prophets (Isa. 11:10–16; Jer. 30:3; 33:7). It will not be any evanescent restoration either, for the **children** [of Ephraim] **shall see it and rejoice. Their heart shall exult** [*yagel* a jussive, implying subjective interest] **in the Lord** (vs. 7). The joy is not only pictured as intense, but centered in the true, unfailing source of joy, the Lord Himself (Ps. 92:4 [5]).

III. THE SECOND ADVENT OF ISRAEL'S SAVIOR-KING AND THE FULL RESTORATION OF THE NATION (Zech. 10:8–12)

As the prophet brings the first section of the first great prophetic oracle (chapters 9–11) dealing with the advent of Messiah (chapters 9, 10), to a close, he ends this important section on a grand climactic note, spanning the era that preceded the first advent and painting in panoramic view the second advent as it pertains to Israel's full restoration. Although this first prophetic oracle (chapters 9–11) deals mainly with the first advent, the results of that coming are also catalogued. Hence, before the dramatically somber note of chapter 11, recounting Israel's rejection of Messiah, is struck, Zechariah reaches a high watermark of joyful hope as he had done after the night visions (Zech. 6:9–15) and after the question of the fasts (Zech. 8:20–23), opening the prophetic vista to show the full restoration of the nation.

1. *The Lord Will Gather Israel out of Its World-wide Dispersion* (Zech. 10:8, 9). The glowing promise of Israel's final world-wide regathering is dramatically couched in the first person (vss. 8–10). The Lord Himself announces the grand prophesied event. **I will whistle for them.** The form of the verb is cohortative, expressing determination. The verb whistle, "pipe" (*sharaq*), is employed to denote the shrill noise made with the lips to gather a swarm of insects. In this sense it is said, "The Lord will *whistle* for the fly that is at the sources of the streams of Egypt and for the bee which is in the land of Assyria" (Isa. 7:18), the figure denoting the gathering together of invading enemies from Israel's ancient foes Assyria and Egypt for the purpose of chastising God's disobedient people for their sins. The same figure occurs again. "He will raise a signal for a nation afar off and *whistle* for it from the ends of the earth; and lo, swiftly, speedily it comes!" (Isa. 5:26).

Zechariah, however, uses the word "whistle" not in the sense of a shrill noise to call insects which are symbolic of the enemies of Israel, but with the signification of "pipe," alluding to the signal a shepherd gives with a rough reed or bamboo pipe to gather together his scattered flock. This usage occurs in the Song of Deborah. "Why did you tarry among the sheepfolds, to hear *the piping for the flocks [sheriqoth 'adarim]*?" (Judg. 5:16).

Because of the rampant demonism and deception of the era preceding the advent of Messiah (Rev. 9:20, 21), especially occultism and contamination with pagan divination (Zech. 10:2, 3; cf. 13:1–5), the people who went their way "like sheep" and who "are afflicted for lack of a shepherd" are now gathered by the true Shepherd who "will pipe for them and gather them" into the illumination and blessing of the millennial fold.

The reason for their restoration is assigned by a causal clause, **for I have redeemed them.** The word **redeem** (*padah*, Assyrian *padu*, Arabic *fada*) means to "ransom" or *free from the ownership of another* by payment of an assessed price (Exod. 13:13, 15; Lev. 27:27); from violence and death (I Sam. 14:45); from exile (Jer. 31:11; Isa. 35:10); from individual calamity, iniquity or death (Ps. 26:11; 31:5 [6]; 44:27 [27]; 49:15 [16]).

The redemption here announced by the Lord Himself is a full and complete ransom, not only from exile but from all iniquities (Isa. 53:4–6), so that "they shall be called the holy people, the Lord's redeemed ... Sought out, a city not forsaken" (Isa. 62:12). The regathering and restoration will be on the basis of the infinite redemptive price paid by the Son of God, Israel's Messiah, on the cross at His first advent.

The promise also includes multiplication in numbers. **And they shall increase as they have increased. They shall be as many as of old** (R.S.V.). Just as Israel persecuted in Egypt increased phenomenally despite their enslavement (Exod. 1:8–22) and became a mighty people prior to their redemption out of the land of the Nile, so they are prophesied to increase as their future greater redemption draws near, to become a mighty nation on the earth. The past two centuries in particular have witnessed a striking increment in the population of world Jewry, from not more than three million at the beginning of the eighteenth century to about sixteen million at present, despite the millions put to death by Adolf Hitler. Besides

10 I will bring them again also out of the land of Egypt, and gather them out of Assyria; and I will bring them into the land of Gilead and Lebanon; and place shall not be found for them.

10   I will bring them again also out of the land of Egypt, and gather them out of Assyria; and I will bring them into the land of Gilead and Lebanon; and place shall not be found for them.

this, the growing power of the Israeli State is another indication of the fulfillment of the promise of Israel's increase in population as her final regathering and redemption draw near.

Though I scattered them among the nations, yet in distant countries they shall remember me, and with their children they shall live and return (vs. 9). The verb should apparently be pointed with *waw consecutive wa᾽ezra῾em* (not *waw* connective as in the Masoretic Text), and having concessive force. The time will come when they "shall remember" the Lord, as the Lord will remember them, and His covenants and promises to them. The entire prophetic ministry of Zechariah, as well as the very name of the prophet himself, signifying "The Lord remembers," constitutes a guarantee of this fact.

Furthermore, it is predicated of Israel that **they shall live with their children.** Ezekiel had had a revelation of this grand spiritual regeneration and revival when, in his explanation of the resuscitation of the nation in the vision of the dry bones, he climaxed the whole with the declaration, "And I shall put my Spirit in you, and you shall live [spiritually], and I shall place you in your own land: then shall ye know that I the Lord have spoken it, and performed it, saith the Lord" (Ezek. 37:14). The spiritual regeneration and the return of the Jews to the land are described both by Ezekiel and Zechariah.

The concluding verses of this chapter set forth the last great regathering of Israel.

2. *The Lord Will Bring Israel Back into Their Own Land* (Zech. 10:10). **And I will bring them back**

from the land of Egypt, and gather them from Assyria, and I will bring them to the land of Gilead and to Lebanon, so that there will be no room for them (vs. 10). The verb, **I will cause them to return,** or "bring them back," is the causative of the stem *shubh*, "to return," "to come back." Egypt and Assyria are geographical terms which are used since Zechariah has in mind the same promise as the former prophets, especially Isaiah (cf. Isa. 11:11–16), where Egypt and Assyria figure prominently in the same context of the final regathering and establishment of the kingdom.

Gilead and Lebanon are listed to show the larger confines of Palestine embracing the full territory promised under the Abrahamic Covenant (Gen. 15:18), the Palestinian Covenant (Deut. 30:3–5), and the Davidic Covenant (II Sam. 7:16; Ps. 89: 30–37 [31–38]). The promise, **And they shall be numerous as they have been numerous** (vs. 8) will result in the fact that even with these larger borders **space shall not be found for them** (vs. 10).

Then shall be fulfilled the words of Isaiah concerning Zion:

The children born in the time of your
                bereavement
  will yet say in your ears:
The place is too narrow for me;
  make room for me to dwell in.
Then you will say in your heart:
  Who has borne me these?
I was bereaved and barren,
  exiled and put away,
  but who has brought up these?
Behold I was left alone;
  Whence then have these come? (Isa. 49:
                   20–21).

The answer to the great increase of Israel's population is given by the Lord Himself:

11 And he shall pass through the sea with affliction, and shall smite the waves in the sea, and all the deeps of the river shall dry up: and the pride of Assyria shall be brought down, and the sceptre of Egypt shall depart away.

11 And he will pass through the sea of affliction, and will smite the waves in the sea, and all the depths of the Nile shall dry up; and the pride of Assyria shall be brought down, and the sceptre of Egypt shall depart.

Thus says the Lord God:
Behold, I will lift up my hand to the
nations,
and raise my signal to the peoples,
and they shall bring your sons in their
bosom,
and your daughters shall be carried on their
shoulders (Isa. 49:22).

Because of the great final regathering of her children Zion is called upon to rejoice:

Sing, O barren one, who did not bear;
Break forth into singing and cry aloud,
you who have not experienced travail!
Because the children of the desolate one
will be more
than the children of her that is married,
says the Lord.
Enlarge the place of your tent,
and let the curtains of your
habitations be stretched out;
hold not back, lengthen your cords
and strengthen your stakes.
For you will spread abroad to the
right and to the left,
and your descendants will possess the
nations
and will people the desolate cities (Isa.
54:1–3).

3. *The Lord Will Remove Every Impediment in the Way of Israel's Full Restoration and Deliverance* (Zech. 10:11). Once more having in mind Isaiah's great prophecy of Israel's final regathering and the establishment of the Davidic Kingdom (Isa. 11:11–16), Zechariah refers to God's marvelous intervention in behalf of His people in the past as the basis of the prophecy of what He will do for them in the greater deliverance in the future. **And he** [the Lord] **shall pass through the sea** as when He led them forth from Egypt and went before them in a "pillar of cloud" by day and "a pillar of fire" by night (Exod. 13:21, 22). Many critics, however, such as Wetzstein, Nowack, Kittel, following the Septuagint and the

Targum, read, "They [*averu*, the returning exile] shall pass through the sea" (so the Revised Standard Version). But the prophet apparently presents the idea that the Lord Himself will march in the van of His people so that no obstacle might be able to interfere with their miraculous conduct back to Zion.

Should any impediment present itself, even as great as the Red Sea, **He shall pass through the sea of affliction** [*yam, sarah,* "sea of trouble"] **and strike the waves in the sea, and all the depths of the Nile shall dry up** (as when Israelites went over the Jordan dry shod) (vs. 11). The Authorized Version construes "affliction" as an adverbial accusative and translates, **He shall pass through the sea with affliction.** Modern critics contend that attempts to construe or emend the Masoretic Text have proved unsatisfactory, and have returned to Secker's conjecture that here, as in Isaiah 11:11, the text originally read *beyam misrayim* "through the sea of Egypt," which may be the case since it makes excellent sense. **They** [or he] **shall pass through the sea of Egypt.** The prophet obviously has the Isaiah passage clearly in mind throughout. **The pride of Assyria** [Israel's former formidable oppressor from the North] **shall be brought down. The pride** (*ga'on* from *ga'ah,* "rise up," Aramaic and Ethiopic "be proud, boastful") is here used in a bad sense (cf. Job 35:12; Prov. 8:13; 16:18; Ezek. 7:20; Zeph. 2:10; Isa. 16:6). The overweening pride of Assyria as "the giant among the Semites" was proverbial and her cruelty was indescribable. **And the sceptre of Egypt shall depart.** The **sceptre** (*shevet,* "rod, staff, club, truncheon") is as an emblem of

12 And I will strengthen them in the Lord; and they shall walk up and down in his name, saith the Lord.

12   And I will strengthen them in Jehovah; and they shall walk up and down in his name, saith Jehovah.

authority (cf. Assyrian, *shabaṭu,* "smite, slay," and *shibṭu,* "rod, sceptre"). No longer shall the *governmental power* of Egypt be able to enslave or to hold back the people of God.

4. The Lord Will Effect Israel's Complete Spiritual Renovation (Zech. 10:12). But the phenomenal regathering of His people out of their worldwide dispersion and settling them in their own land, at the same time removing every obstacle in the way of their return, is only part of the divine undertaking for them. In their own land they shall experience a copious outpouring of the Spirit that will enable them to do marvels in God's name. I [the Lord, as in verse 6], **will strengthen them in the Lord and in his name shall they freely walk here and there** – it is the oracle of the Lord.

Numerous critics following Wellhausen have rejected the Masoretic reading, **I will strengthen them,** *gibbartim,* and pointed the reading *gevurtam,* "... *their strength* shall be in the Lord," imagining a difficulty in God referring to Himself in the third person. But often this mystic inner speaking of the godhead in Zechariah displays the latent truth of God's triunity (cf. 2:8, 9 [12, 13]).

The expression **walk up and down** recalls Zechariah 1:10, 11; 6:7 three times. Just as the scouts carefully went to and fro in the earth to search out its state (Zech. 1:10, 11) *relative to* and *before* the setting up of the kingdom, and to administer the divine judgments necessary to such establishment of the Davidic rule (6:7), so after the kingdom has been set up, God's people Israel converted and spiritually empowered will similarly **walk up and down in His** [the Lord's] **name,** as His messengers and representatives to witness to the blessings

of Messiah's salvation among the nations as "priests of the Lord" when the whole nation is reinstated in its high-priestly dignity as dispenser of the knowledge of God throughout the millennial earth (cf. Zech. 3:1–10).

The *hithpael* form of this verb here and in the other instances in Zechariah carries with it the sense of "walking to and fro" i.e., "here and there" *freely* and *unrestrictedly.* Having been set free by the Messiah, God's Son, Israel shall be free indeed (cf. John 8:32, 36). With holy boldness and tremendous spiritual zeal and power, saved Israelites shall be the evangelists and Paul-like missionaries to the nations of the kingdom age.

Following the Septuagint and the Syriac, a number of scholars (Nowack, Marti, Kittel, Revised Standard Version) read *yithhallalu,* "they shall glory" for *yithhallaku,* **they shall freely walk here and there** (to and fro)." But the difficulty is largely an imaginary one and the Masoretic reading connects the second part of the prophecy (chapters 9–14) with the first part (chapters 1–8) as a unit by the appearance of this unusual expression in both parts of the book. Moreover, the more difficult reading is also capable of a satisfactory exegesis in the light of both its immediate and remote context.

This grand prophecy of the future of Israel under her Shepherd-King Messiah (chapter 10) with the unfolding of what He shall do for the covenant people, is appended by **says the Lord.** These concluding words, as it were, form the divine seal and signature assuring the certainty of the fulfilment of this whole prophetic panorama. The tragedy is that so many Christian scholars have appropriated these and other great promises to Israel made by Zechariah to the nation Israel and applied them to the Christian Church, thus "mysticalizing" their plain meaning (so Keil, Pusey, Wright, Chambers, etc.). More recent writers who do the same are Theodore Laetsch (*The Minor Prophets*, 1956), H. C. Leupold (*Exposition* of Zechariah, 1956), Martin H. Woudstra (*Zechariah* in *The Biblical Expositor* II, 1960). Moreover, in so doing, these scholars fail to see, or refuse to accept the fact, that despite the difficulties which stand in the way of the literal fulfilment of these promises in their simple meaning, God pledges His own sure word and infinite power that they will yet be realized in the plain and obvious sense in which they have been recorded.

CHAPTER ELEVEN

ISRAEL'S REJECTION OF THE GOOD SHEPHERD AND ACCEPTANCE OF THE WORTHLESS ONE

(ZECH. 11:1–17)

ZECHARIAH ("Whom the Lord remembers"), in accordance with his name, is strikingly *a prophet of hope*, as noted periodically throughout this exposition. His vision, spanning the centuries, gravitates resistlessly to Israel's glad future to be realized in her coming Deliverer and King. Chapters 9 and 10 dwell on this joyous theme, showing how the nations surrounding God's people would be judged, while Israel would be preserved for the coming of her King (Zech. 9:1–8), both in His first advent (vs. 9), as well as in His second (vs. 10) with consequent blessings and victories outlined in 9:11 through 10:12.

But suddenly the prophet of hope, since he is also a prophet of truth and reality, glimpses the fearful episode of the nation's apostasy manifest in the rejection of the good Shepherd (Zech.

1 Open thy doors, O Lebanon, that the fire may devour thy cedars.
2 Howl, fir tree; for the cedar is fallen; because the mighty are spoiled:
howl, O ye oaks of Bashan; for the forest of the vintage is come down.

---

1   Open thy doors, O Lebanon, that the fire may devour thy cedars.
2   Wail, O fir-tree, for the cedar is fallen, because the goodly ones are
     destroyed: wail, O ye oaks of Bashan, for the strong forest is come down.

11:1-14) and acceptance of the worthless shepherd (Zech. 11:15-17). In doing so he distills the quintessence of Israel's sorrow and woe in the fact of the nation's refusing their true Shepherd-Messiah at His first advent and their taking up with the false shepherd in the time of their greatest woe previous to the second advent of their Deliverer and King. Both events, starkly tragic in their ominous gloom, must, however, be catalogued by this *prophet of hope*, because both events form a necessary prelude to the glorious blessings he sees for the nation and form the dark and dismal storm that clears into the resplendent millennial day.

Similarly in the first part of the prophecy (chapters 1-8), "the good and the comfortable words" (1:13) form the grand and glowing theme of the eight night visions (1:7-6:8), eventuating in full kingdom blessing typified by the crowning of Joshua, the high priest (6:8-15). But again the *prophet of hope* is a prophet of reality and truth, and against the bright promises of grace presents the dark warnings of the active curse going forth against sin in the vision of the flying scroll (5:1-4) and the sure judgment of ecclesiastical and commercial Babylon in the vision of the woman in the ephah (5:5-11).

I. IMPENDING DEVASTATION OF THE
    LAND DUE TO THE REJECTION OF
    THE GOOD SHEPHERD (Zech. 11:1-3)

The tragic note of this dark chapter is struck in the opening verses which form a prelude to the sinister events narrated in it. The desolation depicted is couched in stirring language, "in words arranged with great rhetorical power, full of poetic imagery and

lively dramatic movement" (Chambers, *Zechariah* in Lange's *Commentary*, II, p. 83). One can feel the severity of the judgment visited upon the land (and inevitably upon the people also) which prepares the reader for the description of the heinous crime of Israel that provoked such severe visitation of wrath.

1. *The Devastation Starts in the Lebanon Region* (Zech. 11:1, 2a). **Open your doors, O Lebanon, that fire may devour among your cedars. Wail, O cypress, because the cedar has toppled, for your glorious ones** [trees] **are destroyed.** In very vivid and striking apostrophe the prophet addresses majestic Mount Lebanon on the borders of Syria and Palestine, over fourteen thousand feet high with its highest ridge perpetually snow-covered. The epithet "White One" is vocative and without the article in a poetic section, but always with the article in prose *hallebanon*, "the white one," or "the white (mountain)," which the Arabs style "the mountain of snow."

The mountain is not only addressed as a person or animate being but figuratively as a fortress or fortified city so doomed to certain desolation that it is commanded without useless resistance to throw open its **doors** (*deleth*, "door," Gen. 19:10; II Kings 4:4, from *dalah*, "to hang or swing," denoting the part of the door that swings open to admit someone, and not *pethah*, the mere "opening" itself). The opening doors are to give access to decimating fire that will ravage unrestrictedly and at will **among** [its] **cedars**, where the preposition "among," *be*, "denotes that the action of the verb will be unrestricted" (*Int. Crit. Commentary*, "Zechariah",

3 There is a voice of the howling of the shepherds; for their glory is spoiled: a voice of the roaring of young lions; for the pride of Jordan is spoiled.

3 A voice of the wailing of the shepherds! for their glory is destroyed: a voice of the roaring of young lions! for the pride of the Jordan is laid waste.

p. 302, cf. Gesenius-Kautsch, *Hebrew Grammar*, section 119). The finest and choicest trees (the **cedars**) will not be spared by this devastating conflagration advancing from the north upon Palestine. How much less the inferior **fir tree** (A.V.), probably one of the coniferous trees is meant, or perhaps the "cypress" (R.S.V.). Because the **glorious trees are destroyed** (the prophetic perfect indicating that so sure is the judgment that the desolation is viewed as having already occurred), the humbler **fir tree** is commanded to **wail** its sealed fate.

The adjective **glorious** (*'addirim*, from root *'adar*, "be wide, inflated") means "large, great, mighty" (Isa. 33:21; Ps. 93:4), "powerful" (Ps. 136:18; Ezek. 32:18), "glorious," (Ps. 8:1 [2]). It is used substantively of "princes," "nobles" (Judg. 5:25; Jer. 25:34; II Chron. 23:20; Neh. 10:30). Zechariah uses it substantivally of **glorious trees**.

2. *The Devastation Sweeps On to Bashan* (Zech. 11:2b, 3a). **Wail, O oaks of Bashan, because the impenetrable forest is felled. Listen!** [Hear] **the wailing of the shepherds for their glory is destroyed!** Bashan was the northern part of the territory across the Jordan river consisting of a plateau contiguous to the Lebanon region on the north (Ps. 68:15 [16]; I Chron. 5:23) and bounded on the south by the wadi Jabbok and Mount Gilead (Deut. 3:10; Josh. 12:4). Taken from the Amorite king Og by the invading Israelites, it was partitioned to the half tribe of Manasseh (Num. 21:33; 32:33). It was renowned for its splendid forests of oaks (Isa. 2:13; Ezek. 27:6), as well as for its verdant pastures and abundance of cattle (Deut. 32:14; Ps. 22:12 [13]; Amos 4:1; Ezek. 39:18). The Arabic *bathnatun*, "level, sandy soil," seems

to indicate the original meaning of the name, often occurring with the article, but omitted here in poetry, although in the vocative case.

The prophet apostrophizes **Bashan's** [famous] **oaks** and dramatically commands them to **wail** as he did the **firs** of Lebanon. **Wail** (*helilu*, imperative; from the onomatopoetic root *yalal* in causative meaning to "lament," "howl," "cry out" [Isa. 13:6; 15:3; 23:1; Jer. 25:34; Amos 8:3]) here captures the notion of the wind wailing through the trees, fanning onward the fiery judgment sweeping over the land.

The reason assigned for the **oaks of Bashan** to howl is because [*kî*] the **inpenetrable forest is felled**. The reference is to **Lebanon** because its elevation and steep, densely wooded slopes made it difficult to reach. If its glorious cedars and its firs on its inaccessible heights had succumbed to the fury of the fiery judgment, well might the more easily accessible **oaks of Bashan** howl and lament.

The adjective **inaccessible** in the *qere* reading is *batsir* from root *batsar*, "to cut off," "gather (grapes)," and occurring as a noun "vintage" (Lev. 26:5; Isa. 24:13; 32:10; Jer. 48:32), but here only in a doubtful reading as an adjective. The preferred reading *kethiv* is *batsur*, the *qal*, passive participle from *batsor*, hence, "cut off," "inaccessible," "impenetrable," employed of very high walls (Deut. 28:52; Isa. 2:15); of cities stoutly fortified (Num. 13:28; Deut. 3:5; Josh. 14:12); and aptly describing the **inaccessible** forests of Lebanon.

It is interesting to note the article is omitted with the modified noun, when the attributive adjective has it in the phrase, "the inaccessible forest" (*ya'ar habbatsur*, instead of normally *haya'ar habbatsur*). But this occurs elsewhere in Zechariah (cf. 4:7; 14:10) and evidently lays pre-eminent stress upon the force of the articular adjective "the *inaccessible* mountain" (cf. Genesius, *Hebrew Grammar*, 126, 5R[a]).

The conflagration now sweeps down from the plateaus to the plain where the shepherds see **their splendor,** i.e., their lush pasture lands in which they were accustomed to tend their flocks (Deut. 32:14) **destroyed,** the grass scorched and devoured by the spreading flames. Above the crackle of the consuming fire comes the cry, **Listen!** [*qol*, "voice, sound," used interjectionally, Hear!] **the wail of the shepherds!** The excited style is abbreviated and the imperative "hear" is omitted and to be supplied in thought. **The shepherds' wail,** *yelalah*, is their lugubrious "lament," their "howling" like an animal, their "yelling" in distress (Isa. 15:8; Jer. 25:36) over the tragedy that has befallen them.

3. *The Devastation Descends to the Lower Jordan Valley* (Zech. 11:3b). **Listen!** [hear] **the roaring of the young lions, because the pride of the Jordan is destroyed!** Once again the excited style is elliptical with the noun *qol*, "sound, voice," an interjection **Hark! listen!** (Gesenius 146, 1, remark 1) and the verb "hear" omitted for brevity and force, but implied. **The pride of the Jordan** (i.e., "ornament," *ga'on*, "glory, splendor" from *ga'ah*, "raise up oneself, be exalted" [Isa. 4:2; 14:11]) is a poetical reference to the thick, jungle-like growth that adorns the narrow Jordan valley in its central and lower sections south of the Sea of Galilee. This rank growth which flourishes in the moist tropical climate, consisting of tamarisks, willows, and luxuriant grasses and cane, was a favorite haunt of lions. After the captivity of the Northern Kingdom these wild beasts began to multiply there (II Kings 17:25; Jer. 49:19; 50:44) and continued as late as the close of the twelfth century after Christ. **The young lions,** *kephirim*, were

those already weaned and which had begun to raven to satisfy an almost insatiable appetite (Judg. 14:5; Ps. 17:12; 104:21) and hence were agile and fierce. Their **roaring** is because the decimating judgment of God upon the land not only destroyed their lairs but their food.

Prominent in the graphic and poetical recital of the impending devastation of Syria-Palestine due to the rejection of the good Shepherd (vss. 1-3) is the thought of (1) destruction, the verb **destroy,** passive intensive of *shadad*, occurring three times, once in verse 2, twice in verse 3 and the thought of "wailing" or "howling," occurring twice and forcefully as an imperative (vs. 2) and once as a noun (vs. 3). (2) Prominent too is the interjectional idea **listen!** with the **wail** of the shepherd and the **roaring of the young lions,** the distinguishable sounds or cries heard, all of which speaks of the severity of the divine judgment in the destruction and suffering it causes.

The passage (vss. 1-3) is accordingly to be taken literally in agreement with the context but, of course, within the scope of the poetic figures it contains. Nothing more than a literal interpretation is needed, and there is not the slightest reason to make the trees signify either nations or men despite such references as Isaiah 10:34; Ezekiel 17:8; Jeremiah 22:6, etc., where trees represent nations or men. As Leupold (*Exposition of Zechariah*, p. 206) correctly states the case, "A literal interpretation . . . carries us far enough. For surely, if the land is so completely devastated as is here described, all greatness and great men will also have been involved in the universal ruin."

II. PREDICTION OF THE REJECTION OF THE GOOD SHEPHERD (Zech. 11: 4-14)

The decimating judgment of God sweeping down from the north on Palestine, so graphically depicted in verses 1-3, is now explained with

4 Thus saith the Lord my God; Feed the flock of the slaughter;
4 Thus said Jehovah my God: Feed the flock of slaughter;

regard to its *cause*. Underlying it is a crime which represents unbelief and crystallized wickedness of such colossal proportions that the fiery judgment which prefaces the description of it is made a divine necessity.

1. *The Prophet's Commission to Enact a Prophetic Parable* (Zech. 11:4). **Thus the Lord my God says, Shepherd the flock destined for slaughter.** Zechariah is divinely instructed apparently to act out a parable or similitude to enforce a prophetic truth. The question is: (1) Did the prophet actually assume any religious or civil function in discharging his commission (as Von Orelli thinks)? (2) Or, was it literal and actual, purely in the sense of an object lesson presented to a restricted audience for a limited time? (3) Or, was it merely an "inner, visionary (in the good sense) experience?" (Leupold, *op. cit.*, p. 207).

While Von Orelli's idea seems scarcely plausible, Leupold's view, following Horst and Pusey, is certainly possible. Actions presented by the prophets, it is true, were not always understood as actions but as predictions, as Jeremiah's being "set over the nations . . . to root out and to pull down, and to destroy and to throw down and to build, and to plant" (Jer. 1:10). Compare the same prophet's being commanded to "take the wine cup" of God's fury "and cause all the nations," to whom the Lord sent him, "to drink it" (Jer. 25:15–38).

But wheras actions presented by the prophets were *not always* understood as actions, but purely as predictions without any action on the prophet's part, *often* the predictions were enforced by symbolic actions, and there is no valid reason to deny that such was the case in this prophetic parable involving Zechariah. He is to be thought of as dressing in the garb of a shepherd, taking two staves, acting out a ministry to the people, later breaking the staves, and even asking for his wages, to receive from taunters and mockers, who despised his action, and his prophecy, thirty pieces of silver. Taking the episode as literal and actual is much simpler than confusing it with an "inner visionary experience." This episode is no more a vision (or visionary) than the crowning of Joshua as priest in Zechariah 6:9–15, which is an *actual historical occurrence*, climaxing the eight night visions, but not one of them.

Another problem closely akin to the nature of the parabolic action, whether literal and actual or merely visionary in the inner experience of the prophet, is the question whom Zechariah impersonates – "the prophetic office" (Koehler), "the angel of the Lord," i.e., Messiah (Hengstenberg), or the Lord Himself. The latter view is correct, as Keil shows (*in loc.*), since the acts executed could only be done by the Lord Himself through "the angel of the Lord" (Messiah); compare verses 8, 12, 13.

Thus the divine injunction, **Tend the flock destined for slaughter** is a genuine commission laid upon the prophet to be acted out before his contemporaries, and which would receive such a negative reception as to make it a proper vehicle for the momentous prediction of Messiah's future rejection by the nation. The imperative **tend** from the word *ra'ah* is a very common word in the Old Testament and indicates "the doing of a shepherd's task in its broadest sense," caring for, feeding, leading, nursing, etc. the sheep (Ps. 23:1–6).

The flock of slaughter is the covenant nation presented under the common figure of sheep (Ps. 95:7; 100:3; Ezek. 34:30, 31), but here containing many goats, or unfaithful

5 Whose possessors slay them, and hold themselves not guilty: and they that sell them say, Blessed be the Lord; for I am rich: and their own shepherds pity them not.
6 For I will no more pity the inhabitants of the land, saith the Lord: but, lo, I will deliver the men every one into his neighbour's hand, and into the hand of his king: and they shall smite the land, and out of their hand I will not deliver them.

---

5   whose possessors slay them, and hold themselves not guilty; and they that sell them say, Blessed be Jehovah, for I am rich; and their own shepherds pity them not.
6   For I will no more pity the inhabitants of the land, saith Jehovah; but, lo, I will deliver the men every one into his neighbor's hand, and into the hand of his king; and they shall smite the land, and out of their hand I will not deliver them.

---

ones. The **flock of slaughter** (*ts'on haharegah*) means "the flock intended or destined for butchering," *haregah* from *harag*, "to kill" (of persons, Gen. 4:8; Exod. 2:14, but here referring to the slaughter or butchering of animals, Isa. 27:1; 22:13; Num. 22:29). Note that the genitive **of slaughter** in the construct chain is practically equivalent to an infinitive of purpose (*Int. Crit. Com., in loc.*, Gesenius, 128q.). Compare "flock of slaughter" (Ps. 44:22 [23]), i.e., "sheep for slaughtering." This is the covenant people given over to God's judgment as a result of sin, but which Zechariah, personating the role of the Lord Himself, makes a final attempt to reclaim.

2. *The Prophesied Punishment of the People* (Zech. 11:5, 6). **Whose buyers [owners] slaughter them and do not feel [hold themselves] guilty [as in Hos. 5:15] and their sellers [to a man] say, Blessed be the Lord, for I have become rich, and none of their shepherds have pity upon them.** Henderson is correct in saying, "that by the buyers and sellers of the Jewish people, we are not to understand the Romans, but their own unprincipled teachers and rulers . . ." (*The Minor Prophets*, p. 420). This is suggested by the following observations: (1) These traffickers say, **Blessed be Yahweh** which would be an incredible statement on the lips of a Gentile, especially a Roman. (2) The corresponding term *ro'ehem*, **their shep-**

herds, is merely expletive of what the buyers and sellers were officially, and not in a category in contrast to them. (3) The historical facts of the case bear out this conclusion. The avarice of the Pharisees was colossal, "yet they had the bare-faced hypocrisy to thank God for their ill-gotten wealth, and because they were not punished, they imagined they might persevere with impunity" (Henderson, *loc. cit.*). The participles appearing in the terms **whose buyers** and **sellers** suggest the unceasingly active and avaricious exploitation of Jew by fellow Jew as an element in the divine punishment of unbelief and sin that culminated in the rejection of the Messiah when He appeared. The clause is added, **for I have become rich,** literally "I made (causative) riches" from *'ashar*, "*prosper*," "*be happy*," specially "to be rich" (Job 15:29; Hos. 12:9), *hifil* "become rich" (Prov. 10:4; Dan. 11:2).

The construction of the plural nouns **their buyers, their sellers** and **their shepherds** with singular predicates **say** and **pity** (*ad sensum* as opposite to grammatical agreement) is an emphatic mode of construction, by which the individuals specified in the plural are singled out and represented as performing individually the action in question (cf. Gen. 27:29; Exod. 31:14; Prov. 3:18). The masculine suffix (*hem,* "their") attached to **shepherds,** is in *ad sensum* agreement with "people" understood, while the feminine suffixes are in grammatical agreement with the idea of the people as *tso'n*, "sheep," probably considered as a flock of helpless ewes. Textual emendation is therefore rendered unnecessary (*ro'ehem* to *ro'ehen*).

In the recital of the people's sufferings the severity of the judgment incurred is accentuated by the repeated idea of the pitilessness of their plight. **Their shepherds** [i.e., their rulers to a man] **do not pity them. For I will no longer pity the inhabitants of the land** (i.e., Palestine). Calamity enough it is that their own rulers do not have compassion on them. Infinitely worse and the acme of their woe when the Lord Himself declares, **I will no more have compassion** on them! **Have compassion on** (*yahmol, 'ehmol*) is from the root *hamal*, "to be mild, gentle," Arabic *haluma*, "be gentle, longsuffering" and means "to pity, have compassion on" (Exod. 2:6; I Sam. 23:21). This compassion or pity is shown in sparing one from suffering, calamity, or judgment. Hence "to spare" (I Sam. 15:3, 15; II Sam. 21:7; Jer. 50:14). Henderson (*in loc.*) renders, "And none of whose shepherds spareth them. For I will no more spare the inhabitants of the land.... But lo! I Myself will deliver the men each into the hand [power] of the neighbor and into the power of his king, and they shall beat the land to pieces and I will not rescue [them] out of their hand [power]."

The Lord announces very dramatically by the use of the *future instans* (interjectional adverb *hinneh*, plus *separate* pronoun *'anoki*, here very emphatic, plus the participle) that not only will He not **pity** or "spare" His people from the impending calamity about to engulf them for their iniquity culminating in the rejection of Messiah, but He Himself in lively manner will actively deliver them over to one another in factional strife and mutual antagonism, which became a terrible reality within the city of Jerusalem among the Jews themselves in the Roman siege that eventuated in the fall of the city in A.D. 70. But as though this tragedy of civil discord and the attendant evils were only the beginning of their sorrows, the Lord Himself declares, **I will deliver the men** [plural] **each** [singular]... **into the hand of his king.** Here again the phenomenon of individualizing the plural, so common in Hebrew, accentuates the thoroughness of the action of the verb **deliver** upon the object of that action – the **men** (*each one* of them).

That the king alluded to is the Roman emperor is obvious (1) from the historical context and (2) from the acknowledgement of the Jews themselves, "We have no king but Caesar" (John 19:15), (3) although a wider reference to earlier kings such as the Hasmonaeans, Herod the Great, etc., is not excluded.

And they [i.e., the armies of the foreign ruler] **shall destroy** (*kitteth*, from *kathath*, "beat," "hammer," "forge" [Isa. 30:14; Joel 3:10 (4:10)]; "beat to pieces" as with repeated blows of a hammer; cf. II Kings 18:4; II Chron. 34:7; Isa. 2:4). This verb "beat" or "hammer to pieces" is most graphically selected to express the destructive measures the Romans used to crush the Jewish state. The stark tragedy of this, insofar as the Jews were concerned, is summarized in the two terrible declarations of this passage **I will no more pity** [spare]... **neither will I deliver from their power.**

3. *The Parabolic Representation of the Lord's Final Endeavors to Reclaim Israel* (Zech. 11:7, 8). So [*waw* consecutive expressing logical result] **I tended the flock destined for slaughter, particularly the poor of the flock. And I took two rods for myself. The one I called Graciousness and the other Unity. Thus I tended the flock. Thereupon I cut off the three shepherds in one month. After that I grew impatient with them and they also loathed me.**

Twice repeated, and not without

7 And I will feed the flock of slaughter, even you, O poor of the flock. And I took unto me two staves; the one I called Beauty, and the other I called Bands; and I fed the flock.

8 Three shepherds also I cut off in one month; and my soul loathed them, and their soul also abhorred me.

---

7 So I fed the flock of slaughter, verily the poor of the flock. And I took unto me two staves; the one I called Beauty, and the other I called Bands; and I fed the flock.

8 And I cut off the three shepherds in one month; for my soul was weary of them, and their soul also loathed me.

---

purpose, is the declaration, **So I** [the prophet] **tended the flock of slaughter ... thus I tended the flock** (vs. 7). This most emphatically asserts what most critics deny, that Zechariah actually performed this symbolic act to his own age and generation. In addition, the repetition, moreover, declares he performed the ministry in accordance with the significance of the two rods he employed, namely, Graciousness and Unity. The symbolic act, however, was not *fulfilled*, of course, until the earthly ministry of our Lord.

Again the designation **the flock of** [i.e., destined for] **slaughter** is mentioned (cf. vs. 4), which is a peculiarly apt term, not only to describe numerous Jews who suffered death in the Maccabean wars and under subsequent Maccabean and Herodian rulers, but particularly under the Romans at the fall of Jerusalem, when more than 1,100,000 Jews perished, and almost a half million more died during the course of the war and siege.

So I tended the flock destined for slaughter, particularly [*lakhen*] **the poor of the flock.** The difficulty with this passage lies in the rendition of *lakhen*, which (1) Leupold takes in the sense of "and so" or "particularly" (*op. cit.*, p. 210). (2) Henderson (*op. cit.*, p. 421) derives it from the Arabic *kun*, "to be," in the sense of a participial noun implying *reality* and used adverbially, signifying "truly," "verily." In this he follows Kimchi, Jarchi, Starr, De Wette, and Ewald. (3) The Septuagint reads *lachen* with the following word *likna'aniyye* "for

the merchants [traffickers]." Nowack, Marti, Kittel, etc., have espoused this doubtful reading and have been followed by the Revised Standard Version. "So I became the shepherd of the flock doomed to be slain *for those who trafficked in sheep*." But this rendering, besides being linguistically weak, glibly avoiding a difficult but correct reading, is colorless in its meaning, both in this verse and in verse 11 where it occurs again.

The ministry of the good Shepherd is "truly," "verily" (or perhaps "particularly") in behalf of the **poor of the flock.** The designation **poor,** *'oni*, comprises the "afflicted" or wretched" of the Lord's covenant people, especially those who were pious and believing (Exod. 22:24; Deut. 24:12; Ps. 10:2, 9; 14:6; 18:27 [28]). The passage refers to "the common people" who heard our Lord "gladly" (Mark 12:37), including His disciples and those who believed on Him at His first advent and received the benefits offered by His ministry (John 10:14).

In tending "the doomed flock" (Moffatt) the prophet, in acting out the parable, **took two rods** or "staves." The Eastern shepherd carried a rod or stout club hewed from a tree to beat away wild beasts attacking the sheep and a crooked staff for retrieving the sheep from difficult places. "Thy *rod* and thy *staff* they comfort me" (Ps. 23:4). The two staves, in Zechariah's case, were given names symbolic of the treatment which the Hebrews had received under the protecting providence of God.

One of the staves was denominated

Pleasantness or "Graciousness" (*noʿam* from *naʿem,* "be pleasant, lovely," [Gen. 49:15; Song of Sol. 7:7; Prov. 24:25]; cf. the Arabic *naʿima, naʿuma,* "delight or have pleasure" in anything). Naomi, "my pleasantness," was the appropriate name of Ruth's mother-in-law (Ruth 1:2). Naaman, *naʿaman,* "pleasantness," was the name of the Syrian general (I Kings 5:1). Calling one staff by this name bespoke the good Shepherd's loving, kind, gracious, tender care for the sheep of His flock (Israel).

The other staff was called Unity (*ḥobhelim,* plural of *ḥobhel* a participle properly denoting a "tying or binding" from *ḥabhal,* "to tighten," "twist" a cord, hence "bind"). Thus the Dutch translators and other render *ḥobhelim,* "Binders" or "Bands" (R.V.). expressing "ties" which unite people together, the plural being used to express forcefully the abstract singular, "Unity" or "Oneness." The naming of the other staff by this symbolic name stressed the unifying and edifying ministry of the good Shepherd, whose goal was ever *"one* fold and *one* shepherd" (John 10:16). Tregelles (Gesenius' *Lexicon, in loc.*) pictures this shepherd's crook to be actually made or covered with "cords or bands." In such a case the very appearance of the staff would suggest the shepherd's efforts to heal the harmful division which had plagued the nation since the days of Rehoboam.

The last clause of verse 7, **I tended the flock,** repeats the first clause of the verse to emphasize the gracious, loving, unifying character of the Shepherd's ministry, so magnificently fulfilled in Him "who went about doing good and healing all that were oppressed by the devil" (Acts 10:38).

Further notices, however, are given in the parabolic representation of the coming Messiah's ministry as the good Shepherd to show His faithful endeavors to reclaim Israel. **Then I disowned** [*ʾakhḥidh,* "cut off" in the sense of "disavow," not necessarily in the

sense of destroying or putting to death (Exod. 23:23; Hos. 5:3)] **the three shepherds in one month** (vs. 8). Leupold, following Kyle, seeks to make the category indefinite to escape the largely fruitless task of identification, witnessed by more than forty diverse interpretations from Moses, Aaron and Miriam (Jerome), to the Roman emperors, Galba, Otho, and Vitellius.

However, the Hebrew reads **the three shepherds** despite the temptation which this rendering offers to project numerous bizarre identifications. Henderson (*op. cit.,* p. 442) cannot be far afield though when he declares, "The only construction which is at all entitled to any notice, is that which regards the language as descriptive of the three orders of rulers in the Jewish state — the priests, the teachers of the law, and the civil magistrates." These were the people of influential prestige by whom the nation's affairs were managed and to whose wickedness, which reached its acme when they crucified the Messiah, the destruction of the state is to be ascribed. The **one month,** *yeraḥ ʾeḥadh,* can best be understood as referring to the period of culminating unbelief just before the national leaders crucified our Lord and thus sealed the fate of the Jewish state. During this period the nation rejected our Lord, and the Lord rejected the nation by disowning its leaders.

The last part of verse 8 points out the mutual dissatisfaction and disgust with which the wicked rulers of the Jewish nation and the Messiah regarded each other. **After that** [the cutting off of the three shepherds] **I grew impatient with them, and they loathed me. I grew impatient with them,** is literally "My soul" [an intensive ego, I] "became *short* [tempered] *at them,*" i.e., "I lost all patience with them." In the idiom, "My soul was *shortened,*" the word *qatsar* is used of "cutting off" grain, hence "reaping" or "harvesting" (Lev. 19:9; 25:5; Jer. 12:13). The stative

9 Then said I, I will not feed you: that that dieth, let it die; and that that is to be cut off, let it be cut off; and let the rest eat every one the flesh of another.

10 And I took my staff, even Beauty, and cut it asunder, that I might break my covenant which I had made with all the people.

11 And it was broken in that day: and so the poor of the flock that waited upon me knew that it was the word of the Lord.

---

9   Then said I, I will not feed you: that which dieth, let it die; and that which is to be cut off, let it be cut off; and let them that are left eat every one the flesh of another.

10   And I took my staff Beauty, and cut it asunder, that I might break my covenant which I had made with all the peoples.

11   And it was broken in that day; and thus the poor of the flock that gave heed unto me knew that it was the word of Jehovah.

---

verb means "to be or become cut off or shortened" (Isa. 28:20; 50:2; 59:1). Hence "My soul became shortened" means "I lost all patience" (Judg. 10:16; 16:16). Compare our expression "short-tempered."

The reaction of the Jewish leaders toward our Lord is graphically prophesied, And they loathed me. The expression loathed means "were nauseated" (cf. the Syriac *beḥilah*, "nauseating," "suffering from nausea," an extremely strong word showing that the rejection of the good Shepherd was prompted by great disgust, the verb *bahal* occurring only here and in Proverbs 20:21, where it refers to a possession "got by *greed* or *avarice*" and there connects with Arabic "to be greedy, avaricious" where it has a different meaning from Zechariah's use).

4. *The Parabolic Representation of God's Final Abandonment of Israel* (Zech. 11:9–11). Then I [the Messiah] said, I will not shepherd you. That which is dying, let it die, and that which is being cut off, let it be cut off. And as for those that are left, let them devour each other's flesh. Then I took my staff Graciousness and cut it to pieces in order to break my covenant, which I had made with all the peoples. So it was broken in that day and thus the poor of the flock, who were giving heed to me, knew that it was the word of the Lord.

The national rejection of Israel by the good Shepherd is most dramati-

cally set forth in this turn in the prophetic parable, acted out by the prophet Zechariah impersonating the future Messiah. The setting aside of the nation is climactically and summarily contained in the good Shepherd's words, I will not shepherd you. This decisive announcement indicates that the broad comprehensive care of the Lord for Israel contained in the term shepherd, *ra'ah*, "tend," would cease. Features of that tender care are enumerated to show the tragedy such drastic action would bring to the nation.

That which is dying (*hammethah, moriens*, the articular participle) indicates a continuous action in the present, the act of expiring, and describes the sheep that is so dangerously ill or wounded that it is in a dying condition. Instead of following the natural procedure of a good shepherd of binding up the sheep's wounds, or giving it medicine or taking it to shelter from the cold, the shepherd abandons it to death with the words of judgment, Let it die! the jussive expressing a movement of the Shepherd's will.

That which is being cut off [the same word used as in the case of "the three shepherds" whom the good Shepherd "cut off" in verse 8], let it be cut off. Disowned and disclaimed by the good Shepherd, the sheep is exposed to destruction by its enemies. But the tragic fate of such abandonment by the good Shepherd of Israel is so terrible that it surpasses in horror anything that could normally befall a sheep. **And let those that are left devour one another's flesh.** By an act of His will (jussive mood) the Shepherd gives up "the survivors" of death and destruction to starvation and cannibalism (*hannish'aroth*, plural passive participle, "to remain, be left as a survivor" [Gen. 7:23; 42:38; 47:18; Zech. 9:7]). Ezekiel illustrates this graphic passage. "He that is far off shall die of the pestilence, and he that is near shall fall by the sword; and *he that remains* and is besieged shall die by the famine: thus will I accomplish my fury upon them" (Ezek. 6:12). However, Zechariah's lurid prophetic parable goes farther. It predicts the cruelest famine, fulfilled in the siege of Jerusalem by the Romans in A.D. 70 and amply attested by Josephus' account of this disaster in which survivors of other calamities actually ate each other's flesh.

Then I took my staff Graciousness and cut it to pieces in order to break my covenant which I had made with all the peoples (vs. 10). At this point the prophetic parable sets forth in lively symbolism the removal of the restraint which the Lord had exercised over the nations to prevent them from overrunning and destroying His people Israel. This restraint is spoken of broadly as a **covenant** (*berith*, "an agreement," from root *barah*, meaning either "to cut up" sacrificed animals to seal the contract [Gen. 15:10] or "to eat a banquet together," the latter among Orientals being equivalent to making a covenant of friendship [Gen. 31:54]). The word *berith* is used variously of contracts between God and men (Deut. 4:23; 29:24), between individuals and friends (I Sam. 18:3; 23:18) and between nations (Josh. 9:6). Here the term **my covenant** is used in an unrestricted sense of the divine restraint placed upon the nations which hindered them from decimating Israel. Elsewhere this holding in check of forces inimical to

God's people is spoken of under the figure of a covenant (Job 5:23; Hos. 2:18 [20]; Ezek. 34:25).

The plural expression **peoples,** *'ammim,* here refers to the "nations," but the singular is employed of Israel as the people of God (*'am Yhwh,* Exod. 15:13; *'am qadosh,* "a holy people," Deut. 7:6, etc.) in distinction from the *goyim* or "nations." However, the plural, *'ammim,* here refers *not* to the tribes of Israel (Calvin), but as commonly to all "peoples"(Exod.19:5; Deut. 28:10; Isa. 8:9; Neh. 9:22, 24).

Representing the Lord's kind and loving protection of Israel was the good Shepherd's crook called "Graciousness" or "Pleasantness." To demonstrate the removal of this aspect of divine providential care, the good Shepherd took this particular staff and "chopped it to pieces." The word used is a strong one, the root in Arabic being used of "cutting off bodily members, mutilating" (cf. I Sam. 2:31; Lam. 2:3). It is employed of "cutting down [slaughtering] men in battle" (Judg. 21:6; Isa. 10:33), under the figure of "hewing down" trees or "chopping off" boughs (Isa. 9:10 [9]; 14:12). This stern action in telling fashion portrays the exhaustion of the good Shepherd's patience and His giving the nation over to judgment and the manifestation of divine wrath in the invasion of Roman armies and the terrible sufferings ensuing in the destruction of the city of Jerusalem and the polity of the ancient people of God.

Verse 11: **So it [the covenant] was annulled in that day, and thus the poor of the flock, who were giving heed to me, knew that it was the word of the Lord.** The anticipated accomplishment of the prediction, symbolized in the prophetic parable, is believed *both* by a faithful few from among those who saw Zechariah enact this object lesson in his day, and by the faithful few who saw the historical fulfilment of the prediction toward the end of our Lord's earthly ministry (cf. Matt. 23:1–39).

12 And I said unto them, If ye think good, give me my price; and if not, forbear. So they weighed for my price thirty pieces of silver.
13 And the Lord said unto me, Cast it unto the potter: a goodly price that I was prised at of them. And I took the thirty pieces of silver, and cast them to the potter in the house of the Lord.

12   And I said unto them, If ye think good, give me my hire; and if not, forbear. So they weighed for my hire thirty pieces of silver.
13   And Jehovah said unto me, Cast it unto the potter, the goodly price that I was prized at by them. And I took the thirty pieces of silver, and cast them unto the potter, in the house of Jehovah.

The judgment the symbolic action of the cutting to pieces of the staff sought to portray actually occurred as an historical event. Those who recognized the fulfilment of the word of the Lord set forth by it are called the poor of the flock, as in verse 7. Since the lowly and wretched usually more readily consider delighting in God's Word and God's ways, they are described as those who were giving heed unto the Lord, that is, "they were watching" (Gen. 30:31), in the sense of "attending upon" or "listening to" the Lord (I Sam. 1:12), thus "honoring" or "worshipping" Him by the proper exercise of faith in his word (Hos. 4:10). "Since those who regard God closely have deeper spiritual insight" (Leupold, op. cit., p. 215), "they knew that it was the word of the Lord" and not just a fortuitous event or bad piece of luck that the nations were able to advance against Israel to afflict and overrun her, and finally to blot her out as a nation when the covenant was annulled, tuppar passive of parar, "break, break in pieces," figuratively of a covenant (Lev. 26:44; Isa. 33:8; Ezek. 17:16), "to be made invalid or void" (Isa. 8:10; Jer. 33:21).

5. The Reason for the Final Abandonment of the Nation — the Rejection of the Messiah (Zech. 11:12, 13). Then I said to them, if it is good in your sight [eyes], give me my pay; and if not, pass it by. So they paid me my pay — thirty pieces of silver. But the Lord said to me: Throw it to the potter, the fancy price that I was valued at by them. So I took the thirty pieces of silver and threw them in the house of the Lord to the potter.

This last action in the prophetic parable concludes the good Shepherd's relations with the flock. It demonstrates the people's reaction to what He had done for them as a faithful Shepherd and also acts as a test of their exact feeling at His refusal to act further in that capacity. So He requests such pay from them as His faithful pastoral labors in their behalf merited in their estimation. He puts His request hypothetically, since so far as the flock is concerned, after its contemptible treatment of their Shepherd, it is questionable whether they will acknowledge any obligation. If it appears proper to you, give me my pay. Literally, "if it is good in your eyes." But their eyes were blinded to any good.

However, the Shepherd proves that He is not a mercenary hireling by His concluding words: If not, don't bother! literally, "if not" (i.e., an abbreviated conditional clause, see Gesenius-Kautzsch, 159 dd), "if it is not good in your eyes, desist" (hadhalu, "leave off, cease" [Gen. 11:8; 41:49; I Sam. 12:23], "leave it undone," i.e., "do not do it; forbear doing it" [I Kings 22:6; Ezek. 2:5; Jer. 40:4; Job 16:6]).

By this abrupt termination of His pastoral relationship the Shepherd is more concerned in making the flock realize that it is being abandoned, and thus cause it to arouse itself to the seriousness of the situation, than He is interested in personal remuneration for His faithful labors.

So [as a result of the Shepherd's

request] they paid me my pay – thirty [shekels] of silver. Their reply is as shamelessly insulting as their general reaction to His ministry as a whole, and shows how utterly unworthy they were of His pastoral solicitude. The sum they paid (weighed) Him represents more of an affront than if they had paid Him nothing. It was a wickedly calculated amount designed to give vent to their scorn and venomous hatred of Him, being the sum paid for a *slave* gored by an ox (Exod. 21:32), not even the price of a freedman. This last terrible touch, laying bare the full measure of Israel's depravity, proved the nation was ripe for judgment, as the Amorites were when Israel entered Canaan (Gen. 15:16).

Then the Lord said to me [Zechariah], Fling the fancy price that I was valued by them to the potter. So I took the thirty [shekels] of silver, and flung them to the potter in the house of the Lord (vs. 13). After this scurrilous treatment of Zechariah, impersonating the Messiah, the prophet is enjoined to cast the thirty shekels of silver (ironically called the fancy price to accentuate the despicable meanness of the whole transaction) to the potter in the house of the Lord.

An acute difficulty of interpretation attaches to the expression to the potter, 'el-hayyotser, which modern criticism, following the Syriac rendering, bit gaza, "the treasury," tends to emend, "cast it in the treasury," 'el-ha'otsar, (cf. C. C. Torrey, The Journal of Biblical Literature, 1936, pp. 247–255). But (1) besides involving an arbitrary emendation of the Hebrew text, (2) this proposed solution is objectional on moral grounds. With what propriety could such tainted money be divinely directed into the temple treasury rather than to be lost? (3) Besides, the meaning of the verb hishlikh, "to throw or fling away in contempt" (Gen. 37:22; Num. 19:6; Deut. 9:21, etc.) is at variance with the idea of depositing the money in the treasury.

(4) Moreover, in the actual fulfilment of the prophecy in Matthew 27:3–10 the thirty shekels never were so deposited. (5) Nor did the Septuagint so understand it, rendering the expression "into the smelting furnace" (eis to choneuterion), nor yet the Vulgate, rendering statuarius, "a maker of statues."

Having decided, then, that the money was actually flung to the potter, the problem still remains what relation the potter sustained to the money. The solution commonly offered is that the phrase, cast it to the potter, was merely an idiomatic proverbial expression like German zum Henker gehen (Leupold, op. cit., p. 217) or our "throw it to the dogs" when alluding to the disposition of something utterly disgusting or contemptible. This simple explanation would rule out seeking for a particular potter, either with workshop in the Valley of Hinnom (Jer. 18:1–3; 19:2) and employed about the temple, as Hengstenberg maintains, or as even being in the temple (Feinberg, op. cit., p. 210) when the prophet contemptuously cast the money down there. The potter was one of the lowliest of the common laborers, a worker whose products were so trifling in value that they could be replaced with little expenditure of cost or toil. Under this view "to throw anything to the potter" would apparently be tantamount to saying, "throw it to a poor dog," i.e., "get rid of it."

But this explanation can scarcely be viewed as satisfactory. "Casting it to the potter" must be a pregnant construction (abbreviated for terseness and effect) and meaning throw it down [i.e., in the house of the Lord] to ['el, i.e., "to go to"] the potter – that it may wind up in the possession of a potter. Compare Num. 25:1; Ezek. 16:29 for similar pregnant uses of the preposition 'el.

That this interpretation is correct is shown by the fact that: (1) The flinging was done in the house of the Lord (vs. 13) which would scarcely directly involve a lowly potter present within the holy precincts, since the whole transaction was divinely enjoined to be performed both officially and publicly both in the presence of the Lord, and before the eyes of the people (certainly through the priests, their representatives) since the act was one involving in a most serious way the nation's standing before God. (2) It would have been pointless to have flung the tainted money *directly* to a potter, even if he should have happened to be in the temple at the moment, since he lacked any official connection with the act, would not have understood it if performed in relation to him, and would have construed such contemptuous casting of money to him, though poor, as a gross insult, if not the jesting of a fool.

(3) The fulfilment of this prophecy in Matthew 27:3-10 is proof enough that the money was flung down in the temple and immediately taken up by the priests to purchase a field *of a potter* for a burying ground for the poor. (4) That the money *promptly* passed into the hands of "the potter" is clear both from the Mosaic law which provided that dishonorable money could not remain in the temple (Deut. 23:18 [19]) and from Matthew's account of how the "chief priests took the silver pieces, and said, It is not lawful to put them into the treasury, because it is the price of blood. And they took counsel, and bought with them *the potter's field* to bury strangers in" (Matt. 27:6, 7).

Two other difficulties appear when Zechariah's enacted prophetic parable is compared with its fulfilment recorded in Matthew 27:7-10. The first concerns alleged discrepancies between the details of Zechariah's parabolic prophetic symbolism and the account of their historical outworking in Matthew's account and the second centers in the fact that Matthew ascribes to Jeremiah the words he obviously quotes from Zechariah.

With regard to the first and less serious difficulty it may be said that

the problems encountered are not greater than those met with in several other New Testament quotations from the Old Testament and do not in any sense affect the end the prophet or the evangelist had in mind. Matthew does not strictly quote Zechariah for the simple reason he must interpret the latter's prophecy since it is couched in the figurative language of a parable and acted out in the first person. Therefore, it was *necessary* for the evangelist also to apply the prophetic truths set forth in the prophecy. As Henderson correctly notes, "The very changes which he [Matthew] introduces into the phraseology are such as his position as a historian required" (*op. cit.*, p. 423). Hence, instead of the wording **at which I was estimated by them** (Zech. 11:13), Matthew has, "at which he was estimated by the sons of Israel" (Matt. 27:9). Instead of **And I took the thirty pieces of silver** (Zech. 11:13), we find "and they took the thirty pieces of silver" (Matt. 27:9). Instead of **And I flung it,** the gospel has "and they gave them" (Matt. 27:10) but interestingly and "he [Judas] *flung* the pieces of silver in the temple" (vs. 5).

The second difficulty that Matthew ascribes to Jeremiah the words he obviously quotes from Zechariah is much less amenable to satisfactory solution and is still a matter of great perplexity to critics. The Latin Vulgate follows the Greek in ascribing the quotation to Jeremiah, but the Syriac omits the prophet's name entirely, simply saying, "by *the prophet* who said."

Although all other quotations from Zechariah in the New Testament, like the Syriac rendering of this one, do *not* mention the prophet *by name*, viz., Matt. 21:4, 5 (Zech. 9:9); Matt. 26:31 (Zech. 13:7); John 12:14 (Zech. 9:9); John 19:37 (Zech. 12:10), the Syriac can scarcely be correct, since the oldest Greek manuscripts have the name Jeremiah.

Henderson (*in loc.*) suggests that Matthew originally wrote his gospel

14 Then I cut asunder mine other staff, even Bands, that I might break the brotherhood between Judah and Israel.

---

14   Then I cut asunder mine other staff, even Bands, that I might break the brotherhood between Judah and Israel.

---

and this passage in Hebrew (*beyad hannabhi*) "by the prophet" (just as in Matthew 1:22; 2:5, 15; 13:35; 21:4; 27:35) and that his Greek translator simply mistook the very similar letter *d* (daleth) for *r* (resh), which he considered was a contraction for *beyirmiyahu*, and so rendered it "through Jeremiah the prophet." This would account (if one *assumes* a Hebrew or Aramaic original for Matthew) for this reading having thus found its way into the first Greek manuscript, and its consequent practically universal propagation. But the thesis of a Hebrew original for Matthew's gospel has never been established.

Views that account for Matthew's reference as (1) a simple slip of the memory (Augustine, Luther, Beza, Wright, Keil, and numerous recent writers), or (2) that his quotation was from an originally Jeremian prophecy which somehow got included in the book of Zechariah, are wholly unsatisfactory and fail to deal with the problem. The same is true of the assumption (3) that the citation is made from an apocryphal book of Jeremiah. That such an apocryphal book existed, but is late and spurious, and was rejected by Jerome, is certain. Portions of this writing existed among the Nazarenes, and are extant in a Sahidic Lectionary and in Coptic (cf. Henderson, *op. cit.*, p. 424, for a translation of the apocryphal passage).

Plummer's idea (4) that "the prophecy, though attributed to Jeremiah ... may be influenced by Jeremiah 18:2 and 19:11, and hence be quoted as from Jeremiah" (*Exegetical Commentary on the Gospel according to St. Matthew*, p. 386) is scarcely credible; (5) nor are Hengstenberg's and Edersheim's variations of this hypothesis (*The Life and Times of Jesus the*

Messiah, II, p. 576) plausible that Matthew blended both Jeremiah and Zechariah and used the former's name as being the more prominent. (6) The contention that the contraction *Zriou* for *Zachariou* was mistaken by an early copyist for *Iriou* (Ieremiou) is also inadmissible inasmuch as such contractions are foreign to the oldest manuscripts (cf. C. H. H. Wright, *Zechariah and His Prophecies*, p. 337).

The most satisfactory explanation is that Matthew actually cites the prophet Zechariah, but labels the citation from Jeremiah because that prophet stood at the head of the prophetic roll he used, according to the ancient order preserved in numerous Hebrew manuscripts and familiar from Talmudic tradition. A similar usage occurs in Luke 24:44 when the book of Psalms gives its name to the entire third section of the Hebrew canon.

6. *The Final Abandonment of the Nation* (Zech. 11:14). **Then I cut to pieces my second stave [crook] Unity in order to break up the brotherhood between Judah and Israel.** This final stage of the prophetic parable represents the complete severance of all relations between the Shepherd and His flock Israel. Accordingly, both staves as symbolizing His shepherd care, must be destroyed. The first, **Graciousness**, already having been destroyed, there remains the disposal of the second, **Unity.**

The Hebrew designation of this second stave **Unity**, *ḥobhelim*, is instructive (see comments on verse 7). The prediction made here involves the utter breaking up of those social and religious "ties" (Hebrew "bindings") that had always united the people of Israel into a solidly knit-together people. This fearful dissolution of their own national solidarity was

15 And the Lord said unto me, Take unto thee yet the instruments of a foolish shepherd.

15 And Jehovah said unto me, Take unto thee yet again the instruments of a foolish shepherd.

occasioned largely by the internal dissensions brought about by the conflicting parties which prevailed among them, which at the last pitilessly pitted brother against brother, and was more cruel and destructive than the suffering occasioned by the besieging Romans, as Josephus, the Jewish soldier-historian, luridly narrates.

The chopping to pieces of the staff **Unity** signified that God would no longer interpose to check disunifying factors. His favor having been withdrawn in the destruction of the first staff, one of the conspicuous areas manifesting that lack of favor would be in their social and political contacts with each other. The term **brotherhood,** *'aḥavah*, is a denominative from *'aḥ*, "brother," and is a *hapox legomenon* meaning "the condition or state that exists among brothers."

III. PREDICTION OF THE ACCEPTANCE OF THE BAD SHEPHERD (Zech. 11:15-17)

The full fate of Israel is not recounted in the rejection of the good Shepherd God raised up to tend them. The complete tale of their woe centers in their acceptance of the bad shepherd God will raise up to destroy them. The one dark episode centers in the events of Messiah's first advent and death, followed by the dissolution of the Jewish state (Zech. 11:1-14). The other tragic experience will occur in the events connected with Messiah's second advent and glory, and deals with the nation's final time of unparalleled trouble (Zech. 11*15-17) previous to her entrance into kingdom blessing.

1. *The Prophet's Commission to Enact a Second Prophetic Parable* (Zech. 11:15). **Then the Lord said to me, Once more take for yourself the**

equipment of a foolish shepherd. The expression **once more** (*'odh*, adverb "again") refers back to what is recorded in verse 7. The prophet is **once again** [to take the] **instruments,** *keli*, the collective singular for *kelim*, here denoting the articles usually belonging to a shepherd, such as crook, club, bag or wallet for food, a pipe or reed, a knife, etc., but commonly used of any "implement, tool, utensil or weapon" (Gen. 31:37; Judg. 18:11; I Sam. 14:1; Isa. 39:2). Usually this equipment helps the shepherd to care for the flock, but in this context it is intended to harm the sheep.

The shepherd the prophet is now called upon to impersonate before the people is called **foolish** (*'ewili* from *'awal*, "to grow thick,") describing a person who has grown obtuse and insensible to higher purposes and aspirations, in this instance foolishly callous to the Lord's purposes with His people, and by implication signifying "wicked," as wickedness is often represented as folly in the Old Testament (Prov. 5:23; 14:16).

This **foolish shepherd** does not represent all the rulers of Israel from the decline of the Maccabean period to the crucifixion of Christ (Lowe), nor Herod (Kimchi, Henderson) nor the Roman Empire (Wright), nor "every unbelieving Jewish teacher" ever since Zechariah's day (Leupold), but *the personal Antichrist* (Baron, Dennett, Pusey, Feinberg).

2. *The Prophecy of the Character of the False Shepherd* (Zech. 11:16). **For, lo, I will raise up a shepherd in the land** — those which are being cut off, he will not visit; neither will he seek out the young, nor heed that which is injured, nor feed that which is sturdy; but he will devour the flesh of the fat ones and will tear their hoofs in pieces.

The diabolic cruelty and insa-

16 For, lo, I will raise up a shepherd in the land, which shall not visit those that be cut off, neither shall seek the young one, nor heal that that is broken, nor feed that that standeth still: but he shall eat the flesh of the fat, and tear their claws in pieces.

17 Woe to the idol shepherd that leaveth the flock! the sword shall be upon his arm, and upon his right eye: his arm shall be clean dried up, and his right eye shall be utterly darkened.

---

16   For, lo, I will raise up a shepherd in the land, who will not visit those that are cut off, neither will seek those that are scattered, nor heal that which is broken, nor feed that which is sound; but he will eat the flesh of the fat sheep, and will tear their hoofs in pieces.

17   Woe to the worthless shepherd that leaveth the flock! the sword shall be upon his arm, and upon his right eye: his arm shall be clean dried up, and his right eye shall be utterly darkened.

---

tiable rapacity of the foolish shepherd are set forth. He is described first in negative terms to show his callous selfishness and blatant unconcern for the sheep, and then in positive terms to delineate his more terribly aggressive destructiveness.

For, lo, I [emphatically the Lord] **will raise up a shepherd.** The lively form in Hebrew (future *instans*) graphically sets forth the divine determination moving to punish the sinful people. The participle **raise up** (*meqim*), like similar verbs in the causative stem, however, does not denote any direct moral excitement to action, but the outworking of concurring circumstances under the divine government, as a result of which certain events are brought about by responsible human agency. Moreover, the raising up of the shepherd **in the land** can only refer to Israel's land contextually, but does not rule out the foolish shepherd's sway far beyond this limited sphere.

Several classes of sheep in dire distress are enumerated, to show the false shepherd's heartless unconcern for the welfare of the sheep. First, **that which is being cut off,** *nikhedeth,* or in some way "in the process of perishing" or "being destroyed" by isolation from the flock, cold, wild beasts, etc., the false shepherd will not "visit" or look after. Next **he will not seek out the young,** *na'ar,* "young of

the human species," but here certainly used of sheep [cf. Isa. 40:11], contrary to Henderson's derivation from an Arabic root "cast out," i.e., "that which strays" (*in loc.*). Next he will not **heal** the helpless sheep with broken bones (*nishbereth,* "shattered, broken"), especially needing the shepherd's case to set and bind up the injured member.

Next is enumerated the **robust sheep,** *nitstsavah, nifal* participle from *natsav,* "stand," i.e., "the one standing," or with Baron, Driver, and Briggs (*in loc.*), "that which stands firm." So worthless is this shepherd that even the well and strong among the sheep, which require a minimum of effort, **he will not sustain,** *yekalkel,* "support or nourish" (Gen. 45:11; 50:21; II Sam. 20:3; Ruth 4:15).

The description now passes from the negative note outlining the indolent and worthless characteristics of the bad shepherd to his positive criminality. He not only will neglect the sheep, but actively destroy and prey upon them as a wolf. **But the meat of the fat sheep** [emphatic by word order] **will he devour.** His incredible greed will goad him to feed on the sheep instead of feeding them. His unbridled rapacity will prompt him to eat the fattest and best sheep. But this detail, as lurid as it is, is not the worst. The final touch to the picture of this repulsive antithesis to the good

Shepherd is that he will **tear off** [the very] **hoofs** of the poor sheep in avaricious search for the last edible morsel.

The verb **tear off** (the intensive form of *paraq*, "break," Arabic *faraqa*, "split, divide"), speaks of the horribly greedy ferocity of this wicked shepherd. He will tear to pieces the sheep's hoofs. The word is used of a great wind "tearing" or "rending mountains" (I Kings 19:11), of branches *violently broken off* a tree (Ezek. 19:12).

Such is Zechariah's prophetic foreview of the Antichrist, the "little horn" of Dan. 7:24-26; the "desolator" of Dan. 9:27 and Matt. 24:15; "the man of sin" (II Thess. 2:4-8), earth's last and most terrible tyrant (Rev. 13:1-10), Satan's instrument of wrath against God and the Jewish saints of the end time. Jesus warned Jews of His day of the peril of rejecting Him (the good Shepherd). "I have come in my Father's name, and ye receive me not: if another [the Antichrist] shall come in his own name, *him ye will receive*" (John 5:43). Jesus' warning will find fulfilment in the rise of Zechariah's **foolish** [wicked] **shepherd.**

3. *The Prophecy of the Doom of the False Shepherd* (Zech. 11:17). **Woe! Worthless shepherd, forsaker of the flock! Let the sword be against his arm and against his right eye! His arm shall be completely dried up and his right eye shall be completely blind.** The Lord pronounces terrible doom upon the false shepherd. Although He Himself will raise him up as His instrument to punish His sinful people, His infinite holiness demands the full punishment of this diabolical personage after his task is completed. Accordingly, the Lord addresses him directly, **Woe, worthless shepherd, forsaker of the flock** (two nominatives of direct address occur in a dramatic face-to-face encounter. **Woe!** (*hoy*) is an onomatopoeic interjection, commonly used in laments (I Kings 13:30; Jer. 22:18; Isa. 1:4), and is employed in this context to arrest attention

preparatory to a declaration of judgment as in Isaiah 17:12; 28:1; Amos 5:18; Habakkuk 2:6. Thus the Lord Himself addresses the false shepherd directly and arrests his attention by the introductory interjection.

Worthless shepherd (*ro'i ha'elil*) is actually "shepherd of worthlessness," the ending *i*, indicating the construct (Gesenius-Kautzch, *Hebrew Grammar*, 901-n). The noun *'elil* is from the root *'alal*, "to be weak, insufficient" (cf. Arabic *'alal*, "to fail") and means "insufficiency," or "worthlessness" (Job 13:4). **Worthless shepherd** is apt and accurate and succinctly describes the sinister character the prophet predicted in his second parabolic action.

Having dramatically accosted the foolish shepherd in direct address and thus having aroused his attention, the Lord does not confine His pronouncement of doom to him, but in lively fashion changes to the third person, and announces judgment upon the enemy of His people both to them and to all the world. **Let a sword** [jussive of command] **be against his right arm and against his right eye,** or, "A sword shall be [declaration of fact] against his right arm and against his right eye." Since the shepherd used his arm not only not to fend for the sheep but to fleece and destroy them and employed his eye not only not to watch over them, but seek their utter ruin, divine vengeance calls the sword of destruction upon these members.

If the avenging sword fails in its work upon the wicked shepherd's arm and right eye, these members will nevertheless be blighted by the inescapable curse of God. **His arm** [emphatic by word position] **shall be completely dried up and his right eye** [emphatic] **shall be completely blind.** The infinitive absolute employed with each of the last two verbs accentuates the verbal idea, rendered in English by "completely" or "utterly." The shocking cruelty and wickedness of the foolish shepherd will meet with the *undiminished* punishment of God (Rev. 19:20; 20:10).

The verb, **dried up,** "become shrivelled," is employed of a hand or arm atrophying or withering, as in I Kings 13:4 and also here. The verb "to be or become blind" is from *kahah,* "to grow dim or faint," and refers to the loss of sight, and in the present context of complete loss of vision (Gen. 27:1; Deut. 34:7; Job 17:7).

With this climactic scene the first prophetic burden describing the first advent and rejection of Messiah, the Shepherd-King (chapters 9–11) comes to a close. The way is thus opened for the second burden and the second advent and acceptance of Messiah, the King (chapters 12–14).

CHAPTER TWELVE

ISRAEL'S DELIVERANCE AND NATIONAL CONVERSION

THE FIRST SECTION OF THE SECOND PROPHETIC ORACLE

(ZECH. 12:1–14)

ISRAEL'S rejection of the good Shepherd prophesied so graphically in the preceding chapter (Zech. 11:1–14), which now, of course, has become history, is followed by the prophecy of the nation's acceptance of the worthless shepherd (Zech. 11:15–17), which still remains a future unfulfilled event. However, both of these great events, although separated by the extended hiatus of the present church age, form a prelude and a necessary introduction to the great prophecy of Israel's deliverance and future national conversion recounted in chapters 12 and 13, which belong to the age to come.

The rise of the Antichrist (Zechariah's worthless shepherd) must precede the nation's deliverance, for it is the cruel career of this sinister character foreseen so luminously by the prophet in its stark and hideous reality that plunges the nation into its greatest and most severe time of testing, foreseen by Jeremiah as "the time of Jacob's trouble" (Jer. 30:5–7) and by Daniel as "a time of trouble, such as never was since there was a nation, even to that same time . . ." (Dan. 12:1). Moreover, the deliverance Zechariah describes in chapters 12 and 13 is inseparably connected with this time of trouble initiated by Israel's worthless shepherd, for Daniel adds "and at that time shall thy people [Daniel's people, the Jews] be delivered, every one that shall be found written in the book [the elect remnant]" (Dan. 12:1).

As Israel's future deliverance grows out of the fearful regime of the false shepherd, so the nation's conversion not only eventuates out of these events and because of these events, but more specifically connects with the rejection and consequent death of the Good Shepherd. These great events form the basis of Israel's future national conversion, so vividly set forth in this present section (Zech. 12:1–13:8). Without a rejected and

1 The burden of the word of the Lord for Israel, saith the Lord, which stretcheth forth the heavens, and layeth the foundation of the earth, and formeth the spirit of man within him.

1 The burden of the word of Jehovah concerning Israel. Thus saith Jehovah, who stretcheth forth the heavens, and layeth the foundation of the earth, and formeth the spirit of man within him:

---

crucified Messiah as an object of faith at His second advent, the nation could never be converted and established in the millennial ministry and glory so glowingly predicted throughout this grand prophetic book, especially in Zechariah 3:1–4; 14:9–21.

I. THE FUTURE SIEGE OF JERUSALEM (Zech. 12:1–9)

The second part of Zechariah (chapters 9–14) consists of *two prophetic oracles*, setting forth the great Messianic future of the nation Israel. The *first prophetic oracle* or **burden** (*massa'*, see Zech. 9:1) extends from Zechariah 9:1 to 11:17 and focusses the prophetic spotlight upon the first advent of Messiah, the Shepherd-King (chapters 9–11). The first part of the first oracle deals principally with events of the first advent but blends its view, as is common to Old Testament prophecy in general, with events of the second advent as inextricably connected with it (chapters 9–10). The second portion of this first prophetic oracle deals with the rejection of Messiah, the Shepherd-King at His first advent (Zech. 11:1–14) as a necessary prelude to the nation's woe in the choice of the worthless shepherd (Antichrist) shortly before the second advent (Zech. 11:15–17).

The *second prophetic oracle* predicting the second advent and acceptance of Messiah, the King, extends from Zechariah 12:1 to 14:21. The first section of this second prophetic oracle, giving the future deliverance and the national conversion of Israel, extends from Zechariah 12:1 to 13:9. The second section of the second prophetic oracle outlining the second advent of Messiah in glory runs to the

end of the book (14:1–21). It is the first section of the second prophetic oracle that now claims attention (Zech. 12:1–13:9).

1. *The Authentication of the Second Prophetic Oracle* (Zech. 12:1). **The oracle of the word of the Lord concerning Israel is the declaration of the Lord who stretches out the heavens and lays the foundation of the earth and forms man's spirit within him.** This caption introducing the second great predictive oracle of Zechariah's prophecies is arresting in its emphasis upon the authority that supports the message it enunciates. In a fourfold manner it stresses the divine origin of the prophecies it contains: (1) By the use of the term **burden** (*massa'*). This indicates a divine message freighted with woe and judgment (Isa. 14:28; 15:1; 17:1; Ezek. 12:10; Nahum 1:1) which may also contain important and weighty promises of deliverance and blessing after the cleansing judgments it contains are passed through (Zech. 9:1; 12:1). (2) By the terms **Word of the Lord** (3) and the "declaration" or **utterance of the Lord** (*ne'um Yahweh* [Zech. 8:17; 10:12; 11:6; 12:1, 4; 13:8] compare Arabic *na'ama*, "to groan, sigh"). This common word nominalized from a past participle "that which is uttered" refers to the "utterance" or "revelation" of a prophet *in the inspired state* (Num. 24:3, 15; II Sam. 23:1), but principally before the divine name when the prophet cites the work of God given through him (Isa. 14:22; 30:1; Mal. 1:2, etc.).

It is not without significance that this prophetic oracle, so widely disbelieved in its panoramic predictions, should be so strongly buttressed with the divine authority. Further to

2 Behold, I will make Jerusalem a cup of trembling unto all the people round about, when they shall be in the siege both against Judah and against Jerusalem.

3 And in that day will I make Jerusalem a burdensome stone for all people: all that burden themselves with it shall be cut in pieces, though all the people of the earth be gathered together against it.

---

2 Behold, I will make Jerusalem a cup of reeling unto all the peoples round about, and upon Judah also shall it be in the siege against Jerusalem.

3 And it shall come to pass in that day, that I will make Jerusalem a burdensome stone for all the peoples; all that burden themselves with it shall be sore wounded; and all the nations of the earth shall be gathered together against it.

---

overcome all the doubts which unbelief might suggest respecting the possibility of the deliverance here predicted (4) a sublime description is given of the omnipotent Creator by whom it would be effected, which constitutes the fourth means by which the authority of the message given by the oracle is strengthened.

The divine Author of the oracle is portrayed by three participles which refute the deistic error that God created the universe and then left it to itself and suggest the immanence and activity of the Lord not only in the heavenly and earthly realms but His definite interest and activity in His plans and purposes for *men* on the earth. Who stretches out the heavens [*noteh shamayim*, showing His omnipotent sway in the celestial sphere], and lays the foundation of the earth [*yosedh 'arets*, demonstrating His absolute control in the terrestrial realm], and forms the spirit of man within him, setting forth His sovereign operation in human affairs (cf. Isa. 42:5; 44:24; Heb. 1:3). It is this omnipotent and omniscient One who utters this oracle (burden) which concludes Zechariah's prophecies (12:1–14:21) and comprises one of the most magnificent eschatological vistas to be found in the Word of God as well as one of the *most disbelieved portions of Holy Writ*.

2. *The Nations Attack Jerusalem* (Zech. 12:2, 3). Lo, I will make Jerusalem a goblet of staggering to all the peoples round about, and likewise

with Judah shall it be in the siege against Jerusalem. (3) And it shall come to pass in that day I will make Jerusalem a burdensome stone to all peoples. All who lift it shall grievously injure themselves. And all nations of the earth will assemble themselves against it.

The same omnipotent Lord who just announced Himself as continuously active in the world of nature and men, now speaks in language of lively vigor, as He shows Himself undertaking for His ancient people Israel under the names Jerusalem and Judah. The future *instans* (*hinneh 'anoki sam*) is given an impending or imminent meaning by the R.S.V. Lo I am about to make Jerusalem a cup of reeling. Better, perhaps, is the thought of determination, "I Myself [emphatic] *will* make . . . ."

The word cup, *saph*, Akkadian *sappu*, Phoenician *saph*, denotes a "basin, bowl" such as that in which the Passover blood was held (Exod. 12:22); "basin" for ordinary use (II Sam. 17:28; Jer. 52:19); temple "bowl" (II Kings 12:14). The cup of reeling, *ra'al* from root to "quiver, shake, reel," as in Syriac and Aramaic, denotes "a goblet of wine that causes intoxication and staggering." Although *saph* also means a "threshold," Henderson (*The Minor Prophets*, p. 427) is correct in rejecting the Septuagint reading *hos prothura saleuomena*, "a shaking threshold," as well as Hengstenberg's contention that *saph* is never used to denote "a cup."

The figure is an expressive one. **I will make Jerusalem a goblet of intoxication** [metaphor] **to all the peoples,** *ʿammim,* i.e., the Gentile nations who come against the city (as in Zech. 11:10; cf. 8:20, 22). Their attacking Jerusalem will be like men greedily draining a wine goblet in pleasure but in the end finding themselves helplessly drunk and unable to take the coveted prize. The divine punishment of Israel's foes will be that they will become besotted and foolish, so that their defeat will be assured.

And likewise shall it be concerning [ʿal] **Judah in the siege against** [ʿal] **Jerusalem** (vs. 2b). This is the only reading of this difficult passage that makes sense, involving two different but common meanings of the preposition ʿal, "against," "concerning." This rendering of the Masoretic Hebrew Text would mean that just as the Lord will make Jerusalem a **cup of intoxication** to those who come against her, so will He likewise make Judah such a **goblet of staggering** to those who overrun her in the siege against the capital city.

A second striking metaphor is employed to demonstrate the defeat and ruin that will engulf those who advance against Jerusalem in the city's last terrible siege. Not only will the Lord make Jerusalem a **goblet of staggering,** He will also make the city **a stone of burden,** that is, "a heavy stone, hard to lift" (Brown, Driver and Briggs, *in loc.*). What is evidently meant is "stone such as was used in weight-lifting contests" (Robert C. Dentan, "Zechariah" in the *Interpreter's Bible,* 6, p. 1106). The figure is apparently borrowed "from one of the sports of the young men in Palestine described by Jerome as still subsisting in his day" (Chambers, *Zechariah* in Lange's *Commentary* on the Minor Prophets, 14, p. 91).

All those lifting it [the stone] **shall grievously injure themselves.** The plural participle **those lifting** is from the verb ʿamas, Ugaritic, ʿms, and

Phoenician "to load," (Gen. 44:13; Neh. 13:15), "carry" a load (Isa. 46:3; Neh. 4:11), in this context used of "lifting" a load (Koehler, *Lexicon in Veteris Testamenti Libros, in loc.*). The stone is "a stone of a load," *maʿamasah.* The Hebrew is "those carrying," i.e., *loading* (themselves) "with the stone of a *load*" (paronomasia).

The divine penalty for those nations who will try to lift the heavy stone (Jerusalem) is that they **will grievously injure themselves** (*nifal* reflexive) or "be grievously injured" (*nifal* passive). The idea of **grievously** "seriously" is expressed by the infinitive absolute intensifying the verbal idea **injure** (*saraṭ* which is used in the sense of "making incisions" or "tattooing" in Lev. 21:5; cf. the noun *sereṭ,* "incision, tattoo" in Lev. 19:28). Brown, Driver, and Briggs and Koehler in their lexicons take the sense of Zechariah 12:3, "scratch one another severely" (Koehler), "be severely scratched, lacerated" (Brown, Driver, and Briggs). But this can scarcely be the sense in this context. The meaning is rather "to rupture oneself, suffer sprains or dislocations" rather than lacerations, as in the Akkadian word *saraṭu,* "tear to pieces, rend." Those who lift the stone (Jerusalem) **shall tear themselves to pieces,** do themselves irreparable injury.

The proud overweening Gentile nations, who think to take Jerusalem and destroy God's people Israel, are here described as **all the nations of the earth.** These are represented by their invading and besieging armies, and, it is said, **they will assemble themselves** [*nifal* reflexive] **against her** (Jerusalem), both of these latter thoughts being emphatic in their word order in the Hebrew.

All this is said to take place, *bayyom hahu',* **in that day,** an eschatological phrase that reverberates with remarkable frequency through the second prophetic burden (chapters 12–14); compare chapter 12:3, 4, 6, 8, 9, 11;

4 In that day, saith the Lord, I will smite every horse with astonishment, and his rider with madness: and I will open mine eyes upon the house of Judah, and will smite every horse of the people with blindness.

4   In that day, saith Jehovah, I will smite every horse with terror, and his rider with madness; and I will open mine eyes upon the house of Judah, and will smite every horse of the peoples with blindness.

chapter 13:1, 2, 4; chapter 14:4, 6, 8, 9, 13, 20, 21. This prophetic time indicator is equivalent to "the day of the Lord" and denotes precisely *that future period when the Lord will openly and publicly manifest His power in delivering Israel from her enemies and establishing her in millennial peace and prosperity.*

Inseparably connected with Israel's deliverance are her enemies, the nations (*'ammim*, "peoples"), who are also very prominent in these eschatological passages (Zech. 12:2, 3, 4, 6, 9; Zech. 14:2, 3, 12, 14, 16, 17, 18, 19). The place (Jerusalem) where the deliverance is effected is also necessarily featured (Zech. 12:2, 3, 5, 6, 7, 8, 9, 10, 11; 13:1; 14:2, 3, 12, 14, 16, 17).

3. *Jerusalem's Enemies Confounded* (Zech. 12:4). In that day, is the declaration of the Lord, I will strike every horse with terror and its rider with madness, and I will keep my eyes open upon the house of Judah, and I will strike every horse of the peoples with blindness. The direct interposition of the Lord in behalf of His people is vividly continued in the first person. I will strike every horse with terror . . . I will keep my eyes open . . . I will strike every horse with blindness. . . .

Special emphasis is laid upon the horse (*sus*), to show the power and resources of Israel's enemies. Poor Israel could scarcely dream of such military equipment as fleet squadrons of numerous cavalry, in which her foes excelled. But against this very formidable area of strength, the power of God will be exerted. I will strike every horse with terror . . . I will strike every horse . . . with blindness. The thorough destruction

of the entire cavalry is shown (1) By the repetition of the thought, I will strike. (2) By the inclusion of every horse (*kol sus*). (3) By the inclusion of every rider. Horses are useless for battle if stricken with terror, more so if stricken with blindness, worse than useless if the rider is stricken with madness. The very calamites that befell Israel in her unbelief and worldwide dispersion (Deut. 28:28) shall now be visited upon her enemies.

Maddened riders mounted upon consternation-stricken and blinded steeds can only destroy themselves, as in similar divine deliverances where "everyone's sword was against his brother" (cf. Judg. 4:15; 7:19–22).

The unusual word terror, *timmahon*, "bewilderment," is from the root *tamah*, "be dumbfounded," "be stupefied," (Gen. 43:33; Job 26:11; Isa. 29:9; Hab. 1:5) and in the noun form occurs only here and in Deuteronomy 28:28 in the sense of "stupefaction." The word madness, *shigga'on*, with which the riders are smitten is from *shaga'*; cf. Assyrian *shegu*, "rage, howl," Ethiopic "be mad" (Deut. 28:34; Hos. 9:7; Jer. 29:26; I Sam. 21:16). To smite with madness is "a figure of wild and helpless panic" (Brown, Driver, and Briggs). The word blindness is from the common adjective "blind," *'iwwer*, and occurs only here and in Deuteronomy 28:28. Smiting horses with blindness, i.e., with "blind staggers," makes them helplessly uncontrolled.

4. *Judah's Faith in the Lord* (Zech. 12:5). And the chieftains of Judah shall say in their heart, The inhabitants of Judah are my strength in the Lord of armies their God. The successful resistance of the enemy by the inhabitants of the capital city will inspire

5 And the governors of Judah shall say in their heart, The inhabitants of Jerusalem shall be my strength in the Lord of hosts their God.

6 In that day will I make the governors of Judah like an hearth of fire among the wood, and like a torch of fire in a sheaf; and they shall devour all the people round about, on the right hand and on the left: and Jerusalem shall be inhabited again in her own place, even in Jerusalem.

7 The Lord also shall save the tents of Judah first, that the glory of the house of David and the glory of the inhabitants of Jerusalem do not magnify themselves against Judah.

---

5   And the chieftains of Judah shall say in their heart, The inhabitants of Jerusalem are my strength in Jehovah of hosts their God.

6   In that day will I make the chieftains of Judah like a pan of fire among wood, and like a flaming torch among sheaves; and they shall devour all the peoples round about, on the right hand and on the left; and they of Jerusalem shall yet again dwell in their own place, even in Jerusalem.

7   Jehovah also shall save the tents of Judah first, that the glory of the house of David and the glory of the inhabitants of Jerusalem be not magnified above Judah.

---

the people of the country districts to find a similar deliverance through divine aid.

The **chieftains** (*'alluphim*) denote "the chiliarchs," "rulers over a thousand," a denominative from *'eleph*, "a thousand" (Gen. 36:15; Exod. 15:15; Zech. 9:7; I Chron. 1:51). What the "leaders" and "rulers" of a people think and say is important. Like leaders, like people. **The chieftains of Judah say in their heart,** that is, they do not speak superficially, but deeply with genuine conviction. "For out of the abundance of the heart the mouth speaketh" (Matt. 12:34). What a confidence is this that animates God's people and panoplies them for victory!

Judah's faith finds expression in the words, **The inhabitants of Jerusalem are my strength** (emphatic by word position) *'amtsah lî*, "are strength to me," i.e., "inspire me with strength," qualified by the phrase, **in the Lord of armies, their God.** The chiliarchs would testify that the real strength of Jerusalem's populace is the Lord Himself and that through Judah's faithful example and testimony, their God became the strength of the Judaean chieftains.

The word **strength**, *'amtsah*, is a *hapax legomenon*, being a feminine abstract noun formed from the root *'amets*, "to be strong or stout." The Septuagint and Targum however read, "Let me be sufficient for the inhabitants of Jerusalem in the Lord of armies, their God," involving a slight emendation of the Masoretic Text. A plausible and meritorious reading is *'emtsah leyoshebhey*, **The strength of the inhabitants of Jerusalem is in the Lord of armies, their God.** This assumes a slight dittography.

5. *The Lord's Response to Judah's Faith* (Zech. 12:6, 7). **In that day I will make the chieftains of Judah like a pot of fire among twigs and as a torch of fire among sheaves, so that they shall devour all the peoples on the right and on the left round about. But Jerusalem shall still be inhabited in its place in Jerusalem. (7) The Lord will deliver the tents of Judah first that the glory of the house of David and the glory of the inhabitants of Jerusalem might not be exalted over Judah.**

Because of their faith in the Lord, the Lord will do exploits through the chieftains of Judah. Two similes describe the operation of God's power through them to the utter rout of their foes. The first is as a **fire pot,** that is a vessel employed to carry hot coals for the purpose of building a

8 In that day shall the Lord defend the inhabitants of Jerusalem; and he that is feeble among them at that day shall be as David; and the house of David shall be as God, as the angel of the Lord before them.

8   In that day shall Jehovah defend the inhabitants of Jerusalem; and he that is feeble among them at that day shall be as David; and the house of David shall be as God, as the angel of Jehovah before them.

fire, the second as a torch of fire among sheaves (Exod. 22:6; Judg. 15:4; II Sam. 14:30). Both the twigs and the sheaves are to be thought of as dry and inflammable, easily set fire to. Just as a "pan" containing burning embers sets fire to twigs of dry wood and as a flaming torch ignites dry grain, so Judah's chieftains will devour all the peoples, i.e., the attacking Gentile nations (cf. Zech. 8:20; 11:10; 12:3).

But through these destructions Jerusalem is described as continuing to be peacefully inhabited in her own place (tahteha, "under her") to demonstrate that all attempts to destroy her have not even disturbed her. She is still quietly inhabited in the place where she has always been. The literal rendering is Jerusalem shall sit, yashevah, i.e., figuratively to "be inhabited" (Jer. 17:6; 50:13; Ezek. 26:20; Zech. 2:8; 9:5; 14:11).

In verse 7 the Lord is said to deliver the tents of Judah first. The picture is of the people outside the city walls, who do not enjoy the protection or the prestige of the dwellers in the royal metropolis and capital. Because more defenseless and exposed, bivouacing in the open country, they shall enjoy God's supernatural interposition first, not only as needing it first in point of time since they would be attacked before the city, but because they needed it first in order that the influential house of David and the proud dwellers of the capital city might not be exalted over them as humble country people.

The word glory (tiphereth, from pa'er, piel "to beautify, glorify") is here used of the eminence of rank. In Esther 1:4 the word described the majesty of the Persian monarch and

in Exodus 28:2, 40 it is employed of the magnificent apparel of the high priest. The glory of the house of David and the glory of the inhabitants of Jerusalem are not to be magnified, tigdal, from gadhal, "become great, grow up," used here as in Psalm 35:27; 40:16 [17]; 70:4 [5]; Malachi 1:5, in the passive sense "to be exalted" or "lifted up" above ('al) anyone. The Lord will manifest Himself in such deliverance as will honor faith, unite His people, and cause them mutually to make their boast wholly in the Lord, instead of partially in themselves.

6. Judah's Triumph in the Lord (Zech. 12:8). In that day the Lord will defend the inhabitants of Jerusalem, so that he that stumbles among them in that day shall be as David, and the house of David shall be as God, as the angel of the Lord before them.

What a gracious promise of God's assistance and deliverance of the Jewish remnant at the end of the great tribulation and the commencement of the kingdom age. So important is this time reference, in that day, so frequent in this general part of Zechariah (see comments on Zech. 12:3), that it is repeated twice in this one verse, which so graphically portrays the direct divine intervention in the affairs of Judah in "the day of the Lord," the day that is conspicuously His (Zech. 12:1), because of His powerful deliverance displayed in it. Thus in that day is tantamount to "the day of the Lord" which is so prominent in the great eschatological portions of the prophets (Isa. 2:12; Joel 1:15; 2:1; Zeph. 1:7; Zech. 14:1).

The Lord's intervention in behalf of His people, the believing Jewish remnant, is set forth as His "defending" them. In that day the Lord will

9 And it shall come to pass in that day, that I will seek to destroy all the nations that come against Jerusalem.

9 And it shall come to pass in that day, that I will seek to destroy all the nations that come against Jerusalem.

defend the inhabitants [*yoshev*, singular participle, used collectively for the plural] of Jerusalem. The verb defend, *yagen*, is from *ganan*, "cover, surround, defend," Arabic *janna* (Isa. 31:5; 37:35; 38:6; II Kings 19:34; 20:6). The word is used by Zechariah (9:15), in the sense of the Lord "hovering protectingly *over* [*ʿal*]" His people, no doubt figuratively as Ashur, the national god of the Assyrians, appears on the monuments as hovering over his embattled people. But in this passage the preposition is not "over" (*ʿal*) but "on behalf of" (*beʿadh*), more strictly, "about." The Lord will *"give protection about"* (Brown, Driver, and Briggs) His harassed remnant.

The *result* of this protecting and covering activity of the Lord *about* His people (expressed by the conjunction "and," *waw*, with the perfect), will be that he that is stumbling from fear, weakness, etc. (the articular participle from *kashal*, "totter, stagger" [Isa. 3:8; 59:14; Jer. 46:6]) among the besieged and hard-pressed remnant shall be as David, the great hero and victorious conqueror of Israelite history, and the house of David [in turn] shall be as God (*keʾlohim*). Some commentators understand this phrase to mean "as angels," rather than as God, following the Septuagint rendering of Elohim in several instances as "angels." That no such idea is intended in this instance is the appended corrective expression as the Angel of the Lord. The house of David was to be as God not in the incomprehensible abstract, but as God manifested to men in His glorious forthcomings under the ancient dispensation, in the Person of the divine Word, the preincarnate Christ who went before the children of Israel as their Almighty Leader and

Protector (Exod. 32:34; 33:15, 21–23; Isa. 63:9; Mal. 3:1). In that day He who was of the house and lineage of David (Luke 1:27–33), shall come as "King of kings and Lord of lords" to conquer His and His people's enemies and establish Israel in millennial blessing. His triumph will therefore be Judah's triumph in that day.

7. *The Doom of Judah's Enemies* (Zech. 12:9). And it shall come to pass in that day I will seek to destroy all nations which will be advancing against Jerusalem. Again the Lord dramatically reverts to the first person and speaks in lively fashion when dealing with the destruction of the enemies of His covenant people Israel. In that day recurs again and stands in striking contrast to former days when God sought to invite enemy nations *against* His people because of their idolatrous disloyalty. But in this future day he will seek to destroy all nations that come against Jerusalem.

Certainly the import of the term to *seek* in reference to the Lord is not "that it will be problematical whether He will succeed" (as Leupold interprets it, *op. cit.*, p. 234), but simply employing human terminology, the Lord will seek, *'avaqqesh*, in the sense of *"aiming at"* (Brown, Driver, and Briggs), i.e., "concentrating full attention upon" the destruction of His people's foes, just like a marksman bends all attention and skill upon hitting the bull's eye, allowing no distracting influence to divert his energy and skill from the goal in mind. (For such a meaning of *baqash* see Num. 35:23; I Sam. 25:26; I Kings 20:7; Esther 2:21; 3:6.) Or, indeed, Zechariah may use the word seek as he had done in chapter 6:7 concerning the steeds who "sought to go to and fro in the earth," i.e., "were restively eager" to go. This would paint a

10 And I will pour upon the house of David, and upon the inhabitants of Jerusalem, the spirit of grace and of supplications: and they shall look upon me whom they have pierced, and they shall mourn for him, as one mourneth for his only son, and shall be in bitterness for him, as one that is in bitterness for his firstborn.

10 And I will pour upon the house of David, and upon the inhabitants of Jerusalem, the spirit of grace and of supplication; and they shall look unto me whom they have pierced; and they shall mourn for him, as one mourneth for his only son, and shall be in bitterness for him, as one that is in bitterness for his first-born.

lively picture of the Lord's zeal and restive energy to destroy His people's enemies who had so cruelly destroyed them, now that the cup of their iniquity was full (cf. Gen. 15:16; Rev. 16:13–21). That such is the case is apparent from the object of the divine destruction — all nations, i.e., in their representative armies, who are seen "coming upon" (*ba'im 'al*, "falling" or "lighting upon") in the sense of "attacking," (as in Gen. 34:27; cf. I Sam. 11:12; Prov. 28:22), the participle vividly portraying the assault as in the process of taking place in the future period specified by the context.

II. THE VISION OF THE CRUCIFIED MESSIAH AND ITS RESULTS (Zech. 12:10–14)

The previous part of the prophecy has been concerned with the Lord's deliverance of Judah and Jerusalem from the furious attack of enemies in the last days of the nation's terrible time of trouble preceding the establishment of the kingdom over Israel. The question now arises, Why should the Lord seek, that is, "be restively eager" to destroy Israel's enemies? What moral and spiritual shift has occurred in the nation that would warrant the change from dispatching foes *against* Jerusalem and Judah to giving *protection about* them and the annihilation of foes advancing against them? The answer is given in the following verses.

The nation enjoys a great spiritual effusion consequent upon a vision of the crucified Messiah (Zech. 12:10)

and undergoes a sweeping national conversion (12:11–14), that thoroughly purges out idolatry and sin (13:1–5).

1. *The Effusion of the Spirit* (Zech. 12:10a). And I will pour out the Spirit of grace and supplication upon the house of David and the inhabitants of Jerusalem.... The prophecy continues in the dramatic first person and foretells that glorious movement of God in behalf of the spiritual needs of the Jewish remnant preserved through the decimating apocalyptic judgments of the period (Rev. 4:1–19:16).

Both Joel in the pre-exilic period and Ezekiel in the exile had foretold this great spiritual visitation upon the Jewish survivors of the great tribulation to equip them for the vast blessings of the kingdom age about to be opened up. "And it shall come to pass afterward, that I *will pour out my Spirit upon* [*shaphakhti ruhi 'al*] all flesh; and your sons and your daughters shall prophesy, your old men shall see visions. And also upon the servants and upon the handmaids in those days *will I pour out my Spirit (shaphakhti ruhi)* (Joel 2:28, 29 [3:1, 2]). Joel likewise connects this spiritual revival with the same eschatological context as Zechariah (Joel 2:28–32 [3:1–4]).

Ezekiel, moreover, envisioned this spiritual outpouring in relation to restored and converted Israel. "Neither will I [the Lord] hide my face any more from them: for I have *poured out my Spirit upon* [*shaphakhti ruhi 'al*] the house of Israel, saith the Lord God" (Ezek. 39:29).

The verb **pour out** (Assyrian *shapaku*, "pour out," especially of earth to form a mound) is employed of *pouring out* water (Exod. 4:9); broth (Judg. 6:20); a libation to false gods (Isa. 57:6); dust (Lev. 14:41); earth to form a mound (Isa. 37:33; Jer. 6:6, like Assyrian *shapaku*); blood (Gen. 37:22); anger (Hos. 5:10); and one's heart (Lam. 2:19). Used in connection with the Spirit of God, the term "pour" or **pour out** denotes copious refreshment, like water poured on thirsty ground.

Peter's quotation from Joel (Acts 2:16–21), which intimately connects with Zechariah's prediction since the latter certainly echoes Joel's prophecy, must *not* be regarded as fulfilled in the Pentecostal effusion. Careful comparison will show that Peter employed the Joel reference merely *as an illustration* that such a spiritual outpouring as had taken place at Pentecost was not fanaticism or drunkenness, as some Jewish taunters alleged, but found a parallel in their own Hebrew prophecies to be fulfilled in connection with the future establishment of their kingdom.

Designated as recipients of this spiritual blessing are **the house of David and the inhabitants of Jerusalem.** The latter term by metonymy stands for the whole covenant people, according to a usage by which the capital represents the whole nation, for example, "Samaria" the capital representing Israel the nation (I Kings 20:34). Many parallels from the ancient Biblical world may be cited, where the name of the capital and the country are identical, such as Ashur, Hatti, Damascus, Hamath, etc.

The former term **house of David** signifies that portion of the covenant people of high or royal status in distinction from the lowly or common inhabitants of the city. Both terms represent *all classes of the preserved remnant* who will receive the full benefits of the blessing apart from human distinctions of rank, or social or economic status, in line with the specific declarations of Joel 2:28–32 [3:1–4]. Leupold declares that there is no

warrant in this passage "for the conclusion that the whole Jewish nation would become penitent," but he gives no reason other than to assert that this is "a tenet taught neither here nor elsewhere in the Scriptures" (*op. cit.*, p. 235). But such a declaration is scarcely tenable, for instance, in the light of the Apostle Paul's dealing with this very subject in Romans 9–11, and his summary statement: "And so *all Israel shall be saved*: as it is written, There shall come out of Zion the Deliverer and shall turn ungodliness from Jacob: for this is my covenant unto them, when I shall take away their sins" (Rom. 11:26, 27). Compare also Isaiah 27:9; 59:20, 21; Jeremiah 31:31–37.

According to the prophets, the nation Israel, regathered from all nations, restored to Palestine and converted, is to have her greatest earthly exaltation and glory at the second advent of her Messiah (Ezek. 37:1–28; Isa. 11:1–16; 35:1–10; Mic. 4:1–8, etc.). Zechariah here envisions what the former prophets had seen so clearly (Amos 9:11–15).

That which the Lord is said to **pour out** effectually and copiously is **the Spirit of grace and supplication,** that is, the Holy Spirit of God. Koenig is incorrect in noting that the term **grace** specifies the *motive* energizing the outpouring of the Spirit and the expression **supplication** points to the *result* that will ensue (*Messianische Weissagung*, p. 214).

Grace, *hen,* is a "demonstration of favor," "a show of graciousness," and is from the root *hanan,* "to show favor," "act graciously toward" one, Arabic *hanna,* "be merciful, compassionate," "be favorably inclined toward," Assyrian *annu,* "grace," "a kindly disposition." The word is used frequently, especially of God (Gen. 6:8; 18:3; 19:19; Exod. 33:12; 34:9; Num. 11:11; Judg. 6:17; Prov. 3:4; Jer. 31:2). **The Spirit of grace** is God's covenant favor and promised graciousness toward His people Israel in the day they turn to their Messiah and have their sin of unbelief removed. In Hebrews 10:29 the Holy Spirit is called "the Spirit of grace," reminding one of this passage.

The Spirit of grace (*ḥen*), moreover, produces **supplication** (*taḥanunim*, from the same root *ḥanan*), an intensive plural form denoting a singular abstract idea, "favor," "supplication for favor," "pleadings," the result of receiving grace (I Kings 8:52; II Chron. 33:13; Jer. 36:7; 37:20; Dan. 9:20). The Lord's gracious movement toward His repentant people in that day will eventuate in their gracious movement toward Him in supplicating prayer.

2. *The Revelation of the Pierced One* (Zech. 12:10b). **And they shall look unto me, whom they have pierced and shall mourn for him as the mourning for an only son, and shall bitterly lament for him as a grievous lamenting for the first-born.**

He unto whom **they shall look** and **whom they have pierced** *is the Lord*, who will have poured out upon them the Spirit of grace and intensive supplication. **I will pour out upon them the Spirit . . . they will look unto me, whom they have pierced.** That God is *pierced*, although obvious from the text (only a very small ·minority of manuscripts read "to him" for "to Me," *'elay*), has occasioned difficulty not only for Jewish exegetes but for Christian scholars as well. The former have advanced the strange notion of a dual Messiah — one from Judah, the other from Ephraim or Manasseh. This second one, "Messiah, the son of Joseph," is bizarrely associated with death in connection with the clash with Gog and Magog (Ezek. 38).

But some Christian scholars (Calvin, Grotius, Gesenius, Maurer), have also balked at the full literal force of God's being pierced by man. Following these, Leupold, for example, takes the position that the verb **pierced** must be employed "in a figurative sense and not literally, for God cannot be literally pierced" (*op. cit.*, p. 237).

However, in the light of the incarnation, which is a prerequisite to the actual fulfilment of this prophecy, such a statement can scarcely be evaluated as unarbitrary. Nor does Leupold's contention that "pierce" (*daqar*) has a parallel in Leviticus 24:11, 16, where we find the idiom "to pierce [*naqab*] the name of God," having the meaning to "profane His name," have any more force than a pure supposition. Not only are the words for "pierce" different, but the idiom of Leviticus is different.

Moreover, the incisive manner in which John quotes the *fulfilment* of this prophecy, "They shall look on him whom they pierced" (John 19:37), in the closest connection with the Roman soldier's piercing the side of Jesus and the importance made of this in the Fourth Gospel's authentication of the death of our Lord (John 19:34–36), strongly militate against the watering down of the meaning of the word *daqaru* to mean "wound by insulting or reviling," despite the Septuagint reading *katorchresanto* ("reviled" or "insulted"). The Greek translators very likely also were imbued with the erroneous notion that the literal rendering of the word was out of place here, since they similarly avoided it in rendering Zechariah 13:3, where it is correctly rendered both by the A.V. and the R.S.V. "and his father and his mother who bore him shall *pierce him through*," and by the Vulgate, *confixerunt*.

Besides the plain meaning of the word *daqaru*, "pierce, transfix, thrust through," it is used in its literal and obvious sense in all its other occurrences (Num. 25:8; Judg. 9:54; I Sam. 31:4; I Chron. 10:4; Isa. 13:15; Jer. 37:10; 51:4; Lam. 4:9; Zech. 13:3), being equivalent to "pierced" to death (*meholal*) in Isaiah 53:5. In addition, the *historical* fulfilment of this prophecy clearly demonstrates that the Jews did more than merely "insult" or "revile" the Messiah. They rejected Him and handed Him over to the Romans to be crucified and pierced to death. Added to this the *prophetic* sequel to the "piercing," the deep penitence and unprecedented sorrow of Israel, are left without a satisfactory explanation if the nation only actually and historically "insulted" their Messiah. Moreover, the dramatic figures of the loss of an only son or a first-born and the piercing lament over the good King Josiah, are left pointless except in the presence of literal death, the very reality of which is demonstrated by the sword-piercing recounted in John's Gospel (John 19:34, 35).

This interpretation of Zechariah 12:10, however, does not introduce the Messiah in this passage "in an unmotivated way that is difficult to account for," as Leupold contends (*op. cit.*, p. 237). The first person occurring over and over again in this chapter (vss. 2, 3, 4, 6, 9, 10) in every case refers *to the Messiah.* It is He who in His glorious person and second advent will effect Israel's deliverance, both temporal and spiritual, so graphically set forth in this whole section. All through the great eschatological passages of the Old Testament (Mic. 4; Ezek. 37, etc., as well as the New Testament, Matt. 24, 25; II Thess. 2; Rev. 19, etc.) it is the returning Christ as "King of kings and Lord of lords" who fulfills the magnificent promises of Israel's coming glory. The Lord (Yhwh) of the Old Testament is He who became incarnate in Jesus of Nazareth to die for the sin of the world and eventually to restore Israel to a place of national blessing.

What a prophecy! **They** [Israel] **shall look unto Me, whom** ['*eth 'asher*] **they pierced.** The sign of the definite accusative '*eth* is placed before the relative pronoun, "whom," '*asher*, more clearly to define it as an object of the verb and to obviate such impossible interpretation of unbelief as Kimchi's construing it as a causal conjunction "because." The verb **they shall look unto,** *hibbiṭu '*el, is used both of physical and mental vision (Num. 23:21; I Sam. 2:32; Isa. 5:12)

frequently as here, with the thought of beholding "with confidence in the object "gazed upon" (Num. 21:9; Isa. 22:11; 51:1). Hence it means not merely to "look upon" (A.V.) but to "look to" in confidence and faith. It is significant that the same verb "look unto" is employed of the Israelite, who when bitten by a serpent (type of sin) "*looked unto* the serpent of bronze" (type of Christ "made sin for us" [John 3:14, 15; II Cor. 5:21]) and "lived" (Num. 21:9). In exactly the same way and with the same result, the remnant of Israel shall "look *unto* Him whom they pierced" at Calvary and live spiritually and nationally.

However, like Thomas, who was not present when our resurrected Lord appeared to the disciples the first time, Israel in unbelief says: "Except I shall see in his hands the prints of the nails, and put my finger in the print of the nails, and thrust my hand into his side, *I will not believe* (John 20:25). But when they shall *look unto* Him **whom they pierced,** and behold the scars of His love for them, like Thomas their excruciating and inexpressibly penetrating cry of deepest contrition will be, "My Lord and my God!" (John 20:28). Then the storm that broke upon Israel for the crime of Calvary and has raged with unmitigated fury these long tragic centuries, shall suddenly subside and burst into the glory of the glad millennial day.

The remainder of verse 10 graphically sets forth the results which follow the Jewish remnant's looking to the pierced One. **And they shall mourn for him.** The third person **for him** (not the first person "for Me," as we would expect) represents a common enallage of persons, met with frequently in Hebrew (cf. Gesenius, *Hebrew Grammar*, 135*o*; 144*a*). The rendering "they shall mourn *for it*" is entirely indefensible contextually. Mourning for an only son is represented in the Old Testament as the acme of sorrow that

11 In that day shall there be a great mourning in Jerusalem, as the mourning of Hadadrimmon in the valley of Megiddon.
12 And the land shall mourn, every family apart of the house of David apart, and their wives apart; the family of the house of Nathan apart, and their wives apart;
13 The family of the house of Levi apart, and their wives apart; the family of Shimei apart, and their wives apart;
14 All the families that remain, every family apart, and their wives apart.

---

11   In that day shall there be a great mourning in Jerusalem, as the mourning of Hadadrimmon in the valley of Megiddon.
12   And the land shall mourn, every family apart; the family of the house of David apart, and their wives apart; the family of the house of Nathan apart, and their wives apart;
13   the family of the house of Levi apart, and their wives apart; the family of the Shimeites apart, and their wives apart;
14   all the families that remain, every family apart, and their wives apart.

---

may invade a home (Amos 8:10) and the death-wail over the first-born became proverbial in Israel from the time of the tenth plague in Egypt and the Exodus (Exod. 11:6).

The word mourn, *saphadh*, employed of Israel's penitent contrition when she believingly looks to her Messiah at His second advent, primarily means to "strike" the breast in deep grief, then to "wail" or "lament"; cf. Assyrian *sapadu*, "to mourn," *sipdu*, "mourning," Ethiopic "a dirge." The action signified is "wailing or mourning" with profuse smiting of the breast, loud cries, and deeply moving, emotional demonstrations, especially for the dead (I Sam. 25:1; 28:3; I Kings 14:13; Jer. 16:6). In the sense of "wailing *over*" (*'al*; cf. II Sam. 1:12; 11:26; I Kings 13:30) it is employed here of the expression of the most moving repentance of the Jewish remnant at the revelation that He whom the nation rejected and crucified at Calvary was their Messiah and Redeemer. Then they shall mourn for him as the mourning [*mispedh*, "wailing," same root, Gen. 50:10; Isa. 22:12; Joel 2:12; Zech. 12:11] for an only one.

The parallel verb to be in bitterness is from the root *marar*, "to be bitter." In the *hifil*, it occurs transitively "to make bitter" (Job 27:2; Ruth 1:20) and intransitively "to display bitter

sorrow." The intransitive sense occurs in connection with Israel's bitter remorse at the realization of their fearful crime of crucifying their Messiah and Redeemer. These expressive verbs "mourn," (*saphadh*) and "evince bitter sorrow" (*hamer*, infinitive absolute for the finite verb) emphasize the godly contrition that will seize the remnant as they recite the moving strains of the great penitential dirge of the converted people contained in Isaiah 53:1–12: "Truly it was our sorrows he bore and our griefs he carried. Yet *we* reckoned him struck [with a plague], punished by God, and humiliated. But *he* was pierced for our transgressions, he was crushed for our iniquities. The chastisement eventuating in our peace was upon him, and by his stripes healing has come to us" (Isa. 53:4, 5).

3. *The National Repentance* (Zech. 12:11–14). In that day the lamentation shall be great in Jerusalem like the lamentation of Hadadrimmon in the valley of Megiddo. And the land shall mourn family by family in private; the family of the house of David in private and their wives in private; the family of the house of Nathan in private and their wives in private; the family of the house of Levi in private and their wives in private; all the families that are left family by family in private and their wives in private.

In addition to the general illustration of intense lamentation and mourning furnished by the death of an only son, the prophet Zechariah adduces an actual historical instance of a memorable occasion of national grief that in later centuries became proverbial. In that day of Israel's conversion incident upon the second advent of Messiah, the prophet declares Jerusalem's mourning is going to be similar to the mourning [*mispedh*, "wailing," "lamentation," same word as in verse 10] of Hadadrimmon in the valley of Megiddo. The reference is patently to the sorrow occasioned by the mortal wounding of the godly King Josiah in a clash with Pharaoh Necho of Egypt near Megiddo in the plain of Esdraelon in 609 B.C. (II Chron. 35:20–24). This tragedy occasioned such a tremendous display of grief that it furnishes a peculiarly apt illustration of the same emotion that will sweep over the people when they finally repent and turn to their long-rejected Messiah.

The word Hadad-Rimmon has occasioned some difficulty inasmuch as the brief historical sketch of Josiah's defeat and death does not mention this place, but tradition evidently preserved the exact locality of the good king's wounding here recorded by inspiration, whereas history only preserves the name of the more prominent nearby city of Megiddo. Hadad-Rimmon is apparently identifiable with the village of Rummaneh some four miles southeast of Megiddo. Jerome refers to such a town in his day which was then called Maximinopolis. The wailing of Hadad-Rimmon was, accordingly, the mourning in Jerusalem and elsewhere occasioned by the thought of the tragedy that occurred near Megiddo.

The old impious view of Hitzig and Movers that the name Hadad-Rimmon is a reference to idolators weeping for the god Tammuz (cf. Ezek. 8:14, 15) has been entertained widely in the present day. Besides being utterly unsuitable in the context of Israel's great national conversion, the hypothesis rests on tenuous arguments that link the Babylon-Aramaic weather deity with Tammuz, i.e., Adonis of the Greeks and Syrians.

The remaining verses of this chapter are devoted to showing how universal, as well as individual, will be Israel's national mourning on her great Day of Atonement when in deepest contrition she looks to her Messiah-Redeemer and the penitential strains of Psalm 51 are experienced by God's ancient people on a national scale. And the land shall mourn [not only the capital city], family by family, distributively for each and every family. Grief so terrific as this demands the utmost heart-searching and privacy. Accordingly, every member of each family will lament in private, wives apart from their husbands, husbands apart from their wives. Individual by individual will face his own deep sin before God. Contrition so overwhelming will demand complete seclusion for its expression and outpouring. The vision of a crucified Redeemer will excite the deepest repentance.

The passage seeks to emphasize the fact that all, without exception, will mourn. The house of David and the house of Nathan (if the son of David is meant), denoting the royal line and the house of Levi and the house of Shimei, denoting the priestly line. Verse 14 constitutes a summary of this passage (vss. 11–14). All the remaining families [shall mourn], family by family apart, and their wives apart. Thus concludes this section (vss. 11–14) which by its somewhat monotonous form suggests a litany for the dead, and the deep grief connected with it. Only in this case the grief will be occasioned by a vision of One "that liveth" "who was dead," and is "alive forevermore" (Rev. 1:18). Moreover, the sorrow will be for sin, and deep personal and national iniquity in putting to death the One who was resurrected and has "the keys of hell and death."

CHAPTER THIRTEEN
ISRAEL'S NATIONAL CLEANSING
(ZECH. 13:1-9)

THE FIRST SECTION OF THE SECOND PROPHETIC ORACLE
(Continued)

THIS chapter continues and concludes the first section of the second prophetic oracle, bringing it to a dramatic climax in Israel's national conversion at Messiah's second advent. In the preceding portion of the oracle (chapter 12) Israel's deliverance and national conversion are set forth, prefaced by a solemn divine authentication of the entire oracle as a whole (12:1). The future siege of Jerusalem (12: 1-9), followed by the great effusion of the Spirit granting spiritual illumination and recognition of the Crucified One and the consequent national repentance of Israel (12: 10-14), prepare the way for Israel's national cleansing (13:1-9), the latter section continuing the context without a chapter division (as in modern Bibles). The first section of the second prophetic oracle, accordingly, extends without a break from Zechariah 12:1 to 13:9.

The inseparable connection of this section (13:1-9) with chapter 12 appears not only in the fact that it belongs to the first section of the second prophetic burden and, as such, concludes it, but also in the added circumstance that the same time is designated by the term **in that day** in 13:1, as well as the same persons by the terminology **the house of David and the inhabitants of Jerusalem** (cf. 13:1 with 12:9). The whole prophetic burden 12:1–13:9 has been commonly claimed to be fulfilled in

1 In that day there shall be a fountain opened to the house of David and to the inhabitants of Jerusalem for sin and for uncleanness.

· 1 In that day there shall be a fountain opened to the house of David and to the inhabitants of Jerusalem, for sin and for uncleanness.

other than the *literal restoration and conversion of Israel* at the second advent of the Messiah. But the consistent eschatological context of the entire book of Zechariah into which this prophetic oracle fits, the often reiterated time designation **in that day** in this particular oracle, always referring to the period of Israel's final restoration and conversion, as well as the clear geographic names (Judah, Jerusalem) and personal allusions **(house of David and the inhabitants of Judah)** preclude such an interpretation. Only a literal application of these prophecies to the restoration and conversion of the Jewish nation at the second advent of Christ can satisfy the scope of these prophetic disclosures. Other interpretations ignore the true scope of Zechariah's prophecies as a whole, violate the immediate context, resort to pointless mysticalizing, and end up in a morass of uncertainty and confusion.

I. THE PROPHECY OF ISRAEL'S NA-
TIONAL CLEANSING (Zech. 13:1-6)

The supreme need of the Jew throughout the Christian centuries has been cleansing and spiritual regeneration. Since they rejected and crucified their Savior-Messiah, they have been under a heavy load of guilt and defilement and kept from God's salvation by hardness of heart and pitiable unbelief. The Apostle Paul succinctly describes the essence of their woe. "For they being ignorant of God's righteousness and going about to establish their own righteousness, have not submitted themselves unto the righteousness of God" (Rom. 10:3). In this prophecy Zechariah sees the Jews when Christ becomes "the end of the law for righteousness" to them as they look to the nail-pierced One and believe.

1. *The Prophecy of Israel's National Cleansing Realized — the Fountain of Cleansing Opened* (Zech. 13:1). **In that day a fountain shall be opened for the house of David and for the inhabitants of Jerusalem for sin and for uncleanness.** The apt figure of a **fountain** portrays Israel's Messiah-Savior, whom the Jews shall "look to" and whom they "pierced" (cf. Zech. 12:10). The word for **fountain,** *maqor,* is from the root *qur,* "to bore, to dig," Arabic *qāra,* "scoop out, cut a round hole in" (II Kings 19:24; Isa. 37:25). The expression was originally applied to a "well" that was dug, but came to be employed of a natural "spring" or "fountain" of water (Ps. 36:9 [10]; Prov. 10:11; 13:14; 14:27; Jer. 2:13; 17:13). In Hosea 13:15 the word is used figuratively of the *source* of life and vigor (cf. Jer. 51:36), and in Leviticus 20:18 of the *source* of menstruous blood and in Leviticus 12:7 of the *flow* of blood after childbirth.

In Zechariah 13:1 the word *maqor* is employed of a **fountain** or "spring" as a figure of abundant cleansing from sin. The periphrastic construction (*yiyeh niphtah,* future tense of the verb *hayah,* "to be," plus the *nifal* participle of *pathah,* "to open"), denotes continuousness and permanency. Not only **shall the fountain be opened,** but remain opened, that is, be perennially available as a medium of purification from uncleanness. The figure embraces the forceful thought that while the Jews continue in unbelief and Christ rejection, the fountain of God's cleansing power opened to the world by Christ's death on Calvary remains closed and unappropriated by them, as water shut up in subterranean cavities is unavailable and unappropriable by men for cleansing and other purposes.

The fountain will be opened **for the house of David and for the inhabitants of Jerusalem**. The preposition *lamedh* with the genitive case denotes "for the good or benefit of," corresponding to the Latin dative of accommodation (Gen. 2:18; 8:9; I Sam. 14:6). The **house of David and the inhabitants of Jerusalem** represent the whole nation (see comments on 12:10 and 12:11-14; cf. Ezek. 36:24, 25). In this verse the primary emphasis is on the time of this prophecy's fulfilment, **in that day**; second, on the *existence* of a "fountain of cleansing"; third, on the "fountain itself"; fourth, on its "being opened," i.e., being made available as an agency of cleansing for Israel; and lastly, the purpose of the cleansing fountain appears *"for* sin and *for* uncleanness." The *lamedh* in this case denotes *the cause* or *the occasion* of the fountain being opened (Lev. 11:24; 19:28; Deut. 14:1).

The words **for sin** with respect to Israel's guilt are significant. The term *ḥaṭṭa'th* is from the root *ḥaṭa'*, "miss" (a goal or way), "sin," "go wrong." Cf. Arabic 2 and 4 conjugations "miss the mark, miss the way" (Prov. 19:2; Exod. 5:16; I Kings 18:9). The word is employed of sin against man (Gen. 31:36; 50:17; Num. 12:11; I Sam. 20:1), but elsewhere of sin against God (Lev. 4:14; I Sam. 2:17; Isa. 3:9; 30:1; Jer. 5:25, etc.). Its use in the Pentateuch of purification from sins of ceremonial uncleanness suggests its aptness in this great passage dealing with Israel's cleansing (Num. 8:7; 19:9, 17), where "water of purification from sin" is emphasized.

The word for **uncleanness**, *niddah*, designates basically "that which is to be fled from or shunned," being from the root *nadad*, "flee," "depart," Arabic *nadda*, "flee," "run away," Aramaic "abominate, shrink from." (Cf. Isa. 21:15; Nahum 3:7; Ps. 64:8 [9]; Esther 6:1.) The noun is employed of ceremonial "impurity" of women in menstruation (Ezek. 18:6; 22:10; Lev. 12:2; 15:19; 18:19) and of ceremonial defilement contract-

ed by touching a dead body. Hence the "water of impurity," *me niddah*, was water which ceremonially removed this type of impurity (Num. 19:9, 13, 20). Figuratively, as a memento of its ceremonial usage, the word *niddah* denotes an "impure thing" (Ezek. 7:19, 20; Ezra 9:11). The happy choice of the Hebrew words for **sin and uncleanness** accentuates the deep guilt of Israel. Not only has she missed God's way, but she is guilty both of ceremonial and moral impurity. Only the sacrifice of Christ, His vicarious death on Calvary, can avail. It is the fountain of cleansing water (not "blood" as in Cowper's hymn, "There is a fountain filled with blood"). The shed blood (death of Christ) is the basis of the cleansing but the *cleansing itself, not* the basis of it, is portrayed in graphic figure by the prophet, for fountains are filled *with water, not blood*.

When our Lord died on Golgotha's brow, the cleansing fountain was opened potentially for Israel and the whole world. But because Israel has rejected this fountain, it will not be opened to her experientially until **in that** [future] **day**. In the light of the larger prophetic context here, and this clear and emphatic time designation, Chambers' view that the prophecy refers to no specific period, but to the general reception of the gospel, is in direct violation of both the immediate and remote context of this prediction (*op. cit.*, p. 100).

2. *The Prophecy of Israel's National Cleansing Illustrated — Idolatry Exterminated* (Zech. 13:2-5). **And it shall be in that day, is the utterance of the Lord of armies, I will cut off the names of the idols from the land, so that they will no more be remembered. And I will likewise banish the prophets and the spirit of uncleanness from the land. (3) And it shall be if a man still prophesies, then his father and his mother who gave him birth shall say, You shall not live, because you have spoken falsely in the name of the Lord. And his father and mother who gave**

2 And it shall come to pass in that day, saith the Lord of hosts, t h a t I will cut off the names of the idols out of the land, and they shall no more be remembered: and also I will cause the prophets and the unclean spirit to pass out of the land.

3 And it shall come to pass, t h a t when any shall yet prophesy, then his father and his mother that begat him shall say unto him, Thou shalt not live; for thou speakest lies in the name of the Lord: and his father and his mother that begat him shall thrust him through when he prophesieth.

4 And it shall come to pass in that day, t h a t the prophets shall be ashamed every one of his vision, when he hath prophesied; neither shall they wear a rough garment to deceive:

5 But he shall say, I a m no prophet, I a m an husbandman; for man taught me to keep cattle from my youth.

---

2   And it shall come to pass in that day, saith Jehovah of hosts, that I will cut off the names of the idols out of the land, and they shall no more be remembered; and also I will cause the prophets and the unclean spirit to pass out of the land.

3   And it shall come to pass that, when any shall yet prophesy, then his father and his mother that begat him shall say unto him, Thou shalt not live; for thou speakest lies in the name of Jehovah; and his father and his mother that begat him shall thrust him through when he prophesieth.

4   And it shall come to pass in that day, that the prophets shall be ashamed every one of his vision, when he prophesieth; neither shall they wear a hairy mantle to deceive:

5   but he shall say, I am no prophet, I am a tiller of the ground; for I have been made a bondman from my youth.

---

him birth shall pierce [transfix] him when he prophesies. (4) And it shall be in that day, everyone of the prophets shall be ashamed of his vision when he prophesies, neither will they put on a mantle of hair to deceive. (5) But each one shall say, I am no prophet. I am a farmer, because I was sold [as a bondman] from my youth.

The cleansing of God's people through the fountain provided at Calvary at Messiah's first advent and opened up to Israel at the second advent portrayed in verse 1 is followed by the thorough purging of Israel's land (vss. 2–6). In this latter remarkable passage Messiah is the speaker (as in 12:2–6, 10) and declares that He will exterminate Israel's ancient besetting sins, *idolatry* and *false prophecy* together with their *demonic dynamic* ("the spirit of uncleanness"). **I [the Lord] will cut off the names of the idols ... and the prophets ... and the spirit of uncleanness (vs. 2).**

The word employed for **idol** ('*otsev*

from '*atsav*, "mould, shape, fashion," Arabic '*adaba*, "cut off," hence the idea of "carving, fashioning") accordingly, denotes "the image of the false deity" moulded or shaped (Ps. 106:36; 115:4; I Sam. 31:9; I Chron. 10:9; Hos. 4:17; 8:4; 13:2; Isa. 10:11; 48:5; Mic. 1:7; Jer. 50:2). Singularly, a similar root means to "hurt, pain, grieve" (Gen. 45:5; I Sam. 20:34; II Sam. 19:3; Isa. 54:6) and some scholars as Robert Young (*Concordance, in loc.*) connect it with "grief," "a cause of grief" (Isa. 14:3; Ps. 139:24; I Chron. 4:9); and it is not impossible that both the idea of the moulded image and the grief the worship of it caused its devotee were in the minds of the pious, at least, in Israel.

The **prophets** whom the Messiah announces He will **cut off** ('*akhrith*, "destroy," "exterminate," "cut down") are idolatrous seers. Compare the "cutting off" of spiritists (I Sam. 28:9; "sun-pillars," Lev. 26:30) and other things connected with idolatry

(Nah. 1:14; Zeph. 1:4; Mic. 5:12). The Hebrew word for "prophet," *nabhi'*, is related to Accadian *nabû*, "to call or announce," either passively, as W. F. Albright holds, "one who is called" (by God), (*From the Stone Age to Christianity*, pp. 231 ff.), or actively, with Koenig, "an announcer" (for God), (*Hebraisches und Aramaisches Wörterbuch zum Alten Testament*, p. 260), or perhaps preferably with Guillaume, "one who is in the state of announcing a message which has been given to him" (by God), (*Prophecy and Divination*, pp. 112f.).

The **prophets** Messiah will cut off are obviously false prophets (Deut. 18:20-22; Jer. 14:14, 15), demonstrated by their association with idolatry and their being dominated by **the spirit of uncleanness.** "The spirit of uncleanness," as Chambers (*in loc.*) correctly notes, is "not merely a pervading principle, but an active, conscious agency, standing in direct contrast with the Spirit of grace (12:10)." The term is here employed of the demonic dynamic which energizes idolatry (I Cor. 10:20, 21) and of the prophets or diviners associated with idolatry (I Kings 22:21-23). Idolatry with the variegated occult phenomena connected with it (Deut. 18:9-14), including paganistic prognostication or divination (Deut. 13:1-5), is energized by demons or evil spirits (I John 4:1-5; I Tim. 4:1-3; II Thess. 2:8-10). The false prophet spoke in the name of the Lord to deceive and lure his dupes into demon-controlled paganism. **The spirit of uncleanness** is a collective designation standing for "the spirits of uncleanness" (so correctly the A.V.) since these wicked spirit energizers of false prophets are notoriously unclean (cf. "unclean spirits," Mark 1:23; 3:11; 5:2, etc.). These evil spirits or demons are not only unclean because they drive their victims into sexual and other types of impurity, but because they, through the false prophets they energize, misguide their devotees into all the unclean practices

and ritual of idolatry (Rev. 9:20, 21).

Idolatry, false prophets, and **the spirit of uncleanness** (inspiration by unclean spirits or demons) always exist together. In the idolatrous reign of Ahab and Jezebel there were over 450 prophets of Baal (I Kings 18:22) each of whom was under demonic dynamic and inspiration (I Kings 22:21-23). And so shall it be in the fearful demonic outburst that is prophesied to occur before the second advent of Messiah (Rev. 9:1-11), resulting in the immoralities and violence of the crudest, demon-inspired idol worship (Rev. 9:20, 21) and precipitating the battle of Armageddon (Rev. 16:13-16). Added to this awesome spectacle Israel will in the last days be sevenfold demon-possessed (Matt. 12:43-45) and will be beguiled into the supreme act of idolatry of her long and checkered history of apostasy—the worship of the Antichrist (John 5:43), the "man of sin" (II Thess. 2:3, 4). It is to Messiah's glorious advent when Satan (and demon powers) will be relegated to the bottomless pit, the prison-house of the demons (Rev. 20:1-3), that Zechariah's prophecy refers; only the prophet couches the conquest of the returning Messiah over the rampant demonism and idolatry of the hour in the first person with the Messiah dramatically presented as the speaker. **I will cut off the names of the idols, and they shall no more be remembered: and also I will cause the prophets and the unclean spirits to pass out of the land.**

The expression, **I will cut off the names of the idols** suggests the *complete extermination* of idolatry. In addition the thought of the *permanence* of the extinction is also emphasized by the added detail **and they** [the names of the idols] **shall be remembered no more.** Zechariah's mode of expression recalls Hosea, "For I will take away the names of Baalim out of her mouth and they shall no more be remembered by their name" (2:17 [19]). Obliteration of the very names of the idols, so that they will no longer be recalled, involves a more thorough and lasting destruction of idolatry than the mere destruction of idols themselves.

The reference to the banishment of **the unclean spirits** out of the land *ha'arets* (primarily Judah's *land*, but secondarily *the entire earth*, as the broader context of the prophecy suggests) is the only passage in Scripture which explicitly refers to the imprisonment of demons during the kingdom age. But since Satan is remanded to the abyss (the prison house of evil spirits) during this era, as is clearly declared in Revelation 20:1-3, it is a necessary corollary that his demon aids shall also share the same fate. This necessary inference is fully corroborated by this interesting eschatological touch (cf. Merrill F. Unger, *Biblical Demonology*, pp. 74, 75).

Numerous critics have pointlessly theorized that this reference to idolatry must be by a pre-exilic author and not Zechariah, since idolatry had passed away from the Jews after the chastisement of the Babylonian captivity. But such criticism ignores the fact that prophecy frequently portrays the future in the terms of the past and is often based on past history as well as contemporary events, and also on revelations of former prophets. Zechariah, as often, echoes the earlier prophetic allusions to paganistic religious practices, false prophetism (Deut. 13:1-5; 18:9-14, 20-22, Jer; 14:14, 15, etc.), and demonic inspiration of heathen seers (I Kings 22:21-23). This form of apostasy represented the quintessence of wickedness in earlier Israel, as it will once again stand for the acme of apostasy in the final phase of Isarel's unbelief before the advent of Messiah. Chambers, in dismissing the literal return of such gross idolatry as is here outlined by Zechariah and corroborated by St. John in the Book of the Revelation, misses the point when he declares this to be interpreting ''an obscure

book by one yet obscurer'' (*op. cit.*, p. 100). If Scripture is not allowed to illuminate Scripture, there is little hope of alleged obscurity being dissipated.

Verse 3 continues to expand the fact that Israel's future national conversion will be deep and real — so deep and real that any attempted revival of idolatrous practices will be dealt with, with the most uncompromising severity. If **any one** [*'ish*, "man,"* used pronominally] **will still prophecy** [*'odh*, "yet,"* in spite of Messiah's cutting off every vestige of idolatry] **then his father and his mother, who gave him birth, shall say, You shall not remain alive, for you are speaking falsehood in the Lord's name.** Love for God, jealousy for His glory alone, and the penetrating repentance so eloquently expressed in chapter 12:11-14, will overrule all human ties and merely human loyalties. The *very parents* of any false pretender to divine inspiration, i.e., **his father and mother** emphasized by the appositional participle, **his bearers** (*yoledhaw*, "those who gave him birth" from *yaladh*, "to give birth to") will be the first to condemn their apostate offspring to death (II Sam. 16:11). Their condemnation, moreover, will be in strict accordance with the original injunctions given the nation to protect it from the degrading heathenism of the Canaanites as they were about to enter the Promised Land (Deut. 13:6-10; 18:20).

The contention of Keil and Koehler that the opening words of verse 3 imply the cessation of prophecy and that the mere act of prophesying will brand the pretender as a deceiver is not only an arbitrary interpretation of Zechariah's words but a gross ignoring of the eschatological warnings of our Lord that in the last days before His second advent false prophets and deceivers would abound (Matt. 24:24; Luke 21:8) as well as the clear intimations of St. Paul (II Thess. 2:7-12) and St. John, who notably features the great false prophet of the end time (Rev. 13:11–18) and stresses the continuous peril of false prophets from apostolic times to the end (I John 2:18, 22; 4:1–6; II John 7).

The parents of the false prophet shall **transfix** or "stab" their renegade son (*daqar*, "pierce," "thrust through" with a weapon, the same verb with the same meaning as in 12:10). That the parents stab the son to death is certified by their declaration **thou shalt not remain alive** which precedes the piercing. Phinehas stabbed the guilty Israelite who married a Moabite woman (Num. 25:7, 8); so every converted Israelite in that future day of Israel's national cleansing will be imbued with a consuming desire for the Lord's honor. As Abimelech, wounded ignominiously by a woman and desiring a speedy death, persuaded his armorbearer to "thrust him through" (Judg. 9:54), so this false prophet was to be dispatched quickly. Compare I Samuel 31:4; Isaiah 13:15; Jeremiah 37:10; 51:4. The reason is given by a causal clause — **because you have spoken falsehood** [noun as object, or "falsely," taken as adverbial accusative and emphatic in either case by word position] **in the name of the Lord.** It is his deception that constitutes his criminality.

Verse 4 continues to demonstrate the genuineness of Israel's future cleansing and conversion by adducing added details of the thorough extirpation of idolatry and false prophecy. Not only shall the false prophets be **stabbed to death** by external foes of idolatry, but they shall be stabbed internally by their own convicting conscience. **And it shall be in that day** [as in 13:1] **every prophet will be ashamed of his vision when he prophesies, and he will not put on a hairy mantle in order to deceive.** Often Hebrew pluralizes and singularizes as here, **the prophets** [plural] . . . **each one** [*'ish*, singular] . . . **his vision.** By this graphic syntactical device the aggregate whole is stressed as well as each individual in the whole, showing

the comprehensiveness as well as the thoroughness of the purging out of idolatrous practices.

The prophets will be ashamed of (1) their false vision and (2) their deceptive garb. The verb **will be ashamed** (*yebhoshu* from *bosh*, "to feel shame," "to be abashed or confused by guilt") indicates conviction concerning some criminal action or indecorous conduct. "The seers shall be disgraced and *the diviners put to shame*" (Mic. 3:7). "The wind shall shepherd all your shepherds, and your lovers shall go into captivity; then you *will be shamed and confounded*" (Jer. 22:22). Compare Jer. 15:9; Job 6:20.

The **vision**, *ḥizzayon*, is that which the false prophet alleged that he had seen, or had in reality seen, that is by demonic inspiration, as contrasted with inspiration by God's Spirit in the case of the genuine prophet of the Lord. The Hebrew word comes from the root *ḥazah*, "to glimpse," in the ecstatic state, Aramaic *ḥaza'* "perceive with the eyes," Arabic *ḥazā*, "perceive with inward vision." The false prophet shall be deeply convicted of his deceptive "oracle or prophecy," the result of his alleged "divine communication by an inner vision" (II Sam. 7:17; Job 4:13; 20:8; Isa. 22:1, 5; Joel 2:28 [3:1]).

The false prophet shall also be abashed with guilt concerning the deception he has practiced by adopting the peculiar attire of a true prophet, the wide garment called *'addereth*, from the root *'adar*, Assyrian *adaru*, "to be wide, great" (Exod. 15:11; Isa. 42:21), and which was frequently just a *mantle* of rough untanned sheep or goat skin, or a *cloak* manufactured of camel's hair. Zechariah calls it *'addereth se'ar*, "a cloak or mantle of hair." Esau is said to have resembled such a "hairy garment" when he was born (Gen. 25:25). Elijah wore such a mantle and cast it upon Elisha as his successor (I Kings 19:13, 19). With this mantle Elijah and later Elisha struck the waters of the Jordan so that they

6 And one shall say unto him, What are these wounds in thine hands? Then he shall answer, Those with which I was wounded in the house of my friends.

6   And one shall say unto him, What are these wounds between thine arms? Then he shall answer, Those with which I was wounded in the house of my friends.

divided (II Kings 2:8, 13, 14). The costly Babylonian mantle from Shinar which Achan took (Josh. 7:21, 24) was such an oriental robe worn by kings and nobles (Jon. 3:6), and in its rustic and austere form as "a mantle of hair" became the characteristic dress of Hebrew prophets, somewhat like clerical garb worn by certain religious groups today.

Like "a wolf in sheep's clothing" false prophets put on the garments of the genuine prophet of the Lord "in order to deceive," *kaḥesh* (infinitive). Thus Sarah "acted deceptively" when she denied that she had laughed at the news that she would have a son in her old age (Gen. 18:15). Israel (through Achan) also "dissembled," "lied" (R.S.V.), i.e., "practiced deception" when they appropriated the spoil of doomed Jericho (Josh. 7:11). The infinitive absolute is translated "lying" and catalogued with killing, committing adultery, and other sins in Hosea 4:2; and in Leviticus 19:11 the finite verb occurs as a prohibition, "You shall not steal, nor deal falsely, *nor lie* one to another [*lo' tekaḥashu*]." (Compare I Kings 13:18; Job 31:28; Hos. 9:2; Isa. 59:13.)

Verse 5 continues the description of the thorough rejection of idolatry and false prophetism in the day of Israel's conversion and cleansing. Not only will every false prophet be ashamed of his vision when he prophesies and will [he] not put on a hairy garment to deceive [by impersonating a true prophet of the Lord] but each one [indefinite third masculine singular construction "*one*"] shall say, I am not a prophet, the predicate of the nominal clause being emphasized by word order. So far from desiring the prophetic office, any connection with

it shall be sedulously denied. I am a tiller of the soil. Again the predicate of a nominal clause is stressed by word order. Connection with the prophetic office will not only be strenuously denied, but *positive* identification with a vocation that precludes the prophetic call will be strongly asserted, so great will be the disgrace into which false prophetism has fallen and so great will be the abhorrence with which it will be viewed when Israel gets a new heart in her great day of national atonement at the advent of her Savior-Messiah.

With the repudiation of the prophetic office and the denial of any connection with false prophetism, the accused suspect of idolatrous contamination not only declares he is a farmer, but gives both the reason for this calling as well as the explanation of the impossibility of the prophetic vocation in the causal clause, because I was sold [as a slave] from my youth. The suspected false prophet asserts that "he had always been in a condition of life in which the exercise of the prophetic office was altogether incompatible" (Henderson, *in loc.*).

I was sold is literally, "One ['*adam,* "man," identical in use with German "man," "one"] sold me," i.e., "I *was* sold," best rendered passively. "Sold" is the causative of *qanah,* "buy," hence "cause to buy," i.e., "sell."

3. *The Cleanser from Idolatry Revealed* (Zech. 13:6). Then some one will say to him, What are these scars on your hands? Then he will reply, Those with which I was wounded in the house of my friends. The boldness and daring of this Messianic prophecy and the *dramatic abruptness* with which it is introduced have frightened most expositors away from its true

import on the supposition that it is inseparably connected with verses 2–5, and therefore, still has the false prophet in mind, and to introduce the Messiah is flagrantly to ignore the context.

But in defense of its Messianic import the following observations are made: (1) *The context is not actually violated.* The entire section 13–1:6 constitutes a prophecy of Israel's national cleansing. Verse 1 presents the realization of the prophecy in the fountain of cleansing opened to Israel. Verses 2–5 present an illustration of Israel's national cleansing in the complete extermination of idolatry. Verse 6 logically and forcefully presents the revelation of the Messiah as the cleanser from idolatry. Rather than violating the context, verse 6, in introducing Him who alone can and will cleanse the nation from that sin which is chosen because it is the most sensitive barometer of the spiritual tone of the nation, beautifully sustains and climaxes the context.

(2) *The grammatical structure of verse 6 does not preclude a Messianic reference.* While the third masculine singular **(Then some one will say to him)** apparently refers to the same person (the false prophet) as in the preceding verse; yet grammatically *it may not,* and the author may *conceivably* have another person in mind. That he does so and resumes the subject broached in 12:10 **(They shall look unto me whom they pierced)** is suggested by the *evident connection between these two passages* (the intervening context being parenthetical, and delineating the effect of Israel's exercising faith in the Pierced One).

(3) *The prophetic Scriptures offer numerous illustrations of such extended parentheses.* An example is Revelation 7:1–17, inserted between the sixth (Rev. 6:9–17) and seventh seals (Rev. 8:1). Another example is Revelation 10:1–11:14 inserted between the sixth trumpet (Rev. 9:13–21) and seventh trumpet (Rev. 11:15–19). Revelation 16:13–16 constitutes another paren-

thesis between the sixth bowl (Rev. 16:12) and the seventh bowl (Rev. 16:17–21). Daniel 9:26, setting forth the *terminus ad quem* of the sixty-nine weeks, is separated from verse 27 describing the seventieth week by the extended gap of time involved in this present age between Jerusalem's desolation in A.D. 70 and the age-end rise of the Antichrist. The Anointed One of verse 26 refers to Christ, but the "he" of verse 27, *contrary to the normal grammatical indication,* refers to the Antichrist, as the broader prophetic context shows.

(4) *Expositions of verse 6 as a reference to false prophets are not wholly satisfactory.* Two views prevail. The first construes the scars as those self-inflicted in idol worship and "the lovers" (*piel* plural participle of '*ahev,* "to love") as denoting sinful idolatrous loves (Hos. 2:7, 9, 12, 14, 15; Ezek. 16:33, 36, 37; 23:5, 9, 22; Jer. 22:20, 22; 30:14; Lam. 1:19) and here having reference to the venerated idols themselves. So Leupold, "the 'lovers' are the idols loved" (p. 249). This position would construe the statement of the false prophet as an inescapable admission of guilt and an unavoidable confession that the accusation is valid. It must be confessed this view is possible, but it fails to plumb the evident depth of the passage which, like Zechariah 12:10, bears an indelible Messianic stamp that cannot be brushed aside by less satisfactory exegesis.

The same criticism, although less cogent than the first, can be made of the second general view which refers the verse to false prophets. This interpretation renders the participle *me'ahavay* as "friends" (instead of idolatrous "lovers") and construes the wounds received as the result of discipline from relatives or parents, ostensibly in childhood, and the general reference as an evasion rather than a confession of idolatrous complicity (Keil, Wright, Baron, etc.). Henderson translates "friends" and interprets "the scars" as mutilations on the hands "in token of grief for departed relatives" (*op. cit.*, p. 434). Compare Deuteronomy 14:1: "You are the children of the Lord your God; you shall not cut yourselves or shave your forehead *for the dead.*" But it is not necessary, as Baron seems to hold (p. 469), to end this section with a persistent evasion of guilt on the part of the false prophet, when his crime has become so obvious.

(5) *The mediating view that verse 6 alludes indirectly and typically to Messiah under the figure of His being condemned as a false prophet* (A. R. Fausset, *Commentary*, p. 733) *is also unacceptable.* It sees that there is an apparent Messianic allusion, but fails to discern the context is that of the revelation of Israel's Cleanser from idolatry at the second advent (13: 1-6), and not His rejection as a prophet at His first advent.

(6) *The word used for wounds in Zechariah* 13:6 *is not the technical word for the self-inflicted "cuttings" connected with idolatrous ritual.* This word is *gedudah*, from the root *gadad*, "cut." "For every head shall be bald, and every beard clipped; upon all the hands shall be cuttings [*gedudoth*]," (Jer. 48:37). The verb (in *polel*) is used commonly of "cutting oneself" as a pagan practice. So the priests of Baal on Carmel *cut themselves* with knives and lancets till the blood spurted out (I Kings 18:28), and mourners following heathen customs "cut themselves" and made themselves bald (Jer. 16:6, cf. 47:5) for the dead in direct violation of Deuteronomy 14:1, "Ye shall not cut yourselves [*lo' yithgodedu*] nor make any baldness between your eyes for the dead."

The term here employed, *makkoth*, denotes any "wound" whether unhealed or healed and remaining only as a "scar," which is the result of an accident or violence done one (from root *nakah* in *hifil*, "to strike," "smite," "inflict an injury" on an enemy, Arabic *nikāyatan*). Thus to "smite to wound" (II Kings 8:28; 9:15; II Chron. 22:6; Hos. 6:1; Jer.

30:14), "to strike" fatally (Exod. 21:12; Josh. 10:26; II Sam. 2:23, etc.). Ahab's fatal wound (I Kings 22:35) and Joram's wounds received from the Syrians at Ramah (II Kings 8:29) are examples of common wounds. Isaiah describes such wounds of very recent infliction as "new or fresh" wounds (Isa. 1:6). Although Pusey (*in loc.*) correctly differentiates these wounds from idolatrous "cuttings," he has no proof that they only refer to fresh unhealed wounds themselves, not to the later scars (*Minor Prophets* II, 443, note 11). Certainly Isaiah 30:26 and the various metaphorical uses of the word do not always require unhealed wounds, and even Pusey's application of the prophecy to the first advent would necessitate the meaning of "scars."

(7) *The word for "friends" is not here used of idolatrous "lovers."* When it is so used (see under point 4), it uniformly occurs under the metaphor of male and female. As Pusey points out "of fourteen times in which it occurs . . . it is united with the feminine pronoun . . ., three times in the first person of the city personified" (*op. cit.*, p. 443, note 11).

The verse, accordingly, is *not* united to what immediately precedes (an illustration of the main subject), *but to the main subject itself*, Him whom they pierced, for whom they are to mourn and by whom they are to be cleansed when they realize the wounds "between His hands," i.e., "in His hands," are those which He received on Golgotha's cross. The **wounds in the hands** are thus in harmony with the piercing of Zechariah 12:10 which precedes, and the smiting of the Good Shepherd, which follows, and concerning which David prophesied when he said, "They pierced my hands and my feet" (Ps. 22:16 [17]).

Unsuccessful attempts have been made to make **between thy hands** mean something other than "*in* thy hands" — between the shoulders (Rashi), the breast between the hands (Wright), the breast or chest (Feinberg, who

7 Awake, O sword, against my shepherd, and against the man that is my fellow, saith the Lord of hosts: smite the shepherd, and the sheep shall be scattered: and I will turn mine hand upon the little ones.

7   Awake, O sword, against my shepherd, and against the man that is my fellow, saith Jehovah of hosts: smite the shepherd, and the sheep shall be scattered; and I will turn my hand upon the little ones.

cites II Kings 9:24 as an analogous case [*God Remembers*, p. 244], following Chambers (*op. cit.*, p. 100), but II Kings 9:24 is "between the arms" and is not the same as "between the hands."

By whom will it be said, **What are these wounds in thy hands?** The answer is in the word, **And one** [indefinite third masculine singular] **shall say to him.** The **one** represents *each individual* of the remnant of Israel who shall look to Him whom they pierced (12:10) when He appears at His second advent. Like Thomas (John 20:25) they shall not only see "in his hands the print of the nails" but thrust their finger into His side and cry that long-awaited cry that always should have been Israel's, "My Lord and my God" (John 20:27, 28).

He with infinite grace and majestic pathos will reply to the heart-rending cry of His repentant people, with **these I was wounded** [smitten] **in the house of my friends** (*me'ahavay*, "in the house *of those who loved Me*"). It is to be carefully observed He does *not* say, "With these I was wounded *by* those who loved Me," for this was not true. The Jewish leaders who put Him to death, on the contrary, hated Him diabolically. But it was dramatically, even pathetically true, that His wounds were those with which He was wounded "*in the house of* those who loved Him," for it was "the house of Abraham, Isaac, and Jacob," yes, of Isaiah, Jeremiah, Daniel, and Zechariah himself who loved Him, looked for Him, and foretold His coming. It was the house of Simeon, Anna, His own mother Mary who bore Him and tenderly nursed Him, of Joseph who lovingly provided for

Him, and the house of Peter, James, and John, who although they denied and forsook Him in the hour of supreme trial, nevertheless passionately loved Him, despite their human failure and weakness.

II. THE PROVISION FOR ISRAEL'S NATIONAL CLEANSING (Zech. 13:7a, b)

Verse 7 continues the subject of Messiah, introduced in verse 6 in such a startingly abrupt and dramatic manner. However, the difference is that the preceding prophetic reference is to Messiah's presentation to Israel as her Savior and Purifier from idolatry, which will be as sudden and lively an event in history when He returns in power and glory, as it is here presented in prophecy, and also as an occurrence to be looked forward to. This present reference to Messiah, on the other hand, is to Him (1) in His *death* and (2) in His *deity*.

1. *The Death of Messiah* (Zech. 13:7a). **Awake, O sword, against my Shepherd . . . smite the Shepherd!** The Lord is the speaker and the Messiah is the person spoken of. Such views as make the person addressed Zechariah himself (Calvin), Judas Maccabaeus (Grotius, Eichhorn, Bauer, Jahn), Jehoiakim (Maurer), Pekah (Ewald), appear little short of frivolous in the light of our Savior's express and decisive application of these words to Himself (Matt. 26:31), and in view of the context by the clearly discernible identity of the subject dealt with in chapter 11:4, 7, 10–14, which is resumed and treated as it was there in connection with the destruction of the Jewish state. Henderson, however, who owns the above-mentioned contextual relation-

ship of verse 7, is wrong in declaring that "the prophecy contained in this and the following verses has no coherence with what immediately precedes, and was evidently delivered upon a different occasion" (*op. cit.*, p. 434). Leupold is of the same opinion (*op. cit.*, p. 252).

So far from this being the case, these words are an explanation from the divine side, of the wounds in the hands of the Messiah by which He was wounded in the house of His friends. Human hatred, with free rein could nail the Messiah to a cross, even among those who prophesied, looked for, and loved His appearing. Yet man's wickedness could do no more than the Lord's own hand and counsel "determined before to be done" (Acts 4:28). He who knew no sin was "to be made sin for us" (II Cor. 5:21) "and become obedient unto death, even the death of the cross" (Phil. 2:8) so that the Father was to hide His face from the Son (Ps. 22:1 [2]; Matt. 27:46; Mark 15:34). This is the prophetic import of the divine command, **Awake, O sword, against my shepherd . . . smite the Shepherd.**

Hebrew syntax by word order emphasizes the **sword. O sword** [vocative], **awake** [imperative]! The prophet graphically states what will be (the *death* of Messiah) by a *command* that it should be, with the added emphatic touch of the first person with the Lord Himself issuing the command. The **sword** is here the figure of the *death* (of Christ), since this weapon is commonly used figuratively for any means of taking away human life (as in Exod. 5:21; II Sam. 12:9; Ps. 17:13). Moreover, the **sword** was figuratively "asleep" until it was "awakened" or "aroused," (*'uri* from *'ur,* "arouse oneself, awake"), that is, "become alert and active," used of the Lord's arm (Isa. 51:9), of a stone idol (Hab. 2:19). The **sword** became active against the Lord's Shepherd *as the divine will permitted* the enmity of Satan to be manifested against His sinless life, the diabolic opposition

of the Scribes and Pharisees to move against His wonderful ministry, the scorn of Herod and the cowardice of Pilate to allow Him to be condemned to death (Acts 2:23). Then the Shepherd was divinely smitten.

Forceful indeed is the apostrophe addressed to the sword. In similar fashion Jeremiah apostrophizes the sword of the Lord. "O thou sword of the Lord, how long will it be ere thou be quiet? Put up thyself in thy scabbard, rest, and be still" (Jer. 47:6). But in the case of the beloved, sinless One, the Messiah to come, whom the Lord addresses, "My Shepherd," the divine sword is appropriately seen as sleeping, i.e., completely passive and inactive, for why should the divine sword be in any other state with regard to One who was eternally the delight of the Father? Only His becoming the Sin-Bearer and Savior could elicit the terrifying divine command of *death.* **O sword, awake, against my Shepherd! . . . Smite the Shepherd!** Let those who see His wounds realize this. By this let them know how it came to be that **He was wounded in the house of those who loved him.**

2. *The Deity of Messiah* (Zech. 13:7b). **Sword, awake against my shepherd and against the man my equal.** This is an unmistakable Old Testament reference to the deity of the Coming One, the Lord's Shepherd, and the expressions employed are extremely significant. The Messiah is first designated **my Shepherd,** that is, "the Shepherd of the Lord," to set forth the relation He sustains to God (the Father) in the plan of redemption. Even more arrestingly He is termed **the man of my union,** *gever 'amithi,* i.e., "a human being closely conjoined or united to Me."

The Hebrew word for man employed here is not the common one, but refers to man in his strength, *gever,* "a strong man" from *gavar,* "be strong, mighty." The term distinguishes man in his strength from women, children, elderly people, and non-combatants whom he protects (Exod. 10:11; Num. 24:3; Josh. 7:14; Deut. 22:5; Judg. 5:30; II Sam. 23:1; Isa. 22:17, etc.).

The term **the man of my union** is rendered by Hengstenberg "a man, my nearest relation," by Leo Juda (*virum coeqalem mihi*), "a man coequal with me," and remarkably by De Wette, the rationalist, "the man my equal," and by Arnheim, the Jew, "the man whom I have associated with myself." The Hebrew word employed, *'amith*, is used to denote persons associated together under common love for the enjoyment of common rights and privileges. The root is *'amah* (compare Assyrian *emû*, "be united, associated," *emûtu*, "family, family connection"). Hence the word *'amith* means "relation, associate, fellow," apparently originally a feminine abstract noun, "association." In Leviticus 6:2 [5:21] it is employed of one lying "*to his neighbor*" (cf. Lev. 19:11). In Leviticus 24:19 it is similarly used of one causing "a blemish *in his neighbor*." In Leviticus 25:17 it is used pronominally, "Ye shall not oppress *one another*." In all cases it is used of "an equal," "an associate," or "neighbor" (cf. Lev. 18:20; 19:15, 17; 25:14, 15).

Thus in the light of the meaning of the word, "fellow, associate, neighbor, one associated with another on an equal status," in Leviticus (where the word occurs only, outside of Zechariah 13:7), it is apparent that De Wette's rendering of *gever 'amithi*, as "the man my equal" or Arnheim's "the man I have associated with myself" reflect very closely the real meaning of the term, which undeniably foretells the deity of Messiah. Moreover, the objection that such is not the case because our Lord was not put to death by a sword is pointless in the light of the obvious figurative use of the word in the passage, the import of which is further highlighted by the appended words, **says the Lord of armies**. The divine witness to the death and deity of the prophesied

Messiah makes this verse one of the most significant in the entire Old Testament.

How clearly this passage predicts the wonderful *association* the Messiah, the Son, was to sustain to the Father in assuming a human nature in the incarnation. For the union prophesied is that of the two natures in a theanthropic Person, and not of the divine nature or substance, as the use of the word *gever*, "man," proves. It was the foretelling by the Spirit of prophecy of that ineffable uniting of the divine with the human, resulting in the birth of Immanuel, one with the Father, who could say, "I and my Father are one" (John 10:30).

III. THE PRELUDE TO ISRAEL'S NATIONAL CLEANSING (Zech. 13:7c-9a)

Not only must the Messiah become incarnate and die by crucifixion (12:10; 13:6, 7), but judgment terrible and irremediable must fall upon the flock who rejected their Shepherd. The sad events following the smiting of the Shepherd were to form with that pivotal and climactic event the prelude to the eventual conversion and restoration of the sheep.

1. *The Sheep Scattered* (Zech. 13:7c). **Smite the Shepherd, and the sheep shall be scattered.** It is interesting that the imperative smite, *hakh*, "strike with plague, death or judgment" (same root underlying the "wounds" in Messiah's hands, vs. 6) is masculine, while the **sword**, *herev*, is feminine. Hitzig is correct in referring the grammatical anomaly to the agent handling the sword, but incorrect in referring it to a human agent instead of the divine. The Hebrew form would accentuate the important fact that the smiting of the Redeemer-Shepherd was in the most real sense the act of God in accordance with His eternal plans and purposes, and not merely the culmination of Satanic malignity and human treachery.

The result of the smiting to death

of the Shepherd-Messiah is indicated in the clause **and the sheep shall be scattered.** It is evident that the smiting of **the sheep,** *tso'n,* "flock," cannot be restricted to the faithful disciples of the Savior. The manner in which our Lord appropriated the prophecy (Matt. 26:31), however, furnishes a striking type of the general dispersion of the Jewish people after A.D. 70, which is the slant of the prediction as uttered by Zechariah.

The Hebrew word for **sheep,** commonly used of small cattle, is a feminine *singular* collective. It is used frequently metaphorically of Israel to show both the unity of the "flock" as the covenant people of the Lord and their helpless dependence upon the Lord, their Shepherd (cf. Ps. 23:1). It is interesting that the verb **shall be scattered,** *tephusena,* is not third feminine *singular* (stressing the unity of the sheep) but third feminine plural, emphasizing the fact that in the consequent diaspora that unity shall be destroyed, and the *individual* sheep shall be dispersed far and wide. The verb "to scatter," *puts,* is apparently to be related to Arabic *fadda,* "break in pieces, scatter." It is used in several passages of Israel's being scattered among the nations under the figure of a flock as here and in Ezekiel 34:5 (twice), and particularly of "enemies" being dispersed (Num. 10:35; I Sam. 11:11; Ps. 68:1 [2]).

Zechariah's remarkable prophecy of Israel's diaspora embraces the worldwide scattering of Israel from the dissolution of the Jewish State under Titus and the Roman armies till the regathering toward the end of the age preceding the restoration of the kingdom to Israel (Acts 1:6). How remarkably this ancient prediction has been verified is demonstrated by the history of the Jew during the Christian centuries.

2. *The Faithful Sheep of the Flock Warned of Persecution and Death* (Zech. 13:7d). **And I will turn my hand upon the little ones.** The speaker (the Lord) is not only the same as He who commanded the sword of death to awake against Him who was in His redemptive plan to become the incarnate Son and vicarious sin-bearer of the human race, but the message to **the little ones,** the faithful of the flock, was of similar import. As their Shepherd-Savior by the divine will was to be subjected to persecution and death, so the little ones who would believe on Him and follow Him, would likewise in the divine economy be exposed to suffering and martyrdom.

Although numerous commentators construe the idiom, **turn my hand upon,** in a good sense and the passage as offering "this one brief touch of comfort" (Leupold, *op. cit.,* p. 255; cf. Henderson, *op. cit.,* p. 435), this position can scarcely be correct for the following reasons: (1) *The context does not favor it.* The thought of the passage is the rejection and death of the Messiah as an event in "the determinate counsel and foreknowledge of God" (Acts 2:23). There is no reason to suppose that the same thought is not in view with regard to His faithful followers, especially since the passage is an inseparable part of the divine utterance comprising verse 7, enforced, but *not divided* by His statement, "says the Lord of armies."

(2) *The consistent use of the idiom "to turn one's hand upon" does not support the idea of "protection in time of calamity"* (Henderson). The expression is uniformly employed in a bad, or at most, a negative sense. Amos speaks of the turning of God's hand *against* Ekron (Amos 1:8). Ezekiel describes Israel's great enemy Gog turning his hand *against* restored Israel (Ezek. 38:12). The Psalmist speaks of God's turning His hand *against* Israel's foes (Ps. 81:14 [15]). Even in Isaiah 1:25 (cited by both Leupold and Henderson as an example of the use of the idiom in a good sense) the thought is cleansing *by* affliction rather than protection *from* it. As Pusey says, "It were in itself improb-

8 And it shall come to pass, that in all the land, saith the Lord, two parts therein shall be cut off and die; but the third shall be left therein.

9 And I will bring the third part through the fire, and will refine them as silver is refined, and will try them as gold is tried: they shall call on my name, and I will hear them: I will say, It is my people: and they shall say, The Lord is my God.

---

8   And it shall come to pass, that in all the land, saith Jehovah, two parts therein shall be cut off and die; but the third shall be left therein.

9   And I will bring the third part into the fire, and will refine them as silver is refined, and will try them as gold is tried. They shall call on my name, and I will hear them: I will say, It is my people; and they shall say, Jehovah is my God.

===

able that here alone" the idiom "should be in a good sense" (op. cit., p. 446, note 3).

(3) The objects of God's action do not necessitate construing the idiom in a good sense. The term the little ones does not necessarily suggest "creatures who are in need of pity" (Leupold). It merely suggests the believers in, and followers of, the crucified Messiah: accounted "insignificant" and "despicable" by both the Jews and pagans of their day. The little ones, hatstso'rim, a participial substantive, is formed from the root "to be (or grow) insignificant" (Assyrian ṣeḥeru, Arabic ṣaghura, "be small or little," Syriac, "be despicable, insignificant"). Thus the little ones are the lowly persecuted followers of the Savior (both Jewish and Gentile believers) who were despised and accounted as insignificant by their Jewish and pagan non-believing contemporaries. Nothing in the term of itself suggests they were "in need of pity" or that this was a promise of protection or escape from persecution and death.

(4) The fulfilment of the prophecy is against a good interpretation. Three centuries of almost relentless persecution by Rome in which countless "little ones" suffered martyrdom, and the papal inquisition and other atrocities against the true saints in later centuries down to the communist war against Christ's followers in the twentieth century constitute sufficient fulfilment of the prophet's words.

(5) The warnings of our Lord to His own constitute a refutation of a good interpretation. Our Lord forewarned His own small band of despised followers: "The servant is not greater than his master. If they have persecuted me, they will also persecute you" (John 15:20). "Then shall they deliver you up to be afflicted and shall kill you, and ye shall be hated by all nations for my name's sake" (Matt. 24:9). "They shall lay hands on you and persecute you, delivering you to the synagogues, and into prisons . . . (Luke 21:12). (Compare Luke 21:17; Matt. 10:17, 18: Acts 4:1, 2; 5:17, 18; 8:1, etc.)

3. The Great Tribulation and the Deliverance of the Remnant (Zech. 13:8, 9a). And it shall be in all the land, is the declaration of the Lord, two-thirds in it shall be cut off and perish; but the one-third shall be left in it. (9) And I will bring the third part through the fire, and I will refine them as silver is refined, and I will try them as gold is tried. . . . Henderson refers these verses to the destruction of two-thirds of the inhabitants of Judea during the Jewish War of A.D. 67–70. The remaining one-third preserved he says "after having been submitted to very trying and afflictive processes, should come forth out of the furnace a regenerated and spiritual people" (op. cit., pp. 435, 436).

But this interpretation (1) ignores the fact that the remnant of Jews who survived that furnace experience did not come forth "a regenerated and spiritual people." On the contrary, the preponderating majority of them, scattered world-wide, have consistently remained in unbelief and spiritual darkness, with only a *very few* believing and constituting "a remnant according to the election of grace" (Rom. 11:5).

This interpretation also (2) neglects to take into account the full scope of chapters 12:1-13:9, which embrace the second advent and the events ushering in the kingdom over Israel. Failure to take this fact into consideration has misled Leupold into the inaccurate statement that "there is no reference" in these verses "to any particular time or situation" (*op. cit.*, p. 256). In the light of the elaborate Scripture revelation concerning Israel's time of trouble and purging previous to her cleansing and establishment in kingdom blessing (Ps. 2:5; Rev. 7:14) called by Jeremiah, "the time of Jacob's trouble" (Jer. 30:5-7) and fully described in Revelation 11-18, these events apply most specifically and definitely to a particular time and situation.

The "time," as noted, is the Great Tribulation, the era of world-wide trouble and hatred of the Jew preceding the second advent of Messiah, seven years in length, according to Daniel 9:27. It is inaugurated by a Jewish treaty with the head of the revived Roman Empire, who in the middle of the seven years breaks the treaty and turns in deadly hatred against the Jews to destroy them utterly. It is in connection with these end-time events that the confederated armies of the nations under the Antichrist move against Palestine. Then in all the land [Palestine] ... two-thirds in it [the land] shall be cut off and perish (*yiqwa'u*, "expire, die," Arabic *ja'a*, "be empty, be hungry"), hence, die by hunger, sickness, the sword, or from natural causes (Num. 20:29; Josh. 22:20; Job 3:11; Lam. 1:19). These two-thirds involve the Jews in Palestine. The one-third is left *as a* remnant, *yiwwather*. This descriptive word comes from the root

yather, "to remain over," Assyrian, *ataru*, passive, "be left over, remain over as a part or portion surviving" (I Sam. 25:34; II Sam. 9:1; 17:12; Amos 6:9).

It is precisely to this Jewish remnant which survives the age-end judgments that Zechariah refers and concerning which the Lord declares, And I will bring the third part through the fire, and I will refine them as silver is refined and try them as gold is tried (vs. 9). These survivors are identical with those "who look unto him whom they pierced" (Zech. 12:10) and who "mourn for him, as one mourns for his only son" (12:10-14), unto whom the "fountain" of cleansing is opened (13:1), who are cleansed and converted (13:2-5), and who inquire of the Messiah, "What are these wounds in thine hands?"

The fire through which this saved remnant is brought is the Great Tribulation (Rev. 11-18). Refine as silver and try *as* gold, refers to the purging out of their sin and unbelief and their conversion at Messiah's advent. The term for "refining" silver, is literally, "I will *smelt* them," *saraphtim*, from *tsaraf*, "to smelt metals," "refine" by removing dross by heat, "test." In Assyrian *surrupu* means "refined," *sarpu* is "silver," and *nasraptu* is a "crucible" for melting metals under high heat for separating impurities and alloys (Jer. 9:7 [6]; Isa. 48:10; Dan. 11:35; Ps. 17:3; 26:2).

I will test them as gold is tested. The verb here is *bahan*, "examine, scrutinize, try, test" (so in Aramaic, Syriac, and Arabic, 8th conjugation). "Try, test or prove" with the metaphor of gold also occurs in Job 23:10, and the figure of God testing people (Jer. 9:6; 17:10; Prov. 17:3; I Chron. 29:17). The smelting of precious metals constitutes an apt illustration, for the trial will be the greatest and most severe in intensity Israel has ever had to endure (Dan. 12:1; Matt. 24:21, 22; Rev. 7:14; cf. Jer. 30:5-7), but the issue will be the conversion and restoration of those who pass through the furnace of fire, and who will be made like pure silver and gold, and constitute the nucleus of the millennial kingdom.

The third part will likely be the 144,000 of the Tribes of Israel sealed in Revelation 7:1-8 and 14:1-5. Like the three faithful Hebrews in Babylon they will not worship the beast's image (Rev. 13:1-18), but will successfully pass through the furnace of the Great Tribulation, heated seven times (cf. Mal. 3:2, 3; I Pet. 1:7), coming forth from the crucible like purified silver and gold.

IV. THE APPROPRIATION OF THE PROVISION FOR CLEANSING (Zech. 13:9b-d)

Chapter 13 ends in a dramatic climax as the Jewish remnant, brought safely through the crucible of the Great Tribulation, calls on the Lord. The Lord in turn hears and answers them with the result that they are restored and give joyous testimony of their salvation.

1. The Remnant Calls on the Lord (Zech. 13:9b). He will call on my name.... He (hu', the separate pronoun in addition to the pronominal subject contained in the finite verb, "he will call") is emphatic. The expression is literally, He, h e, will call. The use of the singular instead of the plural "they" is also arresting. As Chambers remarks, the singular masculine "he" (not the neuter "it") is "more idiomatic and vivid" (op. cit., p. 103). Since the singular pronoun stands for the same remnant described in verses 8 and 9, and thus refers to a collective entity, its use stresses the unity and solidarity of this faithful purged remnant as God's very own.

The idiom call on the name of the Lord means "to invoke the Lord Himself," the Lord's name denoting the Lord Himself. So men began "to call on the name of the Lord" in Enos' day, that is, they began to earnestly supplicate the Lord by means of His name. Abraham likewise "called on

the name of the Lord" at the altar he built at Bethel (Gen. 12:8). Elijah on Mount Carmel cried to the pagans: "Call on the name of your gods, and I will call on the name of the Lord" (I Kings 18:24) so they "called on the name of Baal" (I Kings 18:26); that is, they implored or earnestly supplicated Baal. Compare II Kings 5:11; Jeremiah 10:25; Isaiah 65:1; Psalms 79:6. Zechariah, accordingly, foresees the Jewish remnant of the last days, cleansed and converted, and embued with "the Spirit of grace and supplications" (Zech. 12:10) calling out to God in the name of the Messiah, Jesus. Such praying as this will be unique for its fervency and efficacy, and is dramatically described in chapter 12:11-14.

2. The Lord Hears and Answers the Remnant (Zech. 13:9c). He will call upon my name and I will answer him, I will say he is my people. The he and the I are emphatically set over against each other, the separate pronoun I, 'ani, occurring in addition to the suffixed pronominal subject of the finite verbal form, like the he with which it is in emphatic contrast. The object him, 'otho, is also in its separate (not suffixed) object form, giving it also a touch of emphasis.

The he of this passage is the nation at long last redeemed, purged, and revealed in true sonship. The people about to be redeemed from Egypt out of Pharaoh's power accordingly were styled the Lord's "son." "And thou [Moses] shalt say unto Pharaoh, Thus saith the Lord, Israel is my son, even my first-born: And I say unto thee, Let my son go, that he may serve me ..." (Exod. 4:22, 23). "When Israel was a child, then I loved him and called my son out of Egypt" (Hos. 11:1). The Apostle Paul summarizing his great dispensational revelation concerning the relation of unbelieving Israel (Rom. 9-11) to the gospel of grace in this age (Rom. 1-8), concludes with the same remnant and the same time-period in view, as Zechariah has in this passage: "And so *all Israel* shall be saved: as it is written, There shall come out of Sion the Deliverer [Isa. 59:20, 21] and shall turn away ungodliness from Jacob" (Rom. 11:26). All this is in accord with the teachings of the prophets. Israel, regathered from all nations, restored to her own land, and by regeneration brought into national sonship, will yet have her greatest exaltation and glory.

Brought into vital spiritual relationship to the God of their fathers, Abraham, Isaac, and Jacob, through faith in the crucified, risen, ascended, and returned Messiah, the prayers and intercession in Messiah's name (Jesus) shall bring the immediate and overwhelming answer of the Lord to their prayers, with glorious deliverance and spiritual blessing. **He will call upon my name and I will answer him!** The answer is a thrilling one, its terseness giving the ring of an exclamation of delight. **I will answer him, I will say: He is my people!** he, not "it," as A.V. and most commentators. The he (*hu'*) is the personalized remnant, as is the case throughout this context, the regenerated nucleus of the nation. **My people** (the predicate in a nominal sentence) is emphasized by word-order, being placed before the subject, he (*hu'*).

Zechariah, in this passage, as so frequently is true of his entire prophecy (chapters 1–14), in inspired fashion echoes and reiterates the former prophets. Jeremiah in similar context (Jer. 32:37–42) writes: "And they shall be my people, and I will be their God" (Jer. 32:38). Likewise Ezekiel declares the same great conversion (Ezek. 37:23–28) "... but I will save them out of all their dwelling places, wherein they have sinned, and will cleanse them: so shall they be *my people*, and I will be their God" (Ezek. 37:23).

Hosea likewise foresaw this national cleansing and reinstatement of Israel into her status as an elect nation: "Yet the number of the children of Israel shall be as the sand of the sea ... and it shall come to pass, that in the place where it was said unto them, Ye are *not my people* [Hos. 1:9; Rom. 9:25, 26], there it shall be said unto them, Ye are *the sons of the living God*" (Hos. 1:10 [2:1]).

3. *The Remnant Testifies to Salvation* (Zech. 13:9d). **And he shall say, The Lord is my God!** He is once again emphatic because of the use of the separate pronoun, and once again refers to the preserved and regenerated remnant of Israel. Spiritually restored as a *son*, linked to God by vital faith in the Messiah, this remnant will have a superbly fervent and genuine testimony of radiant salvation: **The Lord is my God!** will ring from heart and lip, reminding one of Psalm 23:1: "*The Lord* is my Shepherd." In that glad day the nation will be regathered under the Shepherd of Israel (Ps. 80) and will enter into all the blessing of the great Shepherd's psalm. The covenant relation between the Lord and His people, interrupted for so many weary centuries of suffering and persecution, but never abrogated, will be established again in fullest blessing.

The tragic divine pronouncement of judgment for persistent sin and breaking of the covenant relation on the part of the nations — *lo-'ammi* — "not My people" — will give way to the blessed word *'ammi* — "My people" (Hos. 1:9–11 [1:9–2:2]). Then "shall the ransomed of the Lord return and come to Zion with songs and everlasting joy upon their heads: they shall obtain joy and gladness and sorrow and sighing shall flee away" (Isa. 35:10).

THE SECOND ADVENT
OF MESSIAH IN GLORY

THE SECOND SECTION OF THE SECOND PROPHETIC ORACLE

(ZECH. 14:1–7)

I. The last triumph of the nations over Jerusalem (Zech.
14:1–3)

   1. The Time of the Last Triumphant Siege of Jerusalem — the
   Day of the Lord (Zech. 14:1)
   2. The Enemy Triumphant in the
   Last Siege of Jerusalem (Zech.
   14:2a)
   3. The Plight — Threatened Total
   Destruction of the City and the
   Remnant (Zech. 14:2b)
   4. The Deliverer of the Remnant —
   the Lord (Zech. 14:3)

II. The personal advent of messiah (Zech. 14:4–7)

   1. The Place of Messiah's Advent
   — the Mount of Olives (Zech.
   14:4a)
   2. The Result of Messiah's Advent
   — a Gigantic Earthquake Effecting Topographical Changes
   (Zech. 14:4b)
   3. The Purpose of Messiah's Advent — to Deliver His People
   and to Destroy Their Foes
   (Zech. 14:5a)
   4. The Manner of Messiah's Advent — with His Saints (Zech.
   14:5b)
   5. The Time of the Second Advent
   More Fully Described (Zech.
   14:6, 7)

CHAPTER 14 continues and concludes
the second oracle of Zechariah (chapters 12–14). The first oracle (chapters
9–11) in setting forth the first advent
and rejection of Messiah is foundational and preparatory to the second
oracle predicting the second advent
and acceptance of Messiah (chapters
12–14). The first section of the second
oracle in outlining the future deliverance and national conversion of
Israel (chapters 12 and 13) in turn
prepares the scene for the return of the
Messiah in glory and the establishment of the kingdom over Israel
(chapter 14). This last chapter is
climactic and is *in strict agreement
with the scope of Zechariah's entire
sweep of prophetic prediction.*

Just as the eight night visions
(chapters 1–6) and prophecies spring-

ing out of the question of the national
fasts (chapters 7 and 8) all have their
fulfilment in events leading *up to and
into the kingdom* (without an exception), so chapters 9–14 likewise comprehend *the same great Messianic future
of Israel.* Failure to recognize this
simple fact of the full scope of Zechariah's visions and prophecies has
plunged many of the commentaries,
dealing with the book as a whole but
especially with the concluding chapter, into a labyrinth of confusion.

Chapter 14 is still *wholly prophetic*
and commentators who struggle vainly
to apply it to some past historical
event or events either in whole or in
part, such as the Babylonian conquest
of Jerusalem or its destruction by
Titus and the Romans in A.D. 70
(Henderson, *The Minor Prophets,* p.

436, and many early writers), or to the whole of this present age, only with special emphasis on its consummation (Hengstenberg, *Christology of the Old Testament*, IV, p. 107, and Leupold, *Exposition of Zechariah*, p. 259) not only violate the prophetic scope of this chapter with respect to the other thirteen chapters, but must honestly confess with Lowe, following De Wette, "that this chapter defies all historical explanation" (*Commentary on Zechariah*, p. 131). The same is true whether the application to the past is in whole or in part, or whether the method of interpretation is literal, spiritual, allegorical, or mystical.

Chapter 14 is *wholly prophetic* from the standpoint of the present age, and the only method of interpretation that will unlock its meaning is the *literal*. Feinberg (*God Remembers*, pp. 248, 249) with acute precision correctly declares that when this passage "is interpreted in the literal sense, it harmonizes with all that Zechariah has revealed thus far and with the prophecies concerning the consummation for Israel found throughout Scripture."

Too much stress can scarcely be placed upon these two guiding stars of correct interpretation: (1) harmony with the *immediate context* of Scripture; (2) harmony with the *entire context* of the revealed Word of God. *Sane literal* interpretation guided by these two balancing criteria of truth and dealing discriminatingly with figurative language as a graphic vehicle for presenting such literal truth, cannot fail to lead to happy results in exegesis. Spiritualizing and mysticalizing interpretation, on the other hand, dictated by the exigencies of *deductive* principles superimposed upon Scripture rather than literal interpretation the natural result of inductive principles springing out of Scripture, are bound to produce endless confusion.

Chapter 14 of Zechariah is, in a sense, a testing ground demonstrating the vast difference between the literal and inductive interpretation of prophecy and the mysticalizing and deductive interpretation. The methodology of one is to seek to know what the Word of God says concerning the future by building up general truths from particulars (the inductive method). The other starts with general statements (alleged to be true) and seeks to impose them on the particulars, and where they do not fit *mysticalize* them, i.e., give them an incomprehensible or obscure connotation, making them merely emblematic or allegorical, by attaching some secret meaning to them, and so explain them away rather than explain them.

This is essentially what Hengstenberg (*op. cit.*, pp. 131–132) does in referring Chapter 14 "to the whole of the Messianic era," by which he means the present church age, and Leupold also (p. 239) when he writes: "Our verses do not, therefore, apply to any one situation. They do not describe a siege, capture, and captivity which actually occurred. By means of a figure they describe a situation which obtains continually through New Testament times. God's people shall continually be antagonized and suffer bitter adversity at the hands of their foes and shall in consequence be brought low; but there shall always be an imperishable remnant, and that not so extremely small."

Several very obvious fallacies in this interpretation are to be noted: (1) There is nothing but pure supposition to support these verses as a "figure." (2) Applying them "through New Testament times" violates the entire context of Zechariah's visions and prophecies, which concern the future hope of *Israel*, not the Christian Church. (3) The remnant in chapters 12–14 is the Jewish remnant regathered to Palestine at the end of this age and not a Christian remnant. (4) This interpretation clashes with the overall eschatological context of the revealed Word of God. And (5) it robs the passage of its simple and obvious sense, giving it one (so far as any fulfilment in history is concerned) which is nonsense.

Kliefoth, Keil, Pusey, Wright, and many of the older and later expositors who reject the *literal* interpretation of Zechariah 14 as involving a still future siege of Jerusalem with a Jewish remnant in Palestine preceding the second advent of Christ, do so by lumping it together with the error of so-called "Jewish Chiliasm." But the heresy of Jewish millennial hopes was *not* that Israel looked for a Messianic kingdom of peace and righteousness on the earth with Jerusalem as its capital and radiating center. *Zechariah features this theme in his entire prophecy from chapter 1 throughout chapter 14,* and if they were in error in this hope, then Zechariah himself was in error, an error imbedded not only in his prophecy, but in his very name, "God remembers," i.e., He remembers His covenants and promises to Israel involving their future kingdom.

"Jewish Chiliasm" was wrong *only* in the fact that it *overlooked the prophesied rejection and death of the Messiah as the indispensable prelude to His manifestation in kingdom glory.* Moreover, this truth of Messiah's second advent to establish an earthly kingdom over restored Israel is *so resplendently emblazoned* in the prophets and on the pages of Zechariah, particularly chapter 14, that it is one of the inexplicable conundrums of the history of Christian doctrine that it should be so widely denied by Christian scholars and Bible expositors. In fact, a tragically striking parallel obtains between the rejecting of Messiah and His atoning sufferings and death by the ecclesiastical intelligentsia at His first advent and the rejection of His kingdom glory over restored and converted Israel at His second advent by the Biblical commentators of the present age. Chapter 14 records the events following upon the return to the land of a remnant in unbelief, their time of trouble previous to their conversion, and

establishment in glory under the returning Messiah.

I. THE LAST TRIUMPH OF THE NATIONS OVER JERUSALEM (Zech. 14:1-3)

Chapter 14 in presenting a prophetic portraiture of full kingdom blessing and worship (vss. 8-21) first recapitulates the pivotal events leading up to this grand consummation of Israelite hopes (14:1-7); namely, the last siege of Jerusalem (vss. 1-3) and the personal advent of the Messiah (vss. 4-7). Already these climactic episodes have been presented in chapter 12 — the siege and deliverance (12:1-9), and the second advent (12:10), but from a different point of view, from a slightly different point of time (although in "the day of the Lord") and for a different purpose. In chapter 12 the siege is presented in its later developments when divine interposition has been vouchsafed. Chapter 14 presents the siege in its earlier more drastic and cataclysmic phase of apparent hopelessness and helplessness, when only divine intervention could save the day. Therefore, the coming of the Lord to Olivet in power and glory working deliverance is portrayed over against His coming in grace and salvation, effecting the spiritual regeneration of the remnant (12:10-13:6).

1. *The Time of the Last Triumphant Siege of Jerusalem — the Day of the Lord* (Zech. 14:1). **Lo, a day is coming** [which is] **the Lord's when thy plunder shall be distributed in the midst of thee.** Leupold (*op. cit.,* p. 260) holds that this **day** is not the one that in Old Testament prophecy goes under the name of "the day of the Lord" and is so rendered by the Authorized Version. That this is not the case, but the reference is emphatically to "the day of the Lord" *par excellence* is suggested (1) *by the Hebrew idiom employed (yom-ba' leyahweh),* literally **a day is coming — the Lord's,** i.e., "distinctively and pre-eminently His." The *lamedh* before Yahweh (the Lord) thus denotes possession, "belonging

1 Behold, the day of the Lord cometh, and thy spoil shall be divided in the midst of thee.

1 Behold, a day of Jehovah cometh, when thy spoil shall be divided in the midst of thee.

to, of" (Isa. 2:12; 22:5; 28:2) being a circumlocution for "the day *of the Lord* is coming," because the author wished to accentuate the *certainty* of the coming of the day, employing the *future instans* and therefore attaching the participle *directly* to "day," *yom*, so making a construct chain impossible, but achieving an added stress on "a day — *the Lord's*" or "*to the Lord*" by substituting an adjectival phrase for the construct (genitive) relationship.

That Zechariah 14:1 refers emphatically to **the day of the Lord** in a special sense is also unmistakably suggested (2) *by the context*. **The day of the Lord** is that period immediately preceding the second advent of Messiah when God *directly* and *publicly* manifests His power to dispossess Satan and wicked men from their usurpation of the earth (Rev. 5:1–19:16), delivers His people Israel (Zech. 12:1–9), and establishes His mediatorial kingdom of righteousness and peace throughout the world (Isa. 2:12; 4:1, 2; 11:10, 11; 13:9; Amos 9:11; Joel 1:15; 2:1, 2; Mal. 4:1–5 [3:19–23]). This is precisely the subject of Zechariah 14:1–3, indeed quintessentially so (which accounts for the emphatic terminology to designate "the day of the Lord" — "a day — the Lord's"), since it describes the most terrible and desperate condition to which the Jewish remnant will be reduced, which, in turn, calls for the direct and supernatural intervention of the Messiah.

Leupold's translation, "Lo, a day is coming *for* the Lord," although possible grammatically, and in the light of the true second advent context would not be at variance with pointing to the well-known prophetic "day of the Lord" is, however, utterly untenable in suggesting, as far as time is concerned, "the whole New Testament era," as he maintains (*loc. cit.*). Such a deductive interpretation not only ignores the place of this passage in the over-all Scripture testimony of "the day of the Lord," with which it dovetails perfectly, but also fails to reckon that this expression is identical in its time implications with the frequently recurring phrase in chapters 12–14 in **that day**, which *in every case* denotes "the day of the Lord" in its future eschatological significance with reference to Israel's deliverance from her final time of trouble just prior to her conversion and establishment in kingdom blessing. To apply it to "the whole New Testament Era" is to apply it to a concept that is not once in view in Zechariah, chapter 14.

The last clause of verse 1, introduced by **and** (*waw*) is temporal (Gesenius-Kautzsch, 164:1[a]) and shows the desperate plight of Jerusalem overrun and completely plundered by the victorious armies of the nations invading the Israeli state. **Lo, a day is coming — the Lord's — when thy spoil shall be distributed in the midst of thee.** The pronoun second *feminine* singular, refers to Jerusalem personified. **Thy spoil** ("spoil *of thee*," objective genitival idea), accordingly, means *not* the plunder Jerusalem takes in the battle (subjective genitive), but the booty the besieging enemies take from her (objective genitive). This spoil will be distributed among Jerusalem's conquerors, leisurely and deliberately in the very city itself. This initial touch shows the desperation of Jerusalem's situation, and the terrific straits to which she has been reduced. But her dire extremity (further detailed in verses 2 and 3) becomes God's opportunity (dramatically set forth in verses 4–8 in the glorious advent of her Deliverer and Savior).

2 For I will gather all nations against Jerusalem to battle; and the city shall be taken, and the houses rifled, and the women ravished; and half of the city shall go forth into captivity, and the residue of the people shall not be cut off from the city.

2   For I will gather all nations against Jerusalem to battle; and the city shall be taken, and the houses rifled, and the women ravished; and half of the city shall go forth into captivity, and the residue of the people shall not be cut off from the city.

2. *The Enemy Triumphant in the Last Siege of Jerusalem* (Zech. 14:2a). **For I will assemble all the nations against Jerusalem to battle....** Once more, and for the last time, in line with the phenomenal nature of this great eschatological section (Zechariah, chapters 12-14), *the Lord Himself* speaks in the *first* person (cf. 12:2-6; 12:9, 10; 13:2, 6, 9) to reinforce the amazing and confessedly almost incredible predictions made. This He doubtless does to help render inexcusable numerous Christian scholars who resolutely not only refuse to believe these tremendous prophecies *literally* (which is the only way to *believe* them, although not the only way to interpret them), but who also resolutely persist in excoriating those who do.

The **for** (the explicative conjunction *waw*, "and") presents the reason (explanation) for the immediately preceding statement that Jerusalem's booty should be distributed within her walls by her triumphant enemies. It is arresting to note that the explanation given is not that the enemy was overwhelmingly superior in power or that his advance was uncheckable, but that the whole episode was providential. *God not only allowed it, but actively interposed in bringing it to pass.* The case is succinctly stated: **For I will gather all nations,** demonstrating that God's purposes are not only sovereignly assured even though wicked nations may seem to triumph over His people, but His plans for the ordered ages of redemptive history, so far from being set aside and thwarted by Satan, demons, and rebellious men (and

these evil agents have a large part in these end-time activities [Rev. 9:1-20; 16:13-16]) are actually carried out by them to the glory of God and in accordance with His "definite plan and foreknowledge" (cf. Acts 2:23, R.S.V.).

It is important to note that the enemy is precisely defined as **all nations,** *kol-haggoyim,* which designates the nations of the earth in distinction from the Jewish people, whether as a free and autonomous people till the Babylonian captivity, or under the suzerainty of a foreign power till A.D. 70, or scattered among the nations in the Christian centuries, or restored to Palestine as an independent state, as at present. In any case, the people were prophesied to "dwell alone" and "not be reckoned among the nations" (Num. 23:9). Hence in the prophetic Scriptures the Jews are rigidly differentiated from non-Jewish peoples as being an elect nation, and the *only* people so divinely chosen to be the recipient *as a nation* of the covenants and promises vouchsafed to their fathers (Rom. 9:4, 5; 11:1, 2). Compare also Joel 3:2 [4:2]; Revelation 16:14, 19.

To ignore this indispensable distinction in this passage (cf. Zech. 12:9; 14:3, 16) is to plunge the whole into confusion and utterly fail accurately to define the foe or to differentiate him from friend. But when it is said that **all the nations** are gathered against Jerusalem, it is not of course meant that every individual comes, but contingents of the armies of the various world powers, representing them as nations (Rev. 16:13-16).

Moreover the Lord declares, **For I**

3 Then shall the Lord go forth, and fight against those nations, as when he fought in the day of battle.

3 Then shall Jehovah go forth, and fight against those nations, as when he fought in the day of battle.

will gather ['asaph, "assemble," "bring together"] all nations against Jerusalem to battle. The place (Jerusalem) is defined just as precisely as the foe (all nations). To interpret either other than literally is to fly in the face of the general pattern of age-end events, revealed not only by Zechariah (1:14, 16; 2:12 [16]; 3:2; 12:2–10; 14:4, 11, 12, 16), and other Old Testament prophets (Joel 3:2 [4:2]; Dan. 9:27; Isa. 4:3, 4; 31:5), but also New Testament seers (Luke 21:24; Matt. 24:15–22; Rev. 16:19).

3. *The Plight—Threatened Total Destruction of the City and the Remnant* (Zech. 14:2b). And the city shall be captured and the houses plundered, and the women raped, and half of the city shall go into captivity, but the rest of the people shall not be cut off from the city. This verse portrays the moment of direst distress of Jerusalem, when it will appear that the city and its inhabitants are hopelessly doomed. This is the acme of "the time of Jacob's trouble" (Jer. 30:5–7), just before "he" (i.e., the remnant) "is saved out of it," here described by Zechariah as the rest of the people (*yether ha'am*). The word remainder, "remnant" (*yether* from the root *yathar* "to remain over," Assyrian *ataru*, "remain over as a small part"), is used of what an enemy or scourge may leave behind (Joel 1:4), particularly of a surviving portion of Israel or Judah rescued from a foe (Mic. 5:2; Zeph. 2:9; Jer. 39:9; 52:15; II Kings 25:11).

Although this remnant *in the city* constituting *half* of its population is not "destroyed" at this time, yet "*in all the land*" of Palestine *two-thirds* shall be cut off. The remaining *one-third* is brought through the fire to be a purged and refined remnant to become '*ammi*, "my (i.e., the Lord's)

people" (Zech. 13:8, 9), prepared for kingdom blessing and leadership in the new spiritual order established at the second advent of Messiah.

The dire straits to which the city is reduced is given in four statements. (1) The city shall be taken, *nilkedhah*, perfect passive of *lakhadh*, "capture, seize," take by lot, or by siege, Arabic *lakada*, "strike, push." The verb commonly occurs of "capturing" or "seizing" a town in war (Judg. 1:8; Josh. 8:21; Deut. 2:35; II Sam. 8:4). (2) The houses shall be plundered, *nashassu*, from *shasas*, "spoil, rob, plunder," used actively (Judg. 2:14; I Sam. 17:53; Ps. 89:41 [42]) and passively here and in Isaiah 13:16, "their houses plundered" in a passage (Isa. 13:12–16) which treats of the same subject, namely, the Jewish remnant in the Great Tribulation. (3) The women shall be raped, *tishshagalnah*, *nifal* passive from *shagel*, "violate, rape, ravish" (Deut. 28:30); passive, (Isa. 13:16; Jer. 3:2). The Masoretic editors considered the word obscene, and substituted a needless euphemism *shakhav*, "to lie with," in the *keri* (marginal reading) both here and in Deuteronomy 28:30 and Jeremiah 3:2. (4) Half the city shall go into captivity (*baggolah*, carried away as prisoners of war and transported to another country).

4. *The Deliverer of the Remnant— the Lord* (Zech. 14:3). And the Lord shall go forth and fight against those nations as when he fought in the day of battle. The whole passage indicates such a direct personal interposition of the Lord Himself as constitutes this pre-eminently a day which is the Lord's (14:1); that is, "the day of the Lord *par excellence*, when He is predicted throughout the prophetic Word to interpose in the affairs of

men, terribly with respect to wicked men and gloriously on behalf of His own, to establish His righteous kingly-priestly reign on the earth in the coming age (see comments on Zechariah 14:1).

In the hour of terrible exigency when the enemy is brutally triumphant and the remnant of God's ancient covenant people is in danger of total extinction, and the covenants and promises made to the fathers in peril of being unfulfilled forever, **then the Lord shall go forth and fight against his and his people's foes.** In the hour of the apparent triumph of anti-God and anti-Christ forces bent on ousting the name of God and His Christ from the earth, and destroying the Jewish remnant in whom God's purposes for the earth in the coming age center, **the Lord will go forth and fight ... as when he fought in the day of battle.** The most gigantic and virulent outburst of demon-inspired anti-Semitism the world has ever seen will at the height of its success be irremediably destroyed by the Lord Himself.

The word **go forth,** *yatsa'*, is very fitting to the Lord who appears once again in behalf of His people as "a man of war" (Exod. 15:3). The word has a technical ring, and is employed of a king going out to war at the head of his troops (I Sam. 8:20), and of the Lord going before His people to battle for them (Judg. 4:14; II Sam. 5:24; Ps. 68:7 [8]; 108:11 [12]; I Chron. 14:15), and to deliver and save them (Hab. 3:13), and of the Lord's hand issuing forth hostilely against anyone (Ruth 1:13). Here it refers to Messiah's personal coming forth from heaven (cf. Mic. 1:3; Rev. 19:11-16) to fight for His beleaguered people on earth.

The Lord will fight for His people **as ... in the day of battle** (*qerav*). This expression denotes a "warlike or hostile approach" from the root *qarav*, "to draw near, approach," Assyrian *karabu*, "come near," Arabic *qaribu*, *qarubu*, "be near, come near." Hence

the word means a "battle," "war." In Psalm 68:30 [31] it occurs in the plural accusative, "people who delight *in battles.*" In Job 38:23 it is used of "the day of battle [*qerav*] and war [*milḥamah*]." In Psalm 144:1 it is employed of the Lord "who teaches my hands to fight," literally, "for battle [*qerav*], and my fingers for war [*milḥamah*]." Compare Psalm 78:9; Ecclesiasticus 9:18.

The allusion to the Lord's special interposition under the figure of fighting **as ... in the day of battle** (hostile encounter with Israel's enemies), although it certainly includes the conflict in behalf of His people at the Red Sea (Exod. 14:14), can scarcely be confined to this famous deliverance, but embraces such signal triumphs as Joshua's victory at Gibeon when "the Lord fought for Israel" (Josh. 10:14), the general conquest of Canaan (Josh. 23:3), Barak's defeat of Sisera (Judg. 4:15) and Jehoshaphat's discomfiture of the Moabites and the Ammonites (II Chron. 20:15) and similar outstanding instances where the Lord in a special manner fought in behalf of His hard-pressed people.

II. THE PERSONAL ADVENT OF MESSIAH (Zech. 14:4-7)

Verses 1-3 form a fitting introduction to the present section by presenting the *drastic need* which only the omnipotent Person, introduced so cataclysmically in verses 4-7, can meet. It is interesting to note how Hebrew prophetic style accentuates the desperation of the situation in verses 1-3. The emphasis appears in verse 1. The certainty of the coming of a day which is peculiarly the Lord's is declared and coupled with the need for such divine undertaking as that day signifies; namely, Jerusalem conquered and despoiled. Thus "the outcome," as Leupold notes, "is at once stated in headline fashion" (*op. cit.*, p. 259). Then the details are given in verse 2, with an intimation of how the situation is to be met in verse 3.

4 And his feet shall stand in that day upon the mount of Olives, which is before Jerusalem on the east, and the mount of Olives shall cleave in the midst thereof toward the east and toward the west, and there shall be a very great valley; and half of the mountain shall remove toward the north, and half of it toward the south.

---

4   And his feet shall stand in that day upon the mount of Olives, which is before Jerusalem on the east; and the mount of Olives shall be cleft in the midst thereof toward the east and toward the west, and there shall be a very great valley; and half of the mountain shall remove toward the north, and half of it toward the south.

The actual order of events in this day peculiarly the Lord's is: (1) the nations assembled to war against Jerusalem (vs. 2); (2) the city captured and plundered, etc. (vs. 2); (3) the spoil of the city divided within its walls (vs. 1); (4) the Lord's intervention (vs. 3).

1. *The Place of the Messiah's Advent — the Mount of Olives* (Zech. 14:4a). **And his feet shall stand in that day on the Mount of Olives, which is before Jerusalem on the east. . . . His feet** are the Lord's feet, as verse 3 demonstrates. How can the Lord's (Jehovah's) feet stand on the Mount of Olives? Because they are the feet of His resurrected, glorified humanity, which ascended to heaven from the same locality, and because *"this same Jesus* who was taken up . . . into heaven shall *so* come *in like manner"* as the disciples witnessed Him "go into heaven" (Acts 1:11). The "so" and "in like manner" evidently also mean, in the light of Zechariah 14:4 that He ascended from Olivet personally and visibly in His glorified humanity and will so return to the same spot personally and visibly in His glorified humanity.

The time of this earth-transforming event is designated **in that day,** which so far from being "the most general possible designation of time," as Leupold contends (*op. cit.,* p. 261), denotes very precisely "the day of the Lord." If the glorious second advent of Messiah is not "the day of the Lord," *what is?* In fact, the phrase **in that day** occurs over and over again in the prophets, designating Israel's

final period of trouble, eventuating in the appearing of her Messiah and the consummation of national blessing under His earthly rule (cf. Isa. 4:1, 2; 12:1; 24:21; 26:21).

This designation of time **in that day** occurs remarkably frequently throughout Zechariah's second burden (oracle), in chapters 12–14 (at least seventeen times), and it is obvious that *one period is described,* which is the *very same* era to which the former prophets, Isaiah, Jeremiah, Amos, Micah, etc., allude, and is identical with "the day of the Lord." Featured also in Zechariah 12–14 are the city of Jerusalem (mentioned at least twenty-two times), the nations (referred to at least thirteen times), and the name of the Lord (the Tetragrammaton YHWH). The conclusion is plain. This period denominated **in that day** deals with both Israel and the nations of the earth relative to Jerusalem, in the light of age-end events and the restoration of the kingdom to Israel (Acts 1:6), involving the personal intervention and deliverance effected by her Savior and Messiah. A simple comparison of the events prophesied by Zechariah **in that day** are identical to those prophesied to take place in "the day of the Lord" or "in the last days" (Isa. 2:2) by the former prophets.

At His glorious advent Messiah's **feet** [once nail-pierced] **shall stand** on the Mount of Olives. The word **stand,** *'amedhu,* with "feet" as the subject and the preposition "on" (locative use of *'al,* denoting place) can only mean "touch" or "rest firmly on." Messiah's feet shall "come in contact with" or "rest on" the Mount of Olives. A *person* is commonly said to "stand," i.e., "be erect," not sitting or reclining. But here the feet are said to "stand" to emphasize the personal, bodily return of the Lord to the earth, for the feet standing can only mean they support the weight of the human body in question. The language is apparently designed to compel a literal rather than a mystical interpretation of the Lord's second coming.

The Mount of Olives, as the place of the Lord's appearing in glory, is said to be **before Jerusalem on the east.** Although this is the only time **the Mount of Olives** is mentioned by this name in the Old Testament (cf. "the ascent of Olives" in II Sam. 15:30), this can scarcely be the reason for the topographical notation describing the location of the site. The mountain was so dominant and in such close proximity to the holy city that it was well known, being plainly visible to every eye. Why then, the appended geographical description? The following reasons may be suggested. (1) *From this mountain the glory of God departed and will return to Jerusalem.* "The glory of the God of Israel" (Ezek. 11:22), also called "the glory of the Lord," left Jerusalem *by the east* previous to the Babylonian captivity and the beginning of "the times of the Gentiles" (Ezek. 11:23), and *from the east* the same glorious symbol of the divine Presence is seen to return. "And, behold, the glory of the God of Israel came from the *way of the east* . . ." (Ezek. 43:2), marking the termination of "the times of the Gentiles."

(2) Accordingly, *the idea prevailed in antiquity that from the east salvation would arise,* like the sun, dispensing its salutary light, "even the Sun of righteousness (Messiah) . . . with healing in its beams . . ." (Mal. 4:2).

(3) Moreover Zechariah's prophecy doubtless echoes the Ezekiel passages where similar topographical notations occur. "And the glory of the Lord

went up from the midst of the city, and stood upon the mountain *which is on the east side of the city*" (Ezek. 11:23). "And, behold, the glory . . . came from *the way of the east*" (Ezek. 43:2). "And the glory of the Lord came into the house [millennial temple] by the way of the gate *whose prospect is toward the east*" (Ezek. 43:4).

The Mount of Olives, the central eminence of a mile-long line of limestone hills, rising almost 200 feet above Mount Zion and almost 300 feet above Mount Moriah, thus dominating the skyline on the east, accordingly offered a suitable spot for the revelation of the glorious One who will come to relieve the city. In addition, the declivitous mountain separated from the city by the narrow defile of the brook Kedron offered a serious impediment to a rapid escape from Jerusalem, as in the case of David's flight from Absalom (II Sam. 15:30). Messiah's feet touching the mountain (modern *Jebel et-Tur*) will transform the natural obstacle into a way of escape for the beleaguered remnant.

2. *The Result of Messiah's Advent — Gigantic Earthquake Effecting Topographical Changes* (Zech. 14:4b). *. . . and the Mount of Olives shall be* split through its middle, eastward and westward, by an exceedingly great valley, and half of the mountain shall recede northward and half of it southward. The Lord appears personally and bodily to deal with His people's enemies for *under His feet* the mountain, dislodged by terrific seismographic upheaval, is torn from its foundation, and half of it recedes **northward** (*tsaphonah*, "to" or "toward the north") and the other half of it **southward** (*negbah*, "to or toward the Negev* or south," adverbial accusatives of the nouns with *he* directive, giving the direction of the action).

This is not the only passage in prophecy which connects the day of the Lord and the venting of divine wrath against sinners with violent earthquakes (cf. Mic. 1:4; Nah. 1:5;

5 And ye shall flee to the valley of the mountains; for the valley of the mountains shall reach unto Azal: yea, ye shall flee, like as ye fled from before the earthquake in the days of Uzziah king of Judah; and the Lord my God shall come, and all the saints with thee.

5 And ye shall flee by the valley of my mountains; for the valley of the mountains shall reach unto Azel; yea, ye shall flee, like as ye fled from before the earthquake in the days of Uzziah king of Judah; and Jehovah my God shall come, and all the holy ones with thee.

Hab. 3:6; Ps. 18:7 [8]; Ezek. 38: 19–20). The seventh-bowl judgment of the Apocalypse, in which is filled up the wrath of God and which is coeval with the glorious advent of Messiah, is attended with a world-wide earthquake "such as had never been since men were on the earth, so great was that earthquake. The great city [i.e., Jerusalem] was split into three parts, and the cities of the nations fell . . ." (Rev. 16:18, 19). Although Zechariah describes only the Palestinian quake, doubtless however the most severe since the whole topography of the land is altered, the disturbance is world-engirdling, and unparalleled in its frightful intensity, in fact climaxing the apocalyptic judgments of Revelation 5:1–16:21.

Split latitudinally or breadth-wise through its middle eastward and westward **by an exceedingly great valley** (adverbial accusative), the two halves fall back one to the north and the other to the south. The Mount of Olives shall accordingly dissolve into "a huge valley," *ge᾽ gedholah me᾽odh.* The vast alteration of the physical contour of Palestine will be an accommodation to the center of blessing and activity it will assume with reference to the whole earth in the kingdom age. The city, then the capital of the entire earth, will be situated eminently, the very large valley receding all around it, making it the conspicuous object of admiration, as the city of the great King. **The whole land shall be turned into a plain from Geba to Rimmon. But Jerusalem shall remain aloft upon its site** . . . (Zech. 14:10, R.S.V.). Then Psalm 48 will have its

prophetic aspects fulfilled: "Great is the Lord, and greatly to be praised in *the city of our God*, in the mountain of his holiness. *Beautiful for situation, the joy of the whole earth, is Mount Zion*, on the sides of the north, the city of the great King [i.e., Messiah]. God is known in her palaces for a refuge" (Ps. 48:1–3 [2–4]).

3. *The Purpose of Messiah's Advent — to Deliver His People and to Destroy Their Foes* (Zech. 14:5a). **Then shall you flee by the valley of my mountains . . . as you fled before the earthquake in the days of Uzziah, king of Judah.** This passage conveys the assurance of the effectual means of escape for the pious Jewish remnant within the beleaguered city provided by the cataclysmic earthquake. The word **valley**, *gey᾽*, is an adverbial accusative telling *how* and *where* the remnant shall make their escape both from the terror of the earthquake and the fury of the attacking foe. They shall flee **by** or *"by way* or *means* of the valley.*" This valley is called **the valley of my mountains** or more accurately **my** [the Lord's] **mountain valley** because He formed it by splitting Olivet in two.

Numerous modern critics (such as Nowack, Marti, Kittel, etc.) reject the Masoretic reading, supported by the Vulgate and Syriac, **and you shall flee**, *wenastem*, for the pointing *wenistam*, "shall be closed up" (Septuagint, Targum, Symmachus, Arabic), and emend **the valley of my mountains,** following Wellhausen, either to *ge᾽ hinnon*, "Valley of Hinnom," or *ge᾽gihon*, "Valley of Gihon." The result is they have either one or both of Jerusalem's springs "stopped up" by the earthquake. But Henderson (*op. cit.*) is correct in declaring these emendations "are utterly to be rejected, as unsuited to the connection." Indeed, they give the very opposite thought of added impediment, rather than escape and are pointless in the light of "the very great valley" specified in verse 4, and the vast topographical change in Palestine indicated by verse 10. Moreover, they are ridiculous in the over-all context of prophetic Scripture (Rev. 16:19) which predicts such an earthquake not only in Palestine but in the entire earth in connection with end-time judgments and Messiah's return.

Besides these objections such arbitrary dealing with the text commonly rejects the reference to flight before the earthquake in the time of Uzziah as a gloss. But both this notice and the reading, **valley of my mountains,** are supported by the Septuagint, so that the Masoretic reading is to be sustained throughout.

The proper name **Azal,** moreover, is to be preserved and not made a preposition with a suffix, involving another free emendation. Its very meaning "be joined to, be at the side of, near" suggests its likely origin by being in close proximity to one of Jerusalem's gates on the east. With the newly formed valley extending to it, it would readily be a means of quick exit from the city for those fleeing from the enemy. The "Beth Azel" of Micah 1:11 may be the same location as that alluded to by Zechariah, the *beth* ("house of") often being omitted in place names.

The flight **before the earthquake in the days of Uzziah king of Judah** is doubtless that referred to by Amos (1:1), and must have been of terrible severity to be so vividly referred to more than two centuries later. Josephus relates the catastrophe to Uzziah's attempt to offer incense in the temple against the protests of the priests (*Antiquities* IX, 10, 4; cf. II Chron. 26:16–21).

4. *The Manner of Messiah's Ad-*vent—*with His Saints* (Zech. 14:5b). **And the Lord my God shall come, and all the holy ones with thee.** That the phenomenal cataclysm described in this passage occurs in conjunction with the second advent of Messiah is stressed by the fact that reference to this climactic and age-altering event is made both at the beginning and at the end of the account of the earthquake, **His** [the Lord's] **feet shall stand upon the Mount of Olives** [vs. 4] ... **and the Lord my God shall come and all the holy ones with thee** [vs. 5]. This circumstance alone not only demonstrates the tremendous importance of Messiah's return, but to the reverent student of prophecy offers a completely satisfactory explanation for the entirely supernatural character of the earthquake and the vast geological changes effected by it. If the coming of Messiah is literal, so must this catastrophe be literal, in which no doubt millions of people will lose their lives. The world-wide catastrophe involved in the Noahic flood is used by the Apostle Peter as an illustration of the world-wide catastrophe that will attend the second coming of Christ (II Peter 3:1–14).

Zechariah's designation of the Messiah in both references in this passage on the earthquake stresses the deity of the Coming One. In verse 4, **His feet which shall stand in that day upon the Mount of Olives** are **the Lord's** [*Yhwh's*] feet, as verse 3 proves. In verse 5 the designation of deity is even more pronounced, **The Lord** [Yhwh] **my God shall come,** showing also Zechariah's simple and fervent faith in this fact. Reference to Messiah's feet also focusses attention on His humanity. Rationalistic commentators who refuse to believe these clear revelations cannot be expected to own the possibility of such an earthquake as is here described. Even believing scholars who receive the testimony of Messiah's deity, as here set forth, frequently balk at a literal interpretation of the siege, the deliverance, the earthquake, and the other marvels of this passage, and either mysticalize them altogether or apply them to past events with which they only very inexactly agree. The only true interpretation, as seen, is to relate the entire chapter wholly to the still future "day of the Lord."

The verb used of the Lord's second advent, *bo'*, means "to come, arrive, make one's personal appearance," as in Genesis 45:16, "Joseph's brothers *have come*" (i.e., arrived in person). It is the opposite of *halak*, "to go, go away, leave in person," as in Genesis 16:8 when the angel said to Hagar, "From whence have you *come [ba'th]* and where *are you going [telekhi]*?" Compare I Samuel 20:21, 22. The thought in the verb is *the entrance in person* of "the Lord my God" into the earthly scene of sin and rebellion to deliver His people and establish His righteous rule in the affairs of men in the coming age. This is the quintessential element in the common Old Testament concept of "the day of the Lord" and the reason for the emphatic variant terminology of verse 1, **Lo, a day comes – the Lord's!**

Let those who disbelieve the wonders of this chapter, either by flatly denying their possibility or mysticalizing away their full literal sweep, realize they are dealing with an era that is pre-eminently the time when the Lord Himself, "whom the heavens must receive until the times of restitution of all things, which God hath spoken by the mouth of all his holy prophets since the world began" (Acts 3:21), openly and actively *arrives in person* to perform all the miracles which are a necessary prelude to that "restitution" (*opakatastaseos*). This word occurs only in Acts 1:6 and Acts 3:21, and refers to Israel's restoration to Palestine under a theocracy with Messiah-King-Priest reigning. This is the theme of Zechariah throughout his prophecy, as well as of the other prophets, Isaiah, Jeremiah, Ezekiel, Joel, etc. It is this that the majority of commentators

fail to believe, even resolutely refuse to believe, and scorn those who do believe it.

This passage then deals with the *revelation* of the Messiah in His second advent. It is the grand theme of the book of the Revelation, from chapter 4 to the climactic second-advent passage, Revelation 19:11–16. Zechariah has already given a terse and eloquent resumé of this same scene in 2:13 [17]: "Be silent, all flesh, before the Lord, because he is aroused out of his holy habitation." Now he gives other aspects and details.

The glorious revelation of Messiah is accompanied by the manifestation of others in power and glory with Him. **The Lord my God shall come and all the holy ones with thee!** The term **holy ones** in this context certainly includes angels, but is not restricted to them, as Keil, Von Orelli, Chambers, H. G. Mitchell, (*International Critical Commentary*, p. 344), Leupold, Wright, Henderson, etc., maintain, for the following reasons: (1) In the Old Testament *qedoshim* ("separated ones, those set apart" for holy work, "saints") *is a word employed both of the angels* (Deut. 33:3; Ps. 89:5–7 [6–8]; Job 15:15) *and holy men* (Ps. 16:3; 34:9 [10]; Lev. 11:44, 45; 19:2; 20:26; Num. 15:40; 16:3; Dan. 8:24; II Chron. 35:3). For example, Aaron is called "a saint of the Lord" (Ps. 106:16). Daniel employs the equivalent Aramaic term *qaddish* (intensive of the same root, *qedesh*, "consecrate") to refer to "holy men" (Dan. 7:18, 21, 22, 25, 27), that is, righteous Israelites of the end-time remnant who shall "possess the kingdom." (2) *The New Testament reveals that Christ in His coming again to the earth will be accompanied by an innumerable company both of angels and glorified saints of the church period.* I Thessalonians 3:13 speaks of "the coming of our Lord with all his saints." Jude speaks of the coming of the Lord "with myriads of his saints" (Jude 1:14). (3) *New Testament saints (hagioi) are promised resurrection and*

6 And it shall come to pass in that day, **that** the light shall not be clear, **nor dark:**
7 But it shall be one day which shall be known to the Lord, not day, nor night: but it shall come to pass, **that** at evening time it shall be light.

---

6   And it shall come to pass in that day, that there shall not be light; the bright ones shall withdraw themselves;
7   but it shall be one day which is known unto Jehovah; not day, and not night; but it shall come to pass, that at evening time there shall be light.

---

glorification before Christ's advent in glory. "When Christ, who is our life, shall appear, then shall ye also appear *with him* in glory" (Col. 4:4). Compare II Thessalonians 1:10, I John 3:2. The bride of Christ will be united to Christ in glory (Rev. 19:7-9) before He returns to the earth in triumph (Rev. 19:11-16) and will form part of "the armies in heaven" which follow in the train of the returning triumphant Messiah (Rev. 19:14). These celestial armies "clothed in fine linen white and clean" connect them, in part at least, with the bride, the Lamb's wife, whose garments "of fine linen, clean and white" are said to be *"the righteousness of saints"* (Rev. 19:8). That angels will also be in the retinue of the returning King is also plain from Scripture (Matt. 16:27; 25:31; Mark 8:38; Luke 9:26, etc.), but unfallen angels will not be attired in fine linen. This is reserved for redeemed and glorified sinners.

The prophet in declaring the resplendent prophecy of the second advent of Messiah is so lifted up by the mighty spectacle of the revelation of the Lord with His holy angels and saints that he cries out, **The Lord my God** [not "thy God," as Marti emends, *Das Dodekapropheton,* p. 451] **shall come and all the saints with thee.** Despite the fact that many manuscripts and all the old versions read "with him," *'immo,* instead of *'immakh,* "with thee," the latter is to be preferred, as Chambers (*op. cit.,* p. 109) correctly notes "both as the more difficult reading and as more vivid and expressive." The first personal pronoun suffix on God — **my God** and the lively enallage of the second

masculine suffix with **thee** indicate the enthusiastic joy with which the enraptured prophet hails the appearance of the delivering Messiah. To demonstrate his ecstasy the seer passes from indirect to direct address, a phenomenon often met with in animated Hebrew style.

5. *The Time of the Second Advent More Fully Described* (Zech. 14:6, 7). **And it shall be in that day that there shall not be the light of the luminaries but thick murkiness. (7) Indeed it shall be a unique day — it will be understood only by the Lord — neither day nor night. However, it shall be that at evening time there shall be light.** The subject of verses 6 and 7 is the same as that of verses 1-5 of Zechariah 14; namely, **the day, the Lord's** (vs. 1), that is, "the day of the Lord par excellence," that concentrated part of it in which Messiah's advent occurs, **when his feet shall stand . . . upon the Mount of Olives** (vs. 4) and when **the Lord my God shall come and all the saints with thee** (vs. 5). This great age-altering event which constitutes the dominant occurrence and quintessence of "the day of the Lord," is elsewhere described by celestial portents and physical phenomena, as it is here.

Isaiah prophesies of this day in the following language: "Behold, the day of the Lord comes! It is pitiless, accompanied with wrath and fierce anger, to make the earth a desolation and to destroy its sinners out of it. *For the stars of heaven and its constellations shall not give their light;* the sun shall be dark and its rising and the moon shall not send out its light" (Isa. 13:9, 10, Berkeley). *"Then shall the moon blush, and the sun shall be ashamed;* for the Lord of hosts shall be king on Mount Zion, and in Jerusalem His glory shall be before His elders" (Isa. 24:23, Berkeley).

Joel describing the same period predicts: "... for the day of the Lord is in the valley of decision; *the sun and the moon are darkened, and the stars withdraw their shining.* For the Lord roars from Zion, and from Jerusalem he utters his voice. *The heavens and the earth are shaken;* but the Lord is a refuge for his people and a stronghold for the sons of Israel" (Joel 3:14–16 [4:14–16]).

Our Savior Himself said, "Right after the affliction of those days, *the sun shall be darkened and the moon shall not shed her light; and the stars shall fall from the sky and the forces of heaven shall be shaken. Then shall the sign of the Son of man be shown in the sky* ..." (Matt. 24:29, 30; cf. Mark 13:24, 25; Rev. 6:13; 8:12).

Zechariah sees the day as characterized by the absence of the normal light from the sun, which shall be supernaturally darkened. **And it shall be in that day there shall be no light.** But since this day is not a twenty-four-hour day, but *a prophetic interval of time* embracing the final trouble and deliverance of Israel, leading to her establishment in kingdom blessing, the absence of light affects the night also inasmuch as the sidereal disturbance is world-wide and night would prevail in some parts of the globe. Therefore the *failure of all heavenly luminaries,* as other prophetic passages teach, is in question. Thus the prosaic statement of the *result* of this celestial upheaval, ... **there shall be no light** is followed in the *kethiv* of the Masoretic Text by a poetical statement of its cause; namely, **the bright ones shall wane,** *yeqaroth yigpa'un,* "shall thicken, condense, congeal, contract" (Exod. 15: 8; Zeph. 1:12; Job 10:10), meaning that the celestial luminaries shall cease to function normally.

The bright ones, *yeqaroth,* are lit-

erally, "the *glorious* or *splendid* ones," feminine plural substantive from the adjective *yaqar,* "costly, precious, rare, splendid, glorious." Job applies the word *poetically* to the moon. "If I looked at the sun [Hebrew *'or light*] when it shone or the moon walking *in splendor*" (adverbial accusative of manner). But it is better grammatically to construe *yaqar* as an appositive. "If I looked ... on the moon, *a splendid one walking*" (Job 31:26). Thus with all propriety the word **splendid ones,** *yeqaroth,* may fitly be understood as a poetical term applied to the heavenly luminaries.

Although the *kethiv* reading, **shall wane,** *yiqpa'un,* is preferred by a number of conservative scholars (Chambers, Hengstenberg, Pusey, Baron, Keil, Feinberg) and makes tolerable sense, the *kere, weqippa'on,* is evidently the superior one, if the ancient versions (Septuagint, Syriac, Vulgate, Targum, Symmachus) are permitted a voice (since none of them takes the word as a verb) and if a large number of the best manuscripts (134 of Kennicotts, twenty-two more originally, nine of De Rossi's Spanish manuscripts, reckoned the best) are allowed to speak. Although the noun in the *keri* reading, *qippa'on,* unfortunately turns out to be a *hapax legomenon,* its meaning can be deduced from the verb of the *kethiv,* which gives its etymology to mean "congelation, density, thick murkiness." With this meaning and taking *'or yeqaroth* as a construct chain, the following translation is arrived at: **And it shall be in that day that there shall not be the light of the luminaries but thick murkiness.** This reading has the advantage of retaining the same practical meaning of the *kethiv,* but at the same time appears more defensible in the light of the evidence furnished by the ancient versions and manuscripts, since none of them construes *qippa'on* as a verb.

However, whether the textual or marginal reading is preferred, the sense and scope of the passage are the same—the day of the Lord will be characterized by supernatural celestial disturbances. These heavenly phenomena will make the day unparalleled in the annals of human history. Hence verse 7 proceeds to declare the uniqueness of the day of the Lord with further explanation of why this shall be so.

The uniqueness of the day of the Lord is expressed (1) *by declaration*. Indeed **it shall be a unique day** (*yom'ehadh*, "one peculiar day," "the only one of its kind," "solitary"). Compare Ezek. 7:5: "An evil, a *unique* evil, lo! is coming." Compare Zechariah 14:9 and Song of Solomon 6:9 for this use of the cardinal number.

The uniqueness of this day is also stressed (2) *by statement of its supernatural character*. **It will be known** [only] **to the Lord** and to no one else (whether astronomer or commoner). Better, it will be understood (only) **by the Lord**, common use of *lamedh* of personal agency with a passive verb *yiwwada'*, that is, only "perceived" or "comprehended" by Him (Gen. 41:21; Ps. 74.5) since it is uniquely the time of the manifestations of His power and glory in fulfilment of His purposes, and will be inexplicable to uniformitarian science, being a catastrophic intrusion of divine power into the arena of a logical and law-operating universe.

Further the uniqueness of the day is explained (3) *by its physical nature*. It will be **neither day nor night**. It shall not be day for the natural sources of light will fail, nor can it be night, "for there will be the transplendent light of the glory of the Lord, and the myriads of His holy angels, and the glorified saints reflected on the earth," as Baron notes (*op. cit.*, p. 501). For the same reasons it cannot be the admixture of day and night, nor yet twilight. As Jeremiah cried, "Alas! for that day is great, *so that none is like it . . .*" (Jer. 30:7). It will be utterly distinct and completely different from any day in the history of the world.

The uniqueness of the day is also defined (4) *by its eventual blissful outcome*. **And it shall be at the time of evening there shall be light.** The passage opened with the statement **there shall not be light.** Now it closes with, **at evening time, there shall be light.** Since the day is not a twenty-four-hour interval, but "the day of the Lord," the phrase **at the time of evening** can only mean the concluding part of this period centering in the second advent of the Messiah. But contrary to a normal day which ends in evening and darkness, this day characterized by preternatural murkiness, shall conclude with light. This can only mean, according to the scope of the passage, that the heavenly luminaries which have withdrawn their light shall not only be restored, but with increased splendor in the new order of nature that will be instituted, resulting in the partial restoration of Edenic conditions that prevailed before man's fall.

Isaiah prophesies just such a time of sidereal, atmospheric, and certainly climactic changes. "The light of the moon shall be as the light of the sun, and the light of the sun shall be sevenfold, as the light of seven days, *in the day that the Lord binds up the hurt of his people and heals the stroke of their wound*" (Isa. 30:26). The Apostle Paul also speaks of creation's deliverance from the vanity to which it has been subject because of man's fall (Rom. 8:19-22; cf. Gen. 3:17-19).

Reflected, however, in these literal physical phenomena will be the spiritual renovation of the godly converted remnant of Israel (Zech. 12:10-14), spared to see the glorious "Sun of Righteousness" who shall "arise with healing in his beams" (Mal. 4:2). To them and to all who are spared through the appalling judgments of the day of the Lord **at evening time there shall be light.** This light will be the glory of God revealed in the face of Jesus Christ at His second advent. He, as the light of the world, appearing at evening time, shall usher in the glad new order of things in the millennial earth. His own, like Thomas, will cry out, "My Lord and my God!" and become like the Apostle Paul, who was one to whom the risen Christ appeared "as to one untimely born" (I Cor. 15:8), mighty messengers of God's redeeming grace in the coming age.

What a nightmare of judgment faces this godless world—both Jew and Gentile! What deliverance and glory will be brought by Him who is earth's only rightful "King of kings and Lord of lords" (Rev. 19:16). Not until He comes as such, and is received as such, will earth's woes be alleviated and earth's sorrows healed. His splendid advent involves Israel's destiny and the world's only hope for righteousness and true peace.

Modern criticism by specious though arbitrary and fallacious emendations of verses 6, 7 completely misunderstands it and mistakenly refers it to the subsequent context of the "new era" established, rather than to the interim phase of judgment prerequisite to the new order; i.e., "the day of the Lord" par excellence, which is the subject of 14:1–7 (cf. H. G. Mitchell, J. Powis Smith, Julius Bewer in *International Critical Commentary,* "*Zechariah,*" pp. 346–347). Rejecting the Masoretic reading the heavenly luminaries shall wane, *yeqaroth yiqpa'un,* Mitchell emends to *qaruth weqippa'on,* "cold and frost," following the Septuagint, Vulgate, Syriac, Targum, and Symmachus. But this reading is obviously wrong, not squaring with the remainder of the verse, so the clause "it is known to the Lord," is arbitrarily rejected as a gloss upon the assumption that "the incongruousness of these words is proof that they are an interpolation" (Mitchell, Smith, Bewer, *in loc.*). But the "incongruousness" of these words is due solely to rejection of the correct reading in favor of one which is patently wrong, though attested to in this case by various versions.

THE ESTABLISHMENT
OF ISRAEL'S KINGDOM

THE SECOND SECTION OF THE SECOND PROPHETIC ORACLE

(ZECH. 14:8-21)

WITH this section of the second prophetic oracle the prophecy of Zechariah draws to a climactic close in the realization of the grand finale of Israel's hope for the future – the establishment of the long-promised and long-awaited kingdom of Messiah, to be ushered in by the personal return to the earth of the King. The oracle as a whole works up to this magnificent conclusion. As a prerequisite to this prophetic denouement, the future deliverance and national conversion of the nation have been portrayed in glowing language (Zech. 12:1–13:8), as well as the appearance in glory of King-Messiah (14:1–7). At last the stage is set for the final scene of full kingdom blessing.

I. THE MESSIANIC KINGDOM ESTAB-
LISHED OVER ISRAEL (Zech. 14: 8-15)

As noted in the preceding chapter, modern textual emendation of the preceding verses (Zech. 14:6, 7) distorts their meaning and erroneously places them in this present section describing the new order, rather than in the preceding context dealing with the events preparatory to the new order involved in the cataclysmic aspect of the day of the Lord, called **a day, the Lord's** (Zech. 14:1) accentuating its quintessential phase manifested in the personal second advent of Messiah (Zech. 14:1–7).

Although the term **in that day** continues to occur in this millennial section (vss. 9, 13, 20, 21), as it has occurred over and over again in chapters 12 and 13 to describe the active interposition of the Lord in human affairs in the woes and judgments necessary to the setting up of the kingdom over Israel, nevertheless the events of "the day of the Lord" par excellence are related in Zechariah 14:1–7, and that is the reason the expression is unique in Zechariah 14:1.

Moreover, Zechariah's use of the expression **in that day**, which is tantamount to the term "the day of

8 And it shall be in that day, that living waters shall go out from Jerusalem; half of them toward the former sea, and half of them toward the hinder sea: in summer and in winter shall it be.

8 And it shall come to pass in that day, that living waters shall go out from Jerusalem; half of them toward the eastern sea, and half of them toward the western sea: in summer and in winter shall it be.

the Lord," and which is in agreement with its widespread usage in the former prophets, enables a clear definition of the eschatological concept. "The day of the Lord," accordingly, is *that prophetic period embracing the final phase of Israel's chastisement and trouble, followed by her salvation and deliverance at the second advent of Messiah (the quintessential phase) and extending throughout the subsequent period of kingdom peace and prosperity, commonly called the millennium.*

1. *The Temporal and Spiritual Blessings of the Kingdom* (Zech. 14:8). **And it shall be in that day that living waters shall issue from Jerusalem; half of them toward the eastern sea and half of them toward the western sea. In summer and in winter it shall be.** These **waters** will be *literal* waters although they reflect and imply spiritual blessings. To phantomize or mysticalize them is just as arbitrary and destructive of the real meaning of the passage as to phantomize or mysticalize the capture and deliverance of Jerusalem (vss. 1–3), or the second advent of Messiah, or the earthquake and the topographical changes accompanying it (vss. 4–7).

It is not, however, inconsistent with a *literal* interpretation of such a prophecy to see a *spiritual* meaning behind it, inasmuch as the physical reality presupposes and is based upon the revelation of the Lord, which affects both *land* and *people*, as throughout the great prophecies of Israel's future kingdom status. Compare Isaiah 4:3, 4 with 4:5, 6; Isaiah 35:2–6 with 35:1, 7–10. Compare Ezekiel 36:16–37:28 (restoration of the people) with Ezekiel 36:1–15 (restoration of the land). Jerusalem as the capital of the millennial earth

will be the radiating center of spiritual blessings reflected by the literal physical and climatic transformation of Palestine.

Living waters (*mayim hayyim*) are waters that are in the act of "living" (participle), that is, *manifesting signs of life* by moving in fresh fulness, as in a running brook or river, or gurgling from a perennial spring, or rising up in a well (Song of Sol. 4:15; John 4:10, 11; 7:38). Accordingly, the Lord cries out through Jeremiah, "My people have committed two evils; they have forsaken me, the *fountain of living waters*, and they have hewn out for themselves cisterns, broken cisterns, which cannot hold water" (Jer. 2:13; cf. 17:13). This verse contains a perfect illustration of the difference between mere "water" caught from rain and stored in a lime-calked tank or cistern, a common necessity in the hill country of Palestine, and **living water** gushing from a perennial spring, cold, fresh, and exhilarating to the taste, depicting the true blessings which come from God, in contrast with paltry flat substitutes offered by sin.

Jerusalem and Judah have always lacked what an oriental paradise must have, namely, a copious supply of fresh water. Thus "a river went out of Eden to water the garden" (Gen. 2:10–14). Compare Paradise Restored (Rev. 22:1). Ezekiel graphically describes millennial Palestine as having a life-giving stream, issuing from under the threshold of the sanctuary, flowing eastward with increasing depth, dispensing fertility to the entire desert region (Ezek. 47:1–12).

Joel, likewise, had foretold such a physical transformation of the land. "And it shall come to pass in that day,

9 And the Lord shall be king over all the earth: in that day shall there be one Lord, and his name one.

9   And Jehovah shall be King over all the earth: in that day shall Jehovah be one, and his name one.

that the mountains shall drip sweet wine, and the hills shall flow with milk, *and all the brooks of Judah shall flow full of water, and a fountain shall send forth its waters from the house of the Lord,* and irrigate the valley of Acacias" (Joel 3:18 [4:18], Berkeley).

The psalmist, inspired by the Spirit of prophecy, foresaw this same scene: "There is a river whose streams make glad the city of God, the holy dwelling of the most High" (Ps. 46:4 [5]). Like Zechariah, he too envisioned the mammoth earthquake and other world-engirdling convulsions immediately preceding and accompanying the personal return of Messiah, which will eventuate in the elevation of Jerusalem and the lowering of the whole surrounding country to a plain, so that living water shall flow from the city:

God is for us a refuge and a fortress;
found to be a mighty help in troubles.
Therefore we do not fear *though the earth is displaced,*
though the mountains reel into the midst of the sea;
though its waters roar and foam;
though the mountains shake at its swelling.
(Ps. 46:1-3 [2-4], Berkeley).

Half of the waters issuing from Jerusalem as the result of the earthquake opening up vast subterranean springs will flow toward the eastern sea (the Dead or Salt Sea) and half toward the western sea (Mediterranean). **In summer and winter shall it be.** This passage indicates that the streams shall be abundant and perennial, not drying up as most Palestinian watercourses do in summer. The two-directional flow of these streams will be possible because the elevated city will be on a water-shed plateau.

The Dead Sea is called **the eastern** or "*former sea*" (*hayyam haqqadhmoni,* an adjective from the root *qadem,* "to be in front, to be before one," cf.

Arabic *qadama,* "precede," Assyrian *qudmu,* "front"), since the Oriental faced the east in calculating directions of the compass. The body of water "in front of" him would thus be "the eastern sea" (Ezek. 47:18; Joel 2:20). Accordingly, the Mediterranean sea, which would be behind the observer looking eastward, is called "the rear" or **hinder sea** (*hayyam ha'aharon,* from the root *'aher,* "coming after or behind") i.e., **the western sea** (Deut. 11:24; 34:2; Joel 2:20; Job 18:20). So the Assyrians designated "the western land" of Phoenicia and Palestine, *mat aharru* ("the hinder country").

2. *The Absolute Lordship of the King* (Zech. 14:9). **And the Lord will become King over all the earth. In that day the Lord shall be one and his name one.** The Hebrew word for **earth** (*'arets*) here, as elsewhere, may be translated "earth" or "land" (Palestine). However, it should be translated **earth** in this case, despite the fact that contextually it appears to be limited to the land of Palestine (cf. vss. 1–8 and especially verse 10 where the identical expression, *kol ha'arets,* denotes a part of Palestine) for the following reasons: (1) *The translation "land,"* while certainly in line with the context outside of verse 9 (i.e., vss. 1–8 and 10), *is not consonant with the larger context of the verse itself.* That **the Lord will be one and his name one** only in Palestine is unthinkable. The scope of verse 9 demands the larger meaning of the Hebrew word "earth," and strikes the note of universality in its wording and thought pattern. (2) If the prophet wished to say **earth** instead of land, there is no other way he could have done so in this context, for only one Hebrew word expresses both concepts. Moreover, (3) *the idiom "to become"*

(hayah plus *lamedh), points to the larger meaning* **earth. In that day the Lord will become King,** not be "for King" (Leupold, *op. cit.,* p. 267) or "be king" (R.V.). Although the King establishes the kingdom with its capital in Jerusalem, by means of Messiah's rule (Ps. 2:9–12) and the zealous missionary effort of the converted nation (Zech. 8:23; Ezek. 37:28), Messiah's rule and dominion, as well as the knowledge of the absolute uniqueness of Messiah and His name, will be gradually extended to the ends of the earth. (4) *The larger context of this very chapter calls for the translation of* **earth** *rather than* "land." **And it shall come to pass, that everyone that is left of all the nations which came against Jerusalem shall even go up from year to year to worship the King, the Lord of armies...** (Zech. 14:16).

Moreover, (5) *the larger context of prophecy with which Zechariah 14:9 dovetails requires the concept of* **earth** *rather than* "land." Passages could be multiplied *ad infinitum,* but compare Psalms 2:5, 6; 72:8–11; Isaiah 2:4; 54:5; Zechariah 9:9–10, and particularly Zechariah's extremely significant use of the millennial epithet "the Lord of the whole earth" (see comments on Zech. 4:4; 6:5; cf. Mic. 4:13). Messiah's second advent as "King of kings and Lord of lords" (Rev. 19:16) gives the clue to His universal dominion in Zechariah 14:9, since His same glorious coming is featured in this chapter (Zech. 14:4, 6).

Objections to the concept of **earth** in Zechariah 14:9 instead of "land" (6) *on the basis of arguments that phantomize or mysticalize these great prophecies* have little weight for those who see them in the larger framework of prophetic teaching *concerning Israel.* In this phantomizing category is Chambers' contention that "Canaan here stands as a type of the kingdom of God in its fullest extent in the world" (*Zechariah* in Lange's *Commentary,* p. 111). In the same class is Leupold's insistence on "land" in-

stead of **earth** on the ground that "this picture is painted in terms of the Holy Land," or "the fact" that the Lord "is King over all has always been true" (*loc. cit.*).

Such a declaration as that of Leupold ignores the Scripture revelation concerning the full results of man's fall and the resultant Satanic usurpation of the dominion of the earth and the purpose of the Creator's incarnation not only to redeem man from sin, but *the earth from Satanic sway.* This is the whole scope of the book of the Revelation (4:1–19:16), and the teaching of the Apostle (Eph. 1:14; Rom. 8:18–22), as well as the inspired prophets of the Old Testament (Ps. 2:1–2; Mic. 4:1–13, etc.).

In that day the Lord shall be one (*'ehadh).* The Hebrew term denotes *one only* of its kind, *solitary,* altogether *unique,* Arabic *wahidun,* "only one, incomparable" (cf. Job 23:13; Ezek. 37:17; Song 6:9; Zech. 14:7). This does not mean that the Lord (Yahweh) will be at some future time something He was not always been in Himself and in His divine essence in the past or present. But it does mean *He will be known and adored as the one only Lord,* the absolutely unique and incomparable One, the only wise God and Savior, the Word who was with God and who became flesh (human), that which He always was in the redemptive plan of God and which He became in the incarnation.

As the **one only Lord,** He will be universally owned as such in the kingdom age, and worshipped as the one true God. Never has this been true since idolatry and polytheism have enslaved men from earliest antiquity. It is distinctively not true of the present age of the church, and those who phantomize these prophecies by applying them to the Christian church or the eternal state find this prophecy quite ill-fitting in their scheme and totally meaningless. *Now* there are "gods many and lords many." *Then* alone shall God be worshipped. Monotheism shall be world-wide. Judaism

10 All the land shall be turned as a plain from Geba to Rimmon south of Jerusalem: and it shall be lifted up, and inhabited in her place, from Benjamin's gate unto the place of the first gate, unto the corner gate, and from the tower of Hananeel unto the king's winepresses.
11 And men shall dwell in it, and there shall be no more utter destruction; but Jerusalem shall be safely inhabited.

10   All the land shall be made like the Arabah, from Geba to Rimmon south of Jerusalem; and she shall be lifted up, and shall dwell in her place, from Benjamin's gate unto the place of the first gate, unto the corner gate, and from the tower of Hananel unto the king's winepresses.
11   And men shall dwell therein, and there shall be no more curse; but Jerusalem shall dwell safely.

(rejecting Christ), Islam (giving Him no proper place), and the great ethnic faiths like Buddhism, Taoism, Hinduism, etc., which flourish over vast sections of the earth today, shall vanish. Monotheism will be universal, and the one true God manifested in Christ, will be the sole object of faith, worship, and service.

Not only will the Lord . . . be one (the one only object of faith and worship) with the Jewish Shema (Deut. 6:4) the sole creed, but His name (the revelation of Himself as Jesus, the Christ, the Lord and Savior, King and Redeemer) will be one only. Jesus the Messiah will be the only name known and revered in that glad day of Israel's restoration and ministry to the nations. For the Lord Himself has already declared, "On that day . . . I will cut off the names of the idols from the land, so that they shall be remembered no more; and also I will remove from the land the prophets and the unclean spirit" (Zech. 13:2).

This interesting passage from Zechariah (13:2) is the one Scripture passage that indicates the imprisonment of demons (who are the dynamic of idolatry, I Cor. 10:20) during the kingdom age, although Revelation 20:1-3 clearly teaches that Satan will be incarcerated during this period. Zechariah 14:9 can only be realized (1) by the revelation of the one only Lord and King in His second advent and kingdom reign and (2) by the removal of Satan and demons as the abetters of idolatry and the promoters of false religions (cf. I Tim. 4:1-5; I John 4:1-6; James. 3:15).

3. The Exaltation and Peace of Jerusalem (Zech. 14:10, 11). All the land shall be transformed as the Arabah from Geba to Rimmon south of Jerusalem; and she [Jerusalem] shall be elevated and shall be inhabited in her place, from Benjamin's Gate unto the Corner Gate, and from the Tower of Hananel unto the king's winepresses. (11) And people shall dwell in her, and there shall be no more wholesale destruction, for Jerusalem shall be inhabited in perfect safety.

Zechariah has already given us the cause of this vast topographical change in which the city of Jerusalem is to be exalted above the hills by which she has always been surrounded and overshadowed; namely, the resplendent second advent of Messiah attended by a mammoth earthquake that shall make the entire rugged terrain from Geba to Rimmon "a very great valley" (14:4). The purpose of this vast transformation of the geography of the central highland region of the tribes of Benjamin and Judah is to give Jerusalem, which will be "the city of the great King" (Ps. 48:2 [3]) in the kingdom age, the eminent situation it will warrant as the capital and chief metropolis of the millennial earth, from which Messiah's dominion and rule will issue forth to the utmost bounds of the globe in the coming age.

The land is said to be turned about

[*yissov*] **as the Arabah.** The verb is *nifal* (passive, rather than *qal*) and from the root *savav*, "to turn about," and hence means "to be turned about," that is, "to be changed or transformed so as to become" (a pregnant construction) "like" or "as" the Arabah. The R.S.V. has "turned *into a plain*," but "as" or "like the Arabah" is a simile, and the noun is definite with the article *ka'arabhah* and means **as the Arabah** (not "as *a plain*," A.V.).

The Arabah is the geographical name of the deep rift that extends from the Sea of Galilee and the Jordan Valley through the Dead Sea and on to the Gulf of Aqaba. It is remarkable in that *it is the deepest depression on the surface of the earth*. At the Sea of Galilee it is 652 feet below sea level, at the Dead Sea almost 1300 feet below, and only 300 feet above sea level at a point just west of Petra in Edom (see Denis Baly, *The Geography of the Bible*, New York, 1956, pp. 210–216).

But there is another element that prompted Zechariah to use the comparison "as the Arabah," beside *the depth of this terrain*, and that is *its level character*. Josephus twice speaks of the Ghor or Rift from the Lake of Galilee to the Dead Sea as the "Great Plain" (*Wars* VIII, 2; *Antiquities* VI, 1). But the chief characteristic is its depression, the Greek writers calling it the *Aulon* or Hollow (Diodorus Siculus II, 48, 9; XIX, 98, 4). Zechariah, then, employs the figure **as the Arabah** to stress the depression of the surrounding hills of Jerusalem and their being made level as a plain so that the city might be exalted (cf. Nelson Glueck, *The River Jordan*, p. 72).

The district, thus altered by tremendous earthquake action by being drastically depressed and levelled out, is precisely defined as extending **from Geba to Rimmon, south of Jerusalem.** This geographical note is intended to indicate the whole "hill country" of the ancient tribe of Judah to the

border of Simeon on the south and most of the tribe of Benjamin on the north, since Geba was in Benjamin (Josh. 18:24), about six miles northeast of Jerusalem (L. H. Grollenberg, *Atlas of the Bible*, maps 11, 13, and page 161), and is mentioned in II Kings 23:8 as one of the border towns of Judah.

Rimmon is En-Rimmon (Josh. 15:32; 19:7; I Chron. 4:32), 33 miles southwest of Jerusalem, a few miles south of ancient Ziklag, where the central highland ridge of Judah falls off to the lower-levelled country of the Negeb. En-Rimmon was one of the places reoccupied by the Jews on their return from exile (Neh. 11:29), and so was an inhabited site in Zechariah's day.

The words **Rimmon south of Jerusalem** are appended to distinguish the south Judean border town from a Rimmon in Galilee (Josh. 19:13) and from the Rock Rimmon in the hill range of Benjamin (Judg. 20:45–47). The name **Rimmon** meaning "pomegranate," was thus used of several places.

The purpose of the levelling and the lowering of the entire hill country of Judah is that Jerusalem may enjoy an eminent position, unobstructed by higher heights about her, as has always been the case of the city, with higher hills adjacent. **And she** [Jerusalem] **shall be elevated,** *wera'amah*, an anomalous third person feminine singular *qal*, from *wera'mah* for *weramah* from *rum*, "be high, be exalted" (Deut. 8:14; Isa. 6:1; Ezek. 10:16). Hosea 10:14 is a parallel verse which contains an *aleph* inserted as a *matres lectionis*, or aid to reading.

And shall be peacefully inhabited, *weyashevah* from *yashav*, "remain, dwell," Akkadian *ashabu*, "sit, inhabit," here used of a city in the sense of being "seated in its place" and so figuratively for "be [peacefully] inbabited" (Jer. 17:6, 25; 50:13, 39; Ezek. 26:20; 29:11; Isa. 13:20; Zech. 2:8; 9:5; 12:6; 14:11). **In her** [Jerusalem's] **place** is literally "in her underparts," i.e., "upon that which is under her" (*taḥteha*, on her *ancient historical location*, in contrast to some new site). The city's location will remain the same, but the country around her will be transformed to accommodate the new religious and governmental capital of the millennial earth.

In this bold prediction Zechariah, as is his custom in his *entire* prophetic book, echoes, summarizes, abbreviates, or amplifies the predictions of the former prophets, and notably so in this case. Isaiah had glowingly predicted the same great fact. "And it shall come to pass in the last days that the mountain of the Lord's house shall be established in the top of the mountains, and shall be exalted above the hills, and all nations shall flow into it" (Isa. 2:2). Compare also Micah 4:1 and Isaiah 2:3.

In the case of the topographical details and the description of the cause (the second advent of Messiah and the accompanying earthquake), Zechariah gives important supplementary material not found in the former prophets. However, like them, his prophecies are to be taken in a literal sense, but the literal furnishes the vehicle for the emblematic. These prophecies state physical facts, but also portray spiritual truths. Jerusalem will be the radiating center for the outflow of spiritual blessing and instruction to the entire earth of the kingdom age.

The future enlargement and expansion of restored Jerusalem are indicated in the latter part of verse 10. **But it [Jerusalem] shall be elevated and inhabited in her place from the Gate of Benjamin to the place of the Former Gate unto the Corner Gate, and from the Tower of Hananel unto the king's winepresses.**

The prophet in predicting the future size of the millennial city sees Jerusalem not in the paltry dimensions of the small town of his day, with a struggling remnant and its walls still in ruins, but in terms of the walled city as it had existed in the heyday of its strength in pre-exilic times. The **Gate of Benjamin** was in the north wall and is apparently identical with that called "the Gate of Ephraim" (II Kings 14:13), through which the road ran to Benjamin and thence on to Ephraim, situated to the north.

The "first" or **Former Gate** was apparently in the northeastern corner of the city, while the **Corner Gate** (II Kings 14:13; Jer. 31:38) was at the northwestern extremity. These measurements would then indicate the full dimensions of the city, east and west, on the north beginning at the **Gate of Benjamin**. The **Tower of Hananel** was evidently at the opposite extremity of the **Corner Gate** in the northeastern part of the northern wall (cf. Jer. 31:38). From it to **the king's winepresses,** which were located in the king's gardens south of the city, in or near the Valley of Hinnom, would then give the north-south limits of the city. The over-all measurements present an area of generous proportions adequate for the prophet's prediction of the future enlargement of the city, and the minute topographical details argue cogently for the literalness of the whole prophecy.

Appended to the forecast of the restored city is the prophecy of a restored population (vs. 11). **And they** [indefinite third masculine plural] **shall dwell in her.** The redeemed and restored people of Israel in kingdom status, are thus indicated indefinitely. Hebrew syntax, however, scarcely permits a passive construction. "And it [the city] shall be inhabited" (R.S.V.). The reason adduced is, **for there shall be no more curse** (R.S.V.). The Hebrew is **and a curse** [emphatic by word order] **shall be no more** (a circumstantial clause, which may well be rendered causally, as does the R.S.V.).

The **curse,** *ḥerem,* is a "ban of utter destruction" (I Kings 20:42; Isa. 34:5; 43:28; Mal. 3:24) from the root *ḥaram* in *hifil,* "ban, devote to

12 And this shall be the plague wherewith the Lord will smite all the people that have fought against Jerusalem; Their flesh shall consume away while they stand upon their feet, and their eyes shall consume away in their holes, and their tongue shall consume away in their mouth.

13 And it shall come to pass in that day, that a great tumult from the Lord shall be among them; and they shall lay hold every one on the hand of his neighbour, and his hand shall rise up against the hand of his neighbour.

14 And Judah also shall fight at Jerusalem; and the wealth of all the heathen round about shall be gathered together, gold, and silver, and apparel, in great abundance.

15 And so shall be the plague of the horse, of the mule, of the camel, and of the ass, and of all the beasts that shall be in these tents, as this plague.

---

12 And this shall be the plague wherewith Jehovah will smite all the peoples that have warred against Jerusalem: their flesh shall consume away while they stand upon their feet, and their eyes shall consume away in their sockets, and their tongue shall consume away in their mouth.

13 And it shall come to pass in that day, that a great tumult from Jehovah shall be among them; and they shall lay hold every one on the hand of his neighbor, and his hand shall rise up against the hand of his neighbor.

14 And Judah also shall fight at Jerusalem; and the wealth of all the nations round about shall be gathered together, gold, and silver, and apparel, in great abundance.

15 And so shall be the plague of the horse, of the mule, of the camel, and of the ass, and of all the beasts that shall be in those camps, as that plague.

---

destruction, exterminate" (Josh. 8:26; 10:28; I Sam. 15:18, 20; Jer. 50:26). When a city was placed under "a ban," it was devoted to complete destruction. The inhabitants were put to death and the spoil destroyed or not as the gravity of the situation demanded. Thus in the case of Jericho as an initial warning the ban was complete (Josh. 6:17, 21), and Achan transgressed in appropriating some of the booty. The ban was also complete in regard to the extermination of the Amalekites, Saul likewise sinned in sparing Agag and some of the spoil (I Sam. 15:3). The word occurs on the Mesha inscription, set up by Mesha king of Moab, about 850 B.C., "I devote it [the city of Nebo] to Ashtar-Chemosh" (line 17).

The reason there will be no more "ban of complete extermination" will be the peace and security of the Messianic reign. The rod-of-iron rule of the Messiah will not allow sin and wrong to flourish, all transgressors being dealt with in terrible severity. God's own will be so loyally devoted to Him that there will be no occasion for the Lord to say, "Therefore, I have profaned the princes of the sanctuary, and have given Jacob *to the curse* and Israel to reproaches" (Isa. 43:28).

If an individual or a city in Israel apostatized from the Lord and was lured away to devotion to other gods, they became "a curse" (ḥerem), abandoned to complete destruction (Deut. 7:25, 26; 13:12–17). When the Lord shall become King over all the earth and there shall be one Lord, the sole object of worship, and His name one, the name of no other god acknowledged, then there shall be no idolatry and no apostasy, and hence no more ban of complete destruction.

Jerusalem's millennial security is further described in the clause, And Jerusalem shall dwell safely (vs. 11). The oft-recurring personification of a city "dwelling" (i.e., "being inhabited," as in Zech. 2:8; 9:5) is here qualified by the phrase in safety, *labheṭaḥ* (Lev. 25:18, 19; Judg. 18:7; I Kings 5:5; Isa. 47:8; Ezek. 38:8; 39:6). The noun safety, "security," *beṭaḥ*, is from the root *baṭaḥ*, "to trust," and has the notion of quiet undisturbed confidence and repose, giving a sense of security. Zechariah employs the phrase in its eschatological connotation, describing the peace and safety that shall characterize Israel and Jerusalem in the kingdom age. Thus Jeremiah describes the final regathering of God's people to Palestine, where the Lord "will cause them to dwell *safely*" (Jer. 23:6; 32:37; 33:16) and likewise Ezekiel (Ezek. 28:25, 26; 34:25, 28; 38:8, 11, 14; 39:6, 26). Although the expression is also employed of sinners and enemies of God dwelling in *false* security (Judg. 18:7; Isa. 47:8; Jer. 49:31), it is *never* so employed of Israel eschatologically, when the nation will be regathered and restored to God's favor.

4. *The Destruction of Jerusalem's Enemies* (Zech. 14:12-15). **And this shall be the plague with which the Lord shall plague all the peoples who shall go forth in battle against Jerusalem. Their flesh shall rot away while they are standing on their feet, and their eyes shall be consumed [rot] in their sockets, and their tongues shall rot away in their mouth. (13) And it shall be in that day there shall be a great panic from the Lord among them; so that each one shall grab another's hand and one's hand shall rise up against the hand of his neighbor. (14) And Judah also shall fight at Jerusalem. And the wealth of all the nations round about shall be gathered together, gold and silver apparel in profusion. (15) And the same plague shall be on the horse, on the mule, on the camel, and on the ass, and on the beasts that shall be in those camps — the very same plague.**

Three divinely ordered weapons are described in these verses as unleashed against the last-day enemies of the godly remnant to destroy them utterly just prior to Jerusalem's establishment in millennial glory as the religious and governmental capital of the millennial earth: (1) a deadly plague (vs. 12), (2) a frightful con-

sternation producing mutual annihilation (vs. 13), and (3) the superhuman valor of the remnant of Judah, who shall also fight at Jerusalem (vs. 14).

Chronologically these verses 12-15 follow chapter 14:1-3, which verses in turn are an amplification and a supplement to the same subject discussed by the prophet in chapter 12:4-10. The reason the detailed description of the judgments on Jerusalem's enemies is for the moment passed over is that the prophet did not wish to interrupt the sequence of events setting forth the grand deliverance of God's people and the wonderful transformation of Jerusalem and Judah. But having fully and graphically set forth these dramatic results of the second advent of Messiah (14:4, 5), Zechariah now proceeds with the details of the destruction of Israel's enemies, which are as terrible as the deliverance and exaltation of Jerusalem and God's people are glorious.

And this shall be the plague with which the Lord shall plague all the peoples . . . (the same root *nagaph*, "strike, smite" being used in both the noun and the verb). The noun *maggephah* denotes a "blow" or fatal "stroke" (Ezek. 24:16), that is, a divinely sent "plague" (Exod. 9:14), or "pestilence," as the tumors visited on the Philistines (I Sam. 6:4) or as a divine stroke against the Lord's chastened people (Num. 14:37; 16:48, 49 [17:13, 14]; 25:8, 9; 31:16; II Sam. 24:21; I Chron. 21:22; Ps. 106:29, 30). The word is used also of "slaughter" in battle, with the idea implicit that it was at least by divine permission, if not by direct divine intervention (I Sam. 4:17; II Sam. 17:9; 18:7). Here the "stroke" is wholly supernatural with which the Lord strikes Jerusalem's last and cruelest enemies and invaders.

The **plague** is unparalleled in its severity and terribleness and fits into that end-time period of cataclysmic judgment when "the iniquity" of the nations in their virulent anti-Semitism is "full" (cf. Gen. 15:16) and "the seven last plagues" in which "is filled up the wrath of God" (Rev. 15:1) are poured out in the frightful bowl judgment of the Revelation (Rev. 16:1–21) and emptied upon the earth immediately before the advent of Messiah (Rev. 19:11–16).

The penalty for those who **will come against Jerusalem** (*tsave'u*, a prophetic or future perfect denoting the certainty of the fact, and not a past perfect, since the action is still future) is that the Lord **will make their flesh rot while they stand on their feet.** The stroke is like a horrible leprosy that spreads through the body with shocking rapidity (cf. Lev. 26:16; Deut. 28:21, 22), so that the flesh will rot or "decay" so quickly, that the victim will become a skeleton erect upon his feet, with his flesh a putrid mass about it.

This is a judgment so unparalleled and awful that it is said concerning the victim, **He** [the Lord] **will cause his flesh to rot** (*hameq* being an infinitive absolute employed in lively dramatic style to take the place of a finite verb). "The infinitive absolute is precisely adapted to portray the suddenness of the infliction described and the rapidity with which it will do its work" (Mitchell, in *Int. Crit. Commentary, in loc.*).

Although the *plural* **all the peoples who engage in military combat against Jerusalem** is the subject, the Hebrew original changes to the *singular*: **He** [the Lord] **will cause his flesh to rot while he is standing upon his feet and his eyes shall rot in their sockets and his tongue shall rot in his** [Masoretic Text incorrectly "their"] **mouth.**

This reversion from the plural to the singular is a device to show the thoroughness of the plague, as not only striking the peoples en masse and as a whole, but extending in its terror to each individual person in the aggregate. The word **rot**, *maqaq*, means "to fester" of wounds (Ps. 38:5 [6]; "rot, rot away, consume away" (Zech. 14:12), "pine or waste away" because

of punishment for iniquity (Ezek. 4:17; 24:23; 33:10; Lev. 26:39), "fade away," of the host of heaven (Isa. 34:4).

Never previously will humanity have experienced such a horrible visitation as in this instance of divine justice unloosed against the iniquity of man come to the full. The **tongue** is consumed because it had with wicked impudence blasphemed God. The **eye** is included because it had sought out God's people to exterminate them in one fell final blow.

Beside the deadly **plague** or "pestilence" (vs. 12), another divinely ordained weapon is unleashed against the end-time enemies of God's people; namely, a fearful commotion among those who attack Jerusalem, producing their mutual annihilation. This is called a **great consternation from the Lord.** The word **confusion**, *mehumah*, "tumult, disturbance" is from the root *hum*, "to roar" or "to discomfit," Arabic *hāma*, "to rush about wildly, to be distracted" (Deut. 7:23). The word is used of "tumult" and "confusion" in general (Amos 3:9; II Chron. 15:5), but especially of "tumultuous confusion" and "wild panic" among men, the result of divine judgment (I Sam. 5:9, 11; Ezek. 7:7) and "discomfiture" due to the Lord's interposition in battle in favor of His people (Deut. 7:23; 28:20; I Sam. 14:20; Isa. 22:5). The confusion is said to be **great**, *rabbah*, and **of the Lord,** a subjective genitive, better rendered **from the Lord,** that is, produced by Him "among them" (*bahem*, that is, "the enemy").

This tremendous tumult includes two features. Each attacker will first seize the other's hand with one hand to hold him powerless. Then he will lift his other hand to strike his neighbor, whose hand is also raised against him. Thus they will slaughter one another (cf. Zech. 12:4) in the wildest panic. Similar instances of God's confounding and destroying His people's foes by causing them to slaughter one another in a confused fight to the death at close quarters are found in Judges 7:22, in the case of Gideon's victorious three hundred, and Jonathan's great triumph over the Philistines at Michmash (I Sam. 14:14-16).

Despite the clear time indication, **in that day** of this **great consternation from the Lord**, Leupold (*op. cit.*, p. 271) insists that neither verse 12 nor verse 13 depict "a particular event which was to come to pass on a particular date, but by its specific picture rather portrayed a general principle." So far from such a statement being tenable, the expression **in that day** throughout the great section from chapter 12 through chapter 14 *always* signifies a very precise and definite period, namely, "the day of the Lord," denoting the time of the *direct* divine intervention in human affairs when God judges and removes sinners preparatory to His establishment of Israel in blessing upon the earth at the second advent of Messiah.

Besides the **plague** (vs. 12) and **the great confusion** (vs. 13), a third divinely ordained weapon is let loose against the latter-day attackers of the godly remnant in Jerusalem. This is the superhuman valor of the remnant of Judah, who shall also fight at Jerusalem (vs. 14). **And Judah also shall fight in Jerusalem** (not *against* Jerusalem, as in the Vulgate and Targum), not only defending themselves, but making a successful attack upon the attacking enemy. The expression "to fight against," *nilham be*, signifies to fight *in* or *at* such a place, as in Judges 5:19: "They fought *at* or *in* Taanach," *beta'anakh*, and in Exodus 17:8: "Then came Amalek and fought with Israel *at* Rephidim," *berephidim*.

The collection of the wealth of the invading armies will yield an immense quantity of booty for Israel in the form of gold, silver, and garments. This will come from the well-equipped contingents composing the invading military powers, who will be cast into utter confusion in order to be annihilated (II Chron. 20; II Kings 7:2-8).

Verse 15 describes how the entire encampment of the enemy, including the cavalry and the beasts of burden, will fall under the same "ban of utter destruction" (*herem*), and Jerusalem, it is said, will be forever delivered (cf. vs. 11). The Mosaic law provided that a city which had committed the crime of idolatry and incurred the penalty of the ban, was to be totally wiped out. Its human inhabitants, as well as the animals in it, were to be exterminated, as in the case of Jericho (Josh. 6:17, 18, 21). Achan who disobeyed the law of the ban, was himself visited with its terrible severity. His oxen and other animals were stoned and burned along with himself and his children (Josh. 7:24, 25), demonstrating the awfulness of falling under the curse of God, as those who attack Jerusalem in her final assault.

II. MILLENNIAL WORSHIP AND GOVERNMENT (Zech. 14:16-21)

As a result of the terrible judgments outlined in verses 12-15, the nations who survive will have learned righteousness (cf. Isa. 26:9) by turning in faith and obedience unto the Lord Jesus Christ as Savior and Universal Ruler. Then the Lord shall be king over all the earth; in that day shall there be one Lord, and his name one, as the prophet has already declared (Zech. 14:9). With Israel at last converted and reinstated in divine blessing as a high priestly nation (Zech. 3:1-10) and as the light of the world (Zech. 4:1-14), with Messiah King-Priest ruling in righteousness and peace in the midst of her (Zech. 6:9-15), the nations will then be mightily blessed as they willingly submit and serve the King, the Lord of hosts. This wider extension of God's salvation to the ends of the earth is the happy note with which the final section of the prophecy of Zechariah closes (14:16-21). But amidst the note of world-wide salvation runs the notice of Messiah's rod-of-iron rule

16 And it shall come to pass, that every one that is left of all the nations which came against Jerusalem shall even go up from year to year to worship the King, the Lord of hosts, and to keep the feast of tabernacles.

16 And it shall come to pass, that every one that is left of all the nations that came against Jerusalem shall go up from year to year to worship the King, Jehovah of hosts, and to keep the feast of tabernacles.

which will deal firmly and resolutely with all recalcitrants and sinners who might arise to attempt to destroy the righteousness and world-engirdling peace which will characterize the entire kingdom age (Isa. 11:1-9; Amos 9:11-15).

1. *Jerusalem the Religious Capital of the Millennial Earth* (Zech. 14:16). And it shall be that every one who is left as a survivor out of all the nations that shall come against Jerusalem shall go up annually to worship the King, the Lord of hosts, and to celebrate the Feast of Tabernacles.

Every one that is left [singular] ... **they shall go up** [plural]. Again, as often, Hebrew idiom singularizes the subject to stress the individual and pluralizes it to stress the totality (all the nations). The apparent meaning is that the nations shall come up *representatively, each one* who comes up does so as a delegate from his particular nation, so that the aggregate (all the nations) may be said to attend in the person of their representative.

The prophet also features **every one that is left** as an escaper (passive of *yathar*, "remain over," hence, "be left remaining" [Exod. 10:15; II Kings 20:17]), "be left over as a survivor *from*" (*min*, "*out of*") some calamity (I Sam. 25:34; II Sam. 9:1). This notation gives a hint how decimating and widespread will be the judgments and how wholesale will be the extermination of the wicked preceding the establishment of the kingdom.

The survivors are described as **out of the nations who will come** (*habba'im*, plural participle), "who will be coming" (not "who came"). The prophet is looking at them in *the act of coming* (participle in the future),

and not as already having come in the past or in the context (14:1-3; 12-15).

When shall these converted Gentiles come? **From year to year** (*middey shanah beshanah*, literally, "from the sufficiency of a year in a year," when time has fully completed one year and enters another, i.e., "annually"). What is the purpose of the trip? **To worship** [literally "to bow down to"] **the King, the Lord of hosts,** He who will be known and adored as *the one only Lord* (Yahweh), *the absolutely unique One,* whose name will be *the one only name* of Deity that will then exist (Zech. 14:9). How will these converted and worshipping Gentiles express their adoration of the Lord? They will **celebrate the Feast of Tabernacles.** This is the only one of the seven Jewish festivals (Lev. 23:4-44) which is represented in this prophecy as being observed in the kingdom age.

Many answers have been given why only the **Feast of Tabernacles** or Festival of Booths will be observed in the millennium. The answer is: *it is the only one of the seven feasts of the Lord which at that time will be unfulfilled* typically and the only one which will be in process of fulfilment by the kingdom itself. The Passover (Lev. 23:4, 5) was fulfilled in the death of Christ the Redeemer (I Cor. 5:7; I Peter 1:19). The Feast of Unleavened Bread (Lev. 23:6-8) is being fulfilled in the holy, separate walk of the believer in fellowship with his Savior (I Cor. 5:6-8; II Cor. 7:1; Gal. 5:7-9). The Feast of Firstfruits (Lev. 23:9-14) was fulfilled in the resurrection of Christ (I Cor. 15:23). The Feast of Pentecost (Lev. 23:15-22) was fulfilled in the formation of the Church at Pentecost fifty days

17 And it shall be, that whoso will not come up of all the families of the earth unto Jerusalem to worship the King, the Lord of hosts, even upon them shall be no rain.
18 And if the family of Egypt go not up, and come not, that have no rain; there shall be the plague, wherewith the Lord will smite the heathen that come not up to keep the feast of tabernacles.
19 This shall be the punishment of Egypt, and the punishment of all nations that come not up to keep the feast of tabernacles.

---

17   And it shall be, that whoso of all the families of the earth goeth not up unto Jerusalem to worship the King, Jehovah of hosts, upon them there shall be no rain.
18   And if the family of Egypt go not up, and come not, neither shall it be upon them; there shall be the plague wherewith Jehovah will smite the nations that go not up to keep the feast of tabernacles.
19   This shall be the punishment of Egypt, and the punishment of all the nations that go not up to keep the feast of tabernacles.

---

subsequent to the resurrection of Christ (I Cor. 10:16; 12:12, 13). The Feast of Trumpets (Lev. 23:23-25) will be fulfilled in the future regathering of Israel at the *beginning* of the kingdom (Isa. 18:3, 7; 27:12, 13; Ezek. 37:1-14). The Day of Atonement (Lev. 23:26-32) in its prophetic feature will be fulfilled in the conversion of Israel at the second advent (Zech. 12:10-13; 13:1) and preparatory to the millennium. *Only the Feast of Tabernacles at that time will be unfulfilled in its prophetic aspect as typical of the kingdom rest of Israel after her regathering, and the blessedness typified by that festival will be in process of fulfilment throughout the kingdom age.* Moreover, the joy and blessing foreshadowed in the celebration "will then not only be the portion of saved Israel," as Baron says (*op. cit.*, p. 521), "but shall also pervade all nations of the earth."

There is nothing in this present age to answer to the **Feast of Tabernacles.** It belongs in its anticipative or prophetic character to the time of the future conversion and restoration of Israel as a high-priestly nation (Zech. 3:1-10) and as the light of the world in the millennial age (Zech. 4:1-14). In its primary sense as "the Feast of Ingathering" or Harvest (Lev. 23:33-44; Deut. 16:13-15), it looks forward to the time "when the

Lord of hosts" in Mount Zion "shall make unto all people a feast of fat things, a feast of wines on the lees, of fat things full of marrow, of wines on the lees well refined" (Isa. 25:6).

Three times the **Feast of Tabernacles** is mentioned in these verses (vss. 16, 18, 19). Its place at the end of the cycle of sacred Jewish festivals, which constitute in their typical significance the sacred calendar of the history of redemption, gives it an eschatological significance which the other holy festal celebrations do not possess. Its ritual as laid down in the Mosaic Law (Lev. 23), as celebrated in ancient Jewish tradition, and as described in the Talmud and Mishna, point to its antitype in the millennial peace and prosperity of Israel's future kingdom (cf. Baron, *op. cit.*, pp. 527-530).

Particularly arresting as a feature of the **Feast of Tabernacles** was the eighth day, "the last and great day of the feast," the climactic solemnity when Israel no longer dwelled in the booths but returned to their homes. This feature looks beyond the millennial kingdom to the eternal state when time merges into eternity, and it shall be said, "Behold, the tabernacle of God is with men, and he shall dwell with them, and they shall be his people" (Rev. 20:1). The kingdom age will be characterized by a tabernacling of God with men that will be greater than any previous era. But the eighth day of the Feast of Tabernacles, in prefiguring the eternal state, points to a tabernacling of God that will be endless and absolute. When "God himself shall wipe away every tear from their eyes, and there shall be no more death, neither sorrow, nor crying, neither shall there be any more pain: for the former things have passed away" (Rev. 21:2–8).

2. Rod-of-iron Rule Regulating Millennial Worship (Zech. 14:17–19).

Also it shall be that whoever of the families of the earth shall not go up to Jerusalem to bow down to the King, the Lord of hosts, upon such there shall be no rainfall. (18) And if the family of the Egyptians do not go up and do not appear, then no rain shall fall upon them; but the plague shall befall them with which the Lord will plague the nations who do not go up to celebrate the Feast of Tabernacles. (19) This shall be the sin of Egypt and the sin of all the nations who will not go up to celebrate the Feast of Tabernacles.

The stern note emphasizing the rod-of-iron rule of Messiah struck in Zechariah's sixth vision of the Flying Scroll (Zech. 5:1–4), once again appears in the notice regulating millennial worship. There Messiah's rigid rule is connected with the moral conduct of the inhabitants of the millennial earth. Here it concerns their religious and spiritual behavior. In both cases the severity of millennial administration is accentuated. This aspect of Messiah's kingly rule is featured throughout the prophetic word. The psalmist dramatically foretells it. "Ask of me, and I shall give thee the nations for thine inheritance, and the uttermost parts of the earth for thy possession. Thou shalt *break them with a rod of iron;* thou shalt dash them in pieces like a potter's vessel. Be wise now therefore, O ye kings; be instructed, ye judges of the earth. Serve the Lord with fear, and

rejoice with trembling. Kiss the Son lest he be angry, and ye perish from the way, when his wrath is kindled but a little. Blessed are all they that put their trust in him" (Ps. 2:8–12).

In Revelation 12:5 the woman (Israel) "brought forth a male child [Christ], *who was to rule all nations with a rod of iron.*" Out of the mouth of the returning Messiah "proceeds a sharp sword, that with it he should smite the nations: and *he shall rule them with a rod of iron*" (Rev. 19:15). The overcomer in the Thyatiran church will be given "power over the nations," and in association with the reigning Messiah, "shall rule them *with a rod of iron*" (Rev. 2:27).

In the matter of worship in the day when the Lord shall be universal King and the sole object of adoration, Messiah's absolute rule shall be manifested in withholding rain from the people or nation which refuses to send representatives to Jerusalem to worship the Lord at the annual Feast of Tabernacles. **And it shall be that he who** [singular] **does not go up from the families of the earth to Jerusalem . . . upon them** [plural] **there shall be no rainfall** (vs. 17). The use of the singular points to the individual representative of the people or nation, while the plural has in mind the people or nation itself.

The word **families,** *mishpahoth,* is from the root *shaphah,* "to pour out" (water, blood, semen, Arabic *safaha*). The term comprehends the idea of human reproduction. The word is employed of a "clan," i.e., the family connection of an individual (Gen. 24:38; II Sam. 14:7); or loosely of a "tribe" (Judg. 13:2; 17:7); of the technical divisions of the people of Israel (Num. 11:10; Jer. 2:4); of the tribes of Israel (Exod. 6:14; Num. 3:15; Zech. 12:13). In a broader sense it is employed of a non-Israelite "people" or "nation" (Gen. 12:3; 28:14; Jer. 10:25; Ezek. 20:32; Nah. 3:4), and this is its usage in this millennial passage.

The particular punishment specified

to be visited upon any "nation" or "people" who will display recalcitrance in spiritual obligations is the withholding of rainfall. The word used is not for the "early rain" or autumnal precipitation of Palestine (*moreh*) nor the later winter and spring rains (*malqosh*), but *geshem* (Arabic *jasuma*, "be massive or bulky"), comprehending general copious rainfall suitable for any part of the globe (cf. Zech. 10:1). In Ezekiel 34:26 the word is used figuratively of spiritual blessing, and Zechariah's usage, while literal, does not exclude the spiritual connotation.

It is interesting that the family of Egypt, the Egyptian "nation" (or "people") is singled out for mention, especially when Egypt has notoriously and in striking contrast to Palestine been independent of rainfall and dependent upon the annual inundation of the Nile River for her sustenance. But the fact must not be overlooked that sometimes the Nile failed and Egypt suffered famine, as in the seven-year dearth in Joseph's day (Gen. 41:54) and similar times of extreme scarcity recorded on the Egyptian monuments, as in the time of Zoser. Moreover, the Nile was dependent upon the rainfall in the African hinterland, which could be effected. Then, too, there will be drastically different climatic changes in the kingdom, which will effect all nations, including Egypt.

It is possible, however, that the Septuagint and the Syriac have preserved the original text in this passage, and their reading makes no reference to rainfall. And if the people of Egypt do not come up and appear, upon them [*wa'aleyhem*] shall be the plague with which the Lord will plague the nations who will not come up to celebrate the Feast of Tabernacles.

Of course, the plague (*maggephah*, cf. comments on Zech. 14:12) is apparently the withholding of rainfall in Egypt's case also, but it is possible it may comprehend some other varia-

tion of punishment. This particular chastisement is scarcely the only form the rod-of-iron rule of Messiah will assume in dealing with sinners and recalcitrants in the earthly theocratic kingdom.

The question still remains, however, irrespective of the question of rainfall, why Egypt is singled out of all the millennial nations for special citation both with respect to her existence as a millennial nation and her submission to the Lord, on the one hand, and the rigid government of her by the Lord, on the other. The reason in the first instance is to glorify the grace and kindness of the Lord, and in the second instance, to magnify His holiness and severity. As in the case of His dealing with Jew and Gentile in this age, the purpose is enunciated. "Behold therefore the goodness and severity of God: on them [the Jews] which fell, severity; but toward thee [saved Gentile] goodness, if thou continue in his goodness; otherwise thou also shalt be cut off" (Rom. 11:22).

The refusal of Egypt or any other millennial nation to go up to Jerusalem to celebrate the Feast of Tabernacles will constitute a serious "sin," *hatta'th*. This word (from the root "to do wrong, miss the mark") here means not "sin, or sin offering" as commonly, but "the condition of sin, guilt of sin" (Gen. 18:20; Num. 16:26); or, better, "the punishment for sin" as a result of the guilt. This will be the punishment for sin of Egypt and the punishment for sin of all nations.

The expression, to go up to Jerusalem ('*alah*, "to ascend"), is employed because, as a result of the globe-engirdling earthquakes (Rev. 16:18-20), especially in Palestine (Zech. 14:4, 5, 10), Jerusalem, to accentuate its eminence, will be elevated geographically over all the surrounding territory of the ancient tribe of Judah, which will be depressed as the Arabah. But more than this, Jerusalem will be exalted as the religious and gov-

20 In that day shall there be upon the bells of the horses, HOLINESS UNTO THE LORD; and the pots in the Lord's house shall be like the bowls before the altar.

21 Yea, every pot in Jerusalem and in Judah shall be holiness unto the Lord of hosts; and all they that sacrifice shall come and take of them, and seethe therein: and in that day there shall be no more the Canaanite in the house of the Lord of hosts.

---

20   In that day shall there be upon the bells of the horses, HOLY UNTO JEHOVAH; and the pots in Jehovah's house shall be like the bowls before the altar.

21   Yea, every pot in Jerusalem and in Judah shall be holy unto Jehovah of hosts; and all they that sacrifice shall come and take of them, and boil therein: and in that day there shall be no more a Canaanite in the house of Jehovah of hosts.

---

ernmental capital of the millennial earth as the city of the great King from which the law of the Lord shall go forth. To **go up ... to Jerusalem** will be a glorious privilege, as well as a stern and inescapable duty to the inhabitants of the millennial earth.

3. *Israel's Holiness as a High Priestly Nation in the Millennium* (Zech. 14:20, 21). In that day "Holiness to the Lord" shall be upon the bells of the horses, and the utensils in the house of the Lord shall be as the sacred bowls before the altar. (21) And it shall be that every common pot in Jerusalem and in Judah shall be Holiness to the Lord of hosts! And all who shall be offering sacrifice shall come and take any of them and boil meat in them. And there shall no more be a Canaanite in the house of the Lord of hosts in that day.

Zechariah concludes his grand prophecies of Israel's glorious future on the note of the nation's holiness as a high priestly nation. In his vision of Israel's cleansing for this high and holy ministry (Zech. 3:1-10), the prophet had set forth the basis of this holiness; namely, cleansing from the excrement-bespattered garments of self-righteousness and clothing with the garments of salvation through faith in the redemptive work of Messiah, Jehovah's "Servant, the Branch" (Zech. 3:8).

To illustrate this wonderful priestly restoration of Israel according to

God's original intent for the nation (Exod. 19:5, 6), the prophet selects several details which, although minor and quite incidental, are nevertheless eloquently revealing of Israel's restoration to high priestly status *as a nation*. This is suggested by the employment twice of the epithet, Holiness to the Lord (Exod. 28:36), which was engraved upon "a plate of pure gold" on the turban of Aaron. "And it shall be upon Aaron's forehead," that the high priest might be responsible for every neglect or offence respecting "the holy things" (Exod. 28:38). The designation Holiness unto the Lord was thus in the life of Israel reserved for the highest and holiest position and function imaginable, engraved in gold upon the forefront of the turban of the loftiest spiritual dignitary of the nation and its representative before God to ever remind him to guard the holiness of God in the people's worship and service.

But **in that day** (here embracing the full establishment of the kingdom with Messiah's direct rule and administration in the affairs of men), the epithet Holiness unto the Lord **shall be upon the bells of the horses.** Hebrew word order emphasizes the fact that the most common and ordinary things of life, such as **the bells of the horses** (i.e., every common horse), used merely to decorate the brute animal, shall in that day be as holy unto the Lord as was the high priest's engraved turban. Why? Because the *entire nation*, cleansed from sin by Messiah, the Servant the Branch, shall be in function and purpose, what the high priest was set to be in Israel — the representative of God to the nation. With the *people cleansed*, the *whole land* and *everything* in it, including the bells of the common horse (vs. 20) as well as **every common pot in Jerusalem and in Judah**, are emphatically declared (by the word order) to be **Holiness to the Lord** (vs. 21).

Further to emphasize the fact that *every* phase of life in the kingdom will be sanctified and holy and nothing would any longer be considered secular, the utensils or pots in the Lord's house, to which some degree of sanctity attached, shall be as holy as the strictly sacred *bowls* before the altar. These holy vessels (*mizraqim*, from the root *zaraq*, "to toss, throw, scatter abundantly," Assyrian *zaraqu*, Arabic *zaraqa*, "throw at") were the **bowls** or "basins" for throwing or tossing a liquid, employed to catch the blood of slain victims and from which it was sprinkled according to the ritual of tabernacle and temple sacrifices at the altar (Exod. 27:3; 38:3; Num. 4:14; I Kings 7:40; Jer. 52:18; Zech. 9:15). These **bowls** were also presented by the princes of the people full of flour mingled with oil for a meal or cereal offering (Num. 7:13, 19, 25, etc.).

Every pot in Jerusalem and in Judah [that is, throughout the *Holy Land*] **shall be holy unto the Lord of armies: and all they that sacrifice shall come and boil flesh in them.** Private and domestic life in that glad day shall be as hallowed as priestly ministrations once were in Israel. This will be possible because all such distinctions as profane, secular, holy, and most holy shall come to an end. Everything will be **Holiness to the Lord,** that is, completely sacred in the highest sense of the term, and those who refuse to regulate their lives in accordance with this principle will be summarily and severely dealt with under the stern administration of the King, who "with righteousness shall judge the poor, and reprove with equity for the meek of the earth: and he shall smite the earth with the rod of his mouth, and with the breath of his lips shall he slay the wicked. And righteousness shall be the girdle of his loins, and faithfulness the girdle of his reins" (Isa. 11:4, 5).

But despite the swift and severe discipline of that day, it will be administered only because grace has been rejected or disregarded. The preponderating majority of earth's population will then receive the salvation of Messiah into their hearts and gladly pay homage to Him as absolute King, whose law will be written in their hearts. It is because the "knowledge of the Lord will cover the earth as the waters cover the sea" (Isa. 11:9) with the removal of moral and spiritual defilement that the condition will be removed that first evoked the distinctions between the holy and the profane. All will then be holy when Israel *as a nation* has "Holiness to the Lord" engraved upon her, as once only the high priest had upon his turban.

A final detail illustrating the universally holy character of Israel in kingdom blessing is given. **And there shall be no more a Canaanite in the house of the Lord of armies in that day.** The term **Canaanite** is best taken as a figure of a morally and spiritually unclean person. The Canaanites were degraded when Israel entered the land. The Old Testament references as well as archaeological discoveries (notably the religious epic literature recovered at Ugarit in North Syria, 1929–1937, and dating from the fourteenth century B.C.) agree in painting a dark picture of the gross immorality of the Canaanites, particularly because of their low and degrading religion. This was true to such an extent that the term **Canaanite,** as here, became proverbial in Israel for a profane and morally degenerate person.

In that millennial day the temple at Jerusalem will be a House of Prayer for all nations. As such its holiness will be jealously guarded. Nothing that defiles or works abomination shall be allowed to desecrate its sanctity. As the Holy City of Jerusalem itself, it will be the mecca of the millennial earth, and no profane or wicked person shall be allowed to desecrate its holy precincts. Israel, in high priestly glory and service, will adorn it, and the Holy Land with its holy people will grace it. The grand consummation of Israel's hopes and aspirations which it will symbolize, will attest the fulfilment not only of the age-spanning visions and prophecies of Zechariah, but will vindicate the very name of the prophet himself, Zechariah, "The Lord remembers."

BIBLIOGRAPHY

Aben, Ezra, *Commentary*. (A.D. 1167).

Adams, John. *The Man among the Myrtles*. New York: Scribner's, 1913.

Anderson, Bernhard W. *Understanding the Old Testament*. Englewood Cliffs, N.J.: Prentice-Hall, 1957.

Asada, Eiji. *The Hebrew Text of Zechariah*. 1899.

Baer, S. *Liber duodecim Prophetarum*. 1878.

Barnes, W. E. *Haggai and Zechariah (Cambridge Bible)*. Cambridge: University Press, 1917.

Baron, David. *The Visions and Prophecies of Zechariah* (4th ed.). London: Morgan and Scott, ltd., 1951.

Baumgarten, M. *Die Nachtgesichte Sacharias*. 1854–1855.

Bentzen, A. "Quelques remarques sur le mouvement messianique parmi les Juifs aux environs de l'an 520 avant Jésus Christ," *Revue d'Histoire et de Philosophie Religieuses* 10, 1930, 493–503.

Bechhaus, J. H. *Über die Integrät der prophetischen Bücher des alten Bundes*. 1796.

Bennett, W. H. *The Religion of the Postexilic Prophets*. Edinburgh: T. and T. Clark, 1907.

Blayney, Benjamin. *A New Translation of the Prophecies of Zechariah*. 1797.

Bleek, Friedrich. *Das Zeitalter von Sacharja, Cap.* 9–14. 1852, 1857.

Böhmer, J. "Haggai und Sacharja," *Neue kirsche Zeitschrift*. 1901.

Bredenkamp, C. J. *Der Prophet Sacharja*. 1879.

Brown, Francis, S. R. Driver, and Charles Briggs. *A Hebrew and English Lexicon of the Old Testament*. 1906.

Brown, Lawrence E. *Early Judaism*. Cambridge: University Press, 1920.

Brusten, C. A. *Histoire critique de la litterature prophétique des Hébreux*. 1881.

Budde, Karl. "Zum Text der drei letzten kleinen Propheten," *Zeitschrift für alttestamentliche Wissenschaft*. 1906.

Burger, J. D. F. *Le Prophète Zacharie*. 1841.

Calvin, John. *Commentary on the Twelve Minor Prophets*, ed., Owen. 1846.

Cannon, William W. "Some notes on Zechariah 11," *Archiv für Orientforschung*, IV, 1927, 139–146.

Chambers, T. W. "Zechariah" in Lange's *Commentary*, ed. Philip Schaff, Vol. 14. New York: C. Scribner's Sons, 1874.

Cocceius, J. *The Twelve Prophets*. 1652.

Collins, G. N. M. "Zechariah," *The New Bible Commentary*. London: Intervarsity Christian Fellowship, 1953.

Cornill, C. H. *Einleitung in die kanonischen Bücher des Alten Testaments*, (sixth edition), 1908.

Creelman, Harlan. *An Introduction to the Old Testament*. New York: The Macmillan Co., 1917, pp. 274–279.

Dathe, J. A. *Prophetae Minores*. 1773.

Davis, John D. "The Reclothing and Coronation of Joshua," *Presbyterian Theological Review*, XVIII, 256–268.

Denton, Robert C., and Cleland, James T. "Zechariah 9–14," *The Interpreter's Bible*, Vol. 6. New York; Abingdon Press, 1956.

Dods, Marcus. *The Post-Exilian Prophets: Haggai, Zechariah, Malachi (Handbook For Bible Classes)*. Edinburgh: 1879.

Drake, W. "Haggai and Zechariah," *The Speaker's Commentary*. 1876.

Driver, S. R. *The Minor Prophets II (The Century Bible)*. New York: Oxford Press, 1906.

————. *Introduction to the Literature of the Old Testament*. New York: C. Scribner's Sons, 1910.

Duhm, Bernhard. *Die zwölf Propheten in den Vermassen der Urschrift übersetzt*. 1910.

————. *Die Theologie der Propheten*. 1875.

Eckhardt, R. "Der Sprachgebrauch von Zacharja 9–14," *Zeitschrift für Alttestamentliche Wissenschaft* XIII, 1893.

Ephraem Syrus. *Explanatio in Zachariam*. A.D. 373.

Ewald, Heinrich. *Die Propheten des alten Bundes*. 1867–68.

Feinberg, Charles L. *God Remembers*. Wheaton, Illinois: Van Kampen Press, 1950.

Flügge, B. G. *Die Weissagungen welche heu den Schriften des Propheten Zacharias beygeboden sind*. 1784.

Forberg, E. *Commentarius in Zachariae vaticiniorum partem posteriorem*. 1824.

Frost, S. B. *Old Testament Apocalyptic*. London: Epworth Press, 1952.

Gaebelein, Arno C. *Studies in Zechariah*. New York: 1904.

Gottwald, Norman. *A Light to the Nations*. New York: Harper and Brothers, 1959, pp. 428–442.

Gray, G. B. *Hebrew Proper Names*. 1896.

Grutzmacher, G. *Untersuchungen über den Ursprung der in Zacharja 9–14 vorliegenden Propheten*. 1892.

Hackman, George, G. "The Book of Zechariah," *The Old Testament Commentary*. Philadelphia: Muhlenberg Press, 1948.

Heller, B. "Die letzten Kapitel des Buches Sacharja im Lichte des späteren Judentums," *Zeitschrift für Alttestamentliche Wissenschaft,* 1927, pp. 151–155.

Henderson, E. *The Book of the Twelve Minor Prophets.* 1868.

Hengstenberg, E. W. *Die Authentie des Daniel und die Integrität des Sacharja* (1831), English Translation. Edinburgh: T. and T. Clark, 1848.

————. *Christology of the Old Testament* (London 1872–78). Reprint Grand Rapids: Kregel, 1956, Vols. III, IV.

Hitzig, F. *Die zwölf kleinen Propheten,* ed. Steiner, 1881.

Hoonacker, A. *Les douze petits prophètes.* 1908.

Horst, Friedrich. *Nahum bis Malachi (Handbuch zum Alten Testament).* Tübingen: J. C. Mohr, 1954.

Keil, Carl Friedrich. *Biblischer Commentar über die zwölf kleinen Propheten.* 1873.

————. *Biblical Commentary on the Twelve Minor Prophets* (English Translation). Reprint, Grand Rapids: Eerdmans, 1949.

Kimchi, David. *Commentary.* A.D. 1230.

Kliefoth, Th. *Der Prophet Sacharja.* 1862.

Koehler, Ludwig, and Walter Baumgartner. *Lexicon in Veteris Testamenti Libros.* Grand Rapids, Michigan: Eerdmans, 1951.

Köhler, August. *Die nachexilische Propheten.* 1860–65.

Köster, F. B. *Meletemata in Zachariae,* Cap. IX–XIV. 1818.

Kraeling, Emil, G. "The Historical Situation in Zechariah 9:1–10," *American Journal of Semitic Languages and Literatures* XLI (1924–25), pp. 24–33.

Kremer, Josef. *Die Hirtenallegorie im Buche Zacharias.* Munster, 1930.

Kuiper, A. K. *Zacharia IX–XIV.* 1894.

Laetsch, Theodore. *The Minor Prophets.* St. Louis: Concordia Publishing House, 1956.

Lange, J. P. *Die Propheten Haggai, Sacharja und Malachi.* 1876.

Lapide, Cornelius á. *Commentarius in duodecim Prophetas Minores.* 1628.

Leupold, H. C. *Exposition of Zechariah.* Columbus: The Wartburg Press, 1956.

Ley, J. *Zu Sacharja* 6:9–15.

Lowe, W. H. *The Hebrew Student's Commentary on Zechariah.* 1882.

Lowth, W. *Commentary upon the Prophecy of Daniel and the XII Minor Prophets* (sixth edition). 1766.

Marck, J. *Commentarius in duodecim Propheten Minores.* 1784.

Marti, Karl. *Dodekapropheton.* 1904.

Marti, Karl. *Der Prophet Sacharja der Zeitgenosse Zerubbabels.* 1892.

————. "Die Zweifel an der prophetischen Sendung Sacharjas," *Studien zur semitischen Philologie und Religionsgeschichte J. Wellhausen... gewidmet, Zeitschrift für alttestamentliche Wissenschaft,* 27, 1914.

Mitchell, H. G., J. M. P. Smith, and Julius Bewer. *A Critical and Exegetical Commentary on Haggai, Zachariah, Malachi, and Jonah.* New York: Scribner and Son, 1912.

Moeller, William. "Zechariah," *Illustrated Bible Dictionary,* ed. W. C. Piercy. 1908.

Montet, E. *Étude critique sur la date assignable aux six dernier chapitre de Zacharie.* 1882.

Moore, T. V. *Haggai, Zechariah, and Malachi.* 1856.

Munro, W. D. "Why Dissect Zechariah? *The Evangelical Quarterly* X, 1938, pp. 45–55.

Neumann, W. *Die Weissagungen des Sacharja.* 1860.

Newcome, W. *The Twelve Minor Prophets* (second edition), 1809.

Nowack, W. *Die kleinen Propheten, Handkommentar* (second edition). 1903.

————. *Duodecim Prophetae* in Kittel's *Biblia Hebraica.* 1906.

Oosterley, W. O. E. *Old Latin Texts of the Minor Prophets (Journal Theological Studies V).*

Orelli, C. von. "Die zwölf kleinen Propheten," *Kurzgefasster Kommentar* (third edition), 1908 (English, 1893).

Ortenberg, E. von. *Die Bestandtheile des Buches Sacharja.* 1859.

Peiser, F. E. "Zu Zacharia"; *Orientalische Literaturzeitung.* 1901.

Pemble, William. *A Short and Sweet Exposition upon the First 9 Chapters of Zacharie.* 1658.

Perowne, J. J. S. *Haggai and Zachariah.* 1893.

Pressel, W. *Commentar zu Schriften der Propheten Haggai, Sacharja, und Malachi.* 1870.

Pusey, E. B. *The Minor Prophets* (1885). Reprint, Grand Rapids: Baker Book House, 1958.

Rashi (Rabbi Shelomoh ben Yishak 1040–1105). *Commentary.*

Ribera, F. de. *Commentarius in Libros XII Prophetarum.* 1581.

Riessler, P. *Die kleinen Propheten.* 1911.

Robinson, George L. *The Prophecies of Zechariah.* 1896.

Rosenmüller, E. F. C. *Scholia in Prophetas Minores.* 1836.

Rothstein, J. W. *Die Nachtgesichte des Sacharja.* Stuttgart, 1910.

Rowley, H. H. *The Relevance of Apocalyptic* (second edition). London: Lutterworth Press, 1947.

Rubikam, N. I. *The Second Part of the Book of Zechariah.* 1892.

Sanctius (Sanchez) C. *Commentarius in Prophetas Minores.* 1621.

Sanders, F. K. *The Messages of the Later Prophets.* 1899.

Schegg, P. *Die kleinen Propheten II.* 1854.

Schultz, Samuel. *The Old Testament Speaks.* New York: Harper and Sons, 1960, pp. 411–419.

Sebök, Mark. *Die syrische Übersetzung der zwölf kleinen Propheten.* 1887.

Sellin, E. *Serubbabel.* 1898.

————. *Studien zur Entstehungsgeschichte der jüdische Gemeinde nach dem babylonischen Exil.* 1901.

————. *Die Zwölf Propheten* (third edition). Leipzig: 1929–30.

Smith, George Adam. *The Book of the Twelve Prophets* (Revised edition). New York: Harper and Brothers, 1928, Vol. II.

Stade, B. "Deuterosacharja," *Zeitschrift für alttestamentliche Wissenschaft* 1881–1882.

Staerk, W. *Untersuchungen über die Composition und Abfassungszeit von Sacharja 9–14.* 1891.

Stonard, John A. *A Commentary on the Vision of Zechariah.* 1824.

Theiner, J. A. *Die zwölf kleinen Propheten.* 1828.

Theodoret (A.D. 457). *Commentarius in duodecim Prophetas* (edition 1642).

Thomas, D. Winton, and Theodore Cuyler Speers. "Zechariah 1–8" in *The Interpreter's Bible,* Vol. 6. New York: Abingdon Press, 1956.

Wellhausen, J. *Die kleinen Propheten* (third edition, 1988).

Woudstra, Marten H. "Zechariah" in *The Biblical Expositor,* Vol. II. Philadelphia: The Holman Company, 1960.

Wright, C. H. H. *Zechariah and His Prophecies.* 1879.